village and family in contemporary china

William L. Parish

Martin King Whyte

The University of Chicago Press/Chicago and London

village and family in contemporary china

WILLIAM L. PARISH is associate professor of
sociology, the University of Chicago. MARTIN
KING WHYTE is associate professor of sociology
and associate of the Center for Chinese Studies.
University of Michigan.

The University of Chicago Press, Chicago 60637
The University of Chicago Press, Ltd., London

HQ
684
. P37

Library of Congress Cataloging in Publication Data

Parish, William L
  Village and family in contemporary China.

  Includes index.
  1. Rural families—China. 2. Villages—China—
Case studies. 3. China—Rural conditions. I. Whyte,
Martin King, joint author. II. Title.
HQ684.P37   301.42'0951   78-3411
ISBN 0-226-64590-8

This book is dedicated to our rural informants, who opened up the realities of life in contemporary Chinese villages to our inquiring eyes.

Contents

1
The Setting

2
Institutional Arrangements and the Pursuit of Equality

3

Family Organization and Ritual Life

4

Communities and Change

Acknowledgments

*t*his study is the product of the equal contributions of its two authors, who worked in collaboration but at separate institutions. Many individuals and institutions contributed to the work of one or both of us, and expressing appropriate gratitude to all becomes a rather complex affair.

Funding for this research came from grants to both authors individually from the Social Science Research Council, to Parish from the National Science Foundation, and for Whyte salary support from the Center for Chinese Studies at the University of Michigan. Continuing support from the Center for Far Eastern Studies and PHS Grant No. 5 SO7 RR 0729-11 at the University of Chicago and from the Department of Sociology at the University of Michigan helped to underwrite the data analysis. The facilities of the Universities Service Centre and the Union Research Institute were indispensable to our work in Hong Kong. We are particularly grateful for the extraordinary assistance provided by the entire staff of the former institution, as well as for the aid of Stephen S. K. Chin of the Hong Kong University Centre for Asian Studies and Sidney Liu of *Newsweek*. The kind cooperation of Thomas Y. H. Young and the International Rescue Committee Hostel was also vital to our research. We were both ably assisted in Hong Kong by Yeung Sau-lun and Yeung Sai-cheung. Both Yeungs conducted interviews for us and screened thousands of pages of newspaper clippings to find sources we could use. In effect they also became our teachers, guiding us to a deeper understanding of their native land. Yeung Sai-cheung, in particular, served us with unflagging energy and his customary extraordinary grasp of detail both in Hong Kong and later, informally, after he came to the University of Michigan.

In Chicago Elizabeth Lin Salmon gave many hours of voluntary effort to the coding and initial analysis of our data, while Martin Kong and Cheng-hung Chang helped track down additional sources and saw that things were pushed through the computer. At Michigan Thomas Wilkinson served as a general computer consultant and troubleshooter. The staffs of the University of Chicago Far Eastern Library, the University of Michigan Asia Library, the Columbia University Far Eastern Library, and the Library of Congress Orientalia Division went out of their way to see that needed resources were provided. At the Library of Congress Leo Orleans was particularly helpful in locating fugitive sources.

Many friends and colleagues around the country provided assistance in one way or another. Several made generous gifts of unpublished data: Robert Worth on mortality, fertility, and marriage ages; Janet Salaff on marriage ages; Pi-chao Chen on birth control; Frederick Crook on communes and markets; Michel Oksenberg on village leaders in the 1960s; Gilbert Rozman on leaders in the 1870s; Marc Blecher on income distribution; Dwight Perkins on grain yields; Peter Schran on women's contribution to farm labor; Ezra Vogel with interviews and trip notes; and William Abnett, Byong-joon Ahn, Richard Baum, Graham Johnson, Stephen Levine, Victor Li, and Edwin Winckler with maps and data on commune and county boundaries. G. William Skinner, Myron Cohen, C. Arnold Anderson, Kathleen Whyte, Tom Bernstein, Suzanne Pepper, Rubie Watson, James Watson, and Ezra Vogel gave meticulous readings to all or most of our manuscript, and Norma Diamond, Steve Butler, and Jean DeBernardi to individual chapters. We could not hope to live up to all of their expectations, but their incisive suggestions did much to improve the finished product. Chan Wah-kong kindly donated his time and energy to preparing our map of Kwangtung. An earlier version of Chapter 15 appeared in *Problems of Communism* 24 (March–April 1976). Several typists at the Universities of Chicago and Michigan gave careful attention to earlier drafts of the manuscript while Mrs. Joan Allman put most of a heavily edited final version into readable form. We are grateful to all of them for both their speed and accuracy.

Finally, we are grateful to our families for suffering the disruption of schooling, work, friendships, and a settled home life as we trekked to Hong Kong and back. We appreciate the encouragement given both in listening to many crude early drafts of our work and in adjusting to our tendency to become suddenly unavailable while repairing a failed computer run or tracking down a missing reference. The loyal support of our families was vital to the successful completion of this study.

July 1977   William L. Parish
                                              Chicago

                                              Martin King Whyte
                                              Ann Arbor

Note on Transliteration and Measures

1 mou = $^1/_{15}$ hectare = $^1/_6$ acre

1 chin (catty) = ½ kilogram = 1.1 pounds

1 yuan (Y) = approximately US $0.40 for the early 1970s. This official exchange rate does not accurately reflect differences in purchasing power.

All transliteration of Chinese terms is via the Wade-Giles romanization of Mandarin (p'u-t'ung hua). For ease of reference, terms are rendered in Mandarin regardless of the dialect used at the time of interview. We modify the use of Wade-Giles romanization in two respects, however. With person or place names widely known in another spelling (for example, Canton, Sun Yat-sen) we use these common spellings. We are also more sparing than most in our use of the umlaut, as in yuan above, rather than yüan.

village and

family in

contemporary

china

1

Introduction

China has in the course of little more than a generation moved from being a desperately poor country racked by political and social turmoil to a position as a dynamic, revolutionary society which seems on the way toward becoming a major power in the world. How this transformation occurred is a subject of great interest to scholars, politicians, and many others. The Chinese Communists rose to power through a rural revolution, and they seem to be having some success in ensuring that their drive for economic development will not leave the rural areas completely behind. Given the huge and growing size of the Chinese population, these signs of success fascinate and puzzle much of the rest of the world, both in developed and developing nations. Delegations from all over the globe stream toward Peking for brief tours, many of them hoping to find ideas they can take home to solve their own problems. Despite all of this attention and interest, the dynamics of Chinese society today are still poorly understood. A brief tour of China is not a suitable vehicle for achieving a deep understanding, and no empirical social research is being carried out in China today, either by foreigners or by the Chinese themselves. Thus on some of the most basic points of interest about China today we lack accurate information, and a variety of half-formed ideas and guesses substitute for hard facts.

If we are to achieve a better understanding of China, we need more systematic information about how that society operates and is changing. The aim of this study is to provide such information for one important corner of the Chinese social world. We are interested in understanding and explaining the pattern of continuity and change in village and family life in rural China today.

Something like 80 percent of the Chinese population still lives in rural areas, but if the questions most often addressed to us are any guide, little reliable information exists about contemporary Chinese villages. A few examples will illustrate the diversity of concerns and views. Has the inequality of pre-1949 rural life been replaced in the people's communes by something like the equality of an Israeli kibbutz or a Western commune, or is there more similarity with a Soviet collective farm? Has the Chinese Communist party managed to destroy family loyalties and reorient the peasants toward loyalty to the commune, the party, and Mao Tse-tung? Have traditional kinship ties and cleavages in fact survived, and perhaps taken on new life, under the new labels of team, brigade, and commune? Are the leaders within today's communes simply another "new class," exploiting their neighbors and passing on advantages to their children and kinsmen, or have the Chinese Communists managed to produce a new ethic of selfless devotion to the public good? Can traditional customs and ceremonies honored by Chinese peasants for more than two thousand years be eliminated in little more than a generation? Has the inequality of the sexes been ended in rural China? Do young peasants today still respect their elders as they used to? How much impact did the Cultural Revolution of 1966–69, designated to "touch men's souls" and revolutionize human relationships, have on village and family life? Are Chinese peasants still concerned about such things as carrying on the family line and warding off evil spirits? What methods does the Chinese Communist Party use in its effort to change relatively intimate areas of peasant life, such as how people choose a spouse or decide how many children to have? Has the party been able to use its base of rural support to introduce such changes at will, or have Chinese peasants stubbornly resisted? Does the Chinese case throw any light on how far and how fast the basic solidarities by which people orient their lives can be changed? These are only a few of the concerns of students of Chinese life, questions we feel our research will help to answer.

At the most general level, such inquiries can be reduced to two basic questions that constitute the underpinnings of our study. First, what is the nature of village and family life in rural China today; what elements are familiar from the period before 1949 and what elements are new? Second, if there have been changes in village and family life, how and where have they been introduced, and what have been the obstacles to those changes? To provide detailed answers to these two questions we had to devise research methods of some complexity, given our inability to directly investigate these topics in villages within China. We feel that these methods have enabled us to develop a much more detailed and accurate picture of the nature of contemporary rural China than has previously been available.

Our study is based on intensive, semistructured interviews that we conducted in 1973–74 in Hong Kong. Our interviewees were former residents of sixty-three different villages in Kwangtung, the Chinese province adjacent to Hong Kong whose capital is Canton. Our informants for the most part had lived in these villages until a few weeks or even days before their arrival in Hong Kong. The reader will find a full discussion of our methods of interviewing and analysis in Appendix 1. For those who do not wish to make this detour in their reading now, several explanatory notes and qualifications are important.

First, our interviewees served not as respondents in a questionnaire but as informants ''at a distance'' about events and organizations in the villages from which they came. Thus the unit of our analysis is usually the village, but sometimes it is also a neighboring family or a wedding that was observed, rather than our interviewee himself. We are less concerned with our informant and whether he or she is in some sense ''typical'' than with whether the village or the wedding or whatever has been described accurately. Our methods are basically ethnographic, although they concern not one village but sixty-three different ones, scattered throughout Kwangtung. For each village we asked our informants to provide information on a standard set of topics: on the political and economic organization of the village, on the daily routine of peasant families, on local institutions and policies for education and health care, on recent weddings and funerals, and so forth. The focus is thus on concrete features of village life rather than on our informants' attitudes and values. These detailed descriptions of village life in sixty-three different villages form the core material analyzed in this study.

Second, the focus of our questions was on the post–Cultural Revolution period in China, basically 1969 to 1974. Thus information about earlier periods, which would in most cases be based on recollections from long ago, was covered only sketchily in our interviewing outline. In fact most of our informants were fairly young, and could not be expected to have detailed memories of village and family life in the early 1960s, not to mention the period prior to 1949. (In the next chapter we present a discussion of how we attempt to analyze social change while focusing on this short time frame.)

Third, we use our interview materials to make general statements about contemporary village and family life throughout Kwangtung only when such statements are supported by evidence from interviews from widely differing areas. But we are as much or more interested in variations from one village to another as in the "general picture." To answer our second major question, dealing with the "how" and "where" of change, we coded our interview information on each village both for things we thought might affect the pace of change (e.g., many or few local members of the Chinese Communist party, proximity of the village to a major city) and for whether desired changes have occurred or not (e.g., whether a cooperative health-care plan has been adopted, whether household ancestral tablets have been discarded). Using these two types of coded characteristics (which we refer to as independent and dependent variables, respectively), we are in a position to perform simple statistical tests to determine what sorts of villages have experienced more or less change. We feel that these systematic intervillage comparisons are the most distinctive contribution of our study. They enable us to say more about the actual process of social change in rural China today than has previously been possible. If we have done our work properly, the reader should come away from this book not only with new information on what life is generally like today in Chinese villages, but also with an understanding of the way in which various changes have actually been introduced, and of the forces which are likely to promote or retard further change.[1]

Our study is concerned, then, with examining one corner of rural China, in Kwangtung Province, in order to determine the nature of the changes in village and family life that have occurred there since 1949. In Chapter 2 we discuss a variety of mechanisms that others have used in explaining social change in other contexts. Our purpose in that chapter is to consider alternative conceptions of the change process in order to lay the groundwork for an explanation of the complex pattern of persistence and change which we unfold in succeeding chapters. In Chapter 3 we present basic background facts about Kwangtung province, the regional focus of our study. There we introduce some of the important kinds of variations across villages—geographical, ethnic, economic, and so on—with which we will be concerned in subsequent chapters. We also address there the question of whether our findings reflect peculiarities of rural Kwangtung or might be generalized to other parts of China. In Chapter 4 we discuss the way in which agricultural organizations in Kwangtung were transformed, and the nature of the commune structure that has existed since the early 1960s.

Chapter 4 also focusses on the kinds of political structures which are built into the commune system, and the variations in those structures which we think may be associated with speed or slowness of change in particular villages. Chapters 5 through 8 are concerned with aspects of rural equality and inequality. In Chapter 5 we consider the ways in which the present system of collectivized agriculture acts to maintain or reduce material inequality—inequality within and between villages, and between the peasants and urban residents. There we try to explain how peasant incomes are gained and calculated today, and some of the sources of the economic differences between villages of different types. There we also give a detailed account of the variety of labor remuneration systems that exist in Kwangtung communes today and attempt to explain why some communities use one system rather than another. In Chapter 6 we consider the systems for providing and financing health care, education, and welfare services in Kwangtung communes. We are interested in how these social programs affect equality within villages and why some communities have developed more extensive programs than others. In Chapter 7 we consider the kinds of power and status differentials that exist within Kwangtung villages and the factors that affect access to positions of influence. One issue in that chapter is the extent to which various kinds of favoritism toward kin still operate within the transformed political and economic structures of the commune. Chapter 8 summarizes our findings on rural equality and inequality and attempts to assess the consequences of the commune system for peasant work-motivation and satisfaction. Taken together, Chapters 3 through 8 provide an overview of the new organizational framework that has been created in rural Kwangtung and how and why it varies from place to place. The new organizations and policies described in these chapters can be expected to influence rural family life and ceremonial life and thus form the background necessary for consideration of changes in these areas.

The chapters that follow consider changes in rural family organization and ceremonial life in some detail. In each of these chapters the reader will learn what the "traditional" patterns were, what the government's goals are, how far along on the continuum between old and new Kwangtung peasants have come, and what the reasons are for particular changes or lack of change and for variation from village to village in the amount of change. Chapter 9 describes household composition, and looks at trends in both the number of adults and married couples who choose to live together in one family unit, and in the number of children Kwangtung peasants are having. In Chapter 10 we describe trends in marriage customs, including the age at which people marry, how free their choice of mates is, how they go about finding mates, and the forms of marriage finance that are involved. In the same chapter we discuss divorce in rural Kwangtung today, and the procedures and customs which surround divorce cases. In Chapter 11 we examine three aspects of relationships within the family—how much change or persistence there has been in the division of daily tasks and activities among family members, in the emotional character of various dyadic bonds within the family (father-son, husband-wife, brother-brother), and in the way children are reared. In Chapter 12 we bring together material from earlier chapters on different aspects of the changing role of women in rural Kwangtung. There we are particularly concerned with whether the increasing role of women in agricultural labor has produced a general improvement in their lot. In Chapter 13 we examine a series of traditional ritual occasions: the ceremonies connected with the major events of the life cycle—births, marriages, and deaths. In the following chapter we examine what has happened to another series of traditional ceremonies—those connected with the annual round of festivals. In both of these chapters we are interested in whether the new set of secular celebrations introduced by the government has replaced the traditional rituals, and in analyzing village-to-village variations in the extent of change. Together, these six chapters present a broad survey of changes and continuities in important aspects of rural family and ritual life, with an analysis of current patterns and differences.

In the concluding two chapters we step back and look at village and family change from a broader perspective. Chapter 15 examines what has happened within the commune structure to the kinds of ties and rivalries based upon kinship and marketing relations which used to characterize rural Kwangtung. There we are interested in whether traditional forms of extravillage conflict and cooperation find an outlet within this new structure, or whether new kinds of cleavages and alliances are emerging. We will also be concerned with whether the overall incidence of extravillage conflict and cooperation has increased or decreased. In our final chapter we draw together materials from the entire study to reach some conclusions about the nature of the process of change in village and family life in contemporary Kwangtung. We want to summarize there the general extent of continuity and change that is observable in different areas of social life. We will examine whether there is any general tendency for villages of particular types to exhibit more changes than others. In this final chapter we will also return to our different theoretical frameworks from Chapter 2, in an effort to determine whether any of them present an adequate explanation of the process and pattern of rural social change we have uncovered. We will then move on to construct our own overall interpretation of how and why village and family life in rural Kwangtung have changed. Our study concludes with two appendices, which provide the reader with additional explanations and information enabling him or her to judge the procedures used in the body of the text.

Our study builds, then, from some general background information through descriptions of the economic and political structures of contemporary rural Kwangtung, and then on to family behavior, ritual life, and extra-village relationships. Along the way we continually examine the general pattern of change which emerges, as well as the differences from village to village (and sometimes those within villages). Each separate topic constitutes one piece in our overall puzzle, and brings us closer to our final goal: the presentation of a systematic, empirically based analysis of what Chinese village and family life are like today, and how and why they are changing.

2

Perspectives on Purposive Change

*t*he Chinese Communists achieved national power on the basis of a mobilized peasantry, and after 1949 they shifted many of their revolutionary programs back to the countryside. In a series of dramatic mass campaigns during their first decade in power they carried out rural land reform, collectivized agriculture, and then amalgamated collective farms into even larger organizations called people's communes. Yet in fashion which sets their thinking off from some orthodox Marxists, the Chinese leaders did not assume that these socialist transformations would automatically produce a rural utopia. They wanted not only to end class exploitation and landlessness but to produce an egalitarian society in which individuals would work for the common good rather than to advance the interests of their own family, a society in which power would rest on devotion to national goals rather than on loyalty to particular kinship groups, and in which the freeing of peasants from the bonds of feudal customs and superstitions would release boundless human energies for the building of a more abundant society. Not only basic political and economic changes were called for, but far-reaching social, cultural, and psychological changes as well. Far from being content with the current state of rural life, China's leaders have regularly proclaimed new sets of goals and ideals toward which peasant energies should be channeled. The elite has in recent times mounted a succession of efforts designed to change the face of rural life still further.

In succeeding chapters we will use our interview data to sketch the pattern of changes and continuities in rural life that these elite efforts have produced. But the goal of this study is more ambitious than simply to describe the changes that have taken place in Chinese village and family life. Insofar as possible, we want to try to explain the patterns that emerge, and in particular the reasons why some parts of village culture change more than others and some villages change more than others. Our explanation will be esentially an effort to develop a picture of the nature of the change process that could have produced the patterns we find. There are a number of competing perspectives on how purposive change can penetrate village life, and by considering several here we may gain some insights which will help in developing our own final explanation.

One view of the purposive change process is the official Chinese one, based on Marxist ideas with some Maoist additions.[1] In this view the aspects of village life slated for change—class exploitation, superstition, sexual inequality, the squandering of peasant funds on ceremonial expenses, and so forth—found their basis in the feudal system of property relationships before 1949, in which a rural landlord class controlled disproportionate shares of village land and dominated rural social life. The major step in bringing about change was the elimination of that economic structure, through the kinds of changes already referred to—land reform, collectivization, and the forma tion of people's communes. These changes in rural property relationships had basically been completed by the late 1950s (see the discussion in Chapter 4), with socialist property relations firmly established. Some secondary changes within this socialist system are still needed—particularly the provision of more nursery schools, sewing cooperatives, and other service facilities to free women from domestic work, and fuller implementation of the principle of equal pay for equal work for women. But in the main the basis for traditional kinds of behavior and values in the contemporary economic structure of the communes is gone. Peasants can be expected to react to this new socialist rural structure by changing the way they interact with kinsmen and nonkin, the way they treat their wives, the way they celebrate weddings and holidays, and so on—all toward the official ideals of egalitarian, secular, frugal, and public-spirited behavior.

This is not the whole picture, however. In Marxist terms there is not an automatic alignment between the economic "base" and the social and cultural "superstructure" of village life. Many peasants alive today were raised in the old society and absorbed habits and values from the ideology of that period. Such people continue to operate on outmoded values, ignoring the new structures around them and passing on old ideas to other people. The remnants of the former landlord and rich peasant classes are assumed to cherish the old values more than others and to play a leading role in their continued propagation. To realize the official ideals, the government has to find ways to help the superstructure of values and attitudes catch up with the base of socialist property ownership. For the younger generation this can be done by forceful propagation of the new values through schools and other media. But the older generation is not unredeemable in the Maoist view. Their values can be changed by the sorts of mass campaigns we mentioned in the beginning of this chapter. The government can decide that a certain set of traditional attitudes requires changing. They can then proclaim a special assault on those values. The centrally controlled mass media will then churn out materials describing the outmoded and socially harmful attitudes being attacked, and local political leaders can organize peasants to discuss these materials. In local political study meetings these leaders urge peasants to examine their own attitudes and values and to confess their own failure to fully live by the new ideals. Former landlords and rich peasants can be subjected to public abuse for continuing to cherish outmoded values, and local leaders and party members can lead former poor peasants in these activities. Through group discussion and social pressure, the presentation of model cases of personal reform, and other devices, peasant consciousness can be raised, and a new set of beliefs and behavior more appropriate to a socialist village will emerge. Examples of this sort of effort would be the rural socialist education campaign of 1962–65 in which the "three evil tendencies" of capitalism, feudalism, and extravagance were attacked, and the anti–Lin Piao, anti-Confucius campaign of 1973–75, in which attitudes such as male chauvinism and disrespect for manual labor were targets.

The combination of mass campaigns with proper local political leadership and ideological work among the masses is seen as producing a great force for change. In the official view, this combination will even enable poor and isolated villages to pull themselves up by their bootstraps and become prosperous, which is said to have been the history of the national model Tachai agricultural brigade in Shansi Province.[2] Chinese media tend to portray the rural scene as divided between advanced villages and backward villages. Those that develop proper leadership and ideological work among the masses will prosper economically and produce an egalitarian, secular, and public-spirited set of social relationships. Those lacking proper leadership and ideological work will tend to have economic problems, kinship and sexual animosities, superstitions, and many other negative features, in spite of their socialist economic form. Thus in simplified terms the official view of rural change sees the transformation of the rural economic structure as a necessary first step but one that has to be followed by repeated mass campaigns in order to prevent traditional beliefs and values from regaining strength and subverting rural socialism.

Change in rural China has been seen by others in quite different terms. One competing perspective stems from the theory of totalitarianism and probably has its most forceful advocates today among analysts on Taiwan. In this view officially disapproved traditions—for example, wedding feasts, lineage loyalties and male dominance—are not outmoded "survivals" from a previous era. They are cherished customs which are reinforced by thousands of years of Chinese history, customs which continue to provide a great deal of harmony, security, and satisfaction. The Chinese government is demanding that peasants give up these satisfying customs and social arrangements for new forms that are much less satisfying—loyalty not to kin but to distant party elites, politicized and dull official holidays in place of boisterous traditional festivals, and so forth. Given this sort of option, peasants will not make the indicated changes unless they have to. The government thus has to exert pressure on local party, police, and other authorities to coerce peasants to adopt the new ways. Peasants will then have to change some of their behavior to avoid official coercion, but their attitudes and values will not really change, and in those areas of life where they can escape detection and punishment they will try to maintain traditional ways. The main force for change in this perspective is officially mobilized coercion. A modified version of this argument would allow that peasants might change their behavior not only to avoid coercion but also if it were made rewarding enough to them. Thus the offering of new kinds of material rewards for altered behavior might produce some compliance, although, again, the underlying peasant values and attitudes would not change. The image is of a conservative peasantry unwilling to depart from time-honored ways unless the official carrot and stick are powerful enough.

Still a third perspective on social change has not been as explicitly applied to the rural Chinese scene (although it is implicit in many treatments). This is the perspective presented by Western modernization theory.[3] In this perspective certain social structures are more "modern" than others in the sense that they promote the kinds of behavior and relationships common in modern industrial societies: familiarity with modern machinery and technology, authority based upon competence and knowledge rather than upon age or sex, cooperation across kinship and ethnic boundaries, participation in the planning of complex activities involving large numbers of people, and so forth. The preeminent examples of such modern structural environments are cities, bureaucratic agencies, factories, and schools, Peasants in such modern milieus have to engage in activities and become exposed to values which are far different from those that characterize traditional villages. As a result of such exposure, peasants lose confidence in old ways and values as the only correct way to live, and they begin to change in order to reflect their new environment.

Change can occur not only by taking peasants out of their village setting and exposing them to modern social structures; change can also come by introducing parts of these modern structures into the rural scene. New village schools and rural factories can be established; farm machinery, agricultural extension agencies, and new credit facilities can be introduced; and rural cooperatives can be set up to organize farming, marketing, health care, and other activities in a modern manner.[4] As these new structures and activities are introduced into rural life, peasants will experience some of the modernizing influences that they would have received if they had gone off to the school, factory, office, or city; and while remaining in the village they will begin to change. In some varieties of modernization theory, social change can occur not only by taking peasants out of their villages or by changing the structures in which peasants spend their lives, but also by the seeping into the village of other kinds of modern influences. Villages and individuals exposed to radio broadcasts and other mass media, to individuals who come from more modern urban areas, and to new manufactured goods may, by the "demonstration effects" of such exposure, begin to act and think in new, more modern ways.[5]

In their emphasis on altered rural social structure and the impact of new ideas coming from outside, modernization theories are superficially similar to official Chinese ideas of social change. But there are important differences in the ways these mechanisms are portrayed. Current modernization theories adopt a much broader (or perhaps vaguer) view of which structural alterations provide the motive force for change. No key role is assigned to the change in property relations, or even to the organization of economic activities. Rather, changes that in the Marxist view are seen as part of the superstructure are seen in these views as important motors for change—more rural schooling, better health care, new forms of village government, opportunities for migration, and so forth. By the same token, stability in such noneconomic realms could retard change in other areas of village life. As a consequence of this broader focus, a modernization theorist would not assume that all structural obstacles to officially desired change would have been removed by the socialization of agriculture and related economic changes in the 1950s.

We have described three different perspectives that could be used to explain the pattern of purposive village change, and these do not exhaust the logical possibilities. However, these three perspectives provide sufficient diversity for us to deal with a more concrete question. What specific change mechanisms can be used to produce village change? If we dissect our three perspectives, we can see that each relies on a distinctive combination of three particular change mechanisms. We shall refer to these as structural transformation, administrative sanctions, and normative influence. The start of the change process in each case is government initiative in favor of certain changes, but this initiative can be translated into either indirect or direct attempts to change village life and peasant behavior.[6] Indirect attempts are pursued by what we refer to as structural transformations. The government can use some or all of its resources—administrative directives, state investment, mass campaigns, and so forth—to bring about some change in the social structure in which peasants live—a change in work organization, in educational opportunities, in migration opportunities, and so on. The assumption behind this mechanism is that, once the structure has changed, peasants will adapt their behavior to it, without any need for exhortation or sanctions. So instead of trying to manipulate peasant behavior directly, one changes the social environment and anticipates adaptive responses by peasants. We have seen this sort of indirect change mechanism stressed in both Chinese Marxist and modernization perspectives, although the two approaches differ in what parts of the structure they see as important for inducing indirect change.

Government initiatives can also be translated into more direct change attempts; here one tries to change peasant behavior and attitudes themselves, rather than relying on peasants to accommodate to a changed environment. Two major types of more direct change mechanisms can be used: administrative sanctions and normative influence.[7] The government can make clear what kinds of behavior and attitudes are allowed and forbidden, and then use the party, police, and other organizations to punish those who do not comply, as our totalitarianism perspective stresses. Similarly, it can make clear its objectives and then give those individuals and villages which comply cash payments, better purchasing contracts, or more fertilizer, machinery, and factories to improve their production. Though usually deemphasized in totalitarian theories of change, this is the carrot half of the carrot and stick model of administratively induced change. Alternatively, the government can use normative influence by relying on things such as exhortation and an appeal to higher moral principles, and by treating noncompliance not as a punishable offense but as a sign of moral weakness, or failure to meet community obligations. Here there are at least three subtypes to note. The first is communications. The mass media and other devices are used to forcefully expose the population to new ideas and their rationale, and to urge adoption of them. The second subtype is childhood socialization—new members of the community are systematically trained in the official values. The third subtype is mobilized social pressure—people in a village are organized to praise and criticize individuals in order to get them to comform to new values.[8] We see all of these normative influence mechanisms stressed in the official Chinese change perspective, and to a lesser extent in some modernization perspectives.

This analysis shows that our three purposive change perspectives use as their building blocks different combinations of more specific change mechanisms: indirect change through structural transformation (economic or general), direct change through administrative sanctions, or direct change through normative influence (with its subtypes).[9] Beyond illustrating the variety of purposive change theories possible, we want to use this discussion to prepare the way for our effort to explain the pattern of change and continuity in village life uncovered in succeeding chapters. We do not assume that we will be able to "prove" that one of our three perspectives is right and the others wrong, or that one change mechanism can explain all the changes that have occurred. Instead we hope to draw insights about the theoretical possibilities from this discussion and then use the insights in constructing our own explanatory framework in the final chapter.

The key to the effort to build a coherent explanation of our findings is our recognition that there should be different patterns of change produced by each change mechanism. By considering which parts of village organization and of family life have changed most and least, which villages show the most change, which individuals show the most change, and how the pattern of change has varied over time, we may be able to reason backwards to discover the change mechanism or mechanisms that could have produced the resulting pattern. For example, if administrative sanctions have been the key change mechanisms, only those officially espoused changes that are backed up by specific enforcement procedures and sanctions should occur, and change will be most apparent in those villages possessing strong political infrastructures to apply those sanctions. If normative influence has been crucial, then changes will be concentrated during the "high tides" of mass campaigns, and villages with the best-developed means for transmitting such influence—political study meetings, schools, nursery schools, and mass media exposure—should have experienced the most change. If structural transformations have been the primary motor, then changes should be concentrated during the period when the major alterations in village social structure occurred (primarily 1949–56) and should be less apparent later. We will not attempt detailed predictions for each change mechanism here but will simply state that from systematically analyzing the pattern of change and continuity in village and family life in later chapters we expect to be able to discover what sort of change process has been at work.

Our procedure in analyzing our results is something like piecing together a puzzle. While we deal with a number of other themes in this book, starting in Chapter 5 we will begin to present information on the extent and pattern of change in many different areas of rural life. To deal with our first major question from the previous chapter—the "What has changed?" question— we will compare particular current practices and customs both with Chinese goals and ideals (as reflected in the Chinese press, legal documents, the writings of Mao Tse-tung, and so on) and with the situation in Kwangtung villages before 1949 (as conveyed in village studies, surveys, and other reports from this area).[10] These comparisons, though crude, allow us to assess the extent of change and persistence in particular areas of rural life. To deal with our second major question—the "how and where" of change—we will use the systematically coded information from our interviews, as described in Chapter 1, to see whether some kinds of villages have experienced more change than others. For a few practices we also will be able to present information on the pattern of change over time since 1949 and on variation in responsiveness to change within the village population. As we go along we will often pause to compare specific results with what might be expected on the basis of our various change mechanisms. Then in the final chapter, by pulling together our analysis of many different topics, we hope to explain what sort of overall change-process is consistent with, and thus could explain, the variations that we discover. If the puzzle fits together, we expect this analysis also to provide evidence on the forces for, and obstacles to, further change in rural China.

1

the

setting

3

Kwangtung
Province

Since our information about contemporary Chinese rural life comes largely from the single province of Kwangtung, we need to acquaint the reader with several basic facts about this locale. We are particularly concerned with the kinds of variations within Kwangtung which we expect may produce differing responses to official change efforts. We also need to consider how distinctive Kwangtung is in relation to provinces elsewhere in China.

Located on the far south coast of China, Kwangtung is one of the twenty-six provinces that make up the People's Republic of China. Its population totals 50 million—almost half the population of Japan and about one-fourth the population of the United States.[1] About four-fifths of its population are engaged in agriculture. The predominant crop is paddy rice, most places having two crops a year, in the spring and fall. In the winter, some places grow a third crop such as wheat or beans, but in most places winter is the slack season with minor crops of vegetables and sweet potatoes.

The cycle of crops strongly affects the social and political life of a village. In busy planting and harvest seasons, particularly in July when spring rice must be harvested and fall rice planted, people work such long hours from before daybreak until late at night that there is little time for any other kind of activity. During the winter, by contrast, some workers take time for nonagricultural sidelines in other villages or towns—hauling stones for a construction project, doing private carpentry to supplement the family's income, or whatever.

Agroeconomic Regions

Within the overall pattern of paddy rice cultivation, there are subpatterns associated with distinct geographic subregions.[2] The most important region in the province is the Pearl River Delta formed from alluvial deposits of three large rivers which join near the city of Canton. They and their tributaries provide not only much of the irrigation water needed for paddy rice but also the principal arteries of transport. The West River is navigable the year round by boats as large as two thousand tons going into Kwangsi Province. The North and East rivers are sailed by smaller junks for at least part of the year, and a tributary off the East River near Ho-yüan provides much of the hydroelectric power for Canton and the surrounding countryside.

After converging near Canton, the three rivers disperse into a multitude of other streams. The Pearl River takes oceangoing ships of up to ten thousand tons to the port of Huang-pu (Whampoa) outside Canton. At the southwest corner of the mouth of the Pearl River, some one hundred kilometers south of Canton, lies the Portuguese colony of Macao. In the southeast corner of the mouth, some 120 kilometers south of Canton, lies the British colony of Hong Kong, to which Canton is linked by a railroad. Northwards, Canton is linked to Hunan Province and to the rest of China by a railroad completed in 1936. The only other major railroad in Kwangtung (completed in the 1950s) links the far western port of Chan-chiang and the shale-oil-producing city of Mao-ming to Kwangsi Province.

The combination of transport and rich soils permitted the Pearl River Delta to become densely populated, urbanized, and commercialized. Today, half of the urban population of Kwangtung lives in the delta. Canton, with over two million people, has long been an administrative center for South China, and it remains the provincial capital. By 1953, Foshan, Chiangmen, and Shihch'i cities in the delta had over 80,000 population each, while an additional twelve cities had over 10,000 population each. The population density in the delta as a whole is over 600 persons per square kilometer— as great as anywhere in China. With less than 10 percent of the total surface area, the delta contains one-fourth of the population of the province.

The urbanization of the delta was linked not only to productive farms but also to early contact with the West. In 1757, the Ch'ien Lung emperor made Canton the sole port for foreign trade. Though trade had to go through government-appointed Chinese intermediaries, the effect on the countryside was immediate. While foreigners brought in silver, arms, ammunition, glass, and opium, the Chinese supplied silk, tea, and chinaware. The counties (hsien) surrounding and just to the south of Canton were ideally suited for silk production, and the rural economy began to commercialize rapidly. Small markets, many of them that specialized in selling mulberry leaves to feed to silk worms and others that collected raw silk, sprang up between the old, more widely dispersed rural markets.[3] The network of markets continued to thicken through the nineteenth century as peasants grew more and more crops for urban and foreign markets and in turn bought more for their own needs.

Because of more commercialized farming, before 1949 many fields in the delta were used to grow not grain but sugar cane, mulberry trees, fruits, vegetables, and for fish ponds. Gradually grain had to be imported from outside the delta. With their strong belief in local self-sufficiency, the Communists gave more attention to grain production, and by the mid-1950s most counties grew all the grain they consumed. Despite the emphasis on grain, commercialized crops continue to contribute to the high incomes enjoyed by delta peasants. Because of a decline in the world market, silk production has failed to return to the peak of the 1920s. Yet in Shun-te and surrounding counties, many women are still engaged in plucking mulberry leaves, feeding them to silk worms, and then spinning the cocoons into thread. The mulberry trees grow along with sugar cane on dikes around ponds from which men net freshwater fish to be sold not only at urban markets within China but in Hong Kong as well. Because Canton has winters that are almost frost-free, vegetables can be grown year-round, as can bananas, lichees, pineapple, and other tropical fruits. In addition, in most villages ponds allow the raising of ducks and geese, while pigs and chickens supplement peasant incomes.

Another rich delta in the far eastern corner of Kwangtung Province is formed by the Han River as it flows to the sea near the cities of Swatow and Ch'ao-chou. The Han River Delta, with some of the richest rice harvests in the country and a dense population, is only one-eighth the size of the Pearl River Delta. (Since our interviews include only two villages from this smaller area, when we speak of the delta throughout the rest of this book we almost always mean the Pearl River Delta alone.)

Outside the two deltas, village life can be much more difficult. Fully two-thirds of the province is hilly, and although on some flatlands along the coast or along the major river valleys production is good, few areas match the productivity of the delta regions. Since peasants prefer to eat paddy rice, which needs irrigation throughout much of the year, most peasants outside the deltas live in small villages up and down narrow valleys where a reliable water supply is available. Though sweet potatoes and other dry-land crops are grown, much of the land has been weakened as heavy rains have leached out vital organic matter and potassium. Mass plantings of trees have helped slow hill erosion, yet much more afforestation and higher fertilizer applications are still needed.

Because of the poor soil and the dispersion of villages among hills, over most of nondelta Kwangtung population densities are low—one hundred to two hundred people per square kilometer in the rolling hills to the east and west and fifty to a hundred people in the hilliest counties to the north. There are no more than ten cities with populations of thirty thousand and these are so scattered that urban influences are more dispersed than in the delta regions. Though some of the nondelta localities would be suitable for commercial crops, lack of urban contact and poor transport have restricted most areas to growing mainly rice and sweet potatoes.

Overall, among the forty-eight villages in our sample for which we have reasonable information as to terrain, eight are in alluvial delta lands, nineteen are on relatively flat plains, and twenty-one are in hill areas. More commonly, in later chapters, we will dichotomize villages according to whether they are in the Pearl River Delta. The delta region will be broadly defined to include adjacent counties such as Pao-an, Tungkuan, Tsengch'eng, T'aishan, and Hsin-hui that share in the commercialization and urban contact characteristic of the Pearl River Delta. So defined, twenty-nine of our villages are in the "delta region," while thirty-four are outside. The map of Kwangtung shows the locations of the major rivers and cities in the province, as well as noting the counties from which our informants came.[4]

In general we expect villages in the delta to be relatively prosperous and advantaged, and we want to know whether their economic position makes them more responsive to post-1949 changes. (A contrary view could also be entertained. Perhaps localities that were wealthy before 1949 would be more conservative and less willing to undertake changes today.) We also devised more direct measures of relative economic position. One scale that we call "collective affluence" is composed of measures of reported local annual rice-yields, the values of a day's work points, and the supply of brigade machinery. Another scale we will refer to as "household consumption," which includes measures of the percentage of local households owning bicycles, households owning radios, and the supply of team machinery. Finally, we developed a land-labor ratio scale from the reports our informants gave us of the amount of land farmed by their teams and the number of full-time laborers on that land. (For the precise definitions of these scales, see Appendix 2.) All of these measures will be used in later chapters to examine whether the economic characteristics of local communities affect responsiveness to change.

Ethnic Groups

Kwangtung Province is the home of a number of ethnic groups. The inhabitants of the province over a thousand years ago were non-Chinese "tribal" groups which now constitute only a small minority living in isolated places in the hills to the extreme northwest of the province and on Hainan Island. Like the American Indians, these tribal peoples were gradually shoved aside or assimilated into the "more civilized" Han (that is, Chinese) ethnic groups moving in from the north. Slowed by hills which ring the northern border of Kwangtung, the migration of Han Chinese into the province started in the first centuries A.D. and continued gradually over hundreds of years. The earliest Han settlers had ample time to displace the original inhabitants and to form a Cantonese culture and language rather independent of those in North China from whence they came.

These "Punti" migrants from the north later were joined by migrants who kept their own language—the Hakkas. The Hakkas began to move into eastern Kwangtung and neighboring Kwangsi and Fukien provinces during the southern Sung (1127–1280) dynasty. Since the fertile valleys were already settled, the Hakkas were forced into the hills where they eked out a poor living. The earlier migrants guarded their privileged positions and fought off attempts by the Hakkas to move into their territory. These battles were most severe in the nineteenth century, when some Hakkas tried to move into the western counties of the province, but skirmishes continued well into the twentieth century. Although over fifty of the ninety-seven counties in Kwangtung have Hakka populations, the Hakkas are to be found mainly in about fifteen hilly counties to the north and northeast of Canton.

There are many ethnic stereotypes about the Hakkas, including stories that they have six toes on each foot, are uncultured, and possibly are not even Chinese. More interesting is the observation that they were poorer than the typical Cantonese and the view that poverty plus some other ethnic characteristics made them more rebellious. A Hakka led the T'ai-p'ing Rebellion which racked China in the middle of the nineteenth century. They were well represented among the communist revolutionaries. Later, then, we will want to ask whether these people, out of their purported rebelliousness and poverty, have any special affinity for social change. Also of interest is the position of their women. In contrast to other Chinese women, Hakka women

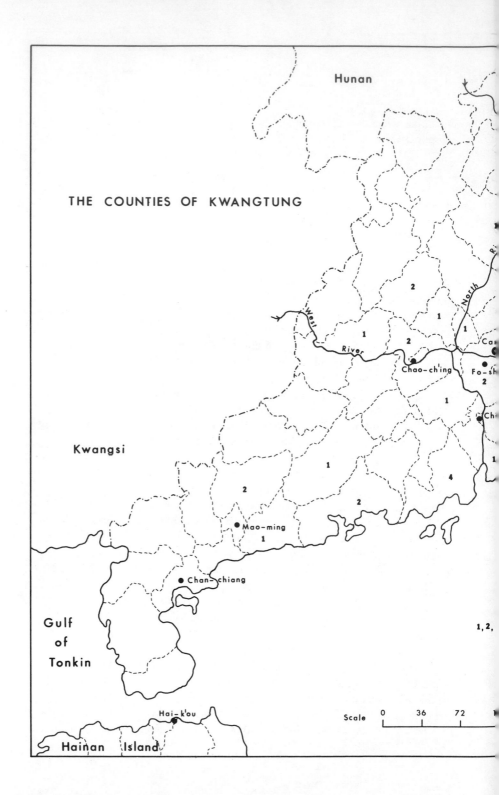

THE COUNTIES OF KWANGTUNG

Hunan

Kwangsi

Gulf
of
Tonkin

Hainan Island

North River

West River

2

1

2

1

2

Chao-ch'ing

Ca

Fo-sh

2

1

Ch

1

4

1

2

2

Mao-ming

1

Chan-chiang

1, 2,

Hai-k'ou

Scale   0   36   72

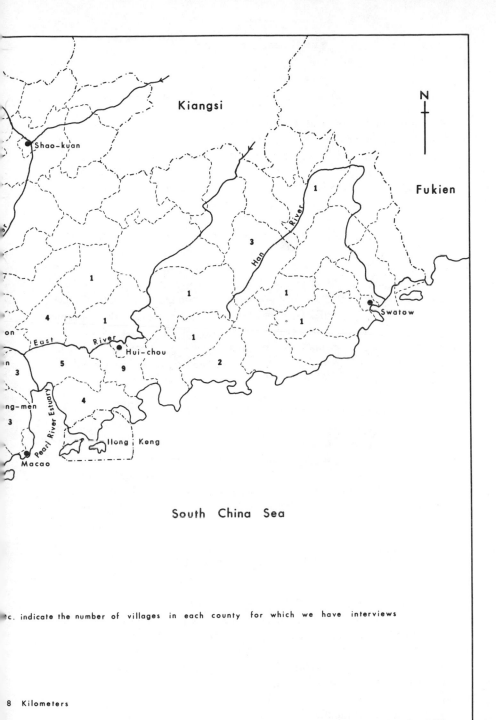

Kiangsi

Fukien

N

Shao-kuan

Han River

Swatow

East River

Hui-chou

on

Pearl River Estuary

ng-men

Macao

Hong Kong

South China Sea

c. indicate the number of villages in each county for which we have interviews

8 Kilometers

W.K.Chan

never bound their feet, and they carried a heavier burden of farm work. Whether these characteristics made them more receptive to Communist appeals for the liberation of women will concern us in later chapters.[5]

In addition to the language difference between the two major ethnic groups, there are differences among the Cantonese themselves. For example, people in four counties to the southwest of Canton—in T'ai-shan, K'ai-p'ing, Hsin-hui, and En-p'ing counties—speak a version of Cantonese which is almost unintelligible to residents of Canton. Despite these regional differences, Cantonese, the language of the provincial capital, remains the lingua franca of Kwangtung. Most young people, regardless of ethnic group, can speak Cantonese. Most young people also speak the national language (Mandarin), now called simply "common language" (p'u-t'ung hua). Though all provincial officials, regardless of background, use the common language in formal discourse, at the county and commune levels Cantonese often predominates, especially in informal social life. There are provincial radio broadcasts in Cantonese as well as in Mandarin. And at the village level, it is always the local dialect (Hakka, Tai-shan, or other) which is used. Mandarin is supposed to be the language of instruction in rural primary schools (at least after the first grade or two). In practice, in many rural schools Mandarin is merely taught, while the local dialect is used for most instruction. Once out of school, a villager who seldom uses Mandarin is likely to lose facility in it. When interviewed in Hong Kong, villagers who were in their twenties could usually understand questions in Mandarin but many of them had difficulty replying in Mandarin. With all dialects being written in essentially the same characters, reading and writing ability is more readily retained.

Overseas Chinese and Remittances

Kwangtung is distinctive in its large emigration to places overseas, which took place particularly from the mid-nineteenth century onwards. Over half of all Chinese who went abroad for work came from Kwangtung. In two counties, Mei-hsien and T'ai-shan, the population from these counties now residing abroad is half as large as the population still in residence.

Many who went abroad became successful workers and merchants and continue to remit, by village standards, impressive sums of money. Those villages which traditionally had the most remittances tend to be materially better endowed, with more elegant ancestral halls, homes, and modern buildings. Similarly, within any village it is frequently those with remittances from overseas kin who have the newest houses, bicycles, watches, and sewing machines.

In the 1950s and 1960s, the Chinese government encouraged remittances. Overseas Chinese could, in addition to aiding their relatives, help endow special overseas high schools in China or invest in the Overseas Chinese Investment Corporation and be paid appropriate interest. In the mid-1950s, remittances by the overseas Chinese who had emigrated from T'ai-shan County (the place of origin for many American Chinese) equaled 120 percent of the value of the annual agricultural production of that county.[6] Before the Cultural Revolution, T'ai-shan, En-p'ing, Hsin-hui, and Nan-hai counties tried to stimulate these remittances by publishing magazines directed towards overseas residents.[7] The magazines were in traditional style: characters were in full form rather than simplified and ran from top to bottom, as of old, rather than in the new, left-to-right pattern. The contents publicized not only higher production figures, new roads, and hospitals but also local scenic sights, recipes for famous local dishes, and rosters of overseas high-school graduating classes. Amid the news of local events there were appeals to come back to visit or to stay and to send money for investment projects funded by overseas Chinese. Both overseas visitors and funds remained a regular part of life in such areas. Antithetical as they might be to the goals of self-reliance and socialism, in the 1950s and 1960s remittances were desperately needed to restore foreign exchange balances. Even in the 1970s the government has not seen fit to abandon remittances. As a result, the prosperity of certain villages and families continues to be greatly affected by a steady inflow of foreign dollars, and this factor may undermine the ability of local cadres to stimulate maximum effort in collective farming.

During land reform in the early 1950s, when class labels were assigned to people, those who had earned most of their income abroad or who still depended primarily on foreign remittances for a living were given the special designation of "Overseas Chinese." There are not many of these people in our sample—somewhat less than 2 percent. There are, however, many who depend on remittances for at least part of their income. The average proportion of village residents receiving remittances in our sample of villages is less than 10 percent. The range, however, runs form zero to 80 percent, the latter for a village in T'ai-shan County. In latter chapters, accordingly, it will be possible to examine the degree to which collective commitment and social change are affected by remittances coming from abroad, and we include a measure of remittance dependency in our indicators of village economic characteristics.[8]

Lineage and History

There are other characteristics of Kwangtung Province that may condition its response to Communist rule. One is the strength of lineages, groups sharing a common surname and tracing their descent through the male line to a common ancestor (often fifteen to twenty-five generations removed). As in much of south China, in certain parts of pre-1949 Kwangtung major lineages controlled not only massive landholdings but also large caches of arms. Often they supported schools and built ancestral halls to serve as ritual centers for their members. The rivalry between lineages dominated the local political landscape.[9] One of the first tasks of the new Communist government after 1949 was to do what no other government in the twentieth century had been able to do—deprive lineages of their weapons and political power and stop the fighting among them. Though first deprived of arms and then, later, of corporate land, lineages were not dispersed but remained clustered in their home villages. In our sample, fully three-fourths of all small villages and neighborhoods within large villages (which make up today's production teams) consist of people belonging to a single lineage. There is reason to believe that strong lineage loyalties might interfere with government programs for change. Accordingly, in later chapters we will compare villages varying by lineage composition to check for the effects of such loyalties. (For the classification used, see Appendix 2.)

Kwangtung has also had a special political history. In the nineteenth and twentieth centuries, Kwangtung acquired the reputation of being a center of rebellion. The leadership of Kwangtung Hakkas in the T'ai-p'ing Rebellion has already been noted. The revolution which overthrew the last imperial government, in 1911, had its early focus in Kwangtung, led by Sun Yat-sen, a Cantonese. In the 1920s both the Communists and the Nationalists did their initial organizing in Kwangtung. After 1927, however, the Nationalists under Chiang Kai-shek were able to extinguish almost all Communist activities as the main Communist units moved first to Kiangsi and then took the Long March north. In the late 1930s, Communist guerrilla units went into operation against the Japanese and then against the Nationalists until the People's Liberation Army arrived in 1949. As the northern main units moved in, they tended to shunt aside the old Kwangtung guerrillas. Outsiders from the north had more seniority in the Communist movement, and some local guerrilla leaders were suspected of being entangled in kinship loyalties and therefore of being unwilling to push violent land reform as vigorously as was thought necessary to break the power of rural landlords and lineages. Though Kwangtung-born officials in Kwangtung were in the majority then, and are today, outsiders tended to get the most powerful posts at each level of administration. The initial inability of these outsiders to speak local dialects, their tendency to take local wives after many years of celibacy in the revolution, and a host of petty complaints and misunderstandings led to ill feelings. The most aggrieved were those guerrillas who felt that they had done just as much to make the revolution as the army coming from the north and that they had been shoved aside for no reason at all or because of simple prejudice against Kwangtung natives. In 1957 some of these guerrillas organized an armed rebellion in the southwestern part of the province which lasted for a number of weeks.[10]

The effects of these difficulties should not be overstated, however. Severe tensions between locals and outsiders were mostly restricted to the upper- and middle-level provincial bureaucracy. At lower levels, outsiders learned local dialects and began to understand local customs. In turn, locals learned Mandarin while becoming more accustomed to practices of the new bureaucracy. Moreover, at the commune and village levels, administration has always been by Kwangtung natives. Local-outsider conflict does not seem to have hindered the implementation of most governmental programs in Kwangtung since the early 1950s. Campaigns such as the collectivization of agriculture occurred just about as fast in the province as elsewhere. Indeed, because of early contact with the West and efforts before 1949, Kwangtung has run ahead of many provinces in health and education programs. Still, we cannot totally dismiss the idea that a heritage of cultural separatism and political rebelliousness may have left an identifiable stamp on the pattern of social change in contemporary Kwangtung.

The great variety that exists within Kwangtung's borders, in terms of agroeconomic regions, ethnic groups, dependence on overseas remittances, and lineage composition, makes the province an excellent site for the study of directed change. Through systematic comparisons of villages with different characteristics, we should be able to say how such conditions foster or retard official efforts to equalize incomes or eliminate "feudal" family practices. Our detailed analysis is meant to apply only to this one populous, complex region, and not to all of rural China. On a number of points, however, we will be able to cite sources which indicate similar phenomena are found in villages elsewhere. The frequency with which we can do this leads us to believe that, for all of Kwangtung's distinctiveness, what we have to say is still relevant for understanding rural change elsewhere.[11]

4

Collective Agricultural Organization

I n order to understand the process of change in rural Kwangtung we need to consider the way in which private farming was transformed into the distinctive Chinese system of collectivized agriculture, and how that system is organized today. Our account of these topics is brief, and interested readers may wish to consult more detailed treatments of these topics elsewhere.[1] We also wish to use this opportunity to describe the variations in organization and channels of influence which we expect may affect the pace of rural change.

Collectivization and Communization

The transformation of agricultural organizations in China occurred in stages. The People's Liberation Army swept into Kwangtung late in 1949 and immediately set about establishing control, disarming the existing local militias and suppressing banditry. After order was restored, land reform was initiated in 1951, directed largely by 123,000 land reform cadres organized into work teams and sent into villages.[2] Peasants were called into meetings and directed to vent their anger against the landlords and rich peasants who had oppressed them. Class labels—landlord, rich peasant, middle peasant, and poor peasant, primarily—were pinned on people at this time, based on their economic position before 1949. Those who had the greatest grievances

30

or who were most active in attacking the landlords were made leaders of the new peasant association, the militia, and the women's federation, and a select few were inducted into the Communist party. The landlords judged most evil were killed in mass meetings, and most of the land of all landlords, and that of corporate lineages, was redistributed to those labeled poor peasants (surviving landlords got a share as well). Though lineage solidarity and conflicts between Kwangtung natives and outsiders caused some problems, land reform was successfully completed by the spring of 1953. The result was an economy of small, private farmers and a new set of rural political organizations and leaders.

Peasants were not destined to retain their newly acquired land for long. The government began immediately to prepare the way for the collectivization of agriculture. The first step, in Kwangtung in 1953, was to form peasants into mutual aid groups composed, on the average, of seven or eight households. Authorities argued that most peasants still lacked sufficient land and other resources to meet their needs, and that exchanging labor, tools, and draft animals with other households would benefit all. Government pressure coincided with both a heritage of similar forms of cooperation before 1949 and the hard fact that each poor peasant family's share of redistributed land was quite small (according to one estimate, for China as a whole less than one acre per family was received).[3] Mutual aid groups spread rapidly, and by the end of 1954 included 60 percent of all peasant households in China. Within these groups each member household retained ownership of its own land and other resources, and if one received more assistance than the others, it was required to reimburse the others.

The second step toward collectivization began in late 1954 and early 1955 when peasants were urged to form cooperatives (lower-stage agricultural producers' cooperatives), each with twenty to forty households. Using studies of a number of experimental cooperatives set up earlier around the country, the government argued that these new organizations would have a number of benefits. By pooling their land, peasants would be able to plow under field boundaries and farm larger fields more efficiently; they would have more manpower and resources to undertake agricultural improvements; and government tax and grain delivery quotas could be managed more effectively. China's leaders also wished to prevent the widening of rural economic differences, which they saw as inevitable as long as private farming remained.

In cooperatives, member households pooled their land, and farm activities were planned by the co-op's management committee on the basis of targets established by the government. Payments to families depended both on the amount of labor contributed during the year by family members and on share payments based on the amount of land or other resources the family gave over to the co-op when it was formed. The cooperative also allocated to each household a small private plot, not to exceed 5 percent of the cultivated land area, whose produce could be sold on free peasant markets nearby. Many farm implements, animals, and fruit trees remained in private hands as well. The government relied heavily on appeals to the former poor peasants in organizing the co-ops, since they not only had benefited most from land reform but could count on still further improvement by pooling together with middle peasants, who still had more land and other resources than the poor peasants. Former middle and rich peasants, although somewhat more reluctant, were enticed both with the promise of a reduction in steep progressive taxes to a lower flat rate and with the security of receiving share payments for the greater amount of property they contributed to the pool. Prodded by new rural cadres anxious to satisfy the cooperativization quotas handed down by higher authorities, peasants began to join the movement in increasing numbers in late 1955.

The third stage of full collectivization began before the previous one had been completed. Wresting the initiative from other leaders, Mao Tse-tung in July 1955 called for larger and more truly socialist collectives (higher-stage agricultural producers' cooperatives). Again, local leaders competed to keep up with the revolutionary tide, and by December of the following year 89 percent of all peasant households in Kwangtung were in collectives. Land now became the property of the collective, without compensation, and the share payments of the co-ops ceased. (Actually, this transformation occurred so rapidly that in many localities no share payments were ever made.) Draft animals, large implements, and orchards were collectivized. However, private plots and free markets remained, and most domestic animals (mainly pigs and poultry) and small tools stayed in private hands. Except for welfare payments, remuneration was now based solely on the labor that members of peasant families contributed to the collective.

The acceleration of collectivization caused some problems. Some peasants killed and ate their animals rather than turn them over to the collectives, and some peasants resisted joining and fled to the cities. The new collectives proved unwieldy, their cadres being insufficiently trained in accounting, labor allocation, and other needed skills, and most were subdivided into more manageable units.[4] Some disbanded altogether, and had to be reor-

ganized later. Nevertheless, in comparison with the violent collectivization
in the Soviet Union in 1929–30, the process in China went relatively
smoothly. A number of factors contributed to this success. Through private
plots, labor-incentive payment systems, nonconfiscatory crop delivery
quotas, adequate purchase prices, and descriptions of the superiority of
collectivized agriculture, the authorities moved to reassure peasants that they
would not suffer economically. The movement toward collectivization in
stages was also important. Peasants could gain familiarity with new forms of
cooperation built upon traditional forms but would be unlikely to develop a
strong commitment to any one stage. Perhaps most crucial were political
factors. Through the land-reform campaign, party organizations and a core
group of cadres and activists were built up in each locality. This indigenous
leadership, grateful for the gains they had made since 1949, could lead and
pressure relatives and neighbors to join the new organizations. Also, the
dangers of opposing the new government were evident, with the killing of
landlords and bandits during land reform still fresh in the minds of the more
reluctant peasants. At each stage, the majority of local peasants—those
labeled as poor peasants during land reform—could calculate that their interests would be served by gaining access to the resources of their more advantaged neighbors and could be persuaded to lead the movement into the next
higher stage. Even those labeled as middle peasants and rich peasants,
whose interests would suffer, could at least comfort themselves with the
thought that the other members of the collective and its leaders would be
their relatives and neighbors, people they had known and dealt with all their
lives. By the end of 1956, then, the vast majority of China's 100 million
farm families had been organized into collective farms.[5]

Scarcely two years later a more dramatic and disruptive shift occurred
with the formation of rural people's communes. After a radical reevaluation
of the faults of the Soviet-style institutions built during the previous years,
China's leaders in 1958 called on peasants to leap into an almost fully
communist society. The new commune was much larger than any previous
unit, embracing in many cases tens of thousands of people. In the most
adventurous locales peasants were drawn from their own villages and organized into specialized production teams which served the entire unit—
plowers, metalworkers, vegetable growers, and so forth. Food consumption
no longer depended entirely on the amount of work performed, with some
provided as free supply and served in the new mess halls that sprang up.
Private plots were eliminated and rural free markets were closed. Nursery

schools and medical care were provided free of charge, and by planning work-tasks and allocating income from the commune center, rural income differentials were dramatically reduced.

Again the impressive political system the Chinese Communists had built was able to lead the peasants into the communes, but it could not make the system work. Everything went wrong. The commune leaders were not equipped to manage the activities of such a huge and complex organization, and in the enthusiasm of the moment they diverted too much labor from farming to a variety of untested schemes: backyard steel furnances, roadbuilding, and large construction projects. Peasants had to work together with people from other villages with whom they had no history of cooperation, and the former poor-peasant allies of the government now realized that those who did not work as hard as they or who lived in poorer villages were reaping undue benefits from the new system. Natural disasters compounded these problems, and as food shortages reached crisis levels, peasants ceased to obey their local leaders and tried to feed their families by any means possible.

Faced with the breakdown of the commune system, national authorities modified that system in an effort to restore production and morale. Communes were subdivided into units one-third to one-half as large. The labor management and income-sharing unit was decentralized, first to the production brigade of 100 to 350 households, and finally in 1962 to the production team of only 20 to 40 households. For the peasants a return to familiar forms was involved, since these units corresponded more or less to the collectives and cooperatives of earlier years, which were in turn based upon natural village and kin-group alignments. Daily work and income sharing now involved only the members of one's own team, and a work-point system keyed to the labor contributed was resurrected. The free supply of grain, mess halls, and nurseries were all eliminated, and private plots and free peasant markets were restored. This revised commune system, essentially the collective of the 1956–58 era, with a higher coordinating and planning level, the commune, added on, was codified in the Work Regulations for Rural People's Communes of 1962 (known as the Sixty Articles), a set of regulations still in force today.[6]

Some of China's leaders were less pleased with this retrenchment than others. To the "radicals" the post-1962 communes, with their private plots, individual incentives, free markets, and limited cooperation, were not adequate for building the communist society of the future. In the wake of the Cultural Revolution (1966–69) there was an effort to use the campaign to study the national-model Tachai brigade to introduce further changes into the commune structure. Work payments were to be as much according to labor enthusiasm and ideology as to skill and work effort; team or brigade as opposed to private raising of pigs was to be stressed; and private plots were to be restricted in size or even abolished. In some villages authorities succeeded in moving the unit of accounting back up from the team to the brigade, following the Tachai practice (although brigades in Kwangtung are much larger). Even though these changes were less sudden and dramatic than those of 1958, peasants saw their interests threatened again by the loss of work payments to the enthusiastic but unskilled and by the necessity of sharing with poorer production teams; they grumbled, and dragged their heels. By the end of 1971 the authorities recognized that this revived attempt to institute a more egalitarian structure was not working, and they gave approval for the changes to be discarded where they did not suit "local conditions."[7] In 1975 radical elements in the leadership again tried to develop support for an eventual return to some of the early commune forms, although with their purge in the following year a major effort of this type seems unlikely.[8]

Administrative Levels

Like other provinces, Kwangtung is divided first into prefectures (ti-ch'ü) and then into counties (hsien). There are seven prefectures, plus Canton and Hainan Island, and a total of ninety-seven counties. In 1973 there were 1,721 communes in Kwangtung, or an average of about 17 communes per county, and about 23,000 people per commune.[9]

The term "commune" may be misleading to readers, since the organization has little in common with communes in most Western societies. Essentially it is both a complex collective farm and a unit of rural government. Though the commune administration is sufficiently distant that most peasants are unclear about its leaders and detailed organization, many of the services which peasants need are available only in the commune seat. If the barefoot doctor in his village cannot cure an illness, the patient gets approval to go to the clinic in the commune town to see a regular doctor. If his children are among those fortunate enough to attend upper middle-school, they will almost invariably have to reside in the commune seat to do so. The commune runs grain mills, oil presses, tractor repair stations, and some small factories, employing people from surrounding villages. Similarly, it is in the commune town that barbers, carpenters, bamboo workers, knife sharpeners, and other service workers are organized into special co-ops for artisans. The commune plays a major role in coordinating the economic plans of subordinate brigades and teams and in collecting state taxes and grain deliveries, and the commune is often the level at which irrigation projects and electrification plans are undertaken. Its activities range from allocating fertilizer and water pumps to issuing marriage permits.

The production brigade (sheng-ch'an ta-tui) tends to encompass a single large village or several small villages. In 1973, there were over twenty thousand brigades in Kwangtung—an average of about twelve per commune. Though some brigades are considerably larger, the average brigade in Kwangtung now includes 450 households, or two thousand people. We expect the size of a brigade to influence its social life—large brigades will have more resources but also more problems of management and financial accounting; small brigades will be more internally cohesive but have fewer resources. Accordingly, in later chapters we compare brigades above and below the average population of two thousand.

The brigade has a number of administrative functions. In consultation with the teams below and the commune above, it helps set production targets and compulsory quotas for grain, animals, and vegetables. It helps to allocate fertilizer, new machinery, and production supplies. It frequently owns and operates small industries, such as brick factories, oil presses, and repair stations for agricultural implements. It is likely to manage and finance at least one primary school, and typically it has a veterinarian and a health station with one or more barefoot doctors and midwives.

The production team (sheng-ch'an hsiao-tui) is a village neighborhood or a single small village. In our Kwangtung sample, a typical team contains 30 to 40 households (150 to 200 people) with 5 to 30 hectares (12 to 74 acres) of land. There are 5 million teams in the country, for an average of seven teams per brigade. It is the production team which is closest to the peasant's day-to-day existence. As noted earlier, it is the team that assigns daily work and at the end of the year divides its income among members, thus being termed the "basic accounting unit" in the countryside. As with brigades, we expect the size of a team to have some influence on its social life, and in later chapters we compare teams with more and less than two hundred people.[10]

Channels of Influence

One of the great strengths of the government in China since 1949 has been the cultivation of leaders in the countryside and the ability to get messages and programs from Peking to the remotest villages. Through many years of guerrilla activities and grass-roots organizing in the revolution prior to 1949, the Communists worked out many ways of organizing and communicating with the peasantry. These channels of influence—operating through the party and government, mass organizations, and communications media— continue to give them close contact with villages today. Villages differ, however, in their exposure to the various channels.

As throughout the national administrative network, rural administration is shared between parallel Communist party and government units, with the party having hegemony. At the level of the commune there is a party committee composed of members elected by party branches at the brigade level. Most of the members also double in commune revolutionary committee administrative roles. As in other Leninist systems, the party secretary is the most prestigious and powerful person in the commune. The secretary is usually from outside the commune, and his seniority and rank give him authority over all other leaders.

Typically, the lowest level at which the party is organized is the brigade. Below this level there are usually not enough members in any one team to form a party cell. The party branch, composed of all party members in the brigade, elects officers for the branch committee, frequently including a secretary, vice-secretary, a women's-work committeewoman who is in charge of the woman's federation, a security officer who may also head the militia, a youth-work committeeman who also heads the youth league, and perhaps others. (The commune party committee must approve the selections.) As at the commune level, the party secretary stands above all the others in power and prestige. Most wear two hats, serving both as party leaders and brigade administrators. Wearing their administrative hats, they carry out the more mundane tasks of day-to-day brigade management.

Party membership in all of China grew from 17 million in 1961 to 28 million in 1973 (and more than 35 million in 1977). Despite this increase in membership, which brought many younger members into the party after the Cultural Revolution, the party is still a fairly exclusive club. In the forty-one teams for which we have information, party membership ranges from a low of no members (in five teams) to a high of about 8 percent. Average membership in the total village population is about 1 percent, though membership among adult males, who are the ones most likely to join the party, is around 5 percent. From reading the press, one would expect these differences in party membership to make a great difference in policy implementation. When new policies are introduced, it is the party members who are called into meetings first and asked to lead the way by becoming living examples. In the area of birth control and family practices, party members are the ones first asked to accept vasectomy, to marry their daughter without receiving a bride price, or to introduce "Mao Tse-tung thought study classes" into their homes. One would expect, then, that those villages with the most party members would be the ones most likely to implement government programs readily.

In contrast to the party structure, which often stops at the brigade, the government structure covers all three levels of subcounty administration—commune, brigade, and team. The commune government typically includes some forty functionaries ranging from revolutionary committee leaders to clerks, accountants, and warehouse keepers. Virtually all these functionaries receive a fixed state salary and a fixed monthly allotment of grain. These help bind them to the state rather than to the village. A second mechanism which helps bind top officers to the state is that some are not native to the commune in which they serve.

Village (brigade and team) leaders are quite different from those in the commune. Village leaders get their income not from the state but from the village. With only a few exceptions, village leaders must work in the fields beside other villagers, and their income and grain go up and down, depending on the year's harvest, just like everyone else's. Similarly, almost invariably they are natives of the village in which they serve. Indeed they are typically not just natives but brothers, cousins, uncles, and nephews of the people whom they attempt to lead. Control of these leaders is, then, somewhat more problematic than central control of commune leaders. Of course, there is ideological control of some leaders. The brigade secretary gets his position because of demonstrated loyalty to the party. A recalcitrant village leader will soon find his village without the supplies of fertilizer, machinery, and other goods that can be allocated only through the state apparatus, and unable to get loans for needed improvements. Should all else fail, more direct means of intervention can be applied. A commune vice-secretary may come to live in the village and temporarily take over village leadership. In production teams suffering a steady drop in production or in teams that cannot agree on a leader among themselves such intervention is farily common. Also, there are special campaigns which bring work teams of two to six outsiders to take over a village. For example, in the Socialist Education Campaign of 1962–65, university teachers, clerks, and officials descended upon villages in such units to dig out corruption and feudal practices. After the Cultural Revolution, the People's Liberation Army joined with officials to supervise the restoration of order in some villages. Still, control of local leaders remains a problem, as we shall see in more detail in Chapter 7.

One channel of negative influence, in the eyes of Chinese authorities, is that stemming from former landlord and rich peasant families residing in the village. They are usually depicted as yearning for the good old days when they dominated village life, and as trying to undermine peasant support for socialism. (For details on class labels and official policy, see Chapter 7.) Within our sample of villages the proportion of such "bad class" families ranged from seven teams that had none all the way to one unusual team which had eighteen former rich peasant families (but no former landlords) out of a total of thirty-two households! The usual range is from 5 to 10 percent of team households with such classifications, and if the government's picture is correct we can expect variations in this figure to affect local responsiveness to change.

Besides the party and government, there are other organizations designed to help implement official policy. They include the Poor and Lower-Middle Peasants' Association, the Women's Federation, the Youth League, and the militia. Though the character of the Poor and Lower-Middle Peasants' Association has changed somewhat since it was formed in 1963, one of its main goals is to heighten class consciousness. The organization is supposed to serve as a reminder that the interests of those labeled poor and lower-middle peasants during land reform are still linked, and that they need to be constantly vigilant against the capitalist and feudal tendencies of class enemies. Originally designed to supervise and criticize local cadres as well, the organization's role is now restricted to auditing village accounts. Even in this milder role, the association or its representative is active in only about half of the thirty-nine villages for which we have information from interviews.[11] Though the function of the Poor and Lower-Middle Peasants' Association has been muted over time, we take the existence of the activity of this association or its representative as one indicator of the degree of class consciousness in a village.

Another organization in the village is the Women's Federation. All women by virtue of their sex belong, and the organization is nebulous in form—there are no special badges, dues, or even a fixed schedule of meetings. At the brigade level, the women's representative dedicates much of her efforts to mass agitation. At meetings on International Women's Day and at occasional meetings through the year, she agitates for planned births and family hygiene. She also encourages women to work in the fields.

Though not formally a part of the federation, the female vice-chief in each team may help assign work to women and helps agitate for things such as planned births.

Youth are mobilized in the Communist Youth League and the militia. Though occasionally a stepping stone to full party membership, membership in the Youth League is considerably less exclusive. After the league was attacked at the start of the Cultural Revolution, many of its village activities stopped. Though it was slowly being reactivated in the early 1970s, in most villages for which we have information the league was still only minimally active in 1973.

The militia is one of the most active organizations in most villages. Except for sons and daughters of former landlords and rich peasants, virtually all men and many women between eighteen and forty-five are nominally members of the regular militia. The regular militia, however, seldom has any activities. The active units are the "basic militia" (chi-kan min-ping), organized at the brigade level, and the "armed militia," usually organized at the commune level. The basic militia consists of ablebodied males and some females in their late teens and twenties. They periodically meet and occasionally perform nightly guard duty around the village, its orchards, and fish ponds. At times they look for saboteurs and people escaping to Hong Kong. Nevertheless, the militia's military role is often secondary to other roles. Its members usually have no more than a gun or two kept at the brigade office, and only sporadically do they practice with guns or live ammunition. It would appear that they are often more important as a study unit. The militia has its own instructional material covering not only military knowledge but also political values, and a well-run unit will devote regular attention to youth indoctrination. In some places, the members of the basic militia also serve as "shock troops" for production emergencies, working around the clock to bring in the harvest before bad weather or working in the mud and rain to hold back a flood.

The armed militia, consisting mostly of retired army men, is usually organized directly under the commune's armed forces department. Its members, who have guns and carry out periodic target practice, guard bridges or railroads on major holidays, but they rarely use their guns. When called out for emergencies (such as brawls between villages), they normally use only batons and manual contact. The average villager has little regular contact with this unit.

Besides formal organizations, there are other means by which information and official policies sift down to the peasant from cities and the central government. Over the years, broadcasting networks have spread ever more widely. Some networks are wired into a central commune station and enable commune leaders to communicate directly with villages. Other networks originate in the brigade. Among the forty-five villages for which we have information, thirty-nine have a broadcast network of some sort or other. Most of these networks have speakers atop posts or buildings in the street. A few broadcast through speakers in each peasant's home.[12] Through these networks, local cadres awaken the peasants early in the morning with martial music, announcements about the day's work, and, occasionally, morning political lessons. Some localities broadcast farm bulletins and revolutionary music intermittently throughout the day.

Though only a few peasants receive regional and national newspapers, almost all teams subscribe to one or more. Usually, both the *People's Daily* and the *Southern Daily,* printed in Canton, are available in the team office. Most brigades and isolated teams are visited at least every few months by a film team showing newsreels and movie versions of new revolutionary operas.[13] Separate spare-time propaganda teams, run by brigade or county, are much less common than immediately after the Cultural Revolution; today they appear with any frequency in only about a third of the villages for which we have information. Where they do exist, the spare-time propaganda teams consist of village youth who practice in the evening after field work and then travel about neighboring villages performing short skits, arias from revolutionary operas, or other pieces of music.

Though widely touted following the Cultural Revolution, team meetings for political study are presently rare in Kwangtung. Only about one-fourth of our villages now have regular study meetings. It simply proved too difficult to make the directives and documents coming down from above relevant and interesting to the peasants. Even in those villages which now have study groups, some of the educated youth who served for a time as study directors in these groups report great exasperation in trying to make political study materials comprehensible to peasants. Enthusiasm and discussion among peasants is reserved for production planning sessions and work-point meetings. New values about cooperation, sharing, and the power of collective effort may be taught in production meetings, but usually it is only by putting things in economic terms that interest can be generated.[14]

Schools provide another channel for government influence. As can be expected in a rural society, some children never attend school and others drop out before completing primary school. Still, in comparison with rates in earlier times, current school attendance is impressive. In about one-third of our villages virtually every child now completes primary school. In almost half of our villages upwards of 90 percent of those children who could be going to school are indeed in school, although not all graduate. Only in the remaining villages, roughly one-sixth of our sample, does a sizable proportion of children never attend school or drop out very early. Socialization of children into new values could begin even earlier in collectively run nurseries. In most villages, children continue to be cared for by grandparents in the home or by neighbors. In about one-fifth of our villages, however, there are now nurseries attended by some children. (For further discussion of rural education, see Chapters 6 and 11.)

Another way central values may sift down to villages is through educated urban youth. Starting in the early 1960s but increasing in tempo after 1968, graduates of urban lower-middle and upper-middle schools have been sent to live in villages, where in theory most were to remain for life. The difficulties of adjusting to reduced living standards and inhospitality by some peasants who can not tolerate "lazy urban manners" have been severe. Many urban youth have slipped back to Canton or even to Hong Kong. Nevertheless, in the village some youth have assumed positions as primary-school teachers, political study leaders, cultural performers, work-point recorders, pig breeders, and occasionally barefoot doctors. Gradually, technical roles for educated youth are emerging, and books about pig breeding, seed selection, and other kinds of agricultural technology, written explicitly for educated youth, are pouring off the presses. In remote areas which previously had little urban contact, urban youth may have great cultural impact.[15] Three factors attenuate the impact of educated urban youth, however. They are sent disproportionately to delta villages near Canton, where they are less likely to be extremely different from the receiving villagers. Averaging less than 3 percent of village populations, they tend not to be a major social group in a village. What voice they could have is attenuated by the inability of many urban youth to match the labor output, or earn the esteem, of the leading native laborers who dominate formal and informal leadership positions in most villages.[16]

Finally, urban influences can penetrate village life directly. Those living in villages close to major cities like Canton and Swatow should not be strangers to urban ways. They may travel to the city periodically on commune or private business, they are likely to have relatives in the city they can visit, and they will share in the general village heritage of close urban contacts established by the pre-1949 process of commercialization.

From our discussion here the reader can see that a distinctive form of collectivized agriculture was built in the Chinese countryside which, even if it does not match the aspirations of some leaders, possesses multiple channels for getting the government's case for change across to peasants. In later chapters we wish to investigate the importance of these channels for producing rural change. From all the topics discussed we managed to construct six separate measures of influence which we will use to analyze our village data (for specific details on their construction, see Appendix 2).

Political Density: a measure constructed from three separate variables—the percentage of local party members, the presence or absence of a functioning Poor and Lower-Middle Peasant Association, and a low or high proportion of former landlord and rich peasant families (note that a *low* proportion of such families is judged conducive to government influence).

Political Study: the presence of a regular political study system or not.

These measures we conceive as tapping the ability of higher administrative authorities to maintain class consciousness in the village and get the party's message effectively communicated. In later analysis we will label these "administrative" variables:

Urban Proximity: proximity to Canton or Swatow.

Urban Youths: a relatively high or low proportion of sent-down urban youths living locally.

Communications: a measure constructed from three separate variables—high or low school attendance, frequent or infrequent movie-team visits, and a well-developed or rudimentary wired radio network.

Nurseries: whether the brigade or team runs nursery schools or kindergartens.

These measures we conceive as tapping more general kinds of normative influences reaching villages from the cities and the mass media. We will in subsequent analysis refer to these as "urban communications" variables. We note that these six measures are not all closely related; a village which has many sent-down youth present is not necessarily likely to have a regular political study system, and so forth. (For the correlations among these measures, see Appendix 2.)

These measures we plan to use to investigate the claims for the importance of normative influences made in both the Chinese Communist and modernization theories of social change. More generally, in combination with our measures of team and brigade size and the ethnic, economic, and other variables introduced in Chapter 3, we now have the means to make systematic comparisons of the pattern of social change in different types of villages, comparisons we expect to reveal much about how such change was actually produced.

2

institutional arrangements and the pursuit of equality

5

Material Equality
and Inequality

O ne of the great promises of socialism has been that it will lead to less inequality. By confiscation of the property of landlords and the urban bourgeoisie, the obstacles to equality in income, power, and status may be reduced and eventually eliminated. Despite this promise, socialist regimes commonly have great difficulty realizing their egalitarian goals, and even introduce new kinds of disparities. A number of reasons for such difficulties have been noted. One is the conflict between equality and efficiency. When market mechanisms (which produce inequality) are forsaken for an administred economy (to secure equality), significant indicators of rational and efficient behavior are lost. Decisions are inevitably centralized, with a growth in administrative overhead and a loss of contact by the administrators with the realities of daily life.[1] In fact, the centralization of power involved may give rise to a "new class" of political bureaucrats who oppress the common people even more than did the old propertied elite.[2] Another dilemma is the conflict between equality and equity. Equality exists when similar rewards are given to everyone, regardless of effort or ability. Equity exists when people are rewarded according to their contribution to an endeavor. In most settings, Western social scientists note, people are in favor of equity but opposed to equality.[3] You cannot have both. The experience of the Soviet Union illustrates these problems and others. In that country the stress on centralization of decision-making and its costs, in terms of efficiency and responsiveness to popular needs, are clearly visible, but equality has not carried the day. Equity as a principle of distribution has been consistently stressed since the late 1920s, and the Stalinist pattern of rapid economic growth and investment in heavy industry aggravated many existing inequalities. Have the Chinese done things differently, though? Certainly a leadership which, long after the revolution, continues to mount a series of sometimes violent mass campaigns in the name of egalitarian goals (and against Soviet "revisionism") seems to be intent on writing a new script. In the chapters that follow we will discuss how China's leaders have dealt with a number of issues involving inequality in the countryside. In particular, we want to know what kinds of inequalities continue to exist or are being modified, and what the sources of continuing disparities are.

We begin, appropriately enough in dealing with a Marxist society, by considering material equality and inequality in Kwangtung villages. Four aspects will be considered here. Does the state expropriate peasant production for the sake of industrial growth? Have the Chinese been able to narrow the gap between rural and urban incomes? How much inequality is there between villages, and what are its sources? How much inequality is there among individuals and households within the same village?

State-Peasant Inequality

The concern with state expropriation of peasant production comes from the Soviet experience of the 1930s and 1940s, when collective farms were used to generate investment funds for heavy industry. Through both taxes and excessively low grain purchase prices, the state siphoned funds out of the countryside for use in the industrial sector. It was only in the 1950s that Soviet collective farms began to be given more reasonable prices for their products and to receive more state investment.

For China, because figures on national expenditures in agriculture have not been published for the 1960s and 1970s, we cannot state precisely how much is or is not being directly siphoned from agriculture into the higher reaches of state administration. From three sources, however, we can get an idea of the general dimensions of the drain or lack of drain. The 1962 Draft Regulations for People's Communes (the Sixty Articles) established limits for various kinds of expenditures.[4] Visitors in the 1960s and 1970s learned the pattern of expenditures in various communes.[5] And in the early 1970s several provinces published new handbooks for rural accountants which gave detailed examples of rural expenditures.[6] The examples in these handbooks, though hypothetical, appear to be sincere attempts to reconstruct the experience of average teams. An example from the Kwangtung accountant's handbook is shown in table 1. In this and other sources production costs (category A) for seeds, fertilizer, machinery depreciation, and so on are typically 15 to 30 percent, with richer, more mechanized teams having higher, and poor teams lower, expenses. State taxes (category B) consist primarily of a grain tax, paid in kind, plus minor taxes on sideline activities, such as pig raising. The grain tax was set at a fixed amount in the 1950s and has not been raised since. Because the tax is a fixed absolute amount, in most teams grain production has increased and the proportion paid in tax has declined. Usually the grain tax ranges somewhere between 3 and 8 percent of the gross income of the team. Even when it is remembered that this is a percentage of gross income rather than of income less production expenses, the amount seems modest.[7]

Table 1	Annual Expenditures of "Hsiang-yang Production Team"		
	Yuan	%	%
A. Production costs	5,280		21.1
B. State taxes	990		4.0
C. Collective withholdings			11.9
Capital accumulation	1,500	6.0	
Cash reserve	500	2.0	
Grain reserve	392	1.5	
Public benefit fund	500	2.0	
Distributions via brigade	93	0.4	
D. Member distributions	15,745		63.0
Total	25,000		100.0

Source: Hypothetical example given in China People's Bank, Kwangtung Province Branch, ed., Nung-ts'un jen-min kung-she sheng-ch'an tui k'uai-chi [Rural people's commune production team accountant] (Canton: Kwangtung People's Press, 1974), p. 111 All figures are stated in cash values, even though they involve some goods which are never converted into cash but distributed in kind. For example, rice distributions to members are calculated at the state, within-contract, purchase price of .098 yuan per catty.

Besides the payments to the state, withholdings must be taken by the collective—the brigade and team (category C). The capital accumulation fund is a reserve for future purchases of draft animals and farm machinery as well as for major water control projects. The cash reserve fund is used to store up money for fertilizer, buckets, and other production expenses that will be incurred between harvests. The grain reserve, restored since the Cultural Revolution and the Sino-Soviet war scare of 1969, provides security against famine or war. The public benefit fund, often translated as "welfare fund" is used partly to provide small, direct welfare grants to members but primarily to pay for education, medicine, and public ceremonial events. Distributions via the brigade are used to pay brigade cadres. Larger amounts are passed up to the brigade through the capital accumulation fund for investment in brigade brick kilns, machinery repair shops, or other enterprises, and through the public benefit fund to pay for the brigade-run health station and school. Typically, these separate withholdings total between 5 and 15 percent of gross income, with richer teams withholding more and poorer teams less.

Team members are usually residual claimants on the balance sheet (category D). Though the state occasionally provides a low-level floor for major downward swings in consumption, minor swings have had to be borne by peasants just as by farmers throughout the world. The proportion of the team budget consumed typically ranges from 50 to 70 percent with an average of about 60 percent.[8] This 60 percent is not too different from what an "average" Chinese peasant retained after paying taxes, land rent, and production costs in the 1930s.[9] But today peasants get more services—education, medical care, agricultural extension services, protection against theft—for the 40 percent that they give up. And, as we shall note later, they earn extra money in the private sector, much of which goes untaxed. Direct payments from peasants to the state and collective, then, do not seem inordinate.

Of greater concern to those who know the history of collective farms in the Soviet Union is whether the state imposes a hidden tax through compulsory grain purchases or through sales of manufactured goods at inflated prices. There are three types of grain deliveries which production teams make to the state. They remit state-tax grain without compensation—this we have already discussed. They sell grain within contract, and they may sell grain above contract. The price paid for grain sold within contract has been raised several times.[10] In Kwangtung before 1966, unhusked, standard grade-three rice was purchased within contract for .089 yuan per catty. Since 1966 that rice has been purchased within contract for .098 yuan per catty. The amount of grain a team is obligated to sell within contract is set in negotiations every three to five years. On the basis of the amount produced in the preceding three to five years, the contract specifies what can reasonably be produced in the coming three to five years and turned over to the state. Under conditions of severe drought, flood, or other hardship the contract may be rescinded. As an added incentive for teams to sell even more grain, the state offers a premium price for any grain sold above contract, which in Kwangtung in 1973 was .12 yuan per catty, an amount about one-fifth greater than the contract price.[11]

While purchase prices were being raised in the 1950s and 1960s, retail grain prices stayed virtually constant. As a result, by the late 1960s, the state had a difficult time breaking even on contract grain, not to mention premium grain. When husked, polished, and transported to Canton, rationed standard grade rice sells for .142 or .146 yuan per catty. Since about one-third of the weight of the rice is lost in husking and polishing, and since there are milling and transport costs, it is easy to believe reports by provincial officials that they must subsidize grain sales.[12] Though the state can make up part of this deficit through grade-one rice exported at some profit each year, the amounts so traded are small compared to total internal grain sales. There is, then, little or no profit in the state grain trade.

A more complex issue is whether the state, even though it makes no direct profit, still imposes a heavy cost on the peasant. What would happen if the grain market were freed of all state controls? There is a black market in grain which in the 1970s brought a price of about .30 yuan per catty of unhusked rice. If urban rationing and rural allocations ended in favor of a free market, would grain prices rise to .30 yuan per catty? Probably not. The black market trade is currently quite small. The urban ration (often about thirty catties per month for male nonmanual workers) is already more than many can eat. Black market grain is used primarily by families who have some special need, such as a wedding where many guests must be fed, and peasants can usually find a black market buyer for only small amounts at a time.

Another government constraint on the grain market is the compulsory planting of low-profit grain when peasants would rather plant high-profit fruits, vegetables, and the like. What would happen if all planting controls were removed? It is difficult to say. As peasants rushed to plant fruits and vegetables, rice prices would shoot up while fruit and vegetable prices would fall. Where they would eventually stabilize is difficult to estimate. What would happen if not only the domestic market were opened up but also the international market? In 1973–74, when international rice prices were high, the Chinese peasant could have done quite well on the international market, but to calculate exactly what would be the peasant's net position after both buying and selling on the international market is again quite difficult. More to the point, speculation about uncontrolled market behavior in grain is so far removed from what most countries, including the U.S., allow, and so far removed from what the Chinese government is likely to allow, that one is reluctant to pursue it further. It seems sufficient to note that, within their own system, the Chinese are attempting to balance the twin goals of using grain sales to assist peasants while guaranteeing a constant flow of cheap grain to cities. In the trade between countryside and city, peasants do not suffer inordinate losses.

Even if the state does not impose a hidden tax through grain purchases, it might do so through the ad valorem tax hidden in the price of tractors, fertilizer, and other goods sold to the countryside. Over the war years preceding 1949, the price scissors—the differential in prices between industrial and agricultural products—moved against agriculture. By the early 1950s, the ratio of prices paid for goods bought to prices paid for goods sold by peasants was about 30 percent higher than in 1936. It took the new government almost ten years to correct this situation, but through successive increases in prices paid for agricultural goods and successive decreases in prices for fertilizer, tractors, and other goods sold in rural areas, the price scissors changed to about 10 percent in favor of agriculture by 1964 (relative to the 1936 situation). With a few additional changes since that time, part of the increasing peasant standard of living is simply the result of changes in prices.[13] Tractor prices, at 2,500 to 3,000 yuan for a twelve horsepower hand tractor, remain high. Agricultural machinery plants visited by foreigners typically have a healthy margin of about 25 percent between costs and selling price. The margin in agricultural goods, however, must be lower than in other goods, for the press reports that local producers are tempted to produce for the urban market rather than for the rural market, which has "no profit." They must be persuaded of the necessity to serve agriculture first. The state does make much more on consumer goods, such as cloth, boots, radios, vacuum bottles, and cooking oils that are sold to peasants, but no more than when these same goods are sold to urban consumers.

Overall, direct payments from agriculture to the state total only 5 percent of all state funds. Indirect payments seem small as well. It is to the profits of urban industry—particularly urban light industry—rather than agriculture that the state must turn to find new investment funds for further economic development.[14] In contrast to the Soviet Union in earlier years, the Chinese are not following a policy of soaking agriculture to pay for urban industry. But this less extractive policy has its own costs as well as benefits, as we shall see subsequently.

Urban-Rural Inequality

The Chinese have a number of programs in addition to price changes for reducing urban-rural inequality: since 1956, urban incomes have been held fairly constant while rural incomes have been allowed to rise. More factories have been built in the countryside, and many factories in small cities have been commanded to produce products which serve agriculture, such as water pumps, tractors, and fertilizer. Rural medical care has been improved, as has rural education. Despite these efforts, a large gap remains. In the 1930s the urban-rural income ratio was about two to one, and in the 1940s and early 1950s it widened somewhat. Though the evidence is spotty, there is some indication that by the 1970s the gap had been brought back to around two to one.[15] To take an example, an average worker in a state factory in Canton will make about 55 yuan per month and receive fringe benefits, such as free medical care and a pension. He will work out of the weather and receive a fixed monthly salary. In Kwangtung countryside, in contrast, the average ablebodied male will receive only about 25 yuan per month, including income in cash and kind from both the collective and private sector.[16] His medical care will be only partially subsidized, and with a few rare exceptions he will receive no pension. He will work outside in the elements, and much of his salary will not be distributed until after the fall harvest, when the sum received will vary depending on the year's weather and other factors. The comparison is crude, but it suggests a sizable remaining difference.[17] The Chinese may be credited with efforts to keep the rural-urban income gap from widening, but the effort to reduce the gap further has proved very difficult.

Regardless of the exact dimensions of the gap, it is sufficient to create a desire among young peasants to move to, and among sent-down urban youth to return to, the city. Many of the youth one interviews in Hong Kong have come there not out of any desire to escape communism but simply out of a desire for an urban job. If they could have done so, they would have preferred to go to Canton. A rural-urban gap and a desire to leave the countryside are common in all developing societies. What is uncommon is that China has been able to contain this desire for migration and partially even to reverse the flow.

In the mid-1950s, there was a great movement of peasants to the city. The government soon became concerned about the disorder and extra expenses this movement could create, and by 1958 they passed strict laws prohibiting uncontrolled migration. Article 2 of the 1958 Regulations Governing Household Registration states,

A citizen who wants to move from the countryside to a city must possess an employment certificate issued by the labor bureau of the city, a certificate of admission issued by a school, or a moving certificate issued by

the household registration office of the city of destination, and must
apply to the household registration office in his or her permanent place
of residence for permission to move out and fulfill the moving procedure.[18]

The concern with urban expenses was so great that even men who were
selected by industry were not allowed to bring their wives and children.
Dependents had to remain in the village. If the dependents left agriculture,
one writer noted, money would have to be spent on additional housing,
food, and social services. "If [this] colossal sum were to be so spent, we
might as well shelve our five-year plans and forget about socialism."[19] In
addition, large numbers of urban residents have been cleared out of the cities
in periodic campaigns and "sent down" to the countryside, including 12
million urban secondary-school graduates in the years 1968–75.

The Chinese effort to limit migration has been largely successful. The
control on grain rations and work permits and the tightness of urban
neighborhood surveillance are sufficient to keep most peasants out of cities.
There are people who live in cities illegally, but these are primarily educated
urban youth who have returned to live with their families. In the countryside, 90 percent of the young males are still in their home villages,
frequently living with or next door to their parents.[20] This contrasts with
Taiwan, where over half of the young village males have left to seek urban
jobs.[21] The Chinese Communists, thus, have tried not only to attack the
urban-rural gap directly but also to limit what they see as its negative
consequences.

Community Inequality

In addition to the income differences between city and countryside, there are
large differences between villages. In places visited by foreigners, the average ratio of high to low incomes among teams in the same commune has
been about two to one, with the highest ratio observed being seven to one.[22]
In our Kwangtung interviews, there are examples of four-to-one ratios
among teams in the same village, and even wider differences between teams
in diverse parts of the province. Suburban villages selling fruits and vegetables to a city provide incomes as high as that of any factory worker. Villages
in hills distant from any city pay incomes several times lower than a city
worker receives. The government has a mixed policy regarding these differences. On the one hand, it emphasizes self-reliance, or doing things on
one's own, which tends to maintain differences. On the other, it occasion-

ally gives special assistance, such as loans to people in substandard housing, which tends to help the very poorest villages. In 1958 and 1969 the government also tried to amalgamate rich and poor teams into larger income-sharing units, without much success, as we saw in Chapter 4. Regardless of the exact policy, the differences between villages are difficult to attack. We noted in Chapter 3 that there are important regional differences in rural prosperity in Kwangtung which have a long history. We investigate the sources of village inequality in greater detail here, using economic variables coded from our interviews.

The importance of natural conditions can be seen clearly in table 2. The level of local grain yields and daily pay for peasant laborers depend to a large extent on the availability of an adequate amount of fairly level, fertile soil and a reliable supply of water for irrigation. The Pearl River Delta is favored in most of these respects, and was also one of the areas first able to adopt new "miracle" rice seeds in the 1960s, since these seeds require ample water and fertilizer. The table also shows that the level of grain yields is closely associated with the value of a day's work-points in a locality (gamma=.92), although the two measures relate somewhat differently to individual characteristics of teams.[23]

Table 2   Reported Grain Yields and Work-Day Values by Ecological Conditions of Production Teams (Gamma Statistics)

	Grain yields	Work-day value	Median number of teams
Work day value	.92*	--	(37)
Ecological Conditions			
Irrigation supply	.61	.16	(35)
Terrain	.40[a]	.44	(36)
Land/labor ratio	.32	.60*[b]	(34)
Delta region	.43	.72*	(41)

Source: Generally, unless otherwise noted, all tables are based on our sample of 63 Kwangtung villages. Because the interview questions were open-ended and varied somewhat over time, not all informants responded to exactly the same set of queries, nor were all informants able to respond to all queries. As a result, the number of informants on whom tabular data are based varies from item to item, with the average base for tabulations being indicated by the "median number of teams" with complete information (hereafter, "median N").

[a] Control by delta region reduces this association to .09. Control for irrigation supply does not weaken the other relationships in this column.

[b] Control by grain yields reduces this association to .22. The other associations in this column are unweakened by controls.

*Relationship likely to occur on the basis of chance alone less than one time in ten (p ≤ .10). This same indication of chance findings is used in subsequent tables.

These regional disparities could be modified if new agricultural inputs, like machinery and chemical fertilizer, were channeled towards poorer villages. Without such a policy, rich villages will still tend to get more than their share of resources. New inputs are not bid for on an open market, but nevertheless quasi-market forces come into play. A certain number of small tractors or pumps may be allocated to a given commune, but poor brigades and teams may calculate that they do not have enough funds to purchase such items and decide to make do with what they have. Wealthier teams and brigades will be in a better position to purchase whatever is available, and may be able to increase their advantage over their neighbors as a result. Because of the policy of not extracting most of the increase in agricultural production from prosperous areas, the state is not able to accumulate large sums to redistribute to poor villages, and disparities are preserved or aggravated.[24] The effects are visible if we examine variations in mechanization within rural Kwangtung.

In recent years much progress has been made in rural mechanization, with ten- to twelve-horsepower hand tractors, water pumps, brigade factories, and electric power lines spreading rapidly. But in 1973–74 there were still marked disparities in the supply of such new resources, with about a third of our sample teams and a fourth of the brigades lacking both tractors and water pumps (N, or the number of villages on which we have information on this point, equals 37). Brigade "factories"—often simply tool repair shops or grain mills—were absent in 40 percent of our villages (N=34), and 20 percent of all localities were still not connected to a regular supply of electricity (N=46).[25] These differences in mechanization are related to team characteristics in table 3. There one can see that villages in the delta region with high work-point and land-labor ratio values are more likely to have team and brigade machinery and, to a lesser extent, to be electrified (brigade factories are not very strongly related to these characteristics). What is cause and effect here is not easy to say, since we have noted that a circular pattern develops, with wealthier communities acquiring more machinery and increasing their advantage still further.

These village differences produce, in the end, differences in the levels of consumption of Kwangtung peasants, as table 4 shows. Four measures are used: the reported proportion of team households that own transistor radios, the proportion owning bicycles, whether the predominant housing construction is of fired brick (rather than sun-dried mud brick), and whether the proportion of households overdrawing their collective account (ch'ao-chih hu)—consuming more grain than they earn through their labors—is low or

Table 3   Mechanization by Team Characteristics (Gamma Statistics)

	Team machinery	Brigade machinery	Brigade factories	Electricity	Median N
Mechanization					
Team machinery	--				
Brigade machinery	.38	--			(29)
Brigade factories	.29	.50	--		(24)
Electricity	.27	.53*	.50	--	(33)
Team Characteristics					
Work-day value	.57*[a]	.78*	.02	.71*	(32)
Delta region	.62*[a]	.52*[b]	.31	.67*	(36)
Land/labor ratio	.34	.51 [b]	.26	.89*	(34)
Median N	(33)	(33)	(30)	(40)	

[a]When controlled one for the other, both these associations remain strong.

[b]When controlled for work-day value, these relationships remain strong.

*p $\leq$ .10

not. All four measures are positively related, though some of the associations are weak (see table 4, upper panel). Both delta regional location and high work-point values are associated with high scores on all four measures of peasant consumption patterns, though again the associations vary in strength. Some peasants rely not only on collective earnings and their private plots for income but also on cash remittances from overseas relatives, and villages with a high proportion of families receiving such remittances show a more complex consumption pattern. Such villages are more likely than others to have many bicycles as well as houses made of fired brick. They are not any more likely to have many transistor radios, which cost much less than the 150 yuan or so for a bicycle and the 1,000 yuan or more for a new house. At the same time they are likely to have many families overdrawing, which means that they shirk collective labor (resulting in low grain yields and low work-point values) and do not earn enough during the year to pay for the grain rations they receive.[26] When this happens families simply repay their debts to the team, using their foreign remittance funds. We see that other factors besides the ecological setting of the village can affect collective production and peasant consumption.

Our review indicates that there are a number of conditions which can affect the prosperity of villages and maintain or even aggravate existing village inequalities. A village located in a barren area, with too many families concentrated on a small area of land, or with many families relying on

Table 4   Consumption by Team Characteristics
                                                 (Gamma Statistics)

	Radios	Bicycles	Housing	Overdrawing	Median N
Consumption					
Radios					
Bicycles	.57				(32)
Housing	.06	.50			(33)
Overdrawing rare[b]	.76*	.43	.17		(26)
Team Characteristics					
Work-day value	.64*	.34	.23	.68*	(31)
Remittances	-.14	.40	.67	-.60	(26)
Delta region	.48	.60*	.53	.35[a]	(37)
Median N	(30)	(36)	(29)	(31)	

[a]Association reduced to .14 when controlled by work-day value. The remaining
associations in the delta and remittance rows are not weakened by work-day controls
and the remaining associations in the delta row are not weakened by remittance
controls.

[b]A high overdrawing score indicates a low proportion of households that are
overdrawn, an indication of the financial health of local peasants.

*p ≤ .10

outside sources of income, will find it difficult to catch up with more
advantaged villages.

We have emphasized the grounding of village affluence in natural conditions that are difficult to change. The influence of "spirit" and leadership
should not be ignored, however. In interviews one is constantly impressed
with variations in individual willingness to work and in leadership skill in
mobilizing collective efforts. One example from our interviews of a four-
to-one differential in income among teams in the same village is based not
on natural but on social conditions. The teams in the village were all given
the same amount and quality of land in a 1961 redistribution. Nevertheless,
large differences in productivity remain. The villagers belong to a single
lineage. The best teams are those belonging to the lineage branch that was
strongest before 1949. Members of this branch still take pride in being
superior; they cooperate well with one another; they keep their trusted leaders; they go to work in the fields early in the morning and return late in the
afternoon. The poorest teams are those belonging to the lineage branch that
was weakest before 1949. Members of this branch still feel oppressed; they
constantly bicker among themselves; they distrust their leaders, turning them
out for new ones every year; and they go to work late in the morning and
return early. Even a commune vice-secretary who assumed leadership of the

poorest team for half a year was able to produce only marginal gains in productivity.[27]

Besides being dependent partly on "spiritual" conditions, differences between villages are maintained because of constraints on migration and tax policies. Before 1949, poor peasants were kept from moving into rich villages by high rents, kin solidarity, and physical aggression. Today, differential prices and rents are gone. Each team holds its land in perpetuity without charge, and, because of their more rapidly increasing output, rich villages pay a smaller percentage of their income in taxes than poor villages, that is, taxation is regressive. We do not know the precise nature of administrative controls on rural migration, but without them poor villages would soon be denuded of their most able workers.[28] In Kwangtung, where lineage feelings remain strong, lineage loyalties help buttress administrative constraints.[29] Though females marrying between villages escape these constraints, males seldom escape, being forced to remain in their home villages while existing income differences are maintained.

Differences in income between villages, then, are deeply embedded in natural conditions and exacerbated by supplies of modern resources and tax and migration policies. Though an emphasis on renewed work commitment and improved leadership could help some poor villages, commitment and leadership problems are so intertwined in old social relations as to make them almost as difficult to manipulate as natural conditions. So long as peasants resist being combined into larger collective units which bridge rich and poor villages, and the state does not extract more of the wealth of rich villages to redistribute to poorer ones, there is not much prospect of reduction in this kind of inequality.

Household Inequality

Besides inequalities resulting from urban-rural and village-to-village differences, the peasant is subject to inequalities within his or her own production team. A major part of this involves differences in income earned from collective labor on the team's fields; we will focus our attention on collective income in this chapter.[30] Calculation of income is according to the socialist principle "From each according to his ability and to each according to his work." In the government's understanding, it will be some time before they can apply the full communist principle "From each according to his ability and to each according to his need." The Chinese system of income distribution, then, is closer to that of the Russian collective farm than it is to that of the Israeli kibbutz. Though differences in payment remain, income disparities within each village would seem more amenable to change than those between villages, and we wish to consider both how those differences occur and what success has been obtained in the effort to reduce them.

The process of income calculation can be best introduced with a hypothetical example, this time drawn from an accountant's handbook from Hunan Province just to the north of Kwangtung (see table 5). A household accumulates income credits primarily through work points but also through manure credits, loan refunds, and welfare payments (rows 1 through 5).[31] From these credits, there must be deductions for payments in kind and cash advances (rows 6 through 12). If a positive balance is left after these deductions, each household is paid the remainder in cash. If the balance is negative, as for Chang Tsu-li and Wang Chin, the household is overdrawn and, as noted earlier, must pay the team back through money earned from other sources—from earnings in the private sector, from money sent back by a son or unmarried daughter working in a city, or from foreign remittances.

There are a number of more general points drawn from the Hunan example that are relevant to later discussions of motivations for marriage, birth control, and household formation. First, accounting is by household. Though the work-point recorder initially records them by individual, points are periodically totaled and entered in the accountant's books by household. The books are kept under the name of the household head—usually the eldest working male—and payment is in a lump sum to this head. Second, most payments from the collective are made only once or twice a year, after the summer and fall harvests. In our Hunan example, only 12 percent of total income and 6 percent of cash income was distributed before December. In real life, more grain is distributed before December, but often cash is distributed only after the fall harvest. For the purchase of daily necessities in the months in between harvests, one must shepherd one's cash carefully and rely on one's family and its private production activities.

Third, the example is designed to accurately reflect the economic situation in real Hunan villages, and seems to represent a situation just slightly above the average for rural Kwangtung.[32] Using other information from this handbook and some additional assumptions, we can gain some picture of the economic world in which the "typical" peasant in this region lives. The annual per capita income in this case is 102.50 yuan (row 16, last column), of which 38 yuan is distributed in cash. Assuming 4.4 persons per household,[33] family income from collective sources would average 451

Table 5

Income from Collective Sources, "Red
Flag Production Team" by Households

	Chang Wei-hung	Chang Tzu-li	Li Keng-sheng	Wang Chin	Ch'en Chien	Total[a]
Income from:						
1. Work points	¥396.00	¥200.00	¥20.00	¥270.00	¥297.00	¥7,200.00
2. Manure	40.00	40.00	15.00	65.00	30.00	860.00
3. Loan refund		40.00		60.00		100.00
4. Welfare			40.00			40.00
5. Total	¥436.00	¥280.00	¥75.00	¥395.00	¥327.00	¥8,200.00
Deductions for:						
6. Rice	¥202.16	¥237.07	¥51.68	¥364.61	¥126.16	¥4,085.00
7. Wheat	5.63	5.21	1.17	9.62	4.03	130.00
8. Cotton	8.00	9.00	2.00	13.00	5.00	160.00
9. Cooking oil	30.00	33.00	8.00	50.00	19.00	600.00
10. Rice straw	5.00	7.00	1.00	9.00	3.00	100.00
11. Cash advances	8.00		2.00		20.00	200.00
12. Total	¥259.79	¥291.27	¥65.85	¥446.23	¥177.19	¥5,275.00
Cash balance:[b]						
13. Surplus	¥176.21		¥ 9.15		¥149.81	¥2,862.50
14. (Deficit)		(¥ 11.27)		(¥ 51.23)		(¥ 62.50)
Other information:						
15. Total cash (11 + 13)	¥184.21	(¥ 11.27)	¥11.15	(¥ 51.23)	¥169.81	¥3,065.50
16. Income per capita (before deductions)	¥109.00	¥ 56.00	¥75.00	¥ 49.38	¥163.50	¥ 102.50
17. Number of members	4	5	1	8	2	80

Source: Adapted from Hunan Province Revolutionary Committee, Agriculture and
Forestry Bureau, ed., Nung-ts'un jen-min kung-she sheng-ch'an k'uai-chi [Rural
people's commune production accountant] (Ch'angsha: Hunan People's Press, 1973),
appendix.

[a]Totals are for all households in the hypothetical team.

[b]The cash balance is the amount to be paid to, or taken back from, each household after row 12 is subtracted from row 5. Deficit values are in parentheses.

yuan, of which 169 yuan would be received in cash and the remainder in
kind, primarily in grain. The addition of income from the private sector,
perhaps about 20 percent of total income,[34] would being annual per capita
income up to 128 yuan, and total household income up to 563 yuan. These
figures, suggestive of the situation of a somewhat better than average
Kwangtung village, place our earlier remarks about the difficulty of purchasing bicycles (150 yuan or so) and new housing (1,000+ yuan) in a clearer
context.

Fourth, most households are not "typical," and even in the five
households used in the table 5 example there is a ratio in per capita income

between the richest and poorest family of 3.3 to 1. Differences in cash income are even greater. These differences stem from the fact that families vary in size and in the work-point earnings of their members. For every day they work, some members of the team earn more than others; some members work more days during the year than others; and some families have a higher proportion of family members working and earning collective income than others. Although factors like outside remittances and private sideline incomes affect the picture, in general the families with the highest "labor-mouth ratio" tend to be the most prosperous in the team. In rural China the typical peasant family seems to have 42.5 percent of its members in the labor force.[35] In our interviews more than two-thirds of those households with more than half their members working in the team's fields were judged to be more prosperous than their neighbors by our informants, while about two-thirds of those families with fewer than a third of their members in the labor force were judged to be poorer.[36] In other words, a careful balancing of births, deaths, ages, and illnesses is critical to family security, and these considerations weigh heavily on peasant minds.

As part of their egalitarian revolution, China's leaders have tried in various ways to narrow the material inequalities that exist within teams. Although much of this inequality is based upon family size, there are still changes in remuneration and grain distribution systems which can modify intravillage differences. There has been an alternation over time in China between periods in which the government has pressured local production teams to adopt new schemes designed in part to reduce inequality and periods in which teams have been largely left alone to find remuneration and grain schemes fitting local conditions.[37] Here we will examine what some of the systems involved are, and how they fared in rural Kwangtung.

Peasants earn work points for their daily labor in a team's fields. Work points may be assigned on a number of bases. Most commonly the point systems, which were hammered out in the 1950s, divide simply into time rates and task rates. Under a time-rate system, workers are ranked once or twice a year according to their ability and then given this number of points each day they report for work. To calculate points, a team accountant asks the point recorder how many days each person has worked and then multiplies this figure by the person's work-point rating. Though there is great variation from village to village, ablebodied males between twenty and forty-five years of age commonly receive nine to ten points per day. Because they do not do plowing but somewhat lighter jobs, such as weeding, ablebodied females without children commonly get seven or eight points a day. Women having to spend an extra hour or two at home with their chores and children commonly get six or seven points a day. A child or an older person tending a water buffalo or inspecting irrigation-ditch levels might get four or five points a day.

Under task rates workers are paid according to the exact amount of work they do.[38] Task rates involve quotas or norms for various jobs. Exactly how fast the quota is fulfilled is up to the individual worker. A team may have determined that a normal worker can plow a group of fields in four days, thereby earning forty work points. The worker assigned to these fields can work very fast and finish the fields in three days, thereby earning his forty points in a much shorter time, or he can stretch the work out to five days. If he finishes early, and if the team does not give him more work, he can spend the extra time on his private plot. Task rates, then, cause work to be speeded up.[39]

Many production teams use neither time rates nor task rates alone, but the two in combination. In the busy planting and harvest season when there is need to motivate people to work very hard from before daybreak until long after dark, the teams use task rates. In the slack season between planting and harvesting, when work such as weeding and the maintenance of irrigation ditches is more difficult to break into separate tasks, and when there is not all that much work to go around, they revert to the simpler time rates. In forty-three Kwangtung production teams in 1973–74, ten had simple time rates, nineteen used a mixture of the two (either by season or type of work), and fourteen appeared to use task rates most of the time.

Separate from these three major variants is the Tachai work-point system, which originated in the model Tachai brigade of Shansi. In the 1960s, the Tachai work-point system had two distinctive components, the first of which changed over time. Initially, the Tachai model called for frequent retrospective assessments of work points. In meetings every day or so, members would report what level of work points they felt they should receive for the previous day's work. The work group then either criticized or approved the self-assessment. By 1967, such frequent assessments had been abandoned at Tachai in favor of semiannual assessments, creating a system analogous to that of time rates, except that rates were retroactive for work already done rather than prospective for work yet to be done. In other words, under this system peasants work in the fields but do not know for sure how many points their work is worth until later. When the model was emulated in Kwangtung starting in 1968–69, villages began with assessments every few days, but this led to so much rancorous conflict and expenditure of time that most teams there also changed to semiannual assessments.[40]

The other component of the Tachai work-point system is that people are ranked not only according to the amount of work they do but also according to their work attitude. A weak worker who exerts maximum effort is rewarded while a strong worker who coasts is penalized.[41] When this aspect of the model was emulated, work attitude was often mechanically linked with political attitude, ideology, and eventually class labels. Peasants whose families had been landlords or rich peasants prior to 1949 were automatically defined as having a bad attitude. They were docked one point a day, reducing their collective income by about 10 percent.

Despite objections by many team members, 90 percent of our Kwangtung villages were pressured to adopt the Tachai work-point system sometime between 1968 and 1971 (N=29). There was wholesale abandonment of the system after 1971, when the government issued directives stating that the Tachai spirit should not be followed mechanically but should be adapted to local conditions (see Chapter 4). By 1974, among twenty-eight teams, one had never adopted the system, eight abandoned it even before the party directive of 1971, ten dropped it in 1972, seven did so in 1973 or 1974, and two were still using the Tachai system when our informants left their villages in 1973 or 1974.

China's leadership has expressed clear preferences in regard to these remuneration systems. Time rates and the Tachai system are seen as promoting equality within villages, and they have been periodically pushed, particularly by "radical" leaders. These leaders oppose paying peasants equally, which would violate the socialist principle of distribution according to labor. But at the same time they are concerned not to have too much emphasis placed on material incentives and the pursuit of more pay, which they label the deviation of "placing work points in command." Task rates, by allowing the strong and skilled to scramble after extra work and income, are regarded as less desirable in this regard, as the following quotation from a leader in the Tachai brigade illustrates:

> Prior to 1960, work points were in command here. We were following Liu Shao-ch'i's policy [Liu was China's chief of state, purged during the Cultural Revolution for fostering "revisionism"]. There were more than 130 different tasks, each with different work-point values. We had ridiculous things, such as the strong taking the easy tasks, which were worth a lot of points, while the heavy tasks were left to the weak.[42]

Mao Tse-tung also went on record as favoring a deemphasis on material incentives, and prefering time rates in particular:

Even if one acknowledges that material incentive is an important principle, it absolutely cannot be the only principle. There must be another principle—the principle of spiritual encouragement in the sphere of political ideology. At the same time, material incentive cannot be discussed in terms of personal interests alone, but should be discussed in terms of collective interests, in terms of subordinating personal interests to collective interests, transient interests to long-term interests, and local interests to the interests of the whole . . . . We hold that the time-rate wage system should be primary and the piece-work [i.e., task rate] system should be supplementary. To emphasize one-sidedly the piece-work wage system will provoke contradictions between new and old workers and between strong and weak laborers. It will promote the psychology of a section of workers "to struggle for the purpose of scrambling for big pieces of work." They will not be concerned first for the collective enterprise, but rather for personal income.[43]

Task rates, then, are seen as undesirable because they foster inequality and a selfish pursuit of individual gain.[44] They are seen as having other undesirable consequences as well. They generally foster individual work assignments and competition, while time rates are more compatible with group work assignments and cooperative work. They allow some former landlords and rich peasants to earn as much or more than other villagers. Also, a great deal of time is required to inspect task completion and to compute points, leaving team cadres with less time to labor in the fields alongside other peasants. But perhaps they are more effective in motivating peasants to work hard, thereby promoting production—this seems to be the view of more "moderate" elements in the leadership. Before we examine what village characteristics have been associated with success in implementing the officially preferred payment systems in Kwangtung, we must discuss how grain allocation can affect local inequality.

The distribution of grain is technically separate from the assignment of work points. Work-point assignments affect a household's credits. Grain distribution affects a household's debits (see table 5 again). After deducting grain sold or given to the state and grain withheld for future collective uses, the team must decide how to distribute the remaining grain. There are three ways in which grain is commonly distributed. First, grain may be distributed on a per capita basis, with set amounts being given according to the age and sex of each individual. Because these amounts remain constant regardless of work performed during the year, grain distributed in this manner is called "basic grain." This system provides a cushion of security. Second, grain may be distributed according to the amount of work performed by household members during the year, or, more precisely, according to the work points they earn. When grain is distributed on this basis (called work-point grain), one must work to eat. Third, a small amount (typically 10 percent) may be given to induce people to turn over manure from their family pig to the team. This is manure or fertilizer grain.

It should be stressed that, regardless of the basis on which it is distributed, all grain must eventually be paid for, if not in this year or this generation, then in the next. The free supply of grain which appeared for a short time in 1958–59 is no more. Nevertheless, the exact distribution policy followed has a significant effect on incentives and welfare. With more basic grain there is less pressure to show up for work every day and a greater possibility for those families with little labor but many mouths to feed to draw grain even though they have no credits to pay for it. A larger proportion of families will become overdrawing households. Equality in consumption is fostered, even though some households are accumulating debts to their team. With more work-point grain, in contrast, there is great pressure to show up for work each day and less likelihood that families will overdraw. Those families with little labor power and many mouths will either go without grain or rely on loans from kin and friends. This system promotes inequality in consumption, based on the ability to pay for the grain received. The proportion of basic or work-point grain is then a matter of intense and volatile debate, with local systems changing with the current political wind and with the changing needs and desires of team members and their leaders. One of the changes fostered by the Cultural Revolution was to have more grain distributed, as in Tachai, on a per capita basis. In the December 1971 call for retrenchment, teams were told to cut back on the great degree of overdrawing to which the high per capita grain policy had led.[45] In Kwangtung there has been some change, though probably there is still more grain distributed on a per capita basis today than before the Cultural Revolution. In twenty-eight Kwangtung villages around 1973, eight distributed all their grain on a per capita basis, eighteen used some mixed system, and only two distributed grain on the basis of work points alone.

Work-point and grain systems do not vary randomly but are patterned according to the conditions of individual villages. This pattern appears when one cross-tabulates point and grain systems with village conditions. We have three measures of point and grain systems: (1) use of task rate, mixed, or time rate work-point systems; (2) use of the Tachai work-point system through at least 1972 or not; and (3) use of 100 percent work-point, mixed, or 100 percent basic grain distribution. (All the measures are scored so that a high value indicates a more egalitarian system.)

Table 6

Work Point and Grain Distribution Systems by Village Characteristics (Gamma Statistics)

	Time rate	Tachai system	Grain system	Median N
Payment and Distribution				
Time rate	--			
Tachai system abandoned late	.08	--		
Grain system	-.23	.12	--	
Administrative				
Political density	-.37	.26	.16	(28)
Political study	.49*	.29	.42	(23)
Urban-Communications				
Urban proximity	.10	.09	.74*c	(29)
Urban youths	-.28	.20	.54	(21)
Communications	.17	.00	.47	(27)
Nurseries	.32	.43b	-.11	(29)
Economic				
Collective affluence	-.20	.55	.30	(31)
(Work-day value)	.02	.77*	.53	(26)
Household consumption	-.18	.63*	.84*	(28)
Land/labor ratio	-.56a	-.42	.55	(26)
Remittances	.33	-.18	.08	(19)
Other				
Brigade size	.18	.48	.63	(23)
Team size	.49*	.43	.10	(29)
Lineage-composition	-.28	-.23	.00	(29)
Non-Hakka ethnicity	.10	-.15	1.00	(29)
Delta region	.21	.07	.86*	(29)
Median N	(41)	(29)	(26)	

aRelationship reduced to -.36 when controlled for team size. In this same column, team size and political study relationships are not reduced when controlled for each other or land/labor ratio.

bRelationship substantially reduced when controlled for team size.

cRelationship substantially reduced when controlled for household consumption. In column three, the relationships with delta region and political study are not reduced when controlled for household consumption.

*p ≤ .10

The relationships of these measures with each other and with selected village characteristics are shown in table 6. This table has a standard format which will be used in most later tables. The first three variables are the dependent variables. The relationships (gamma values) in a triangle at the top of the table indicate how closely the dependent variables are associated with one another. Below these are four sets of independent variables. The administrative variables help answer the question of how much administrative pressure and normative influence through political study promote officially desired changes. The urban-communications variables help answer the question of whether normative influence through exposure to both official messages and urban ways of life promotes change in the village. The economic variables help us see whether more advantaged villages lead the way in change or follow behind. Finally, the independent variables labelled "other" answer the question of how more idiosyncratic village conditions influence change. The way these variables are measured and the interrelationships among them are shown in Appendix 2. Only occasionally will additional variables be introduced. In table 6 we examine separately the associations with the local average work-day payment, but because this payment has already been included in the summary measure "collective affluence" it is enclosed in parentheses. The same indication of redundance will be used in later tables.

The top panel of table 6 shows that work-point and grain distribution systems are not closely related. Villages which now have a time-rate payment system are not necessarily those that held onto the Tachai work-point system for a long time or that distribute grain more equally.

The next four panels of table 6 show the relationship between point and grain systems and village characteristics. Despite the frequent discussion of point and grain systems in ideological terms, administrative or political measures are at best only weakly related to distribution practices. Clearer determinants of distribution practices are physical and economic characteristics such as team size, land per laborer, and affluence.

In the time-rate column, for example, the most strongly related characteristics (gamma $\geq \pm .40$) are political study, land per laborer, and team size. Though we had not predicted the team-size relationship, it is a reasonable one. In a large team, task rates simply impose too great a burden of record keeping on work-point recorders and the accountant. It is much simpler just to multiply the number of days a person reported for work by his daily point rate.

Similarly, though control by team size reduces the relationship somewhat,

teams with lots of land and little labor are likely to use task rates today and to
have abandoned the Tachai system early. Statements in interviews led us to
anticipate these relationships. One youth from a village with lots of land
reported, "We don't have time to sit around arguing about how much each
person's daily work is worth. It is only the nearby villages with lots of labor
and little land who have time for this sort of thing. We have too much to
do."[46] They therefore gave up the Tachai system early in order to get their
work done. They changed to year-round task rates. An educated urban youth
from another village spoke to the other side of the issue: "We used task rates
for only one year, 1973, but the work was done too sloppily and we changed
back, and today we continue to use time rates."[47] This leads to the sugges-
tion that when there is lots of work to be done but a scarcity of labor, teams
will use task rates. Task rates cause people to work very hard but to skimp
on jobs that would take too much time. When there is a shortage of land,
teams cannot afford to have sloppy work. They need to get every rice shoot
planted straight and to have every kernel of rice picked up off every inch of
land. The tendency is for these teams to use time rates.

We might also suggest that when there is little land the competition
introduced by task rates causes a problem. The rate buster who gets up very
early in the morning and works late into the night to earn more points will be
taking work away from others in the team. To make sure that there is enough
work to go around, then, it is advisable to use less competitive time rates.
Also, this kind of rationale could help explain why many teams use time
rates in the slack season even though they use task rates at harvest and
planting. In busy seasons there is too much work and a shortage of labor.
During the slack season there is not enough work to go around and a danger
that task rates will lead certain individuals to take work from others.

Continued use of the Tachai point system, despite its link with ideology,
was less related to political variables than to economic affluence. Though
unanticipated, the latter relationship is also reasonable. It may be that rich
teams can afford to be somewhat more generous and allow points to be
assigned on the basis of considerations other than work effort. This is
suggested in the last column of table 6 which shows that prosperous teams
are likely to share their grain on a more equal, per capita basis. Otherwise,
use of the Tachai system was affected by the same conditions as time rates.
Teams with lots of land tend to switch to task rates. Large teams and
brigades find that the time rate aspect of the Tachai system simplifies accounting problems.

Equal grain distribution systems tend to occur where regular political study systems exist, but the most important determinant of grain sharing is economic affluence. High work-day values, household consumption, and land-labor ratios all support a willingness to share. Though ethnicity is also strongly related, inspection of detailed cross-tabulation tables shows that these results could occur by chance and should not be treated with as much seriousness.[48] Point and grain distributions, then, are associated with a political study system but even more strongly with patterns of landholding, team size, and affluence.

In a more speculative vein, we can suggest that there are several natural conditions that may cause villages to become more egalitarian in their distribution policies in the future. Work-point assignments are highly responsive to land pressure and team size. Grain distribution is highly responsive to affluence of households in the team. Teams tend to grow in population over time, both through natural population growth and through occasional amalgamation of adjoining teams. If team population continues to grow in this manner, but not at a rate so fast as to threaten prosperity, more and more teams will find themselves too large to easily keep track of task rates. They will feel a need to switch to time rates, where individuals simply earn a set amount of points each time they report for work. Also as population grows, pressure on the land will become greater, such that, in an effort to get more careful work on each plot of land, teams may switch to time rates. Similarly, if the moderate increases in village economic well-being of recent years (see Chapter 8) can be sustained, peasants should be more willing to share their grain with their neighbors on a more equal basis. They will still be a long way from the ideal communist state in which grain and other goods are distributed completely according to need and regardless of work effort. Grain will still be paid for, but the tensions created by withholding grain from some families who lack sufficient ablebodied workers will be reduced. With a moderate amount of political pressure, more villages may then be able to nudge just slightly closer to the socialist ideal of equality and community sharing.

Our analysis here notes that efforts to promote intravillage equality through altered remuneration and grain distribution schemes met resistance in the post–Cultural Revolution period, and that these schemes were often abandoned or modified after higher pressure for their adoption was relaxed in 1971. Village comparisons suggest that one important factor operating was that the more egalitarian systems were only suitable in particular kinds of rural settings, not generally throughout rural Kwangtung. When they were introduced in settings where they were less suitable, the result was often less diligent work, more families overconsuming, more grumbling and village acrimony, and a variety of other problems. Lest we end on too pessimistic a note about the difficulty the government has had in promoting village equality, we should emphasize that the changes of an earlier period, of the 1950s, did produce important results in this realm. By confiscating the wealth of the landlords and then collectivizing agriculture, the Chinese Communists eliminated disparities in control of scarce land as a source of income differences within villages. The members of the new village elite which arose at that time, whatever their other advantages (see Chapter 7), did not receive incomes that set them above other villagers. Thus, in comparison with the pre-1949 era, the transformations of the 1950s caused a significant moderation in income disparities within the village.[49] But in more recent years schemes to promote further equality have had limited success.

Summary

We have examined rural material inequality in four dimensions, by considering how extractive the relationship between state and peasant is, how much rural-urban inequality exists, how much inequality exists between villages, and the disparities within villages. Our judgments are somewhat different in each case. We conclude that the state-peasant relationship has not been a notably exploitative one, particularly in comparison with the same relationship in the Soviet Union. As localities have improved their output, the state has not adopted a strategy of extracting most of any surplus, without compensation, to meet needs elsewhere. Partly as a consequence, the gap between town and country, after widening in the early 1950s, has been kept in check, and perhaps slightly reduced in recent years. To reduce the gap still further, however, would require confronting a number of obstacles, such as the limits the official no-inflation policy places on any raises in grain purchase prices, the discontent of urban workers who do not see their wages rising as their output does, and the policy of sharply restricting migration to the cities. Intervillage differences are a different story in our view. These are firmly embedded in natural differences in terrain, water supply, access to urban markets, and other factors; if anything, official policy has served to aggravate these differences in recent years by allowing resources to flow to advantaged areas while issuing exhortations to poor areas about self-reliance. These disparities are also maintained by groups of male kinsmen in wealthier localities, bound to their villages by those same migration policies, who resist joining together with poorer teams into larger income-sharing units, or allowing males from poorer villages to move in. Economic differences within villages are based less on natural and more on human factors, but after initial successses these too have proved difficult to further modify in recent years. Authorities have found it hard to reduce these disparities without alienating the families who have prospered economically under collectivized agriculture, precisely the families who have been the government's most ardent supporters and often the most diligent agricultural workers. Thus some material differences have been reduced or kept in check, while others persist or increase, and remain stubbornly resistant to change.

The remaining income differences have a number of very human consequences for the families that experience them. Those families in affluent teams with many members engaging in collective and sideline labor will receive a fair amount of cash income each year, will be able to accumulate considerable savings, built themselves new and better housing, and will spend considerable sums on festivals, weddings, and consumer durables. They will also have a more than adequate diet, with white rice for all meals, and meat and other sources of animal protein on a fairly regular basis. In contrast, families in the same team who have fewer laborers and many dependents, or families in poorer teams, may receive little cash at the end of the year, or overconsume and go into debt to the team. Unless such families can find profitable outside sources of income they will experience familiar problems of poverty. They will have to make do with the housing they have, they will have little to spend on festivals or consumer durables, and their sons will have difficulty finding brides. Unless their locality has a per capita grain supply system set at moderately high levels, they may have to subsist on a thin rice gruel (congee) augmented by sweet potatoes for many of their meals, with meat to consume only during holiday and wedding feasts. In later chapters we will see the importance of these economic disparities in many spheres of rural social life. Since equality and inequality involve not only income, but also services, status, and power, we need to consider these other realms before we can draw conclusions about the consequences of the pursuit of equality for peasant motivation and satisfaction.

6

Health,
Education, and
Welfare
Policies

a s the previous chapter indicated, the Chinese have been very concerned with fostering equality. Nevertheless, considerable differences in income among individuals and families, among villages, and between urban and rural areas remain. Some of these remaining differences might be narrowed by transfer payments which take from the rich to give to the poor and by more equal provision of health care, education, and other social services.

Any society concerned about these matters must debate the extent to which social services should be distributed equally or as scarce goods, using market mechanisms. Those who argue for equal distribution are likely to contend that a minimum standard of consumption, education, and health care should be provided for everyone. Much as in the debate over income, those who argue against equality of social services contend that equal provision incurs excessive bureaucratic costs and leads to a large state apparatus which threatens individual freedom. It can also be argued that when no market mechanisms are used, social services will be distributed irrationally, with people overusing services which come at no direct cost to them.

Even when members of a society can agree on which services should be distributed equally, there is likely to be disagreement about which administrative unit should be responsible for these services. In order to keep resources to themselves, rich communities are likely to prefer a small unit. For example, affluent American suburbs benefit from small school districts.

Poor communities, such as urban ghettos, benefit from much larger units. Because services supplied from a distance appear to be cost free, both rich and poor communities tend to prefer that a distant national government fund their services. Control of expenses in a society dedicated to social welfare, then, is a difficult matter.[1]

China has had to confront many of these issues. The question of the level of administrative funding has been primarily over whether the state (county and above) should assume responsibility for meeting social welfare needs or reserve its funds for investment in future economic growth. When the state chose not to assume responsibility for social expenses, the issue was whether these expenses should be passed all the way down to families or financed at some intermediate, collective level. The question of mechanisms for allocating services has been whether social services should be distributed freely to everyone or whether rationing devices are needed to prevent overuse of health, education, and welfare services. In this chapter we review the options chosen in meeting the need for social services, and the implications of those options for the pursuit of rural equality.

Public Assistance

The first thorough airing of the debate over the use of state funds for social services versus investment came during 1953–57 when the Chinese had to grapple with hard realities of state financing in the first Five-Year Plan. When the plan was announced in 1955, one central minister after another stood up to apologize for restraints on social expenditures and to urge that local communities think up ways to deal with social services on their own. Repeatedly, those who urged more social expenditures were told that to make such expenditures would mortgage the future for the sake of short-term benefits. In the countryside, this debate was most explicit in the realm of old-age assistance.

As early as 1950, Article 13 of the Marriage Law stated that "children have the duty to support and assist their parents." Support of aged parents by their children was a logical corollary to private family farming in the early 1950s. With the introduction of collective farming in the mid-1950s, one might have expected some change in these arrangements. Indeed, so as to persuade people to give up private landholdings, which were the traditional basis of peasant security, people were told that they could rely on the collective for "five guarantees," namely, food, clothing, medical care, housing, and burial expenses.[2] It soon became apparent, however, that these guarantees were to apply only to old people who had no grown sons to support them—in other words, to those whose traditional family organization had failed them.

This was explained first to the sons and daughters of former landlords and counterrevolutionaries, who had reasoned that, since they were under party orders to "draw a clear line with their parents," they should not support their parents economically. The state would have to assume this responsibility. They were told that "drawing a clear line" implied no such thing. During the revolutionary period, it had been necessary to stress separating oneself from parental ways of thought and behavior. However, in the period of socialist construction one must support one's parents whatever their background.[3]

Later the debate on parental support was broadened. In a 1957 editorial in the *People's Daily,* peasants were told not to artificially divide their households:

some collective members use the "five guarantees" system to divide their family off from their parents as they please. They push the responsibility for the livelihood of the old completely off on the agricultural collective . . . . Those who at their convenience divide from their parents say, "If the family does not take care of the livelihood of the old, they can enjoy the five guarantees from the collective." Among those who so speak, some misunderstand the principles of the five-guarantee system and labor compensation, but most simply use this excuse to escape their own responsibility. It should be pointed out that the behavior of those who do not take care of their parents' livelihood violates our country's morality. Each of us when we were young received our parents' nurture. After we have grown up, each of us has the responsibility to support our parents, who have lost their labor power. We oppose the blind filial obedience of feudalism, but at the same time we support respect and care for the elderly. If anyone violates this kind of social morality and deserts his own parents, this not only is reprimanded by public opinion, but it is also not permitted by national law.[4]

Some unnamed individuals had gone so far as to propose that the state provide social security benefits for all old people. One authority replied to the "dreamers" that if all old people were supported the economy would be in a shambles. For the state to "rear the old" would "seriously hamper the business of socialist construction."[5] The eventual goal was still greater welfare and equality for all, but for the time being socialist construction had to be equated with capital investment. No general state-funded old-age pension system comparable to that enjoyed by urban workers was ever adopted.

According to informants, recipients of five-guarantee support are given a set amount of grain, oil, cotton, fish, and whatever other goods are distributed by their team. The grain allotments they receive are equal to those distributed to other nonworking old people in the team, although five-guarantee recipients do not pay for this grain. In addition to allotments of goods, they are provided with two or three yuan a month in cash, depending on the wealth of the production team. Though some former residents felt this cash to be a terribly small amount, it appears to be no less than the average per capita cash earnings of other team members. Whether an old person receiving five-guarantee support lives securely or not is determined to a great extent by whether he or she can engage in private endeavors, such as raising chickens and tending a private plot.

Today, with improved health and more sons surviving, fewer old people are eligible for old-age support. Some former landlords and other bad class-elements are excluded. And some of those who are eligible conclude they are better off relying on their own private plot and sidelines. Others, who are eligible because they have only daughters, are fortunate enough to marry a daughter into a well-placed family which can take the unusual step of providing support to both parents and parents-in-law.[6]

Whatever the reasons, only a small number of people in Kwangtung villages are receiving this aid. In thirty-seven production teams, eleven have no one getting five-guarantee support, seventeen have one person, six have two, another has three, another has four, and one large team has ten people getting assistance. The average is about 1.24 persons per team, or about 6 percent of all people over age sixty.[7] For the vast majority of old people in rural Kwangtung, support is the obligation of the family, not of the collective or the state.

Besides this support within one's immediate family, there is considerable informal assistance from more distant kin, friends, and neighbors. In interviews, there are frequent examples of neighbors lending a spare room to someone who has no money to repair a tumbledown house, helping to tend a private plot for someone who is ill or lame, and lending cash or grain to those whose supplies have run short. Much of the direct assistance in villages, then, runs in traditional channels, those based on family obligations and individual feelings of compassion.

Despite this emphasis on family and individual aid, there are important new patterns of collective and state aid which should not be ignored. Besides the five-guarantee system, the collective has other support mechanisms.

Most commonly this support is through indirect channels or in the nature of loans. According to informants, a well-run team seeks out extra work for families on the brink of poverty. For example, a poor family's seven-year-old child is given an opportunity to tend one of the team's water buffalo for four work-points a day. An old grandfather in a poor family is asked to oversee water levels in paddy fields for a few points a day. If all else fails, poor families can always go into debt, while still eating, by overdrawing their collective accounts—at least in the majority of teams that distribute part of peasant earnings in the form of "basic grain." In some instances, a team may grant a loan of ten yuan or so to someone who must meet an unexpected expense, with the understanding that the sum will be paid back after the fall harvest. Or a family with unusual hardships may be allowed to borrow from the local savings bank at 4 percent interest. In extreme instances, a team, after discussion, may give direct grants to families in difficulty. These kinds of assistance from the team are handled on a case-by-case basis and depend upon both the financial health of the team and the concern of its members and leaders rather than being based on general statements that poor families that meet certain criteria are entitled to aid.

Most welfare assistance in rural localities depends upon kinship roots or upon the limited resources and willingness of the team. Up until recently the state has not had a major responsibility in this area, in keeping with the preference for decentralization and self-reliance. Some distributions from county budgets are made for injured army veterans and dependents of martyrs of the revolutionary war. County and provincial budgets are also tapped to meet emergency needs caused by typhoons, floods, or other natural disasters. However, there are reports that, starting in 1973, a departure from this pattern began, as selective counties in Kwangtung began to take on the responsibility of providing a minimum diet of thirty catties of unhusked grain per capita for all peasants, with the result that in such localities poor families could increasingly acquire a minimum diet by means of indefinite grain loans.[8] The details and rationale of this shift are not clear, as there has been no public announcement, but if this new effort is maintained and extended it would signify a break with long-standing preferences—both to limit state financial responsibility for welfare assistance and to require peasants to work for the grain they eat and limit "overdrawing" (see Chapter 5). With this one potentially important recent change excepted, though, peasants in need continue to rely on sources close at hand—primarily their own families, and secondarily the nearby families in their production team and their close kinsmen. The number receiving assistance from collective or state budgets has been small, and could not be expected to make a major dent in existing forms of rural inequality.

Education

Education has been a much more contentious area of debate in China than welfare payments, since it involves the training of the young and promising, rather than support of the old and unsuccessful. We will not deal with most of the issues in this debate here,[9] but will focus on how the options chosen affect equality of access to education in rural China.

Kwangtung had more schools and students before 1949 than many other provinces, and after liberation there was some uncertainty about how to combine the existing schools with the system of short courses and mass education that had been developed by the Chinese Communists in Yenan and other guerrilla bases. By 1953, with the start of the first Five-Year Plan (and following Soviet advice), concern for economic growth won out over revolutionary ideals of mass education. The state's need for skilled personnel dictated a stress on quality over quantity, and a concentration of educational investment on those institutions best able to meet immediate personnel needs, primarily urban secondary schools and universities. Throughout the 1950s, educational expenditures by counties and higher levels of the state bureaucracy remained at 2 to 3 percent of national income—comparable to what other developing societies were spending at the time—and these funds were insufficient to provide all villages with schools.[10]

To the extent that they were funded from county budgets, village schools in large, centrally located villages were stressed over smaller schools in many isolated villages. Other places had to start their own community-run and financed (min-pan) schools or do without. Rural youths remained severely disadvantaged in relation to urban youths in competing for places in higher-level schools. In 1955 the minister of education noted that because large, centrally located villages tended to be more affluent, this pattern of funding only exacerbated existing inequalities between villages. For the time being he saw no alternative, since the limited funds had to be spent in the most efficient way possible—primarily on schools in cities and large villages.[11]

This emphasis on well-established and high-quality schools as opposed to equality of educational access came under attack during the Great Leap Forward and again during the Cultural Revolution, and the latter assault produced a number of significant changes in the form and distribution of rural schooling. Of particular relevance to peasants were proposals to shorten the years required for primary and middle-school graduation, and to make most lower-level schools community-run. These proposals were part of a general shift in emphasis toward universalizing forms of primary and secondary schooling which would not encourage aspirations to seek higher education or to leave manual labor.[12] The concern for limiting state expenditures on education remained, however.

Before 1966 most brigades in Kwangtung already had six-year primary schools. Secondary schooling, however, was usually available only at the commune town, or sometimes in the county seat. A fair proportion of rural students dropped out without completing primary school, and even those who graduated had difficulty persuading their parents to part with their labor and the funds needed so that they could go off to attend secondary school. The post–Cultural Revolution reforms called for primary schooling in both urban and rural areas to be shortened from six to five years, and for both lower- and upper-middle schools to be reduced from three to two years (for a total of nine years to complete secondary schooling, rather than twelve). In the cities this policy resulted in a "gearing down" of the existing education system, but in the countryside the effect was different. Most Kwangtung brigades reduced their primary schools from six to five years, but at the same time they added a two-year lower middle-school program. Thus an increasing number of years of schooling was available within most villages, and the rates of attendance and completion increased. Thus, most rural youths were getting more schooling, not less. At the same time, until 1978, graduates of urban middle schools were not allowed to go directly on to a university, but were required to work for at least two years, most often in the countryside. The differences in rural and urban schooling were not eliminated. Upper-middle schooling is still much more available in the cities, and the schools there are no doubt still of higher quality. Also, urban youths still seem to be favored in the competition for higher education after they have fulfilled their labor stints.[13] But the life courses of most urban and rural youths are now more similar (since few of the urban sent-down youths can hope to be chosen for higher education), and these reforms have helped universalize lower-level education in rural Kwangtung, thus reducing somewhat the inequalities in access to schools that characterized earlier periods.

This change in the pattern of rural schooling was not made primarily through large infusions of state funds. Quite the contrary, brigade schools were to be funded primarily out of local resources. This means that the burden falls mainly on brigades and their composite teams, and on parents. In a pattern which may seem odd to Americans, Chinese university education is free, with university students even receiving stipends, while primary and middle schools charge fees. Generally in rural Kwangtung the tuition fee for primary school is five or six yuan a year. Book fees and fees for miscellaneous expenses run another two to three yuan. Fees for lower middle schools are somewhat higher, and parents sending a child off to the commune upper middle school must pay not only still higher tuition fees but the room and board costs involved.[14] Given the meager cash distributions families receive in most teams, these fees could be quite a burden for those with several children in school. However, poor families may receive tuition waivers, and these have reportedly been issued more liberally since 1968. With such waivers, the fees do not constitute a serious obstacle to the completion of the brigade-run schools, although they appear more significant for those thinking about upper middle school. In other words, some important (but unknown) proportion of the cost of rural schools is borne by the parents of students, although the waiver policy keeps this scheme from being highly regressive.

The remaining costs of rural schooling are not borne solely by collective units, that is, by brigades and teams. The state does contribute some funds, although the proportion is again unknown. For example, teachers who worked in rural state-run schools before the Cultural Revolution continue to receive their state salaries even if they now serve in brigade schools alongside newer teachers, who receive their pay in the form of brigade work points. Books and other instructional materials also appear to be subsidized. But the intent of recent policy is clearly to expand schooling as rapidly as possible while keeping state expenditures closely in check. Providing for the growing number of lower middle-school students exclusively by state-financed schools would have been difficult, given the decision not to regularly raise agricultural taxes. The danger in this emphasis on local financing is, as we have stressed before, that intervillage inequalities will be maintained or aggravated, since richer communities can afford to spend more. This tendency would be counteracted only if the state used its educational funds in a redistributive manner, channeling them disproportionately into poorer localities. We do not know whether this occurs in Kwangtung, although there is some indication that this is the policy in the province of Kiangsu.[15]

More precise information is needed on a number of points, but our discussion indicates that we see the changes in rural education as reducing the inequalities in access within villages somewhat, and perhaps also those between city and countryside, but probably having less effect on intervillage differences. A policy that combined a commitment to increased equality with centralized financing and allocation could have reduced differences still further, but here as elsewhere the Chinese opted for a more decentralized pattern.

Though it is difficult to draw firm conclusions about the precise equalizing effects of Cultural Revolution reforms, it is possible through interviews to examine the degree to which the reforms were implemented in Kwangtung. To be more precise about our earlier general statements, informants noted that thirty-two out of thirty-four brigades already had primary schools in 1966. Virtually all these schools were six-year schools, and most of them were started in the 1960s, though some began even before 1949. By 1973, all of the brigades for which we have information had at least one primary school. Some brigades, containing scattered villages, had an additional school or two so that children in remote villages would not have to walk too far. By 1973, in thirty-three brigades for which we have precise information on school structure, seven continued a traditional six-year primary school (two of these had tried five-year schools only to revert to the original form after a year or so). Twenty-five had adopted and kept new five-year schools. One brigade had an abbreviated four-year school (a common pattern before 1949). Prior to the Cultural Revolution, there were almost no brigade-run lower middle schools, but by 1973 three-fourths of our brigades (N = 44) had them. There is no earlier data for upper middle schools, but in 1973 thirty-seven out of forty communes had an upper middle school in the commune seat. In short, the outer forms of Cultural Revolution reforms in education had been largely complied with in the years between 1968 and 1973. By the latter date most brigades ran both five-year primary schools and their own lower middle school.

Because of this high rate of compliance, there is major variation among villages on only two dimensions—the availability of nurseries or kindergartens and brigade-run lower middle schools. In Kwangtung, nurseries and kindergartens are still rare, appearing in only 19 percent of the teams and brigades in our sample (N = 51). The reason they are not more common, according to informants, is that grandmothers and other kin can take care of most children. Those with grandparents to take care of their children do not wish to subsidize those who are without grandparents—even though fees paid by the mother usually cover part of the nursery expenses. In addition

82   **Institutional Arrangements and the**
          Pursuit of Equality

informants say some peasants developed an antipathy to the poorly run collective nurseries of the early Great Leap Forward period and now refuse to support new initiatives for such institutions. To establish nurseries is to move against some strong countertendencies. There is no comparable resistance to lower middle schools, though some informants considered brigade lower middle schools distinctly inferior to those run by the commune or county. Still, establishing a brigade-run lower middle school does entail extra expenses for buildings and for teachers who receive work points. The presence of either a nursery or lower middle school, then, does suggest a special willingness to use public funds to subsidize child care and education.

Contrary to our expectations, villages which are willing to support nurseries are not necessarily willing to support lower middle schools (see table 7). In part there is no correlation because nurseries or kindergartens are usually run by a team while lower middle schools are run by the brigade, and any special collective spirit present in the team may not characterize the larger

Table 7		Collective Education by Village Characteristics (Gamma Statistics)	
	Nursery/ kinder- garten	Lower- middle school	Median N
Collective Education			
Nursery/kindergarten	--		
Lower-middle school	-.11	--	
Administrative			
Political density	-.50	.19	(47)
Political study	.30	-.20	(39)
Urban-Communications			
Urban proximity	.81*	.32	(46)
Urban youths	-.47	-.19	(34)
Communications	.44	.06	(46)
Economic			
Collective affluence	.75*	-.06	(48)
Household consumption	-.25	.12	(45)
Land/labor ratio	-.22	-.04	(41)
Remittances	.07	.37	(33)
Other			
Brigade size	.29	.58	(37)
Team size	.88*	.13	(47)
Lineage composition	-.38	.28	(47)
Non-Hakka ethnicity	-1.00	-.28	(46)
Delta region	.87*	.57	(48)
Median N	(48)	(42)	

*p ≤ .10

brigade of which it is a part. Also, the presence or absence of nurseries, kindergartens, and lower middle schools in unrelated to political density and political study. Rather they are most strongly related to location in the Pearl River Delta region, proximity to large cities, and location within a large administrative unit. Larger teams and brigades, it would seem, have sufficient children without grandparents or wanting to go beyond primary school to make such programs worthwhile, and the delta region, with its greater commercialization, urban proximity, and affluence, simply has a stronger heritage of school development than other regions. Physical conditions, then, are the most important factors in the adoption of these officially espoused educational programs.

Table 8

Education by Year Schooling Begun and Current Age

Schooling began:[a]	-1928	1929-	1949-	1954-	1959-	Total age 16+
			Males			
Education (years)[b]						
12+	0%	6%	0%	17%	8%	6%
7	0	11	29	38	46	21
4-6	28	44	50	38	42	40
3	38	16	14	0	4	16
0	34	24	7	8	0	17
Total	100%	101%	100%	101%	100%	100%
Total N	(29)	(54)	(14)	(24)	(26)	(147)
			Females			
Education (years)b						
12+	0%	0%	0%	8%	0%	2%
7	0	5	9	8	20	8
4-6	0	19	46	54	80	39
3	0	14	18	25	0	11
0	100	62	27	4	0	39
Total	100%	100%	100%	99%	100%	99%
Total N	(20)	(22)	(11)	(24)	(20)	(97)

Source: Kwangtung neighbor sample, 1973.

[a]The year individual would have reached age seven, the normal age for beginning school--i.e., first column is for individuals age 50+, second for those age 30-49, and so on.

[b]12+ = graduates and dropouts from upper-middle school plus a few from teacher
       training institutes and technical schools.
  7 = graduates and dropouts from two- and three-year lower-middle schools.
4-6 = graduates of initial four-year, five-year, and three-year primary schools.
  3 = people trained in classical fashion by a private tutor, self-taught, literate
       through after-hours classes in the 1950s, and dropouts from primary school.
  0 = illiterates.

Finally, we can get some idea of the impact of the broadening of education in rural Kwangtung by comparing different age cohorts. Systematic data on the education of informants' neighbors, classified by age, are given in table 8. These show that Kwangtung school enrollments began to increase even before 1949, but that in the 1950s there was a rapid acceleration in enrollments, when at least half of all males and females were completing four years of primary school or more. By the early 1960s, as many as a third of all males were advancing to lower middle school.

Table 8 overstates the changes in village education. The first few columns omit some people who were educated before 1949 and then left the village for jobs in the city,[16] and it omits also some former landlords (or their children) who were educated and then fled to Hong Kong before or during the land reform campaign. Likewise, because of either sample error or crude reports of education, the final column overstates education in the youngest age group. Even in its most ecstatic moments, the provincial radio claims no more than 95 percent enrollment in rural primary schools—especially no more than this for females.[17] Nevertheless, a striking increase in village education is quite apparent. Primary and lower-middle education have become ever more common, and women now lag only slightly behind men.

Education has been increasing rapidly in all developing societies, but China's record is still impressive. Statistics for about 1970 on the rural population aged 15+ that is literate indicate Kwangtung's relative position:[18]

	Total	Male	Female
India	26%	40%	13%
Turkey	51	69	35
Indonesia	55	67	44
Kwangtung	72	83	61
Taiwan	76	89	62
Thailand	77	86	68
Sri Lanka	79	—	—

Literacy among rural adults in Kwangtung is almost as great as in Sri Lanka, Thailand, and Taiwan and far greater than in Indonesia, Turkey, and India. (The gap of 22 percentage points between male and female literacy found in Kwangtung is among the smaller gaps for developing societies.) In addition to this basic kind of formal education, China has many other programs for training village veterinarians, barefoot doctors, midwives, tractor drivers, agricultural demonstration representatives, and the like which are frequently missing in other countries. The strategy adopted in China for spreading rural education seems to be a fairly effective one, at least as judged by the results in Kwangtung.

Health Care

As in education, the Chinese have made a major commitment to improved health care, and have launched a series of efforts to make medical care facilities more widely available in rural areas. Many of the same strategic issues are also visible here: how to distribute funds and medical personnel between city and countryside, who should bear the major responsibility of meeting medical costs, and how equality can be promoted while medical funds remain limited.

After 1949 there was a rapid growth in hospitals, clinics, and medical personnel, but that growth served rural and urban areas differentially. Medical service to rural areas was not inconsiderable. By the mid-1950s there were hospitals in county seats, and by the early 1960s there were clinics in most communes.[19] Also, informants report that in the early 1960s in some Kwangtung villages there were even small health stations at the brigade level, often manned by traditional herbalists.[20] In most places, however, villagers still had to walk some distance to a clinic, and they might have to wait in line for a considerable time in order to see a doctor. Doctors and clinics were much more sparsely spread over the countryside than they were in cities. In 1967, reporting on the urban bias in medical care, Kwangtung Provincial Radio said that two-thirds of hospital beds, 70 to 80 percent of government funds, and 60 percent of high-level medical personnel continued to serve that 20 percent of the provincial population which was urban. The ratio of doctors to population was one to six hundred in Canton but only one to ten thousand in the countryside.[21]

As early as 1965 Mao Tse-tung criticized the Ministry of Health as the "Ministry of Urban Lords," and in the following years it was decided to allocate more medical resources to the countryside. The change can be seen most clearly in the reassignment of personnel. Urban doctors were sent to serve temporarily in training institutes or to serve permanently in regional hospitals, and a new network of paramedics—barefoot doctors—was created. Under this new system, each production brigade was to have a health station (usually a room or two) with at least a barefoot doctor and a trained midwife (and sometimes other personnel, such as a traditional herbalist). Though they are seldom mentioned in Kwangtung interviews, below the brigade level there might also be team-level health workers to see after emergency first aid and health education. Barefoot doctor, midwife, and health worker are but the lowest rungs in a complex referral network. Cases they cannot handle are referred first to the commune clinic, which has doctors with at least a secondary level of medical training. Cases the commune clinic cannot handle may be referred to the county hospital, which has doctors with a college degree, and if this is insufficient cases may be referred to regional hospitals where there are specialists.

Barefoot doctors, according to Kwangtung informants and visitors, are usually lower-middle or upper-middle school graduates, ideally picked from among fellow villagers because of their dedication to serving the people. Candidates receive three to six months of training at their brigade's expense in either commune clinic or county hospital. Practicing barefoot doctors periodically return to the commune or county for further training. In addition, there is a constant flow of new manuals and also a bimonthly magazine to introduce practicing barefoot doctors to new techniques and the experiences of model areas.

Some sense of the barefoot doctor's work can be grasped from these manuals and magazines.[22] They include sections on public hygiene and birth control, as well as on the diagnosis and treatment of specific diseases. The sections on public hygience explain how to build sanitary pig pens, how to treat human and animal manure so as to make it sanitary, how to eradicate flies, mosquitoes, and rats, and how to keep skin and clothing clean. Birth control sections explain the rationale for family planning and late marriage as well as methods for contraception, sterilization, abortion, and delivery. Sections on diagnosis and disease include discussions of immunization, influenza, jaundice, edema, hookworm, asthma, migraine, fractures, carbuncles, diarrhea, sinusitis, and toothache. According to visitors, a typical barefoot doctor's medicine bag includes not only cotton swabs, syringes, thermometers, acupuncture needles, aspirin, and herbal medicines, but also antibiotics. According to informants, some villagers remain skeptical of barefoot doctor care. Villagers who had access to regular doctor care prior to the Cultural Revolution are particularly wary. Yet Western doctors visiting China have generally concluded that barefoot doctors serve as a useful front line of medical defense.

There is a rough sex balance between barefoot doctors and midwives. All midwives are female. Of the thirty-five barefoot doctors for whom we know the gender, 83 percent are male.[23] Barefoot doctors require more previous education than midwives, putting males at an advantage. Barefoot doctors also require a greater educational investment from the brigade. Villagers fear, we might guess, that if young girls are selected to become barefoot doctors, they will only marry and move away, causing the village to lose its investment. Older, married women selected as midwives, in contrast, will stay. In twenty-nine brigades from our sample, all have at least one barefoot doctor. The average is about 2.5 per brigade, or about one for each eight hundred population, figures which are virtually identical with published reports.[24]

The exact extent to which Cultural Revolution reforms in medicine compensate for urban-rural, community, and household inequalities depends on the manner in which costs are allocated and the devices used to ration access to medicine. More funds and equipment have been shifted to county hospitals and commune clinics. Urban doctors have been sent to work and teach in county and regional hospitals. Urban doctors periodically join special medical teams which travel from one rural area to another. Drug prices have been lowered for both urban and rural dwellers.

Nevertheless, issues remain as to the extent medical expenses should be funded by the state (county and above), brigade, or family. In 1969, a brigade doctor described the debate over collective medical insurance in Liu Lin brigade in northern Shensi Province:

> Yang Kou-shen [a brigade member] was one of those who had been of the opinion that, though in itself good, the reform was also dangerous: "Too many people will come asking for medicines. We'll lose the entire fund. We won't be able to manage it. Even if free medicine is a good idea, it's better that people should have to pay for their own medicines." Only after several meetings was Yang Kou-shen convinced . . . .
> Others thought the State should pay both for medicine and health care . . . . Starting with Chairman Mao, we talked things over until we were agreed it was no good our relying on the State. We must rely on ourselves. Where, anyway, was the State to get all that money from? If we asked the State for money instead of forming our own health insurance fund, it would simply mean we were undermining the national economy. That was not the right way to go about things, was it?[25]

Conveniently, members of Liu Lin brigade agreed with the national policy that medical costs should neither be passed down to families nor paid by the state but kept at the intermediate, brigade level. As with education, one would guess, national planners decided that, with increasing income and a declining agricultural tax, brigades can fund more activities on their own, including medical care.

Aggregating medical services at the brigade level is a significant advance over earlier practices. This not only helps equalize medical services among member families but also among constituent teams. The equalizing effects, however, are limited to people in the same brigade. Differences in income

between city and village and between different brigades are not affected by
this strategy. Affluent brigades, it would seem, continue to have better medical equipment, more manufactured drugs, and more doctor consultations.[26]

The advantage of aggregating medical services and costs at such a low
level is that it makes local-level administrators very aware of costs, and thus
serves as a natural rationing device. Barefoot doctors who must maintain a
balanced budget are unlikely to frivolously prescribe a manufactured drug
when a home-grown herbal variety would do as well, or to refer patients to a
commune clinic when patients might get well at home. Indeed, so as to keep
expenses under control, most brigades require patients to get approval from
their barefoot doctor before going to the commune clinic. To do otherwise
deprives the patient of brigade medical insurance.

Chinese planners are well aware of the need to ration access to medical
care, for attempts to provide free medical care in the 1958–59 Great Leap
period led to long waiting lines at rural clinics and to bankruptcy for many
local medical units. The system adopted since 1965 responds to these problems by also using fees and other market mechanisms to ration user access
and, as a by-product, to limit the redistributive or equalizing aspects of the
system. As to why this should be allowed, a vice-chairman of an affluent
brigade in North China said,

> Though the brigade already subsidizes our cooperative medical program
> heavily, we have not yet reached the point materially or politically
> where we can dispense with all fees . . . . We still have to study and
> prepare ourselves ideologically. If we dispensed with all fees now,
> people would over-use medical care [paraphrase].[27]

Use of market mechanisms, in the Chinese view, is only part of a transitional
phase which will eventually be overcome by better material conditions and
by socializing people into an ideology more appropriate to collective
endeavors.

The major example of the use of market mechanisms is that of medical
expenses being funded from a special cooperative medical insurance fund
instead of being provided directly from a brigade's public benefit fund.
Payments into the insurance fund are not simply according to ability to pay
but rather according to the number of members in a family. Informants
report that fees are the same for both adults and children, and that annual
fees range from a low of zero to a high of six yuan per person. Among
twenty-seven villages in our sample, the average annual medical insurance
fee was a little over three yuan per person.[28] A family with five members

would then pay fifteen yuan a year, which would be about 10 percent of the cash they would get from the collective.

The redistributive aspects of collective medical programs are limited by their being technically voluntary. Those who feel they can do better on their own can opt out of the program, and in some villages informants report that only 70 percent of brigade members belong. Often former landlords, rich peasants, and other controlled elements are not allowed to participate, and in this manner former poor and middle peasants do not have to support "class enemies." There also can be no redistribution in those villages that are without insurance—out of forty villages, three never had medical insurance systems and three others had programs that went bankrupt and were abandoned.[29] In these six villages peasants pay for visits to their barefoot doctor or commune clinic on a fee-for-service basis.

Even where cooperative insurance programs exist, three additional market mechanisms are used to ration access to health care. First, there is usually a nonreimbursable registration fee for each visit to a barefoot doctor, ranging from .05 to .16 yuan, with the most common fees being either .05 or .10. Among twenty-three villages for which we have information, only four charge nothing at all. A referral to the commune clinic usually entails an additional .10 yuan registration fee. With prices for a pencil at .05, a catty of rice at .098, and a bar of soap at .24 yuan, these registration fees are trivial, but they help remind users of the costs involved. Second, certain services are paid directly by the patient. For example, patients who stay in a commune clinic pay for their own food, and brigades do not reimburse them for this expense. Third, some brigade insurance funds make only partial payments. In one brigade, whose medical insurance fund had gone bankrupt in 1972 and had then been revived, the plan paid only 70 percent of drug costs. "Before the brigade paid out too much. Since the registration fee was only .10 yuan, the peasants were running off to get treated every time they had the slightest problem."[30] A more drastic limitation is to restrict payment on major surgical expenses. One brigade pays only 50 percent of surgical costs and nothing for blood transfusions; another pays 70 percent of surgical costs; a third excludes maternity expenses; and a fourth simply cuts off payments above thirty yuan for medical and surgical costs, thus limiting the insurance program to minor medical expenses.[31] Given the low costs for surgery and for most drugs, such limits would probably not be reached too often, and in the last resort both the press and informants report that after public discussion teams may give an extra grant of money to help a severely stricken family. But given the small size of brigade insurance funds, some villages have been forced to make hard choices about medical care. Altogether, of seventeen informants who described their cooperative medical insurance in detail, ten mentioned provisions that in some way limit coverage.

Given the tension between the desire to distribute medical services more equally and the need to ration access to those services, one would expect local health-care systems to differ in their emphasis. Five measures of quantity and equality of medical care are examined systematically in table 9: the ratio of doctors to population; whether cooperative medical insurance was begun before 1970; whether the insurance covers all drug and surgical fees; whether the annual fee per individual is below 3.60 yuan; and whether the fee per visit is below .10 yuan.

Contrary to our expectations, these measures of medical care are not uniformly related to one another (see table 9, top panel). Those programs which began earlier tend to have more doctors and more extensive coverage, and extensive coverage in a cooperative insurance program is surprisingly associated with low rather than high fees. There is very little association among the other measures.

In the next three panels of table 9, most of the associations are weak or inconsistent. With one exception, political study is modestly, but positively, associated with collective medicine, but our political density scale shows quite an inconsistent pattern. Urban proximity is modestly but positively related to our cooperative medicine measures, but other urban-communications variables again show inconsistent patterns. Our measures of local economic conditions are not consistently related with our measures of extensive and egalitarian health care. We had reasoned that profits from brigade factories would yield extra funds to finance collective medicine, but the figures show that if anything brigades with factories are stingier with their funds than those without. Ideas about the effect of political influence, urban contact, and increasing affluence on a village's willingness to share services in a more socialist manner, then, receive only modest support from these data.

Some other hunches fare considerably better. We had thought that both small brigades and single-lineage brigades would be more likely to have the mutual trust necessary to run a cooperative medical program successfully. Both hypotheses receive some support from the data. Though the relationships are not very strong, small brigades consistently have more extensive and cheaper medical care. Though no more likely to have cheap medical care, single lineage brigades were likely to have many doctors and to have begun cooperative medical insurance early. The delta region leads other

Table 9   Collective Medicine by Village
                                           Characteristics (Gamma Statistics)

	Doctors	Early coop- erative medicine	Coverage	Low annual fee	Low visit fee	Median N
Medicine						
Doctor ratio	--					
Early cooperative medicine	.81*	--				
Extensive coverage	a	1.00	--			
Low annual fee	-.09	-.27	.28	--		
Low visit fee	.00	-.33	.85*	.09	--	
Administrative						
Political density	-.41	-.01	.14	-.39	.71*	(24)
Political study	.00	.12	.68	.30	.33	(21)
Urban-Communications						
Urban proximity	.19	.52	.10	.25	.46	(23)
Urban youths	-.11	-.13	.64	-.22	-.33	(17)
Communications	.09	-.01	.14	.16	.68	(23)
Nurseries	.20	1.00	-1.00	.62	-.09	(24)
Economic						
Collective affluence	.25	.33	-.33	.12	-.17	(24)
Household consumption	-.25	-.23	.03	-.45	-.09	(23)
Land/labor ratio	.11	.23	1.00	.04	.19	(22)
Remittances	-.43	.09	-.75	.00	-.11	(19)
Brigade factories	-.33	.58	-.85*	-.82*	-.71	(14)
Other						
Brigade size	-.52	-.28	-.11	.19	-.30	(21)
Team size	.71	-.23	-.14	-.14	.51	(24)
Lineage composition	.64*	.84*	-.56	-.33	-.06	(24)
Non-Hakka ethnicity	-.29[b]	-.08	-.45	.14	-.46	(23)
Delta region	.57	.78	.82*	-.33	-.41	(23)
Median N	(22)	(24)	(16)	(27)	(23)	

[a]Gamma coefficient deleted because the total cases in the contingency table is less than ten.

[b]Relationship substantially reduced by control for lineage composition. The other strong relationships in this table are unweakened by statistical controls for other independent variables or informant characteristics.

*p ≤ .10

areas in the availability of medical care, a pattern of advantage paralleling that shown in several earlier tables. The general thrust of the entire table is toward an interpretation of adoption of particular aspects of the cooperative medical-care system as depending on a combination of local conditions rather than on some general level of political consciousness or moderniza- tion in a village.

As in the realm of education the available evidence suggests that the decentralized options for extending health care chosen by the Chinese have served their purpose fairly effectively. Among those recent visitors who knew rural China before 1949, there is universal agreement that dramatic improvements in popular health have occurred. The difference can be seen immediately in children, who once were undernourished and sickly, but now are generally pictures of health.[32] Improvements are also indexed in scattered reports on death rates. Ravaged first by the Japanese invasion after 1937 and then by civil war in the late 1940s, China's annual crude death rate was close to 40 per 1,000 population. By the mid-1950s, according to some observers' estimates, the crude death rate was down to at least 20 per 1,000 and by the mid-1960s down to about 10 per 1,000.[33]

The infant mortality rate is a sensitive indicator of food and health conditions. Government reports show a rural infant mortality rate of about 200 per 1,000 live births prior to 1949, and probably this was an understatement.[34] By 1955, the rate had declined to 74 per 1,000, and by the early 1970s, medical visitors to villages near major urban centers were estimating rates of 35 to 40 per 1,000.[35] There is one study of infant mortality changes in rural Kwangtung. From interviews of refugee women just after they had arrived in Macao during 1965, the study concludes that infant mortality declined rapidly in the 1950s, when women who had married in the 1940s were still bearing children, and then continued to decline into the 1960s (see table 10). This sort of dramatic decline in infant mortality was not unusual among developing societies during the 1950s, but by 1960 it would appear that China was among the best half of all nations for which infant mortality rates are available.[36]

Table 10   Infant Mortality by Year Mother Married

Year married	Infant mortality[a]	Total births	Total deaths	Reporting women
-1929	.42	226	96	37
1930-39	.32	602	195	92
1940-49	.13	612	80	118
1950-59	.11	285	32	69
1954-58	.07	198	13	67
1959-65	.03	109	3	73

Source: Raw data from 1965 survey by Robert M. Worth, Department of Public Health, University of Hawaii.

[a]Infant deaths (age 0-1) / total births.

Improved rural health conditions were achieved by an emphasis on cleanliness, immunization, and a more equal distribution of food. In the early 1950s, there were campaigns to eradicate four disease-carrying pests: rats, flies, mosquitoes, and grain-eating sparrows (sparrows were later replaced on the list by bedbugs, lice, or cockroaches, depending on the locality). Refuse was removed from around homes, while drainage ditches and sanitary wells were dug. There were massive immunization campaigns against diseases such as cholera, typhoid, scarlet fever, and bubonic plague.

In the 1960s and 1970s, there was evidence of continuing progress in health care. In 1962, one study that examined children in Macao within forty-eight hours after they had come from Kwangtung villages found that immunization campaigns had been successful, and major contagious diseases were under control. Children continued to be afflicted by intestinal worms and tuberculosis, which is not unusual for an Asian society.[37] Similarly, medical visitors in the 1970s reported serious contagious diseases under control but with tuberculosis and diarrhea remaining common.[38] These reports suggest that crowded housing and the handling of excrement are two major remaining public health problems. Since most fertilizer still comes from excrement, or "night soil," fecal contamination can be combatted only through more rigorous composting and curing—a common theme in barefoot doctor publications. Tuberculosis continues to be combatted with BCG innoculations for infants and propaganda from local health workers about personal hygiene.[39]

Though we were only marginally concerned with public health in our interviews, some informants talked about it at length. Urban youths whom we interviewed complained about poor sanitation in villages. They were horrified by families eating from the same bowl, sometimes along with a tuberculous father, and washing with the same rag. In some villages they reported red eyes among middle-age peasants, which may indicate continuing trachoma infections. With surprising regularity, reports of serious tuberculosis turned up in our interview census of neighbors. With as many as one case per team, these tuberculous neighbors were among the poorest families in a village. As others have reported, dental care and eye corrections have low priority. Nutritionally, as in other Asian societies, the diet consists primarily of grain, with some hill villages depending heavily on sweet potatoes, which in the delta regions would be fed only to pigs. In many villages, meat is restricted to festive occasions, and fish is consumed only slightly more often. This would be a boring diet for the average westerner, and Chinese urban youths sent down to the countryside also found it un-palatable. Nevertheless, nutritional studies show that coarsely milled grain combined with beans supplies sufficient protein if consumed in quantity, and, together with vegetables from the private plot, should provide a basic supply of the nutrients needed for good health. Rural health problems have not been eliminated, then, but they have been significantly improved. In-equalities of access to health care have been reduced, but the burden of financing this care does not fall equally on all families and villages.

Conclusion

This chapter has indicated that there are many complexities, shifts, and turns in government health, education, and welfare policies, and any statement about patterns is bound to have exceptions. Nevertheless, it is possible to point to several basic policy trends. As noted at the beginning of the chapter, concerns over government services have centered around questions of the unit of funding, control of access, and consequences for social equality. On questions of the unit of funding, since the mid-1950s it has been consistently decided that state social expenditures should be kept at a modest level. In the 1960s, debates over state social expenditures were not over whether they should be increased or not but simply over how they should be distributed. At the same time, there has been a tendency for collective units (brigades and teams) to take on more social expenditures. This trend of more or less constant state expenditures but increasing collective expenditures seems to have its basis in three givens. First, China is a poor country without many extra resources to spend on social services, and it is a country committed to rapid economic growth. Since the 1950s, its rate of capital investment has been 25 to 30 percent of gross national product, one of the highest rates in the world.[40] Planners interested in continuing this rate of growth do not want state funds diverted to cover current social expenditures. Second, in a man-ner strangely reminiscent of dynasties in earlier Chinese history, the central government is committed to a constant level of agricultural taxes. As popula-tion and economy grow, the central government or state is not getting new funds from agriculture which could then be plowed back into social services in that sector. Brigades and teams, with state taxes becoming a smaller proportion of their gross output, are increasingly in a position to fund social services. Finally, since the mid-1950s the Chinese have been committed to a large measure of decentralization, with local communities becoming as self-reliant as possible. All these factors go together to shape current policies for funding rural social services.

As for control of access, government policy varies by service. In education, the only limits imposed are for students who wish to go to schools outside the village, where strict selection procedures limit access to universities, while both costs and selection procedures limit access to commune upper middle schools. Public assistance payments are still limited by insisting that families assume obligations for many services, including old-age support. Even when assistance is given by collective units, since it is given by close neighbors there is little possibility of receiving excessive benefits, as can occur when the granting agency is a distant bureaucracy. The most complex institutions for limiting access, however, are in health care, where the use of barefoot doctors as "gatekeepers," ceiling limits, and assorted fees tend to keep medical expenses in line.

The consequences of this system of social services for social equality are complex. To an extent this system creates significant transfers of resources which help equalize people's living standards. Health care and probably education expenditures have been redistributed so that the countryside (counties and communes) now get far more in medical services than they contribute in taxes. Within brigades there are also significant transfers, as poor students attend school tuition-free, the sick, both rich and poor, are supported by medical insurance, the old without children are supported by the team, and poor families with insufficient labor are supported by public grain loans. So the system of providing social services does counteract rural material inequalities to some extent.

Nevertheless each of these kinds of transfers has significant limits. Most transfers are still kept within brigades, while major differences between brigades and between villages and cities remain. Urban workers in factories and offices receive state pensions and free medical care while villagers still have almost no access to pensions and must fund medical insurance funds out of their own pockets. Within brigades, while tuition waivers and grain overdrawing policies directly aid the poorest families in a village, other programs, such as medical insurance and old-age support, do not necessarily help the poor. The redistributive aspects of rural social programs, then, are significant but not so great as might be imagined. Peasants must still look to their own family and immediate neighbors for aid in dealing with many of the vagaries of life.

7

Status and Power

Ohne of the major goals of Communist rule has been to establish an effective village administration. In imperial times and even into the twentieth century, formal government pretty much stopped at the county level, and in many ways villages were left to rule themselves. The exact structure of local leadership varied tremendously from village to village and over time. Typically, however, most village decisions were made by informal leaders: groups of village elders (not really so elderly in all cases, with many in their forties) who had sufficient landholdings to be partially leisured and literate. Natives of the villages they led, these men were heads of families—women could not serve and typically neither could a son while his father was alive—and in some villages elders were simply senior members of various lineages. A national examination system that regularly selected talent and provided new sources of wealth, a partible inheritance system that caused the fractioning of estates among multiple sons, and the free purchasing and selling of land made positions as village elders or as members of a broader rural elite far from fixed. Rural power in China, compared to such power in feudal Europe or traditional India, was moderately fluid. Yet, leisure and literacy were highly dependent on landholding or on being part of an affluent lineage, and as a result there was some transmission of village power within families from generation to generation. Local leaders were not paid but served because village leadership gave them authority over others, was a sign of their status, and helped them protect and bolster their own economic interests in a village or wider area.[1]

The imperial government was not content just to accept these informal leaders; from time to time it tried to appoint formal village officers. Whether as heads of mutual defense groups (pao-chia), tax collection units, or in other capacities, the holders of these formal posts were unpopular, and the more elaborate versions of these leadership systems rapidly fell into disuse. Because these posts carried with them little compensation or real influence and many onerous duties, few men were willing to serve. As a result, if filled at all these jobs often fell to poorer peasants, who were but flunkies for village elders, who remained shielded from official exposure and criticism. In the Republican period a formal village headman system was initiated, with headmen controlling increased power and resources, but the problem of weak formal leadership in the villages was not fundamentally solved.

With an open examination system and a flourishing market economy, traditional village elders and local elites in market towns often found that their interests coincided with those of the central government, particularly at the height of dynasties. But the balance between local and national interests was always tenuous, and when times were bad local elites served their own interests and were difficult to penetrate and control.[2] The Communists have tried to change this tenuous balance once and for all by eliminating the landed base for old elites, by attacking lineages and their role in the transmission of elite status, and by promoting into power members of the poorest families in the villages.

The changes in rural political institutions since 1949 raise a series of questions which we will consider here. First, how thoroughly have the organization and personnel of village leadership been altered? In Chapter 4 we described the new formal leadership structures, but we still need to consider the "old wine in new bottles" issue. Has the character of village leadership really changed, or are the same sorts of people rising to the top today? Second, what incentives and loyalties influence today's leaders, and are these leaders in fact tied more effectively into the national administrative hierarchy? Third, what are the consequences of changes in local leadership for the pursuit of rural equality? In particular, has the Chinese form of decentralized administration described in previous chapters produced a new village elite which monopolizes power and privileges, oppresses local peasants, and passes on its advantages to sons and grandsons? The addition of the "new class" tendencies of Leninist political systems to the heritage of strong lineages and nepotism of Chinese culture would seem to pose a particularly serious threat to the egalitarian aspirations of the Chinese revolution.[3] We start our consideration by discussing the way the previous informal village elites were dealt with after 1949, and where they fit in the political scene today.

Old Classes and Class Labels

In rural areas, not only have the pre-1949 village elites not regained their positions, but in many ways in recent years the line against them has hardened and their lot in life has worsened. This has occurred in spite of an official policy which stresses that "bad elements" can and should reform themselves and become accepted.

At the time of land reform detailed instructions were compiled for grouping families into class categories, based upon guidelines worked out by the Chinese Communist party over the years from the time of Mao Tse-tung's first analysis in 1926.[4] The most important labels were the following.

1. Landlords: those who possessed land but did little or no labor, and lived off land rents, hired labor, and engaged in usury.

2. Rich peasants: those who possessed land and engaged in some labor, but also lived by renting excess land to others.

3. Middle peasants: those with more or less enough land for their own needs, who neither rented out land to others nor had to rent land from others to any significant extent (in the 1950s this group was later subdivided into upper-middle and lower-middle peasants).

4. Poor peasants: those who possessed little or no land, and lived primarily on land rented from others.

5. Hired peasants and other workers: those with little or no land, who lived by hiring their labor out to others.

At the time of the land reform classifications, some elements of the rural population were also given the labels of "counterrevolutionary" or "bad element," indicating not their former economic positions but their pasts as members of the local Nationalist political structure, landlords' henchmen, active opponents of the Chinese Communists, or simply bullies and bandits. There were also miscellaneous classifications for those who did not fit into any of the categories above: for example, small land-rentiers, small traders and pedlars, and overseas Chinese—those who depended heavily on remittances from abroad.[5]

In villages today, operative class labels are considerably more simplified than these distinctions would imply. Among informants, only the distinction between former landlords or rich peasants and the rest was consistently clear. Some informants distinguished upper- from lower-middle peasants, but others spoke simply of middle peasant status. Still others lumped former middle peasants with poor peasants. Hired peasants were not distinguished from poor peasants. Given the distinctions with which informants are most familiar, the "old class" labels for 446 neighbors in twenty-one villages are as follows:

Landlord	2%
Rich peasant	4
Upper-middle peasant	3
Middle peasant	13
Lower-middle peasant	4
Poor peasant	73
Overseas Chinese	2
Total	101%

The informants with whom we talked, then, saw most of their neighbors as former poor peasants, while former landlords and rich peasants were a distinct minority.

After agriculture was collectivized in the mid-1950s, these class labels ceased to have any clear connection with prosperity or occupation. As in the Soviet Union after the 1930s, the importance of class labels might have been expected to decline. Indeed, speeches by prominent party leaders in 1956 did suggest that these labels were losing their significance. Yet subsequently, and particularly since Mao's 1962 call, "Never forget class struggle," class labels have taken on a renewed significance.

Today, according to informants, former landlords and rich peasants still under political "control" must visit a brigade or team security officer periodically to report on their activities. If they take a trip outside, they report their destination before leaving and, once they have returned, what they did and who they saw. In each political campaign they are likely to be targets of criticism. If there are untoward events in the village, such as the appearance of an anti-party slogan, they are the first interrogated. They have no right to vote or hold office. Once a month or so they are obliged to contribute a day's free labor to the collective. Earlier we noted that they may be discriminated against in work points and in health and welfare distributions. Not all places are so severe. Some peasants in single-lineage villages never willingly criticized local landlords in the first place. Elsewhere former landlords and rich peasants are judged to have reformed and are "uncapped" (released from political "control"). In such places, they may be accepted into the cooperative medical plan, with little mention made of their former status. Yet, even in lenient places the multitude of class-hatred statements which fill the mass media must make former landlords and rich peasants constantly uneasy.[6]

Though the offspring of "bad class elements" are not under "control," land reform class labels are inherited. And, appropriately for Chinese society, inheritance is through the male line. Daughters who marry into former poor or middle-class peasant families, if they move far enough away, eventually escape their origins, and their children will bear "good" class labels.[7] But sons and grandsons of former "enemy" classes are disadvantaged in a number of ways. They may become targets in political campaigns. In recent years, since the passing of the pressing shortage of skilled personnel of the 1950s, they have found it more and more difficult to get a higher education. They are prohibited from holding political office and are barred from most desirable factory jobs. They often have great difficulty finding brides, given the stigma that comes with being a "landlord wife" and the label the children will bear (see Chapter 10). The Chinese press and radio frequently advocate assimilating those sons of bad class background who are willing to reform and change their ideology. Yet, with the recurring official attempts to revive class hatreds of an earlier generation, the obstacles to assimilation are formidable. To whatever remaining resentments over property lost by the family a generation ago are added the feelings created by a long list of contemporary indignities and harassments. For the most part those who bear bad class labels sullenly go about the business of trying to provide for their families while staying out of trouble. The descendants of the former village leaders have not regained prominence but remain a pariah group to this day.

New Leaders

What of the new village leaders the revolution promoted to power? Do the qualifications for leadership today differ from those of the pre-1949 era? Are today's village leaders set apart from other peasants in income and life-style? The Chinese Communists want to prevent the emergence of a new self-perpetuating and oppressive local elite, but have they found effective ways to do this? We deal with these questions through an analysis of the background characteristics of a sample of team and brigade cadres described by our informants.

One of the first things to note is that there are now many more formal posts available, so that village leadership is not very exclusive. In our sample of village neighbors, among 185 adult males age sixteen and over, fully one-fourth hold posts at either the team or brigade level. Of these, 8 percent are in top secretary, head, and vice-head posts while 17 percent hold lower posts. If people who had once served but are now retired were included, the percentage who have been politically active would be higher. Many villagers, then, know the duties and responsibilities of local office. Since service as a team or brigade officer brings one into regular contact with visiting commune representatives and into periodic telephone conferences with other villages in the commune, many peasants are aware of national policies for agriculture and the specifics of their implementation.

The personal background characteristics of village leaders are described in tables 11 and 12. The cases in the tables are grouped into top leaders (secretary, head, and vice-head) and lower functionaries (accountant, security officer, custodian, and so on) at the brigade and team levels. (The term "brigade head" was commonly used by our informants for the person formally called the chief of the brigade revolutionary committee.) At the far right of each table the distribution of the same characteristics is shown for all adults or adult males.

Except in specifically women's posts there are as yet few females in leadership positions. Women's representation increased throughout the 1960s as the practice of having a woman as one team vice-head became universal, but in most instances women leaders at both team and brigade levels are restricted to "women's work": organizing other women for agricultural labor, birth control, and so forth. In the 1970s there has been an effort in Kwangtung to popularize greater female participation in all posts, but as of 1974, this propaganda had had little effect. Some of the reasons for this scarcity of women in local leadership will be discussed in Chapter 12. Still, women are represented where they were not before.

Both team and brigade leaders are mostly men in their early forties (see table 11). There is a break with the past here not so much in a decline in the average age (we noted earlier that village "elders" were not always very old) as in a restriction of office to men still active in field labor. Today's leaders supervise the daily farm work— the responsibility of family heads in

Table 11   Village Officers by Sex and Age

	Brigade officers			Team officers			
	Top leaders	Women's posts	Lower func- tionaries	Top leaders	Women's posts	Lower func- tionaries	Adult popu- lation
Sex							
Male	37	0	43	61	0	72	277
Female	1	14	2	1	14	3	289
Total	38	14	45	62	14	75	566
Age							
60+	3%		2%	0%		0%	12%
50-59	14		7	26		9	20
40-49	49		25	43		24	17
30-39	27		43	17		24	22
20-29	8		23	13		42	29
Total	100%		100%	99%		99%	100%
Average age	40	42	35	42	34	34	41
(N)	(37)	(14)	(44)	(53)	(12)	(66)	(161)

Notes: Top brigade leaders include 15 Party secretaries, 10 brigade heads, and 13 vice-heads and sideline industry heads. The women's officer is the person in charge of women's affairs. The lower brigade functionaries include 17 militia leaders and security officers, 11 financial officers, 4 clerks (wen-shu), and 15 miscellaneous other personnel. The top team leaders include 36 team heads and 22 vice-heads. The women's officer is simply the women's vice-head. The lower team functionaries include 10 militia leaders and security officers, 20 accountants, 9 cashiers, 19 custodians, 3 financial officers and 16 point recorders. The number of officers with complete data is shown in parentheses following each series of percentages. Two of the lower team officers, a militia chief and a point recorder, are below age 20.

Sources: Last column is from census of neighbors. Other columns from cadre sample.

the past—and are required to take part in field labor themselves. As men lose their physical stamina in their fifties and sixties, they retire from office.[8] Team and brigade functionaries, who fulfill functions that largely were unneeded in traditional villages, are even younger, often in their thirties.

In table 12 are data on the education of village officers paralleling the data on age. The officers in leadership posts clearly have less education than those who hold positions as accountants, financial officers, militia leaders, and the like. Generally, educational differences are explained more by the factor of age than by the special needs of particular posts. What is lacking in formal education can be compensated for by training on the job (although literacy is obviously needed for accounting and bookkeeping jobs).

The policy of excluding old elites has been largely successful. Former landlords and rich peasants hold no offices in our sample. Former upper-middle peasants and overseas Chinese are also underrepresented, appearing only in specialized financial posts.

Most brigade, but only a minority of team, officers belong to the party. Seventy percent of all team heads are members, which allows them to attend party planning sessions at the brigade. (Since vice-heads are usually not members, the average percentage in table 12 is much lower.) But some team heads are accepted into the party only after being elected to their posts, in a form of cooptation. Though party membership among team leaders and functionaries is greater than among all males, the party presence is still not overwhelming at this level.

Among the issues surrounding leadership in socialist societies, undue authoritarianism and the formation of a self-perpetuating "new class" are salient. In China, the government has been very concerned about the quality of village leadership. The Sixty Articles stipulate that brigade leaders should spend at least 120 days laboring in the fields each year and that team leaders should work there full time. To insure that village leaders do not rise above average members, brigade and team cadres receive no state salaries and are to be paid no more work points than the most ablebodied members of the brigade or team. Usually, supplements are allowed only for the expenses of travel to meetings and other public functions, and these supplements are to

Table 12					Village Officers by Party Membership, Class Label, and Education
	Brigade officers		Team officers		
	Top leaders	Lower func- tionaries	Top leaders	Lower func- tionaries	Adult male population
Education					
7+ years	4%	25%	10%	33%	21%
4-6	57	47	40	42	40
0-3	39	28	50	25	39
Total	100%	100%	100%	100%	100%
(N)	(23)	(32)	(42)	(48)	(121)
Class Label					
Poor/lower-middle	100%	90%	95%	88%	75%
Middle peasant	0	10	5	6	12
Upper-middle	0	0	0	5	3
Overseas Chinese	0	0	0	2	2
Landlord/rich peasant	0	0	0	0	8
Total	100%	100%	100%	100%	100%
(N)	(25)	(29)	(39)	(41)	(141)
Percentage Party Members	100%	81%	17%	22%	4-6%
(N)	(30)	(27)	(48)	(49)	(161)

Notes and Sources: See table 11.

total no more than 1 or 2 percent of the distributed income of the team.[9] As a check on corruption, villages are subject to inspection by commune supervisors and outside work teams, such as those that descended on villages in the Socialist Education Campaign of 1962–65 and the "hit-one oppose-three" campaign of 1971. At all times, there is pervasive propaganda reminding officers of the necessity "to serve the people."

These various checks on the performance of local officers seem in large degree effective. In Hong Kong, one hears vague charges about corruption, but, when pressed, most informants can offer only circumstantial evidence—village cadres ate well, they had an extra bicycle, their daughter was in middle school, their children got the best jobs, and so forth.[10] Overall, though our evidence is scanty, it is our impression that periodic political campaigns mixed with checks and counterchecks in accounting and backed up with suspicion by villagers has kept village corruption to a minimum. The restraints on salaries, the absence of material bonuses, and the requirements for work in the fields have also produced a leadership whose income is not too different from that of other peasants.

These assertions can be documented in part by the rough judgments (presented in table 13) our informants made about the relative prosperity of various neighboring households. (Neighbors were judged simply as having incomes higher, lower, or roughly the same as the average for a particular village.) The average team leader does no better than the ordinary former poor peasant household, according to these figures. Because of their better-

Table 13   Household Labor and Income by Current Position and Class Label

	Current position				Class label of agricultural laborers		
	Non-agri-cultural laborers	Brigade leaders	Team leaders	Brigade and team func-tionaries	Poor & lower-middle peasants	Middle & upper middle peasants	Landlords & rich peasants
Labor/mouth ratio							
Average	.62	.46	.54	.54	.50	.51	.66
(N)	(13)	(5)	(17)	(20)	(36)	(12)	(12)
Income							
High	70%	(2)	26%	53%	27%	33%	45%
Average	10	(2)	26	29	29	33	36
Low	20		47	18	44	33	18
(N)	(20)	(4)	(19)	(17)	(41)	(12)	(11)

Source: Combined household sample.

paid jobs and a higher labor-to-mouth ratio, those in nonagricultural jobs do better. Surprisingly, even though they have no excess of labor power, brigade and team functionaries have more income than other households. If this is so, it must be because their sons are more likely than others to take nonagricultural jobs (see table 16) or because they manage family sidelines better than their neighbors, since such functionaries don't receive much more in work points than do agricultural laborers. As for those with "bad class" labels, attempts to invert the old order have had the surprising effect of giving former landlords and rich peasants better than average incomes. Their difficulties in finding brides mean later marriage for sons and delayed childbirth, resulting in a higher than average labor-to-mouth ratio. For those who never marry, however, this prosperity is a temporary phenomenon. In their old age, with no sons to support them and possibly no "five guarantee" support, they will suffer. (However, former landlords and rich peasants may also be more likely than their neighbors to have overseas relatives sending them remittances, which could aid them in their old age.)

How, then, do modern village officers compare with traditional village leaders? First, the government has been successful in formalizing the village power structure. There is not the dichotomy between formal and informal leaders that there once was. There are those considered "respected, older peasants," but for the most part these are men who have known the burdens of formal leadership and then retired, not behind-the-scenes power wielders. Second, there are many more leadership posts today, and these posts are largely the same from village to village. The chances for government penetration through involvement in official service are greater than ever before. Third, the characteristics of today's leaders are not the same. There are women leaders where there were none before. Younger people are more heavily represented, particularly in the lower, functionary posts. Finally, family wealth and education are not necessary prerequisites for service, and today's leaders do not prosper from their posts. (The distinction in this last respect is less marked in comparison with the *formal* leaders of the past, who, we noted, were usually from humble backgrounds and received little pay for their service.) Some things have not changed much, however— particularly the fact that village leaders today are virtually all natives, rather than outsiders sent in by the state bureaucracy. Village leadership today as in the past is also not an important stepping-stone to higher office, since most leaders keep their roots firmly planted in their native villages.

The changes in the village power structure can be seen from another angle, however. We have stressed a certain broadening in participation in village leadership since 1949. But it is also important to note that this broadening occurred in part because today's village leaders perform many more functions than did their predecessors. With the socialization of agriculture and other activities, many decisions which used to be made within individual families are now concentrated in the hands of team and brigade cadres: what crops to plant, when to harvest, who should work where, how much to spend on fertilizer and health care, and so forth. So village power which is shared more broadly may also be seen as power that is increasingly concentrated, with autonomy lost by individual families and their leaders. In this respect the head of a peasant family today may well feel that village power is distributed more, rather than less, unequally than before. Does this alternative perspective mean that positions of village leadership are plums which are widely sought after for the power they bring? We address this question by considering how the changing character of village leadership has affected the motivations of those who serve.

The Motivations and Costs of Leadership

Because of restraints on income and watchful criticism from above and below, the costs and rewards of leadership remain finely balanced, and many people are ambivalent about service in office. As in any voluntary association which does not pay its leaders, people sometimes feel the costs of leadership are greater than its rewards. This situation has been thoroughly analyzed in the Israeli kibbutz, where leaders receive no extra material rewards. In the kibbutz, candidates for office

> often attempt to avoid their nomination, and public pressure is sometimes required for the candidate to take the job ... officeholders in the community tend to experience unpleasant encounters and difficulties causing them high levels of strain. Typical examples are the frequent exposure to criticism from fellow workers including subordinates; the need to depend on committee consensus for important decisions; the need to rely almost exclusively on skills of personal persuasion and informal leadership, since formal sanctions are scarce; and labor days which spread into the night.[11]

With two additions, this same list of complaints is voiced by Chinese village leaders. The two additional complaints are, first, that because of his extra duties the leader may not have time to devote attention to his family's private plot and sideline activities. Often the cadre's wife badgers him about this neglect. Second, besides being criticized from below, the Chinese village leader is subject to periodic criticism from above—from his superiors in the commune or from visiting work teams. The position of a Chinese village leader, then, is somewhat akin to that of a foreman in a factory, who must please both workers and management. Many are reluctant to serve in the position, since a leader receives no extra pay but is held personally responsible for the village.

Despite these problems, posts can generally be filled, and some leaders serve for long periods. Several kinds of motivations and rewards counterbalance the costs of officeholding. The factor usually mentioned in Chinese press accounts is ideological commitment. Informants did not portray their team and brigade cadres as Maoist zealots, but they often did mention commitment of a more subtle sort. A general sense of duty or obligation to the community is frequently noted. A party member reluctant to take a post is told that "a good party member doesn't let the people down." Some cadres whose families suffered greatly at the hands of local landlords serve out of a sense of gratitude for the improvements the revolution made in their lives. The importance of this sort of motivation helps explain the policy of keeping class labels and class struggle alive, although as the years go by it is more difficult to sustain the memories and emotions. The sorts of commitment involved are focused on the local community, however, rather than being oriented primarily toward the state or nation.

Other motivations are also important. Team and brigade cadres lack the coercive power to force peasants to do things they do not want to do, but leaders still initiate most major decisions and arrange day-to-day work. These leaders have more autonomy in their daily routine than ordinary peasants, even though they are required to labor regularly in the fields. They have more opportunity than others to learn new things, to apply their skill and know-how, and to associate with more powerful leaders outside of the village. If they do their jobs poorly, peasants may make their lives miserable with complaints and gossip, but if they perform well their authority and skills will earn them the respect of other villagers. In other words both power and prestige go with officeholding, at least in the important posts, and as in the past these may reflect back on a man's family and kin group. For those with some sense of ambition or service to begin with, the rewards of office are worth the burden.[12]

Judging from our description of rewards and costs and of political and personal motivations for leadership, we would expect tenure of office to vary by post. Brigade party secretaries, with relatively great power and prestige, should serve for long periods of time. Team leaders, with less power and prestige, should serve for shorter periods, and persons such as the accountant and work-point recorder, who can be constantly harassed by people questioning the accuracy of their work, should serve the shortest of all. The Chinese do not have the ideal of a rotating leadership but encourage leaders to serve as long as their service is approved by both the party and the people they lead. In interviews, it appears that those who have served longer are better leaders. One can almost predict how well a team is managed and how prosperous it is simply by asking how often its leadership has changed hands.

The material in table 14 shows that top brigade leaders—secretary, vice-secretary, and brigade head—do indeed remain in office longer than other officers. Some have served in these or comparable posts for fifteen or more years, and over 80 percent have served at least seven years. In other offices at the brigade and team level, there is more turnover. Almost half of the team officers have served for seven or more years, but about one-third have assumed office only in the last year or so. (No difference between team leaders and lower functionaries is visible here, however.) It is difficult to know by what standard this degree of turnover should be judged. In the abstract, it seems to us that service is rather long. In some villages with a multitude of problems, internal conflicts, and falling production, new leaders have to be pressed into office almost every year. But in the majority of more successfully organized and internally harmonious villages, leaders are replaced at an orderly pace as senior leaders die, retire, or move on to other jobs, while an occasional person steps down because of inept decisions or petty corruption.[13]

Brigade and team cadres do not, we have argued, have much chance to enrich themselves or be promoted to higher posts, but given the relative stability of office, which is encouraged by higher authorities, there is some danger of an oppressive leader dominating all major decisions in a village. This is most likely to happen in the case of the brigade party secretary, the

Table 14 — Local Officers by Length of Service

Length of service	Brigade officers		Team officers	
	Top leaders	Lower functionaries	Top leaders	Lower functionaries
7+ years	81%	35%	45%	41%
3-6	12	35	21	24
0-2	6	29	34	35
Total	99%	99%	100%	100%
(N)	(16)	(17)	(29)	(17)

Notes: See Table 11.

Source: Cadre sample.

most powerful man in the village. When it appears that the brigade secretary is going to remain in office, villagers may be wary about opposing him. In one village, some urban sent-down youths began a movement to oust the brigade secretary during the Cultural Revolution. The youths went from house to house in the village seeking support. Though circumstantial evidence implicated the secretary for giving favors to members who cultivated a private plot for him, the youths never got enough evidence to make a case. Some villagers replied that they did not care for the secretary either and hoped that he would be ousted. But they could not afford to give information. Urban youths always had the possibility of going back to the city, but, given the restrictive migration laws, the villagers were stuck there forever. If the attack on the brigade secretary failed, he could make their lives miserable. Other informants offered similar examples of peasants afraid to criticize their leaders openly, even though they might under certain circumstances be willing to voice their complaints to members of a visiting work team or other outsiders. The traditional stress on maintaining the harmony of the village and preventing loss of "face" for others is important here; any serious animosity produced within a small community could persist for generations.

However, peasants do have some fairly effective means of expressing dissatisfaction. For example, if disagreements arise, enough remarks made behind the backs of the leaders in a loud enough tone of voice will make popular grievances known. Social ostracism and other means of passive noncompliance can help get the message across. Envy and gossip are just as much traditions in Chinese villages as the quest for harmony. Nevertheless, the danger of a rise of a new authoritarian leadership exists. As long as rotation in office is not used, the party must rely on such techniques as periodic political campaigns or visits by commune vice-secretaries or work teams to root out bad leaders. Yet, campaigns must not be too severe lest all motivation to serve be destroyed. The government has to balance finely the mix of techniques used in monitoring local leaders.

We have argued that the power and prestige of village leadership are important, in spite of the lack of material benefits. Do the holders of village posts use their power to confer advantages on their families and foster the advancement of their offspring? Given the traditional high value placed on loyalty to kin, some tendency in this direction would not be altogether surprising. Some Western analysts have argued that beneath the new organizational labels and leadership titles rivalry and competition between different kin groups and families goes on much as before.[14] If this view is accurate, it would mean that the party has not been successful in its effort to develop a new style of village leadership, one oriented to serving the people in general, in which individuals are treated and promoted in regard to their contributions and qualifications and not their kinship connections. We can address this issue by examining the extent to which high status in village life is transmitted within families.

Three sets of data—one on education and two on occupation—provide measures of status inheritance. The data on education show, once again, that the government program to invert the old class structure has succeeded (see table 15). Sons of former landlords and rich peasants are falling behind while more former poor-peasant sons advance to a lower-middle education. Sons with middle-peasant labels are in a middle position. Sons of village leaders do have an advantage. The higher a village officer's position, the more likely is the son to advance to lower middle school. Whether by means of nepotism, ambition, or administrative obstacles in the way of bad class elements, there is a perfect linear relationship between education and both leadership position and class labels.

There are also data on occupational inheritance across generations (table 16). According to interviews and press reports, the most desirable jobs are nonagricultural ones outside of one's village—positions in a commune or a county factory, in a commune hospital, a commune purchasing and supply cooperative, or as a commune officer.[15] Even when a commune factory keeps incomes low by paying through a production team, work at a factory lacks the rigors of field work. Service in the People's Liberation Army is esteemed not only in itself but as a possible route to nonagricultural jobs outside one's village after demobilization. Almost as desirable, from the viewpoint of authority and influence rather than income, are jobs as top leaders of a brigade—as secretary, vice-secretary, or brigade head. Positions as team leaders or functionaries are somewhat less desirable. There are also local nonagricultural jobs. As contrasted with agricultural labor, jobs as

Table 15   Sons with at Least a Lower-Middle
                                                  School Education by Father's Position
                                                  and Class Label

Sons	Officer fathers			Class label of non-officer fathers		
	Brigade leader	Team leader	Brigade and team functionaries	Poor peasant/ lower-middle	Middle peasant/ upper-middle	Rich peasant/ landlord
%	100%	72%	57%	54%	47%	27%
(N)	(7)	(18)	(14)	(28)	(15)	(11)

Source: Mobility sample, sons age 16–29 only. In contrast to other samples, this sample includes sons who have left their parental home and sometimes even their parental village.

Table 16   Son's Occupation by Father's Position
                                                            and Class Label

	Fathers				
Sons	Brigade and team officers		Non-officers by class label		
	Leaders	Functionaries	PP/LMP	MP/UMP	RP/LL
1. Outside worker	5%	12%	7%	11%	21%
2. People's Liberation Army	0	19	5	0	0
3. Village officer	14	19	10	0	0
4. Village non-agriculturist	5	12	14	0	7
5. Agricultural laborer	76	38	64	89	71
Total	100%	100%	100%	100%	99%
Total N rows 1-5	(21)	(16)	(42)	(18)	(14)
6. Still in school	28%	16%	7%	5%	0%
Total N rows 1-6	(29)	(19)	(45)	(19)	(14)

Note: The abbreviated classes at the right hand side of the table are poor peasant/
lower-middle peasant, middle peasant/upper-middle peasant, and rich peasant/landlord.
The percentages in the first five rows are for sons who have left school. Total table
is for sons 16 and older only.

Source: Mobility sample

mason, carpenter, barefoot doctor, or village teacher have somewhat more
prestige—they offer a greater variety of work, and sometimes yield more
financial rewards. The differences among these positions are not great, but
from the viewpoint of drudgery and low pay the least-desired position is as a
full-time agricultural labor.

Not all sons sixteen years old and above have yet gone to work. Some are
still in upper middle schools outside their village, and, as seen earlier, this
continuing education favors sons of "good class" families and village leaders (table 16, row six). Among those already at work, the pattern is not so
clearly in favor of one group or another. In the 1950s and early 1960s, when
the restrictions on the education and employment of offspring of former
landlords and rich peasants were not quite so severe, many escaped their
village for jobs in nearby towns and cities. A fairly high proportion of these
individuals, even though they are excluded from the People's Liberation
Army and village office, now hold such desirable jobs.[16] As for new
officers, results vary by the exact position of one's father. Sons of village
functionaries are in desirable positions—only 38 percent of those in our
sample are ordinary agricultural laborers. Sons of village leaders, in contrast, have not parlayed parental power and educational advantage into
superior jobs. Three-fourths of older sons now out of school (who may not
have gotten much education) remain agricultural laborers. Though based on
small numbers which must be treated with caution, these results lend cre-

dence to an explanation of status transmission based on attitudes rather than nepotism. According to this explanation, village leaders (heads, vice-heads) are "locals" who look for power within agriculture and urge their sons to do likewise. Village functionaries are "cosmopolitans" who look for power and prestige in a broader occupational world and urge their sons to do the same. Whatever the exact explanations, though a pattern of educational inheritance has emerged, occupational inheritance is minimal.

A third indicator of transfer of status within families is the correspondence of occupations among brothers. There is not enough data on former landlords and rich peasants to include them, but between the remaining former poor and middle peasants there is little difference in occupational attainment (table 17). For new officers, in contrast, there are distinct differences. If one's elder brother is a village officer, one is no more likely to have joined the army nor to have gotten an outside job, but one is distinctly more likely also to become a village officer. Service in village office, then, runs in families.

Similarly, in more anecdotal evidence, there are some villages with tight kinship interconnections. There are no antinepotism rules to keep family members from serving concurrently in positions of authority. In some villages, gossiping peasants say that family members in positions of authority are doing favors for each other. Nevertheless, much of our data is still in favor of an attitude rather than nepotism explanation of status transmission.

Table 17 — Younger Brother's Occupation by Elder Brother's Position and Class Label

| Younger brothers | Elder brothers | | |
	All village officers	Non-officer poor/lower middle peasant	Non-officer middle/upper middle peasant
1. Outside worker	6%	6%	6%
2. People's Liberation Army	6	3	6
3. Village officer	44	18	10
4. Village non-agriculturist	17	3	0
5. Agricultural laborer	28	71	78
Total	101%	101%	100%
Total N rows 1-5	(18)	(34)	(18)
6. Still in school	5%	13%	5%
Total N rows 1-6	(19)	(39)	(19)

Note: Village officers among elder brothers include one brigade leader, three brigade functionaries, seven team leaders, and eight team functionaries.

Source: Mobility sample.

In one example, a team of about fifty households had a seven-person managing committee composed of team head, team vice-head, female vice-head, stockroom manager, and three nonofficers, and on this committee there were brothers of both the head and vice-head. When queried, our informant—an urban youth sent to live in the village—replied, "No, no one ever complained because these two pairs of brothers served together on the team committee." The problems were entirely different from those an outside observer would have expected:

> One time the older brother [the team head] did tell me that two brothers should not be on the committee together. His brother, he said, had problems in work style, but it would be embarrassing for him to mention this to the brother within a group meeting. Likewise, the younger brother once told me that his older brother had errors in his work, but these errors could not be brought up in a group meeting or even in a separate face-to-face setting. The younger brother, therefore, asked me to intercede and go to his brother with a list of his errors.[17]

This reply indicates not only that traditional interpersonal styles linger on in the village but also that service together in public office may represent something quite different from collusion. Given the occasional hardships of public office, joint service by members of the same family may represent no more than common socialization into a strong ethic of public service.

Altogether, our evidence suggests that high village status results in some educational advantage for sons but not much advantage in terms of jobs. The superior education of officers' children may have to do with the system of recommendation used in the late 1960s and 1970s to pick middle-school students, but occupational position appears to depend more on the aspirations and talents of youthful contenders. In contrast to the practice in the past, then, desirable jobs are not acquired primarily through kinship connections with village leaders.

Our interpretation of these patterns has been influenced by studies of stratification in the West, where the fact that success runs in families does not necessarily prove that nepotistic strings have been pulled. Families differ in how strong an environment fostering achievement aspirations they create, and to approximate total equality of opportunity it would be necessary to remove children from their families at birth and raise them in a uniform manner.[18] This the Chinese have never contemplated doing.

The leaders and functionaries in most villages seem to include representatives from the major kin group residing there (or representatives of various lineage branches, in the case of single-lineage brigades). Moreover, teams and brigades are supervised by, and their leadership selections approved by, the commune leadership, and at this level no single kin group can hope to dominate (in fact, outsiders generally do so). Thus nepotistic tendencies that might be expected to occur are kept within limits. Being born into the family of a village leader clearly has some advantages, but those cadres who show blatant favoritism toward kin are likely to lose their posts and have no privileges to transmit. Power and influence in the village were not all that rigidly structured prior to 1949, but they seem still more fluid today. The evidence presented here does not support either the view that traditional lineage politics continue as usual or that a "new class" has consolidated its control over village power and privileges.

Conclusions

Important changes are clearly visible in village leadership. The old elites have been dethroned and stigmatized, and today a wider range of individuals occupies formal leadership posts. Not only are the new leaders different in important ways from their predecessors, but they are incorporated into a much stronger political structure, one that reaches deep into the countryside and wields powerful resources and sanctions. The policies implemented through this structure provide fairly reliable checks on corruption, nepotism, and other abuses of power. In many respects China's leaders can take pride in having created an effective rural leadership system. Nevertheless, some of the key features of that system, particularly the limits on material rewards and mobility opportunities for village cadres, have their drawbacks as well. With the possible exception of the brigade secretary, village officers find that the rewards of office barely compensate for the costs of extra hours of work and for criticism from villagers below and the government above. Being natives of the village and not very different in background from those they lead, they can fairly easily return to being ordinary agricultural laborers, and when the pressures get too severe, many do so. We have repeatedly stressed that their roots and allegiances remain oriented primarily to their kinsmen and neighbors, and in this respect, at least, the contrast with pre-1949 village leaders is not so marked. The official policies of leadership by natives and relative equality make for solidary communities which are willing to cooperate with the state on many matters, but such policies also impose limits on how readily village leaders can be made to enforce unpopular government programs. We explore these limits in greater detail in subsequent chapters.

8

The Pursuit
of Equality and
Peasant
Satisfaction

In previous chapters we reviewed the evidence on the extent of various
kinds of inequalities in rural Kwangtung and the success achieved in efforts
to reduce remaining disparities. The balance sheet reveals a mixed situation.
Some types of inequality seem to have been kept in check or reduced, such
as the material gap between town and country or the difference between the
powerful and powerless in a village. Other inequalities have remained or
even increased, particularly the gap between rich and poor villages. It may
not be particularly meaningful to try to gauge the overall extent of equality
and inequality in rural Kwangtung today, since so many material and non-
material factors are involved, and no precise measures are available for most
of them. But at the most general level we feel that overall rural inequality
has been reduced since 1949, particularly within individual villages, but that
still things are less equal than is often assumed. Chinese peasants are not all
guaranteed the essentials of life today, and, depending on the resources
available in one's family and village, life is quite comfortable for some and a
constant battle to keep one's head above water for others. Peasant livelihood
is still much more at the mercy of floods, pests, family illnesses, and the
state of cooperation with kin than is the case for urban workers. As regards
family income rural Kwangtung does not seem to have any less inequality
than a number of noncommunist developing societies in Asia.[1] It is not
correct to automatically assume that peasants who live under socialism and

in farms which are called communes must have less inequality than their counterparts elsewhere.

We have noted that conditions in the countryside may change in ways that could incrementally promote certain kinds of equality. In particular, with greater density of population and economic improvement, the officially espoused time-rate work-point system may become more widely suitable. But in this regard it is important to note that, just as there are many aspects of inequality, there are different kinds of rural conditions that foster or obstruct particular egalitarian reforms. The Chinese press sees rural life as polarized between villages with the proper Maoist style of leadership, where sharing is accepted and equality is fostered, and other politically "backward" villages, where no headway is made. Our own village comparisons show that this picture is inaccurate. Villages using time rates tend to be those with political study systems, low land-labor ratios, and large teams. Villages which stressed the Tachai work-point scheme tended to be those that were the most prosperous. Villages with nurseries and kindergartens tend to be large, multi-kin, prosperous villages in the Pearl River Delta region, while villages that adopted cooperative medicine early also tend to be in the delta region, but to be smaller, single-lineage villages which are not particularly prosperous. The political and communications-access characteristics of villages do not consistently support more egalitarian programs, contrary to what press accounts would lead one to suppose. Physical location, wealth, surname composition, team and brigade size—these characteristics are important for the adoption of certain programs but not for all. Our study finds no evidence of a continuum from sharing and equal to selfish and unequal villages. Rather, villages seem to adopt or reject particular programs depending on how these fit local conditions, and in a single village one egalitarian program may be willingly adopted while another is resisted. Our findings also cast doubt on the idea that the movement from socialism to full communism involves the gradual education of the peasantry in officially espoused ideals of selflessness and cooperation. The balance of sharing and stinginess seems to be conditioned more by idiosyncratic local conditions (natural and social) than by some general transformation of peasant values. These are themes to which we will return again after we have reviewed peasant responses to several other kinds of change efforts in later chapters.

Both the limited recent success in fostering broader equality and the absence of a clear sharing-selfish continuum among villages are products at least in part of the decentralized system of rural administration and finance adopted by the Chinese Communists. The primary obligations of village leaders are to their relatives and neighbors, rather than to the state. These cadres reply primarily on local agricultural earnings for both their own pay and the resources to fund village social programs. They are not much more ideologically "activist" than the peasants they lead. The state does maintain sufficient administrative, coercive, and financial power to set clear limits on the range of local policies that can be pursued, and periodic campaigns and work teams are used to collect information on local leaders and enforce these limits. But within this system there is still a substantial amount of flexibility to adapt the government's programs to local conditions, and this often results in the preservation of inequalities which have their roots in prevailing natural and social conditions. The variety of rural social life comes through in spite of the uniformity of directives from Peking.

In the last analysis, then, there are limits on the control that Chinese authorities can exercise over village life, in pursuit of equality or any other goal. We described earlier the conflicts between equality and equity on the one hand and equality and administrative efficiency on the other. In the Kwangtung countryside the emphasis on equity (rewarding the most productive) and efficiency (retaining flexibility and initiative in the hands of those making the daily farming decisions) have clearly been foremost in the minds of Chinese planners. To put this in other terms, since the Chinese system of socialized agriculture was built in the mid-1950s, the pursuit of equality has had to share the stage with several other vital policy objectives: the desire to increase agricultural production, to avoid heavily burdening the state budget, to keep peasants from streaming into the cities, to avoid the inefficiencies and red tape of a fully centralized economic system, and so forth. Attempts in recent years to make more radical shifts in the direction of rural equality have run up against the realization that this cannot easily be done without sacrificing these other objectives. In a crunch, the goal of equality has generally had to take a back seat, and this seems likely to continue to be the case in the future. Like it or not, a fair amount of continuing inequality seems to be built into the agricultural system the Chinese Communists have built.

Peasant Satisfaction

Fundamentally, then, equality goals are sacrificed when they threaten to undermine the efficiency of the Chinese collectivized farming system and the incentives and satisfactions of peasant members and local leaders. But how effectively does the system produce such incentives and satisfactions?

Obviously we are not able to go to China and conduct an objective survey of
reactions to commune life, and our interviews with people who have left
China are not a very good source of direct evidence on this point. But we will
attempt to deal with this question indirectly. We assume that, if the collectivized system provides an acceptable set of incentives and satifactions
to peasants, they will work diligently within it, and statistics on agricultural
output will show improvements. If incentives and satisfactions are deficient,
then peasants will try to shirk collective labor and apply their energies
elsewhere, particularly in their private sideline economic activities. One of
the endemic problems of Soviet collective farms has been the difficulty of
getting peasants to divert enough attention from their private plots so that the
crops in the collectivized fields can be properly cared for. We begin our
consideration of these questions by discussing the nature of private sector
activities within today's communes.

The private sector of the village economy includes the cultivation of
private plots; raising pigs and chickens and other fowl; making baskets,
mats, and hats for sale at the free market; and cutting grass from hillsides for
sale as fuel. There are also a few carpenters, masons, and other laborers who
roam the countryside. Though most of these are peasants who take leave
from their team to do roadwork, carting, or private carpentry only during the
winter slack season, a few operate as artisans year-round. A few others, such
as wandering cloth-dyers, pot-menders, and barbers, operate out of the
market town, pocketing their proceeds much as in a free-market economy.
Most peasants depend in very important ways on their private plots, pigs,
and household sideline activities.

The formal limits on private plots are specified in article forty of the Sixty
Articles. According to this article (and newspaper reports) there are four
kinds of private lands. The principle kind, distributed by the team to its
member households, should be within 5 or 7 percent of the team's total
arable land. Most commonly distributed according to family size, this kind
of land, according to visitors and informants, is fairly tightly controlled. It
is generally near the 5 percent norm, providing the average family with a
square plot measuring about thirteen meters on a side.[2] It tends to be on
poorer land, to be supplemented or cut as a family grows or shrinks, and in a
few villages to be periodically rotated in and out of public holdings. A
second kind is "fodder land," granted according to the number of pigs a
family is raising. A third kind is marginal land around private houses and
along roadbeds or embankments. This "four-margin land" or "five-margin
land" may be used to grow fruit trees and bamboo as well as vegetables.

These latter two kinds of land, though common, are small in amount in comparison with the potentially very large holdings of a fourth kind: land a family brings into cultivation on its own. If it is old land which has gone fallow, a family bringing it back into cultivation can lay claim to it for three years. If the land is new, previously uncultivated land, a family can lay claim to it for five years before it reverts to the collective. This land, which is available mostly in localities with uncultivated hillsides, is formally limited to 15 percent of the total team land, and this makes possible fairly extensive private endeavors. Though informants do not mention cultivations this extensive, they do say that the three- and five-year limits are often ignored. Indeed, most of the 1968–71 effort to limit private plots was directed not at the elimination of the 5 percent of regular private plots but at the larger amount of newly opened lands which had gone beyond their three- and five-year limits, and at marginal lands which had expanded excessively.

Since labor for the team provides little more than grain, cotton, and oil, peasants depend on their private lands directly for vegetables and indirectly for meat.[3] Also, since the collective provides cash only once or twice a year, peasants depend on private sidelines to purchase soy sauce, hoes, and other small items which must be bought throughout the year. Wives feed private-plot produce to family pigs, chickens, and ducks, and sell vegetables in the private market. Chickens, eggs, and ducks are also sold periodically at the free market, while grown pigs are sold to the state purchasing cooperative. Pigs are the largest item in the private sector, each selling for around eighty yuan, or about half as much cash as an average family earns from collective labor over an entire year. It is little wonder that the pig, fed so carefully throughout the year for such a large return, is sometimes popularly referred to as the "farmer's bank."[4]

Our best studies of the role of the private sector date back to the mid-1950s. However, the present team economic system is very similar to that of the 1956–57 collectives, and recent visitor-reports suggest that the role of the private sector has not changed much in most places. Though in North China in 1956 the private sector generated as little as 15 percent of the peasant's total income, in South China this figure was 27 percent.[5] Throughout China in the 1960s and 1970s, foreigners visiting more affluent communes found that the private sector usually generated 10 to 25 percent of total peasant income, though occasional figures as high as 33 percent were found.[6] Though significant, these percentages are still considerably less than in the Soviet Union, where as a result of low grain prices and high delivery quotas in the 1930s and 1940s, private plots produced most of what peasants consumed.[7] This difference may help explain why private sector activities seem somewhat easier to control in China.

In our interviews, though the tension between these private enterprise activities and team labor is a common one, local authorities seem able to deal with it. They keep an eye out for team members who spend too much time off in private pursuits, and may criticize them in team meetings or even try to catch them sneaking off without permission. In recent years, in some areas, market days have been switched by the government from the traditional three-day schedules to new five-day schedules, in order to cut down on the time peasants spend off at markets. (Some of our informants reported, however, that this measure did not reduce the disruption of team labor, since more people at a time would take off from work to attend the less frequent five-day markets than used to take off when markets met every third day.)[8] Some teams also set up rules about the minimum number of days that team members have to work; for example, twenty-eight days a month for men and twenty-six for women. Individuals who do not meet these minima may have cuts made in their grain rations or be subjected to public criticism. Work-point grain allocations may be emphasized so as to penalize those who skip collective labor. Finally, some teams "co-opt" private undertakings of certain types by bringing them under team regulation. The peasant must get permission from team cadres to go outside for work in construction, transportation, and factories requiring short-term laborers. The team gives the individual a certificate indicating he has local approval. Then the individual is required to turn over a certain sum to the team for each month he works outside (say, fifteen yuan). In exchange he (most outside workers are males) continues to receive monthly grain rations and work points from the team and can keep any earnings left over after paying the team's fee.[9] The team is expected to regulate the number and timing of such outside workers so that they do not disrupt farming routines.

The tensions between public and private remain, with families balancing their commitment to the team and their dependence on it for low-price grain against the potential for cash earnings available through private activities. From the standpoint of the team, though, in most places a reasonable balance seems to be struck. Although some of our informants had themselves been "spontaneous elements" (tzu-fa fen-tzu, that is, individuals who run off to earn an outside income without permission, often with forged papers), we did not get a picture from them of team production seriously disrupted by many members deserting collective labor for private pursuits, as occurred in many localities during the early 1960s.[10] Though team cadres have to be constantly on the alert to keep attendance up, and many teams have one or

two perpetual offenders, desertion of team labor was not one of the primary
sources of production problems mentioned to us by informants. Peasants
eagerly pursue private-plot farming, marketing, and other cash income activities, but they do so for the most part outside of the time required for
regular participation in team labor. This conclusion suggests that the collective sector does provide sufficient incentives to motivate peasants to meet
their obligations there, and if so we should see the results in agricultural
output figures.

On the question of productive output, it appears that, except for the Great
Leap interregnum and for minor year-to-year variations in the 1970s, steady
progress has been made. The pattern of growth in Kwangtung can be seen
both in official statistics and in informants' reports on their home villages.
The statistics in table 18 come from government publications in the 1950s
and radio reports in the 1970s. Data on the intervening years are as yet
unavailable. The figures for gross grain output, output per mou, and output
per person all suggest a pattern of reasonable growth.

During World War II and the civil war years, grain output dropped sharply.
It was not until 1952 that the prewar high of some 18 billion catties was
met and exceeded. Output continued to grow through 1957. In the excesses
of the 1958–61 Great Leap Forward grain output nationwide declined by
about 20 percent, accompanied by malnutrition and famine-related deaths.
There were similar problems in Kwangtung, but in the early 1960s with the
dissemination of new dwarf rice varieties production went up sharply, reaching a high of over 30 billion catties in the early 1970s. Similarly, by the
mid-1950s, the highest prewar yield figures were exceeded, and by 1970
Kwangtung had met the target laid down in agricultural plans of the 1950s of
eight hundred catties per mou.

Though seriously interrupted by the Great Leap Forward, this pattern of
growth is quite acceptable in comparison with that of other countries. In
Taiwan, which is considered a successful example of economic growth, rice
yields returned to their prewar highs only in the mid-1950s. Yields, which
were at about 740 catties of unhusked rice per cultivated mou in 1957, grew
sharply in the early 1960s, as new strains were introduced, and then stag-
nated in the early 1970s at about 1,000 catties per mou.[11] The growth pattern
is quite similar to that in Kwangtung. Throughout the world, yields increased by an index of 147:100, when 1970–72 is compared with 1952–56.
One study shows that on this scale China as a whole does not rank very
high.[12] The province of Kwangtung, with an index of about 164:100 for this
comparison, as indicated in table 18, would rank better than average.

Though growth in grain output per capita within Kwangtung was not so

Table 18   Grain Output in Kwangtung Province

	Gross output[a] (billion catties)	Population[b] (million)	Yields[c] (catties per mou)	Output per capita
1949	16.0			
1950	14.0			
1951	15.0			
1952	19.0			
1953	19.4	36.7		
1954	23.0	37.5	479	614
1955	21.9	38.2	456	574
1956	24.1	39.0	502	620
1957	24.7	39.8	514	624
Average (1954-57)			488	608
Average (metric)[d]			3.7	304
1969	32.0	45.8	790	699
1970	33.0	46.7	817	707
1971	30.0	47.7	740	629
1972		48.7		
1973	32.1	49.6	790	647
1974	35.3	50.6	870	697
Average (1969-74)			801	676
Average (metric)[d]			6.0	338

[a]Includes grains, potatoes, and soybeans. Figures for 1954-57 and probably 1949 include data for Chin-chou Special District, which was part of neighboring Kwangsi Province during 1951-54 and after 1965. Data for the 1950s are from Social Science Research Council, Committee on the Economy of China, Provincial Agricultural Statistics for Communist China (Ithaca, N.Y.: Cornell University, School of Industrial and Labor Relations, 1969) and Liang Jen-ts'ai, Kuang-tung ching-chi ti-li, p. 25. Data for the 1970s are from radio reports in C.I.A., China: Agricultural Performance in 1975 (Washington: DOCEX, Exchange and Gifts Division, Library of Congress, 1976), and FBIS, 20 Oct. 1970.

[b]Population as reported in John S. Aird, Population Estimates for the Provinces of the People's Republic of China: 1953-1974, International Population Reports, Series P-95, No. 73 (Washington, D.C.: U.S. Department of Commerce, Bureau of Economic Analysis, 1974), table 2.

[c]Annual output per cultivated mou. 1950s figures are based on the reported 48 million mou dedicated to grain in 1957--Sun Ching-chih (ed.), Hua-nan ti-ch'u ching-chi ti-li [Economic geography of south China] (Peking: Science Press, 1959), in JPRS, no. 14,954, p. 64. Figures for the 1970s are based on 1970 total output divided by reported yield of 817 catties per mou to give a calculated 40.4 million mou cultivated in grain. See SWB, 6 Jan. 1971, p. A6.

[d]Metric equivalents--metric tons per hectare and kilograms per capita.

striking as that for yields and total output, it is within an acceptable range. Between 1952–56 and 1970–72, the index of world growth in grain output per capita was 115:100.[13] The index of grain output in Kwangtung over a similar period was 111:100, that is, there was roughly 11 percent more grain produced per person in the early 1970s than in the mid-1950s (table 18).[14] Already in the mid-1950s, Chinese per capita grain output compared well with that in other developing nations. In the 1970s, the Kwangtung output of 338 kilograms per capita was severely below a developed nation average of

590 kilograms but still comfortably above a developing nation average of just 201 kilograms.[15]

Besides the growth in grain, there may have been even higher rates of growth in other kinds of agricultural activities, such as the raising of pigs, ducks, chickens, fish, fruits, and timber. There are data on increasing pig production. Around 1930 in South China, there was an average of 1.10 pigs per peasant household.[16] As with grain, the number of pigs dropped sharply during World War II and the following civil war but by 1957 had returned to about prewar levels—there were 1.01 pigs per peasant household.[17] With additional incentives, such as extra income and grain allotments for deliveries of pig manure and extra private-plot land for fodder, by 1969 pigs in Kwangtung had increased to 2.89 per household.[18] These pigs produce much of the organic manure which is still so crucial to Chinese agriculture, and because they are owned mostly by individual families they contribute to private income.

Increasing family income is reflected in housing statistics. With only a few exceptions, housing remains in the private sector. Article 45 of the Sixty Articles on commune governance specifies that peasants shall own their houses as well as have the right to buy, sell, and rent them. Children inherit their parents' house, and, when they marry, children may just build an extra room on the family home.[19] Except in some poor tidewater areas, savings institutions do not make loans for housing.[20] Rather families must save from their own finances or borrow from relatives to build houses which, according to interviews, average 1,000 to 1,500 yuan.[21] Besides the difficulties of financing, there is often a shortage of timber for the rafters and sometimes a shortage of bricks. There may be no suitable clay nearby or insufficient fuel for the firing of bricks, or the commune may prohibit digging up valuable rice fields to make sun-dried bricks. Despite these difficulties, housing has improved, at least as estimated by rough judgments of the predominant housing type in two periods.[22]

	South China 1930	Kwangtung 1973
Fired-brick walls	23%	32%
Mixed brick and mud walls	34	60
Bamboo and grainstalk walls	43	8
Total	100%	100%
Number of sample villages	(ca. 20)	(40)

The number of fired-brick houses is not all that much greater today than before. With special assistance to tidewater areas and with a general improvement in living standards for the very poor, however, there has been a dramatic improvement in the poorest housing.

Besides these statistical materials, informants provide a wealth of impressionistic materials implying that living standards in many villages are still very low, but that standards are nevertheless gradually rising. Informants report that water has been brought more and more under control—floods are less severe and irrigation is more widespread. More and more villages are getting electricity each year and electric pumps follow soon after. In recent years, production teams and brigades have been slowly but steadily adding new machines. At the individual level, bicycles are becoming more widespread, as are vacuum bottles, new wash basins, and the like. And at a slower pace, new transistor radios and sewing machines are becoming more popular.

All these indicators point toward increasing output and slowly improving living standards. In part, the increased output is the simple result of new seeds, additional water pumps, and chemical fertilizer. But just as importantly it is the result of long hours of additional human labor expended on water-control projects, leveling fields, weeding, spraying, planting, and harvesting. It is clear that peasants in Kwangtung and elsewhere in China are working many more hours and days each year than they used to.[23] Without acceptable incentives, such efforts would not have been expended. The increased output is, then, an index of the effectiveness of peasant incentives. In turn, the improved living standards which come from this effort should serve as additional incentives for collective labor.

Western social scientists have tended to be skeptical of whether peasants could ever be satisfied with collective farming. Certainly, in China during the Great Leap Forward and to an extent in 1968–71 there were problems with motivation. In the earlier period, with little reward for differential effort, skill, and physical strength, peasants were so unhappy that the best workers slackened in their efforts or even sat down on the job in a massive demonstration of passive resistance. In Kwangtung villages between 1968 and 1971, peasants were very unhappy with the more equal distribution of work points and grain in some villages. In response, they worked shorter hours at a slower pace, often leaving tools in the fields or allowing valuable seed and animal manure go to waste. To them, it was just not right to give money and grain to slackers and incompetent workers. This does not mean that Kwangtung peasants are inherently selfish, but simply that their sense of equity was violated by the new remuneration schemes. But most of the time the incentive system used within communes provides for differential rewards while making some small provision for those who cannot take care of themselves. When this is the case there does not seem to be a particular problem in getting peasants to work hard.

Even if satisfied with collective modes of farming, peasants can be dissatisfied with bureaucratic arrangements which collective farming brings with it. Two of these arrangements which scholars often comment on are the tendency to resort to campaign tactics that ignore local conditions and the difficulty of making rational decisions in the absence of market indicators. Chinese agriculture has certainly suffered from campaign tactics. With untested close planting, deep plowing, irrigation, and other schemes which were appropriate in certain areas but totally inappropriate in others, the 1958–59 Great Leap Forward wrapped all the errors typical of Soviet campaigns into one great movement. The results were devastating, and the Chinese learned their lesson well. With decentralization down to the team level, the basic production and accounting unit became much smaller and more closely tied to natural villages and neighborhoods than its Soviet counterpart. In addition, both the manufacture and ownership of threshers, water pumps, and other machines have been passed to lower units, with the rationale that these units are best suited to design and use these machines in ways that fit local conditions. Though there was some interruption in the 1968–71 radical interlude, and though there have been hints that some central officials would like to reaggregate basic production and accounting units, in the last fifteen years Chinese agriculture has avoided many of the problems of excessive centralization characteristic of Soviet agriculture.

There was also in the post–Great Leap period a great emphasis on local testing. In the early 1960s the press was full of quotes from Chairman Mao saying that one who has not tested his ideas has no right to speak. An agricultural extension network was created which attempts to disseminate new techniques not by administrative coercion but through test and demonstration plots in each county, commune, brigade, and team. In interviews, one occasionally hears of this or that county official pushing a pet scheme which backfires. But these reports are not common, and with the emphasis on officials getting out from behind their desks and investigating in the fields, they should soon learn which of their pet schemes will not work. Since the Great Leap Forward, Chinese problems with farm administration seem to have more to do with introducing unpopular institutional arrangements, such as the Tachai work-point system, than with mandating inappropriate technologies.[24]

There are other kinds of problems which can arise in the absence of market indicators, and some of these do appear in China. Informants report that peasants are unhappy with their poor incomes relative to those of city workers; they are unhappy at being excluded from cities; and they are unhappy that they are forced to grow grain in place of higher-priced fruits, vegetables, and other commercial crops. One can argue that many of these problems would be solved in a free market. Peasants would move to cities in sufficient numbers to drive down urban wages to near the rural level, thus eliminating the quest for urban employment. Peasants would switch from grain to other crops in sufficient numbers to equalize the prices among these crops. Such an answer is too simple, of course. In all developing societies, there is great pressure to migrate from village to city, and this free migration does not eliminate all urban-rural wage differentials.

Chinese officials are by no means unaware of pressures being generated within their system. Urban informants who have lived in villages report that peasants are quite vocal in their discontent, and the press reflects this discontent in articles about the necessity to narrow urban-rural inequalities. Interviews with informants formerly in economic work indicate that through field studies the Chinese bureaucracy does occasionally indulge in fine-tuning via price manipulation of nongrain crops. The Chinese bureaucracy, then, is not so much ignorant in the absence of market information as caught between competing goals. Due to their commitment to keep industrial investment high for the sake of long-run economic growth, they must restrict urban migration and the urban infrastructure expenses that migration would create. From their commitment to avoid the inflation which made the Nationalist regime so unpopular, they must avoid raising grain prices any further while compelling virtually everyone to grow their own grain in order to minimize transport costs. It is more the effort to tightly control the economy than some inherent defects of collectivized agriculture that produce these contradictions.

We judge that the commune system works effectively in spite of these problems. Most of the complaints heard are not with communes per se but with some particular policy enforced within them: the restriction on urban migration, the requirement to grow grain, the discrimination against former landlords, and so forth. We cannot say in the abstract that this is the most efficient or productive way to organize agriculture under Chinese conditions. But we can say that the Chinese have reduced or avoided many of the problems that plague Soviet collective farms and have organized a system that creates acceptable rewards and satisfactions for most peasants and their leaders.[25] The system works as effectively as it does not in spite of the failure to realize more equality but in part because of the remaining inequalities. Those individuals, families, and production teams that devote the most effort to the collective sector have some assurance that it is they, rather than poorer peasants elsewhere or the state, that will receive the primary benefits. As the efforts mobilized within this system produce increases in farm output, average peasant livelihood does slowly improve, and even the most disadvantaged peasants can feel that their situation is less desperate than in the past.

3

family
organization
and ritual life

9

Household
Structure and
Birth
Control

*W*ith the assumption that much of the motivation for family life comes from its community setting, this book has begun with a consideration of collective structures, economic equality, the provision of social services, and power differentials. At this point, our discussion turns to aspects of family behavior.

Household Structure

Though the Chinese government is not very explicit about the ideal structure for peasant households, it would seem to favor relatively large, complex families with grandparents and grandchildren living together. There was talk in the 1958–59 Great Leap Forward of setting up old-age homes and building public housing for peasants, but at other times there has been much more emphasis on how people can keep their private house, how children are responsible for the support of their grandparents, and even how grandparents should be encouraged to care for children so that young mothers can go out to work. On rare occasions press articles have criticized the prevailing patrilocal residence custom, by which daughters marry out of their own families and are incorporated into the families of their husbands.[1] Yet by not making any real effort to break this pattern while discouraging the movement of young males away from their native villages, the government has given tacit support to patrilocal residence. Generally, the government is less concerned about who lives together—household structure—than about the quality of relationships within a family—fathers should not dominate and oppress either their children or their wives. It is the fact of who lives together, however, that helps set the stage for relationships among family members. If children must share the same house and budget with parents far into adulthood, the grounds are laid for parents to have a large say in mate choice and other aspects of the life of a grown child. If daughter-in-law and mother-in-law must use the same cooking pot, the sorts of mother-in-law—daughter-in-law conflicts which were endemic to traditional Chinese families are likely to continue. The description of household structure in this chapter, then, lays the groundwork for the discussion of family relationships in the chapters that follow.

In traditional China, all married sons ideally lived under the same roof with their parents, in a patrilocal joint family structure.[2] Sons were to be filial to their fathers, both before and after death. One of the primary obligations of sons was to provide male offspring in order that the ancestral line might be continued and so that there would always be someone to burn incense for the deceased.

Though some families were able to live up to this ideal, most peasants were sorely pressed to fulfill filial obligations. The greatest threat to the ideal family was simply the high death rates which prevailed in a society yet unexposed to modern public health measures. Though the average woman gave birth to over five children during her lifetime, less than half of these children lived to marry and have children. Even those who had several sons might have to give some of them to a kinsman who had no sons. Extra daughters might receive harsher treatment; sometimes they were killed in infancy or given to other families as prospective daughters-in-law (t'ung-yang-hsi).[3] The rich could occasionally attain the ideal of a large extended family with several sons living together. They could afford to marry early. If the first wife proved infertile or had sons who died, such a family might acquire a secondary wife or concubine. The poor, in contrast, delayed their marriage while waiting for the elder generation to die or for economic fortunes to improve.[4]

High death rates kept the average size of the Chinese family small. Not many families had more than one son who reached marriage age. After marriage, only for a few years did a married son, his spouse and children, and his parents dwell together before his parents' death. Nevertheless, in comparison with Western Europe in the preindustrial age, the family in rural China was rather large and complex. The average family size revealed in Buck's survey in 1930 was 5.0 for South China, compared with a figure of 4.0 for France in 1856, for example. Five members as an average may not seem large, but given the high death rates prevailing in China at the time, a figure of this size indicates that most families who had the opportunity to live in joint families did so (which was not the case in France). At any one point in time many families were nuclear in structure and not very large, but a significant proportion of Chinese peasants lived in extended arrangements for short periods, before death (or disputes between married brothers) reduced things to nuclear form again.[5]

We argue that, except in the cases of child brides and concubines, the government has not been directly concerned with changing the structure of the households in which Chinese peasants live. Have changes occurred nonetheless, so that families are less large and complex than they once were? Today there are contradictory tendencies that may affect the Chinese peasant family. Greater life expectancy brings an increasing probability that lives of family members will over-lap, while restrictions on migration make it likely that they will live nearby. Land reform and collectivization have curtailed the economic authority of the father and his power and desire to keep sons together under his rule. Yet, the difficulties associated with combining collective labor with private sideline activities make it useful for family members to cooperate on different tasks. The high cost of private housing makes it cheaper to add rooms to existing, parental homes than to build a new house for each marrying son. The dependence of the aged on the young makes it likely that parents will want to foster loyalty in their sons and later cooperate with sons in domestic work and child care.

These different tendencies lead to a variety of results. Most commonly, aged parents live with their grown sons and grandchildren as they did traditionally. Brothers, in contrast, are more likely to separate, for there is little incentive for them to maintain a common purse and common kitchen. Nevertheless, brothers often live within the same compound, remaining in intimate daily contact. These and other changes can be seen in three sets of data. First, table 19 shows that, while the average size of peasant families is only slightly smaller than forty years ago, this seeming stability conceals important changes. Family type is defined by whether people share a common budget and eat together. While only one-third of all families were nuclear in the past, over half are nuclear today. In 1973 data, only 2 percent of households are joint—that is, include married brothers. Most commonly, complex families today are stem families, with a grandparent or grandparents living with one married son and his wife and children.[6]

Table 20 shows in greater detail how family size can remain constant while the variety of kin present declines.[7] The table reflects three tendencies.

Table 19   Family Structure

	South China, 1930	Kwangtung, 1973
Average number of members	5.0	4.8
Structure of family		
Single person	3%	12%
Nuclear	34	50
Stem	} 63	37
Joint		2
Total	100%	101%
Total N	(2,422)	(131)

Sources: Lewis, S. C. Smythe, "The Composition of the Chinese Family," Chin-ling hsüeh-pao (Nanking Journal), vol. 5, no. 1 (1935), table 6. Neighbor sample, 1973.

First, lowered infant mortality leads to more children per household (row 3). With the birth rate just now beginning to decline, it would take some time for the number of children per household to approach the American level. Second, since households divide their finances earlier now than forty years ago, there are far fewer children's wives, grandchildren, siblings, and other

Table 20   Persons in Families by Relationship
                                  to Household Head (Persons per
                                  Household)

	South China 1930	Kwangtung 1973	United States 1960
1. Head	1.00	1.00	1.00
2. Spouse	.78	.69	.74
3. Child	1.91	2.54	1.31
4. Parent/parent-in-law	.23	.32	.05
5. Child's spouse	.31	.12	.01
6. Grandchild	.36	.12	.05
7. Sibling/sibling's spouse	.23	.14	.04
8. Other kin	.14	.02	.04
Total per household[a]	5.03	4.95	3.24
Total households	20,066	249	53,024
Total household members	101,018	1,233	171,756

Sources: Adapted from Frank W. Notestein and Ch'iao Ch'i-ming, "Population," in John Lossing Buck, Land Utilization in China (Nanking: University of Nanking, 1937), p. 367. Combined household sample, 1973. U.S., Bureau of the Census, Persons by Family Characteristics, Census of Population, 1960, report PC(2)-4B, p. xiii.

[a]Because of rounding errors, sum of individual ratios will only approximate the total members per household. Only kinsmen and no sent-down urban youth are included in these figures.

kin in the household than previously, despite the fact that kin survive longer now (rows 5 through 8). Third, the headship of households is probably transferred from father to son earlier today than previously. This is in the logic of team accounting, where usually it is the oldest working male who is used for household accounting. Together, these three tendencies make it difficult to predict how many parents of the household head would be found in the modern peasant household—greater longevity and earlier transfer of headship would lead to more parents in the household, while frequent separation of brothers would lead to fewer parents in the household. As it turns out, there are more parents in a typical household today than before (row 4). Finally, Chinese peasant families still remain larger and "more complex" than those in the United States. Household is defined as only those people who eat and budget together. It must also be kept in mind that even when not sharing the same table and same purse, brothers are often in the same compound or in adjacent buildings, as was often the case in the past. The grandmother takes care of the children of several brothers while they and their wives are at work during the day. In emergencies brothers still rely on one another for economic support. Socialism or not, demographically the Chinese rural family has many resemblances with its counterpart in the past.[8]

The third set of data reporting changes in the rural family is derived from table 20, except that more detailed relationships are shown, and for 1973 families are separated according to the gender of the head (table 21). From this table, six observations follow. First, there are probably more households headed by females today than ever before. Surveys in the 1920s and 1930s report only 1 to 8 percent of all rural households headed by women, for women who lost their husbands would traditionally attach themselves to another family or hand the headship over to a son.[9] A few with no close kin left to support them entered Buddhist nunneries. Today, increasing economic security makes it possible for women to live alone, and in our small 1973 sample, 15 percent of all households are headed by women.[10] A second observation to be made from the data in table 21 is that some politically disapproved family relationships are disappearing. Concubines, who existed only in affluent families before, are no more. Infant daughters-in-law, or child brides, have just about vanished.[11] Third, the male line continues to predominate. Within the family, there are more sons than daughters, more sons' wives than daughters' husbands, more sons' children than daughters' children, more brothers than sisters, and more husband's than wife's parents. This predominance shows that patrilocal residence con-

Table 21   Family Members by Relationship to
                                            Household Head (Persons per Household)

	South China, 1930	Sex of household head[a]	
		Male	Female
Head	1.00	1.00	1.00
Spouse	.78	.82	--
Concubine	.01	--	--
Son	1.18	1.45	.84
Daughter	.66	1.07	.56
Child (sex unknown)	--	.21	--
Adopted son	.02	.00[b]	.03
Adopted daughter	.02	--	--
Infant daughter-in-law[c]	.04	.00[b]	--
Father	.03	.07	--
Mother	.18	.27	.05
Spouse's father	--	--	.03
Spouse's mother	.01	.01	.05
Son's wife	.30	.13	.05
Daughter's husband	.01	--	--
Son's child (grandchild)	.35	.13	.03
Daughter's child	.01	.00[b]	--
Brother	.13	.10	--
Brother's wife	.06	.02	--
Sister	.04	.04	--
Brother's child	.08	.01	--
Other kin	.06	.00[b]	--
Total households	20,066	211	38
Total members	101,018	1,134	99

Sources: Same as table 20.

[a]Kwangtung, 1973.

[b]Less than .005.

[c]T'ung-yang-hsi.

tinues to hold sway. Fourth, as one's own children are more likely to survive, there is less incentive to adopt children. Fifth, because mothers live longer, and because headship is still the preserve of males, there are more mothers than fathers of household heads. Sixth, most brothers separate their finances soon after marriage, as we had already surmised. Though the number of unmarried brothers per household continues to be high relative to Western standards, the number of brothers' wives has declined. This table, then, supports the picture to which all our data have been building. The contemporary peasant family is very much a mixture of old and new. There is less variety in family forms than before, for with more children surviving and secure economic conditions there is less need to turn to adopted sons, matrilocal marriages, or child brides. In some ways these changes support old ideal forms of the family. Though brothers divide their finances earlier now, traditionally, with high death rates, few brothers lived together for long anyway. Residence remains partilocal, with virtually all old parents living in the home of a son. The joint family emphasis has given way to a stem-and-associated-nuclear-family combination, but groups of patrilineally related males retain their close links.

Besides giving a picture of family structure in general, our data allow us to examine variation among families and possible sources of change. From a modernization model, one might assume that the greatest tendencies towards nuclear structure would be in households headed by men with high education or in households residing in villages near major cities, with modern communication facilities and a strong economy. Such is not the case. The only strong relationship which appears in comparisons of different types of households and villages is that former landlords and rich peasants are more likely to live isolated from other kin in nuclear and single-person families. This is the result of some landlords being killed in 1952, leaving their widows and children behind, of educated children from such families leaving for urban jobs in the 1940s and 1950s, and of the difficulties that landlord males left in the village have getting married, as we noted earlier. Peasants with other class labels do not differ among themselves in their family structural distribution.[12]

If we eliminate households of former landlords and rich peasants, there are virtually no strong relationships between household structure and characteristics of either the household head or the village in which he or she resides (table 22). Household structure is dichotomized between complex households which include aged parents or other kin and simple households—a single person or a nuclear arrangement. With the latter scored high, a positive association indicates that a background characteristic favors simpler families—a negative correlation indicates the reverse. As a model of modernization would predict, in villages with more household consumption and urban youths, people are more likely to live in simple households, yet collective affluence has no influence on household complexity. And contrary to the modernization model, educated people and people in villages with good communications are somewhat more likely to head complex households. There is also no clear relationship between the household head's party membership or cadre status and household composition, nor between village political density or political study systems and household composition. Taken together, these weak and inconsistent results indicate that a tendency to live in nuclear arrangements rather than more complex forms is not a new pattern diffusing out to Kwangtung villages

Table 22   Household Simplicity by Village and
Household Head Characteristics (Gamma
Statistics)

	Degree of association	N
Village Characteristics		
Administrative:		
Political density	.03	(219)
Political study	.12	(144)
Urban-communications:		
Urban proximity	.18	(213)
Urban youths	.26*	(131)
Communications	-.37*	(193)
Nurseries	.09	(218)
Economy:		
Collective affluence	-.12	(219)
Household consumption	.34*	(198)
Land/labor ratio	.03	(177)
Remittances	-.15	(137)
Other:		
Brigade size	-.11	(165)
Team size	-.14	(219)
Lineage composition	.08	(219)
Non-Hakka ethnicity	-.21	(219)
Delta region	.18	(219)
Household Head Characteristics		
Party member	.09	(219)
Cadre	-.08	(214)
Education	-.26	(160)

Note: Former landlords and rich peasants are excluded from these statistics, as are sent-down urban youths.

Source: Combined household sample, 1973.

*p ≤ .10

under government influence. Simpler forms are best seen as long-standing adaptions to variations in life spans, the numbers of surviving children, and so forth. Important changes in household structure have occurred, but without government pressure and in reaction to the changed circumstances in which peasants now live.

Birth Control

In contrast to its passive stance on household structure, the government is very concerned about birth control. In recent years, the Chinese government has implemented a far-reaching planned-birth program which has received ever more international attention. In selected Chinese cities and certain model villages astonishingly low birth rates have been reported. Though there is no need to trust every figure, there is good reason to believe in the overall success of the urban program. The conditions of urban life, including cramped housing, high female work-participation and the absence of youth sent to the countryside, are conductive to low birth rates. In the countryside, things are more problematic. Some rural conditions continue to support a high birth rate, and government goals for the countryside are more modest than those for the city. We discuss here the structural conditions that both facilitate and hinder the birth control campaign and then several indicators of the success of this campaign in the Kwangtung countryside.

Collective life within production teams has introduced a number of features which should favor any effort to limit births in the countryside. First, with collectivized agriculture, extra sons no longer produce earnings which can be used to buy larger landholdings. Without the control of land, parents and grandparents also lose some of their economic authority and their ability to pressure their grown children to have more offspring. Second, as later chapters will show, collectivization brought more women out to work in the fields. Since only about one-fifth of our villages have nurseries, a larger proportion of women working means that more women experience extra children as a burden. As elsewhere in the world where women work outside the home, one would expect this consideration to reduce the birth rate. Third, with new health programs producing a sharp decline in infant deaths, it is no longer necessary to have two sons simply in order to insure that one survives to adulthood. All these features favor a decline in the birth rate.

At the same time, there are a number of features of the Chinese countryside which continue to favor a moderately high birth rate. First, sons continue to be economically more important than daughters. In day-to-day work in the fields males earn more work points than females, as we have seen. More important, once they grow up girls leave the family to move into their spouses' families. Their services are lost to the families in which they were born. We have seen that it is not daughters but sons who are required to support their parents in old age. As one would expect, the result is that parents are eager to have at least two sons in order to insure a decent level of economic support in old age. This eagerness for sons drives up the birth rate.[13]

There is a second set of features in the countryside which makes children, regardless of sex, less costly than they might be in a different social setting. In most villages until recent years the birth of each new child meant extra rations for the family. Though grain has to eventually be paid for, the birth of an extra child meant that a family could draw more grain from the collective whether or not the family could pay at the time of drawing. Similarly, the family could get extra rations of sugar, oil, fish, or whatever else was being distributed through collective channels. At the end of the year, the family could get a private-plot addition because of the extra child. With collectivized agriculture parents also do not have to fear losing their land and not being able to feed their children.[14] The rural child can begin to serve a number of useful economic functions in the family while still quite young. He or she can help tend the private plot, feed the family pig, cut grass off the hillside to sell on the free market, and earn work points tending a water buffalo. To the family that does not figure its finances closely, these extra benefits may make the child appear almost cost-free.

There are, then, contradictory forces, some encouraging births and other discouraging them. Increasingly in successive campaigns the government has tried to implement programs to tip those forces towards a low birth rate. By 1954, birth control began to be urged by some leaders in the central government, and during 1956–57 some progress was make in urban centers. Initially, there was a shortage of contraceptives, an almost exclusive reliance on the condom (which requires male motivation), and a shortage of medical manpower to implement the program. In 1958 when the Great Leap Forward began, the birth control program was interrupted. Indeed, some leaders took exception to birth control and disputed the argument, stemming from Malthus, that overpopulation was a threat. They argued, rather, that Marx had correctly ascribed world poverty to the dominance of the capitalist classes and to imperialism. Under socialism population was a great resource. This position seemed to be substantiated when in 1958–59 hordes of people were put to work on public-work projects that demanded ever more laborers.

Following the economic difficulties that the Great Leap Forward created, birth control began to be vigorously promoted once again. There were several features of the revived planned-birth program which increased the likelihood that it would have an impact. To oversee the program, special planned-birth commissions were established in each province in 1963. By the end of that year, there was a commission not only for Kwangtung Province as a whole but also for the capital city, Canton, and possibly for other places as well.[15] Local clinics and women's associations were used to agitate for planned births. In a few places there were threats to penalize those who had too many children. This second program relied less on condoms and more on the IUD or intrauterine ring, a device which not only was more convenient but depended on women's attitudes. Weak links in this program were that men were not sufficiently involved and that there were too few local clinics to insure IUD insertion, sterilizations, or abortions for all who desired them.

Some idea of the progress of the campaign can be gained from refugee interviews conducted by Robert Worth in the Portuguese colony of Macao in 1965.[16] By that time the rural women of Kwangtung were already aware of the program for planned births. Of 125 refugee women aged eighteen to forty-four, 95 percent unequivocally approved the idea of birth planning. Sixty percent knew about the IUD, and almost all were interested in learning about additional methods. Sixty percent knew that the government wanted family size to be limited, and they themselves wanted a smaller number of children than did a comparable sample of rural Hong Kong women whom Worth also interviewed. Despite all of this, about as many of the Kwangtung women as of their Hong Kong counterparts were pregnant (15 percent), only 6 percent had spoken with their husband about limiting births, and only 2 percent reported that they knew friends and fellow villagers who used birth control. In addition, family planning services were not always available in these women's villages—only one-fourth of the women knew about them. Therefore, birth rates remained high. By asking women to report on births and deaths in their villages for the previous several months, Worth estimated an annual birth rate between 33 and 46 per 1,000 population and a death rate of only 8 to 11 per 1,000, indicating a very rapid rate of natural population increase—perhaps 3 percent a year or more. In sum, in rural Kwangtung in 1965, there was a growing awareness of birth control and its desirability but not the means to deliver contraceptives effectively or to mobilize peasants to use them.

Like the first attempt, the second attempt at birth planning was just developing momentum when it was displaced by yet another political campaign—the Cultural Revolution. During that campaign (from 1966 to 1968), birth control devices continued to be available and even became more abundant, but provincial leadership was in such disarray that the program was not pushed vigorously. After the Cultural Revolution waned, this situation changed, and ever since 1969 what might be called the third planned-birth campaign has been pushed with ever more vigor. After 1972 there were threats to restrict rations for excess children, and occasionally public meetings were held to criticize those who married too early. By 1973, among the thirty-two villages for which we have reasonable information, in only one isolated hamlet in the hills of northern Kwangtung were planned births not being vigorously promoted.

There are four features of this latest campaign which augur for its success: (1) improved administrative organization, (2) the use of material sanctions, (3) new methods of birth control, and (4) a better network for distribution. In earlier times birth control was the responsibility primarily of the local women's federation officers, and in the male-dominated village leadership these women had little influence. Male leaders periodically filed reports with their superiors on a variety of economic and political matters, but seldom on birth control compliance. The system was designed for producing lip service but not results. Available sources are vague, but it would appear that this situation has now changed. The special commissions in charge of planned births now reach down to the commune level. These commissions apparently set five-year and annual targets for birth control. In Kwangtung, as elsewhere, the target for 1975 was to reduce natural increase in the countryside to 15 per 1,000 population. These commissions demanded annual reports from village (team and brigade) leaders as to the progress of the planned-birth program in their administrative unit.[17] By 1973 planned births were being propogated in meetings by the male leadership in almost half of the villages for which we have information (N=28).[18] A few other villages had received visits from special work teams sent by the county or commune to agitate for planned births.

The second feature which augurs well for the present program is a new willingness to apply negative sanctions or eliminate positive incentives for births. By 1973 sanctions against "excess" children were beginning to be widely applied. The planned-birth program uses the slogan, "One is good, two is enough, three is many, and four is excessive." In slightly under one-third of the villages for which our informants supplied information (eight out of twenty-seven villages), various distributions were eliminated for the fourth child. No regular grain ration would be distributed for the child, and parents would have to pay cash to purchase grain to make up any deficit. The fourth child got no cotton ration, no sugar, oil, or fish distributions, and no extra private plot allotment. In some localities cadres announced that if extra children pulled the family into debt, the team would not loan money.

Other places are even more stringent. Some have forms which must be filled out periodically and which require the statement of one's plans for children, a listing of birth control methods being used or an explanation of why they are not being used. Figure 1 reproduces this type of form from a commune in central China. Where such forms are in use they serve as the basis for both individual and public meetings designed to mobilize village pressure for reduced births. Only a few Kwangtung localities in our 1973–74

Family Planning Form

Name:	Sex:	Age:	Spouse's Name:	Age:	Work Unit:

Present Children	Girls ____ Boys ____	Birth date of latest:

Present and Future Birth Plans	1972	1973	1974	1975	Post 1975	Plan no Births

Males 25 and over; Females 23 and over				
1972	1973	1974	1975	Post 1975

Presently Used Planned Birth Method

Sterilization	Abortion	Pill	Shot	Ring	Other (specify)

Reason Not Yet Using

Present and Future Birth Plans	Months Pregnant	Months Nursing	Other	Planned Marriage

Critical Opinion of the Masses:

Opinion of Leadership Small Group:

Seasonal Inspection	1973				1974				1975				1976			
	1st	2nd	3rd	4th	1st	2nd	3rd	4th	1st	2nd	3rd	4th	1st	2nd	3rd	4th

Year _____ Month _____ Day _____

Fig. 1. *Family Planning Form. The form is captioned as follows.*
This investigative form is distributed in accordance with Chairman Mao's directives—"for mankind to completely disregard regulation in births is incorrect, rather we must have planned births"; and, "mankind should control itself so as to have planned growth"—as well as in accordance with the planned-birth guidelines of the city, province, and State Council in the fourth five-year plan, which proposes that each couple give birth to a total of only two children, that these children be spaced over an interval of four to five years, and that youth respond to the call to marry late. After filling out the form in detail, hand it back in.

interviews used such forms or group-pressure tactics.[19] However, some Kwangtung villages had begun to urge sterilization for those with two or three children or abortion for those who became pregnant with a third or fourth child.

The third promising feature of the current campaign is the greater variety of birth control devices available. In the 1950s there was heavy dependence on the condom and in the early 1960s on the IUD. By the late 1960s, birth control pills and other devices began to be widely distributed in the Kwangtung countryside. These are dispensed through local clinics and brigade health stations. In 1973, IUDs were still more widely used than pills, with local preferences depending on whether there had been a history of bad side-effects in the village with one method or the other. IUD insertions are free, and pills are free or cost only a few cents (fen) for a month's supply. Both tap the greater motivation of women rather than the fickle whim of men. The village midwife and barefoot doctor are trained to distribute these devices. Though infrequently used, suppositories, foam, and condoms are also available.[20]

Sterilizations and abortions are free and usually accompanied by additional incentives. Sterilization—tubal ligation for women and vasectomy for men—is usually done at the commune clinic. Both men and women are eligible for a special "nutrition fee" plus a number of days off from field work without loss of work points. In our interviews, two villages provide a nutrition fee of 3 yuan; one adds five days off work; another gives women thirty days off with pay.[21] Though vasectomy is simpler, by 1973 the tubal ligation, usually performed immediately after childbirth, was by far the more common.[22]

We have some information on sterilizations for eighteen teams. In five of these no sterilizations had been performed, but others had a fair number. One team had a grand total of twelve sterilizations, and another had six. The typical situation is two or three sterilizations per team—not a small number once it is remembered that a team only averages thirty or forty families, and typically only those families with a wife between age twenty and forty-five and three or more children are targets. Sterilizations are, then, becoming moderately common.

It is more difficult to get information about abortion. Since the popularization of simple vacuum techniques, abortions can be performed readily in the commune clinic and on occasion even in brigade health stations. Even taking into account their low visibility, abortions do not appear to be very common. Economic incentives similar to those for sterilization are offered. For an abortion at the commune hospital, one village provides a 15-yuan nutrition fee to the mother plus twelve days of work points. Another village provides 15 yuan plus half a month's work points. In the latter village, the fee alone would be worth more than a month's collective income to the woman.[23]

The fourth promising feature of the current campaign is the dense network of midwives and barefoot doctors that has been created in recent years. These paramedical personnel are available now in every brigade in rural Kwangtung, and their duties include the distribution of birth control advice and devices. Periodically, their efforts are reinforced by teams of doctors and nurses who visit villages and try to dispel myths and fears about the dangers of various birth control procedures—that they will sap one's strength, make one unable to have sexual relations, and so forth. Today many more people than in the past have a stake in the success of the birth control program. In summary, most of the elements foreign experts on family planning say are necessary for a successful birth control program— extensive public health and maternal and child health services, paraprofes- sional as well as professional personnel, special administrative structures, a system of incentives, cheap or free contraceptives, widely available abortion and sterilization, media exposure, statistical reporting and follow-up studies—are utilized in the Chinese effort, with some added features distinc- tive to the Chinese scene.[24] Has the balance then been tipped against those considerations which lead Chinese peasants to desire many children?

As yet there have been no statistics published which would allow us to draw firm conclusions about the success of the planned-birth campaign. We do have, however, four sets of figures which all indicate increasing success of the campaign in the early 1970s. These include (1) official and semi- official figures released to visiting foreigners, (2) the subjective estimates by our sample of informants, (3) a comparison of 1965 and 1973 data on surviving children, and (4) a comparison of 1953 and 1973 age structures.

Most of the official statistics relate only to small and probably unrepresen- tative units. In Kwangtung Province, Ch'en-liao Brigade is currently held up as a successful example of how to implement the planned-birth campaign. In 1965, it had a crude birth rate of 37.6 per 1,000 population; by 1968 it reached a figure near 12 or 13 births per 1,000, which was maintained through 1972.[25] This spectacular a success is unusual, but by 1973 marked changes were being reported for other localities. In a visit to Shunte and Tungkuan counties in the delta region of Kwangtung, Graham Johnson was told that the 1972 natural increase rates were 1.8 and 2.2 percent, respectively—down from reported 1965 rates of 3.4 percent. In these two counties, between 50 and 60 percent of the wives between ages eighteen and forty-five were utilizing family-planning techniques. In Lokang Commune in the suburbs of Canton, only 25 percent of the relevant couples were practicing family planning, but the birth rate had been reduced to 25 per 1,000 in 1972.[26] Another foreign group visiting the family planning commission of Canton in 1973 was told that throughout the province the 1972 birth rate was 26 per 1,000, the death rate 5 per 1,000, and natural increase therefore 21 per 1,000.[27] Numerous questions could be asked about these figures. What is the nature of the statistical system which reports them? What are the pressures on lower-level administrators to falsify reports? Are these sample figures, and were more successful suburban communes over-sampled? Nevertheless, the figures do suggest a definite decline in births. The provincial figure of 26 per 1,000, if accurate, is a significant change from the almost 38 per 1,000 birth rate which prevailed in earlier years.

The beginning of a decline in the birth rate is also suggested by our informants. Among the thirty-one who give an opinion on the matter, 39 percent conclude that in their village the planned-birth campaign is poorly received. They cite the standard reasons: male laborers are needed to make one prosperous; one needs support in old age; or, "they have no other recreation in the village." Some informants bring forth dramatic cases such as the brigade industrial officer whose family consisted of himself, his wife, his old grandmother, seven daughters, and the youngest—a son.

> Before they had the last child, people began to try to convince the husband to use birth control. He opposed them violently because he did not yet have a son. His wife responded to the birth control messages and wanted to stop. Though he was not, she was a party member and had been approached through the party. They ended up fighting, and he smashed in her face with a bottle so that she had to be taken to the commune clinic. He is still very nasty about it, and no one would dare bring up the issue with him again.[28]

Still, there are other informants who are more impressed with local response to the planned-birth campaign. Sixty-one percent report that the campaign is going well in their village or team, particularly among couples who already have a number of children. After three or four children, more can become a burden. A family's well-being is highly dependent on its labor-mouth ratio, as we saw earlier. Too many very young children to support leads families into debt. Young mothers who must work in the fields all day and then take care of the children at night are especially sensitive to the problems involved. As one informant put it,

Old people still feel the more sons the better. Among young couples the males usually feel that three to four children is the ideal, while their wives generally feel that two is already enough. The concept of family size has already begun to change among younger couples. The most important reason is because of family economic problems. It is difficult to support a family of five or six on the income from work points.[29]

The pattern that seems to be emerging is that couples are likely to marry and have two or three children rapidly, without spacing, and then, if at least one of these children is a son, to cease all further reproduction.

Partial success in the planned-birth campaign is also suggested by statistics on surviving children in rural families in 1965 and 1973. The 1965 data come from Robert Worth's study of refugee women mentioned earlier, and the 1973 data come from our asking about neighbors and other individuals in the village.[30] Table 23 shows the average number of surviving children per married woman. Except for the twenty- to twenty-four-year olds, each age set has one-half child fewer in 1973 than in 1965. Since over this eight-year period all indications are that the health of children improved, these data imply a decline in the birth rate.[31]

These findings are similar to reports from Taiwan where there also has been a family planning campaign since 1963. From 1963 to 1973 the crude birth rate there declined from 36 to 24 births per 1,000 population, a decline very similar to that reported for Kwangtung. The decline was reflected in the number of surviving children per woman. Table 24 shows that the decline in surviving children was greatest among older women. Young women continued to have children early with little spacing while older women were much more likely to desist from having further children. The Kwangtung and Taiwan data are not exactly the same, but overall the pattern is similar, giving further support to the view that there has been a significant decline in fertility in Kwangtung.

Table 23				Surviving Children by Age of Married Women, 1965-73	
Age	Surviving children per woman			Number of currently married women	
	1965	1973	Decline	1965	1973
20-24	1.1	.9	.2	(43)	(32)
25-29	2.4	1.9	.5	(70)	(28)
30-34	3.6	3.1	.5	(60)	(29)
35-39	4.5	4.0	.5	(54)	(26)

Sources: Currently married women from 1965 study by Robert M. Worth. Currently married women from 1973 combined household sample.

Table 24   Surviving Children by Age of Married
                                                  Women, Taiwan

Age	Surviving children per woman			Number of currently married women	
	1965	1973	Change	1965	1973
22–24	1.4	1.7	+.3	(380)	(873)
25–29	2.7	2.6	–.1	(975)	(1,472)
30–34	4.0	3.5	–.5	(879)	(1,495)
35–39	5.0	4.6	–.9	(815)	(1,431)

Source: Ronald Freedman et al., "Trends in fertility, family size preferences, and practice of family planning: Taiwan, 1965-1973," Studies in Family Planning 5 (1974): 275, 284.

A fourth sort of evidence comes from analyzing data on the age structure of the population in 1953 and in 1973. Where a population is growing steadily and is unaffected by major catastrophes, we expect a steady shrinking in the size of each age group from birth through old age. Figure 2 shows such a pattern in the 1953 census for the whole of mainland China. Over 26 percent were aged 0–9 and only 18 percent aged 10–19. By 1973, when we asked people to describe the households of their neighbors, the 0–9 category was smaller than the succeeding 10–19-year-old one. Much of this decline in the size of the 0–9 age group we feel comes from a reduced birth rate.

Again, the pattern of change in Taiwan over the same period looks quite similar (figure 3). In 1953, the 0–9 age group constituted 30+ percent of the total population. By 1973, however, after the Taiwan birth control campaign had been underway for ten years, the 0–9 category had shrunk to about 25 percent of the total, just the same as the 10–19-year-olds. The similarity of trends in Taiwan and on the mainland suggests that similar processes are occurring in both places.[32]

Some additional clues to the success of the birth control campaign can be gained from identifying which individuals and which villages show the most headway in the planned-birth campaign. We have two sets of data bearing on this point: data on the number of surviving children per mother and data for individual production teams. The data on individual mothers, presented in table 25, is structured so that a positive association indicates success in the birth control campaign among a given category of individuals. Thus, the first –.31 suggests that the campaign has not been particularly successful among party members. These results could be confounded by differences in

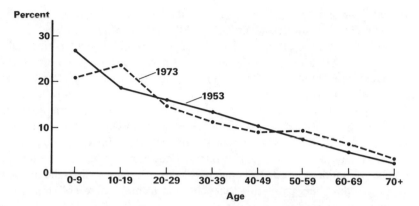

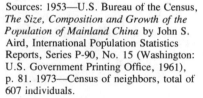

Figure 2. *Age Distributions, 1953 and 1973*

Sources: 1953—U.S. Bureau of the Census, *The Size, Composition and Growth of the Population of Mainland China* by John S. Aird, International Population Statistics Reports, Series P-90, No. 15 (Washington: U.S. Government Printing Office, 1961), p. 81. 1973—Census of neighbors, total of 607 individuals.

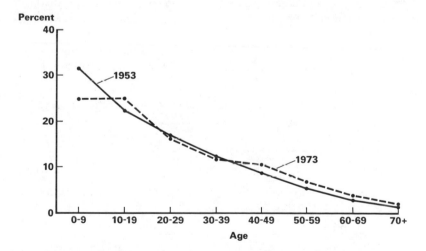

Figure 3. *Age Distribution in a Chinese Population Experiencing Birth Control, Taiwan, 1953–1973*

Sources: Republic of China, Taiwan Provincial Government, Civil Affairs Department, *Household Registration Statistics of Taiwan, 1959–1961,* 1962, table 3. Republic of China, Ministry of the Interior, *1973 Taiwan Demographic Fact Book,* 1974, table 22.

mortality—possibly party members do not have more children but more of their children survive to maturity. All such qualifications aside, it is surprising how little difference individual background characteristics make in fertility. One often hears of cadres and party members who are in the embarassing situation of agitating for birth control when they already have many children. Nevertheless, since they are so often called on to have the first ring insertion or the first vasectomy, one would expect them to have a lower birth rate. That seems not to be true. If anything, those in more privileged positions (by virtue of party, cadre status, or favorable class label) are less likely to have limited their births. Education has no strong effect on number of children nor does the nature of the wife's job. Also, the old saw about grandmothers pressuring their children to have more children is not supported.

We have three measures of the spread of birth control within villages: the degree to which male leaders as well as females agitate for planned births (coded simply as males not involved or involved), the severity of sanctions against the birth of a fourth child (coded as propaganda only or actual sanctions such as cutting normal grain distributions), and the reported response to the planned-birth campaign in the informant's production team (as noted earlier). In addition, we again can tally surviving children per woman, this time according to the characteristics of the production team in which the woman lives.

The three measures of planned-birth efforts are moderately interrelated—male propaganda, severe sanctions, and the reported response to the

Table 25   Number of Children by Individual
                                            Characteristics

	Few children (gamma)	N
Husband in party	-.31	(129)
Husband cadre	-.23	(116)
Husband has poor or lower-middle peasant class label	-.30	(108)
Husband's education	.26	(100)
Wife's education	.12	(68)
Wife in non-agricultural job	.04	(89)
Grandmother at home	.32*	(129)

Note: The dependent variable is based on whether the number of surviving children per married woman age 18-40 is less than would be expected from the regression equation CHILDREN = -3.41 + 0.20 AGE. N is the number of married women.

Source: Married women age 18-40 from combined 1973 household sample.

*p ≤ .10

Table 26   Planned Births by Village Character-
                                            istics (Gamma Statistics)

	Team data			Few children per woman	N (teams)	N (women)[a]
	Male propaganda	Severe sanctions	Village response			
Planned births						
Male propaganda	--			-.40*	--	(81)
Severe sanctions	.64	--		-.44	(20)	(84)
Village response	.45	.74*	--	.07	(19)	(90)
Administrative						
Political density	-.18	-.44	-.22	-.33	(29)	(129)
(Party membership)	.00	-.62	-.19	-.58*	(24)	(100)
Political study	1.00*	-.08	.44	-.28	(25)	(89)
Urban-communications						
Urban proximity	.02	.08	.07	.18	(29)	(125)
Urban youths	.33	.29	-.38	-.19	(21)	(90)
Communication	.15	.11	.22	-.25	(28)	(119)
Nurseries	.40	.21	.33	-.16	(29)	(129)
Economic						
Collective affluence	.38	.26	.31	-.14	(28)	(129)
Household consumption	-.10	.43	.11	-.08	(28)	(119)
Land/labor ratio	.39	.00	-.57	-.42^	(20)	(117)
Remittances	.17	-.40	.14	-.16	(20)	(96)
Health care						
Baby delivery in health station	.90*	.85*	.57	-.32	(27)	(99)
Extensive coverage	.74	.25	-.38	-.70*	(12)	(44)
Low annual fee	.55	.23	.25	-.05	(19)	(80)
Low visit fee	.50	.00	.71	.64*	(14)	(57)
Doctor ratio	.20	-.38	.30	-.10	(15)	(57)
Other						
Brigade size	.04	.04	-.04	.31	(24)	(99)
Team size	-.01	.16	-.01	-.05	(29)	(129)
Lineage composition	-.51	-.31	-.08	.16	(29)	(126)
Non-Hakka ethnicity	.80	.39	.20	.14	(28)	(117)
Delta region	.13	.27	-.22	-.27	(29)	(129)
Median N	(26)	(25)	(27)	--		

[a]Married women age 18-40 from combined 1973 household sample.

*p ≤ .10

planned-birth campaign go together (table 26, top panel). In contrast, the number of children per woman is not positively related to these efforts. Instead those places which have had the most children are the very places where birth control propaganda and sanctions have been most widely applied. It is as though present efforts aim to make up for past failures.

The strongest relationships in table 26 are between medical care availability and planned-birth efforts. Where prenatal care and delivery

occur at the brigade or commune clinic rather than in the home, both propaganda efforts and sanctions have been more extensive. These associations
reflect the important role of rural health personnel in enforcing birth control
targets. Where deliveries occur in a clinic, medical personnel are in a better
position to recommend abortions during prenatal checkups and contraceptives or sterilization after delivery. The associations of these health system
measures with the number of children per woman (column four) are predominantly negative, however, which may simply indicate that these systems have not been in operation long enough to be visible in these figures,
which include the completed fertility of older women.

The positive relationship between village affluence and birth control efforts may mean only that more affluent villages are more likely to deliver
children in a health station. Once place of delivery is controlled, the relationship between affluence and birth control weakens. Other indices of
modern influence (consumption of modern goods, urban proximity, modern
communication channels, and contact with urban youth) show no consistent
relationships. With the exception that villages having political study systems
are more likely to propagandize planned births, the relationships with political characteristics are either nonexistent or the reverse of expectations. If
anything, villages with many party members are more likely than others to
have a large number of children.

Two other findings deserve notice. We had expected that, because of
kinship ties, leaders of single-lineage brigades and teams would be less
likely than leaders elsewhere to push a campaign which some kinsmen
oppose. That notion receives some support (row 22, table 26). By contrast,
we had not expected that births would be related to landholdings, but they
are. Most informants give the impression that the primary basis of the
decision to have more children is a peasant's own family interests, not the
greater interests of the village. Even when land is scarce, some informants
assert, peasants will try to get their cut from a dwindling pie by having more
children. Peasants take a longer or more collective view of things than these
cynics would allow. Where there is less land per laborer, the planned-birth
campaign is reported to be a success and there are also fewer children per
mother (row 13 of table 26—here the negative signs mean more land is
associated with less success). One informant did suggest this pattern:

No one opposed the movement—they have learned their lesson. Before
the brigade population was only 600, but now it is 1,400 plus. So there
has been an increase of over 100 percent in recent years, and everybody
understands the need. The economic difficulties of actual life persuade

them. Now people don't think that many sons will pay off later . . . .
Now the concept of "more sons more wealth" (tuo tzu tuo fu) is
already undermined by practical experience. Women, in particular,
are increasingly afraid of having many kids.[33]

There are tight restrictions on movement from the village to the city. Given
this restriction and the continuing improvement in health, rural land is
becoming scarcer. As a result, it should become easier in the future to
persuade peasants of the necessity to plan births.

Though some speculation is involved, these cross-sectional results
suggest that much of the success of the planned-birth campaign to this point
has been more the result of demand coming from the peasants below rather
than of pressure from the administration above. By 1973, the extreme pressures starting in the early 1970s had not yet had a noticeable impact. Villages with great agitation for birth control were no more likely than others to
have few children. Likewise, politically involved villages had no fewer
children, and neither party members nor village officers—who would be
under the most pressure—were particularly likely to have fewer children than
other peasants. The birth rate reductions which appear in official reports and
interview data have preceded the recent heavy administrative pressure. The
birth control campaign may become even more intensive in the future, but to
this point peasants in Kwangtung seem to have responded more to the
changing cost-benefit ratios of collective living, the realization that fewer
children are needed now to provide the family with surviving sons, the
presence of more midwives and doctors who provide contraceptives, and to
such factors as the shortage of available land.

The Chinese planned-birth campaign appears to be having considerable
success. No single bit of evidence is conclusive in itself, but all of the
evidence together points in the same direction and suggests that there has
indeed been a sharp decline in the birth rate over the last ten years. The
success still falls short of official ideals, as quite a few peasant families,
including those of rural cadres and party members, continue to surpass the
two-to-three-child limit espoused by the government. But our evidence,
particularly the comparisons with the fertility reductions on Taiwan,
suggests that the annual population growth rate in Kwangtung may have
been brought under 2 percent by 1973–74, and even makes possible the
Chinese claim that by 1975 the target of only 1.5 percent growth rate in the
province had been achieved.[34] The birth rate implied by such a figure, of
under 25 per 1,000, is quite impressive in comparison with that of other

populous developing countries like India and Pakistan, where the rate remains around 40 per 1,000.

Conclusions

Our examination of the structure of peasant households in Kwangtung today reveals important changes amid continuities. Parents still expect to live with and be supported by their sons in their old age, daughters still move out at marriage to become members of their husbands' families, and the motivation to have sons remains strong. But adopted sons, concubines, and child brides have all declined or disappeared. The rationale for keeping adult sons bound together in one economic unit to run the family farm is now gone, and therefore peasants rarely go through a joint-family stage these days. Nonetheless, the stem-and-nuclear combinations in which aged parents and married sons live still cooperate extensively. The number of surviving children per family increased noticeably after 1949 but is now being reduced once again—this time by birth control rather than by infant mortality. Except on the issue of child brides and concubines the government has made no real effort to change peasant family structure, yet important changes have clearly occurred. Much effort has been expended, in contrast, to persuade peasants to have fewer children. They are now doing so, although the evidence presented here makes it look as if they are responding to the changing economic and health-care environments in which they live more than to government appeals. The patterns detected for both household structure and family size support the view that changes have occurred primarily through indirect responses of peasants to the structural transformations of rural life rather than through direct change efforts by the government. This is a pattern we shall see repeated in subsequent chapters.

10

Marriage and
Divorce

Since the family is based on marriage, an effort to change the family must alter the way marriages are entered into and terminated. This realization is reflected in the fact that the key post-1949 document expressing the government's ideals and policy for family life is the 1950 Marriage Law, one of the first comprehensive legal documents adopted after the Chinese Communists came to power. This 1950 law is in theory still binding, although recent policies have outdated certain of its provisions. In this chapter we discuss the traditional customs in regard to marriage and divorce in rural Kwangtung, the Chinese Communist policy toward those customs, and the evidence of change and continuity uncovered in our interviews. Our focus is on the process of finding partners and making the commitment to marry (and, in some cases, later to divorce). The wedding ceremonial is treated separately in Chapter 13.

Traditional Marriage Customs
and Official Policy

Before they came to national power the Chinese Communists had experimented over the years with family policy and legislation, so that the provisions of the 1950 Marriage Law had already been largely worked out. This law and the campaigns which surrounded its implementation had as their goal not the "withering away of the family" as some Bolsheviks had sought in Russia during the 1920s but rather an elimination of "feudal" elements in family life so that a new "socialist" form could emerge. Official documents proclaim that China wanted to avoid the development of a "bourgeois" family system, but there is little that is distinctively socialist about the government's ideals. The provisions of the marriage law built upon ideas current among reformers of various stripes since at least the May 4th Movement (begun in 1919), and these provisions constituted only modest extensions beyond the family sections of the civil code of Nationalist China, adopted in 1931.[1] The ideal sought in the 1950 law was by and large the relatively egalitarian "conjugal" family relations characteristic of most modern societies, whether capitalist or communist.[2] But the Nationalist family policy had never been effectively communicated and enforced outside of some segments of the urban population, and the ideals expressed in 1950 were rather far removed from the rural customs of that time. Thus what was in some ways a "moderate" document still called for major changes.

The fundamental fact about rural marriages before 1949 (and probably most urban marriages as well) is that they were arranged. Parents and family elders scouted the field of marital prospects with the aid of relatives and matchmakers, and the desires or even the consent of the young couple were not important to the match. Marriage was seen as a matter between two families, and not just as the joining of a bride and groom. In some, perhaps many, cases the couple did not even meet until the day of the wedding. This was the so-called "blind marriage." In arranging a match the financial status of the families involved was a primary consideration, and substantial exchanges of cash and goods were usually involved. The groom's family presented a bride price to the bride's family, and in many cases the bride's family invested in a substantial dowry which the bride brought with her upon marriage. The Chinese Communists view both strict parental dictation of marriage partners and bride price as "feudal" elements to be eliminated. They term the paying of bride prices "marriage by purchase" and claim that this custom prevented many poor males from marrying, although in comparison with many other societies a very high proportion of both males and females in pre-1949 China did eventually marry.[3] In some cases poor families did have to resort to alternative ways of finding a bride, such as the custom of adopting a future daughter-in-law. Another custom which the Chinese Communists also classified as "feudal child marriage" was the betrothal of two children (with the girl still raised by her parents). Even though the children would not marry until later, the betrothal was considered to be binding on both families. Because the youths were not required to have enough maturity to pick their own mate (and might, in fact, refuse to follow

parental dictates if they were) such early betrothals were socially accepted.)
However, it is not clear to us how common such child betrothals were.
Whatever the case, the pre-1949 average marriage (not betrothal) ages (generally 17–19 for females and 19–21 for males) are not unusually early in
comparison with other peasant societies.[4]

(Customarily, the bride and groom could not be related patrilineally within
the fifth collateral degree in most of China, although even first-cousin marriages on the maternal side were allowed in many regions. In rural
Kwangtung, where it is not uncommon to find entire villages composed of
people of the same lineage (disregarding the inmarrying wives), the
exogamy rule was extended still further, so that marriage was not allowed
within a localized lineage and not with anyone from the same village (even if
of a different lineage). Thus brides had to be sought outside one's village,
among people of other kin groups. These rules tended to reinforce the
solidarity of patrilineal kinsmen and fellow villagers by keeping potentially
contentious ties with in-laws confined to the "outside." Combined with the
patrilocal residence rule noted in Chapter 9, they insured that women were
brought into their husbands' families as strangers, with no local kinsmen to
support their interests and protect them from abuse.)

(After marriage, though retaining some personal possessions (clothing,
jewelry), women did not acquire rights in family property. Divorce was
strongly frowned upon and was available in theory only under extreme
conditions, and then more easily to a husband than to his wife. Most local
accounts testify that divorce was fairly uncommon, although not as rare as
the theory suggests (and desertions did occur).[5] If the husband died, the
woman was entitled to support from her husband's kinsmen, but in theory
she was not supposed to remarry. Virtuous widows were commemorated in
various ways, and a woman who chose to remarry had to overcome the
opposition of her late husband's family. There are indications, nonetheless,
that a substantial proportion of divorced and widowed women, especially the
poor and the young, did remarry, even though they could not take a share of
any property they had helped accumulate into their new home.[6] Moreover,
their children belonged to the husband's lineage and could be alienated from
it only with the approval of his kinsmen. Divorced men and widowers, in
contrast, were encouraged to remarry, and they did not forfeit any rights to
property or children in doing so. As noted in the previous chapter, males
could also take secondary wives or concubines, a right to which the wife had
no counterpart (or legal right to prevent), although only a few wealthy males
could afford to do so.)

(The Chinese Communists set out to change those traditional marriage customs which favored elders, parents, patrilineal kin, and men and the aged in general. The 1950 Marriage Law of the People's Republic of China proclaims that bigamy, concubinage, interference in the remarriage of widows, and the exaction of money or gifts as a condition for marriage are all prohibited (Article 2).[7] Marriage is to be based upon the willingness of the two parties involved, without parental compulsion, and the female is to be at least eighteen and the male at least twenty (Article 4). Registration of marriages is required, and the registrars are instructed to check for compliance with the provisions of the marriage law (Article 6). Women are allowed to retain their own surnames. The law also stipulates that local customs should be followed as to the span of exogamy required for marriages. Women are declared to have equal rights in the ownership and management of family property (Article 10) and its inheritance (Article 12).

Divorce with mutual consent is to be available on demand from a local government office; if only one party demands it, the local court urges reconciliation and, failing that, grants a divorce (Article 17). No specific grounds are stated for a divorce. Custody of children and division of family property are to be decided by agreement between the parties involved; again the local court can dictate a decision if the parties cannot agree (Articles 21 and 23). At least in the case of child custody there is an implicit emphasis in favor of the mother. Nursing children are automatically to stay with her, and other provisions state that the father's child-support payments are reduced in the event that the new husband accepts part of the burden of raising the woman's children (Article 22).

Thus the marriage law called for sweeping changes in many areas of family life, toward an ideal of monogamous marriage based upon free choice, with divorce and remarriage possible without the interference of kin. It should be noted, however, that in some matters the law encouraged adaptation to local customs (for example, in regard to intermarriage among kin), while in other areas no stipulations were made (patrilocal postmarital residence was not attacked).

We will only sketch briefly here the shifting tactics used since 1950 to implement the marriage law and more recent modifications of official policy.[8] The original campaign for marriage reform coincided with the land reform campaign in newly conquered parts of China (1950–53). It was hoped that the two efforts would be mutually reinforcing. Poor peasants, and especially women, were urged (by party, peasant associations, and the women's federation) to rise up to claim property rights and marital rights in one sweeping movement. Extensive propaganda was carried out to acquaint the rural population with the marriage law and to encourage them to follow its provisions. The response was not as positive as the government desired, in part because substantial portions of the poor peasant allies of the new government, particularly older people and males, were less enthusiastic about marital struggle than they were about class struggle. The new rural cadres, who were predominantly male, often saw the provisions of the marriage law as a threat to the integrity of their marriages and to their familial authority, as did many older women. In 1953 the results of the effort to implement the marriage law were declared unsatisfactory, and a new campaign was begun, supervised in Peking by a Central Committee for the Implementation of the Marriage Law. During this campaign the media reported model examples of new-style marriages, local officials were required to submit detailed figures on local compliance, and the Women's Federation and the New Democratic Youth League were mobilized to help young people and women marry and divorce according to the 1950 law. At the same time leaders and cadres were preoccupied with many other activities and concerns connected with the beginning of the first Five-Year Plan, and the editorials in *People's Daily* gave scant attention to the 1953 marriage law implementation campaign.[9] In late 1953 this campaign was concluded, although implementation was still far from complete. According to the final report on the campaign, only 15 percent of the areas in the country had "penetratingly implemented" the law and begun generally to construct new-style marriages; 60 percent of the country had conducted propaganda among the populace generally but had not been able to eliminate strong doubts about freedom of marriage and equality of the sexes; and a final 25 percent of the country had carried out the campaign so poorly that suicide by, and murder of, women as a result of marital disputes still occurred in those areas "to a considerable extent."[10] In spite of such mixed results, Chinese officials turned their attention to other goals, particularly economic ones, and marriage reform was placed on a back burner.

No more specific campaigns for general marriage or family reform have been waged, and the implementation of the 1950 law has been left much of the time to a gradual process of propaganda and education among the masses. The increasing mobilization of women for work outside the home would naturally, it was felt, undermine many traditional features of marriage. In the mid-1950s and again in the early 1960s official spokesmen and court decisions espoused a fairly moderate line toward marriage reform, letting it be known that it was more the spirit of the marriage law than its letter that was important. For instance, parents were not expected to be completely uninvolved in the marital choices of their children, and in fact they were encouraged to prevent hasty or ill-advised marital decisions (marrying too young, marrying someone of questionable political background). Gifts accompanying marriage were deemed acceptable, as long as they were modest and were not a precondition for the match, which would classify it as a case of "marriage by purchase." Celebrations of weddings with family and friends were also deemed acceptable as long as they were modest and unostentatious. Courts also recognized some marriages of youths below the ages of eighteen and twenty as legitimate by allowing continued use of the traditional Chinese systm of reckoning age, under which an individual is one year old at birth and ages another year at each New Year. Thus by Western reckoning females of sixteen or seventeen and males of eighteen or nineteen were sometimes allowed to register marriages. In addition, the courts in effect recognized common-law marriages; couples who lived together as man and wife without registering had the same rights and obligations as properly registered couples.[11] In such moderate periods local cadres were urged to deal with violations of the marriage law by persuasion and social pressure rather than with penalties, fines, or legal action. Ordinary peasants who did not worry about a little criticism for "backwardness" could even ignore much of the spirit of the marriage law.)

During the more militant periods of major campaigns, pressure for closer compliance with official marriage policy develops. Some of this consists simply of more media emphasis on marriage problems. For example, the 1973–75 campaign against Lin Piao and Confucius, in which the male chauvinism of Confucius was one theme, saw a larger than usual number of press accounts of women rejecting parental arrangements, bride prices, and elaborate wedding ceremonies.[12] At the same time the few press articles described in Chapter 9 praising matrilocal marriages appeared. During intense campaigns marriage reform may be pushed with more than just media exposure. For example, in the rural socialist education campaign of 1962–65 two of the evils denounced were "feudalism" and "extravagance." Outside work teams went into villages to guide local peasants in bringing to public notice cases of such evils. In a set of documents from this campaign we are told, for example,

In the Hua-wu brigade at Ao-chiang, eighteen girls of an average age of fourteen years were sold at an average of 750 yuan each. In Pai-sha there is a girl who has been married thirteen times. In some places girls are sold like hogs at so much a catty. Even worse is that some people make a business of buying and selling girls. They get fifty yuan merely for making an introduction.[13]

During this campaign, and during the later Cultural Revolution, cadres and some peasants who had flagrantly violated the marriage law (as well as other official policies) were picked out for mass criticism meetings and in some cases subjected to fines and, in the case of cadres, official reprimands or demotion. In such intense campaign periods there is more danger of public criticism and penalties, but offenders are not generally subjected to legal sanctions. For example, peasants who accept large bride prices may be pressured to return them or threatened with public criticism and confiscation, but they are not arrested, and the marriage will not be voided. Thus over time there have been recurring waves in the marriage reform field, with fairly superficial press accounts of positive models in some periods, and more intensive local pressure, with some sanctions applied to particular negative examples, in other periods

In addition to these cyclical trends of pressure and relaxation, there have been other more long-lasting shifts which have produced clear modifications of aspects of the marriage law, although the 1950 document has not been revised or declared invalid. One of these basic shifts involves divorce. By 1953 a wave of divorces and marital disputes had generated substantial opposition and even violence among the Chinese population, as we have already noted. Since that time a more conservative policy has been adopted toward divorce, although it is not clear how much this was forced on the leadership by popular opposition, or occurred as China's leaders recognized that the period of liberal divorce had served its purpose: women stuck in oppressive marriages formed under the old society had managed to escape in significant numbers, while a new era of economic construction required stable marriages. In any case, the current policy is for local cadres and organizations to mediate and try to resolve family disputes and preserve marriages even if both partners desire a divorce.[14] Only if the dispute continues to cause serious problems after several rounds of mediation and attempted reconciliation should the divorce be allowed. Thus since the mid-1950s official policy has been generally in favor of marital stability in a much firmer way.

Another clear shift is represented by the emphasis on late marriage. First surfacing in 1957, the late marriage policy was largely forgotten during the

Great Leap Forward but has been advocated ever more vigorously since then, as part of the birth control campaign described in Chapter 9. In recent years, and particularly since 1972, rural females have been expected to be at least twenty-three before marriage, and rural males at least twenty-five (in some rural localities even higher minima are reported). Marriage registration officials are instructed not to allow couples below these ages to marry. This late-marriage policy now receives much more emphasis than other aspects of marriage reform.)

We have noted both oscillations and shifts in official policy toward marriage and divorce over the last twenty-five years, but the central aim of that policy remains clear: to foster marriages and families based upon free choice and individual compatibility rather than upon parental or economic compulsion, and within marriage to promote equality of the spouses. Let us now turn to see what the reflection of these policies and other social changes has been in the Kwangtung countryside. In the following pages we will supplement our general statements with two kinds of systematic data from our interviews. One is the judgment of our informants from sixty-three villages about the local marriage customs in general—for example, what the range of bride prices paid in recent years has been. We also have varying amounts of data on 344 specific marriages or couples, data coming from fifty-one out of our sixty-three villages (for details on this sample, see Appendix 1). In the pages that follow we will weave together a narrative of the process of mate choice with detailed analysis of particular findings.

Age at Marriage

The rural surveys conducted by John L. Buck and his associates around 1930 yielded average marriage-age estimates for the double-cropping rice region, which includes Kwangtung, of 20.4 for males and 17.0 for females.[15] Various writers have speculated that marriage age was on the rise after that, but precise figures are lacking. Our figures concern only the post-1949 period, and are heavily weighted toward recent years. In table 27 we present our results and comparisons with data from Buck's Chinese collaborators and from two other studies which used methods similar to ours. All three of the recent studies involved interviews in Hong Kong or Macao with former residents of Kwangtung, who were asked to describe their age and the age of their spouse at marriage (as well as the ages at marriage of other couples well known to them, in the case of our figures only).

Table 27

Average Marriage Ages of Kwangtung Peasants, with Changes over Time (First Marriages Only)

	Pre-1940	1940-49	1950-58	1959-67	1968	1969	1970	1971	1972	1973-74	(1968-74)
Females											
Ch'iao[a] (N)	17.0 (?)	--	--	--	--	--	--	--	--	--	--
Worth (N)	18.6 (129)	19.2 (118)	19.5 (136)	20.5 (73)	--	--	--	--	--	--	--
Salaff (N)	18.4 (8)	18.8 (10)	20.7 (8)	22.2 (16)	--	--	--	--	--	--	--
Parish-Whyte[b] (N)	--	--	20.0 (12)	20.9 (31)	20.8 (16)	21.0 (11)	21.2 (10)	20.8 (13)	21.3 (17)	21.4 (19)	(21.1) (86)
Males											
Ch'iao[a] (N)	20.4 (?)	--	--	--	--	--	--	--	--	--	--
Salaff (N)	21.5 (8)	21.0 (10)	23.6 (8)	25.3 (16)	--	--	--	--	--	--	--
Parish-Whyte[b] (N)	--	--	24.5 (13)	25.3 (29)	24.9 (16)	26.0 (12)	24.0 (11)	24.1 (17)	24.7 (18)	25.3 (22)	(24.8) (96)

Sources: Ch'iao Ch'i-ming and Wang Chung-wu, "Population: in Chung-kuo ching-chi nien-chien [Chinese economic annual] 3d edition, vol. 1 (Shanghai: Commercial Press, 1936), p. B-27; Robert M. Worth, "Recent demographic patterns in Kwangtung province villages," unpublished paper. Information is from 456 women interviewed in 1965 in Macao about their own marriage ages. The raw data supplied by Dr. Worth has been recomputed to fit our periodization. Janet W. Salaff, "Youth, family and political control in Communist China" (unpublished dissertation, University of California, 1972). Data recomputed for us by Dr. Salaff.

[a]Ch'iao's data refer to the double cropping rice region circa 1930, not to Kwangtung specifically.

[b]All cases given in the interviews to illustrate especially early or late marriage have been omitted from these figures.

Several observations can be made about the figures in this table. In general there is a fair degree of correspondence between the results of different studies. (For women, they say that the average marriage age in rural Kwangtung prior to 1949 was in the range seventeen to nineteen, that it was around twenty in the decade 1950–58, and that it had climbed past twenty-one by 1973 (the 1959–67 figure of 22.2 from Salaff's study is the only deviation from this pattern). In other words we see a gradual rise in women's average age at marriage of more than two years over the course of two generations, with perhaps half of this change taking place under the present government. For men the early trend is less clear, with an apparent jump between an average age of about twenty-one and one closer to twenty-four or so occurring between the 1930s and the 1950s, and only slight upward movement since then. The reasons for, and timing of, this pattern for men are not clear from the table, but it does undermine the notion that getting land as a result of land reform in 1950–52 allowed peasant males to marry at earlier ages than before.[16] For both males and females, then, there has been an upward shift in average marriage age over time. For men most of this change seems to have taken place by the 1950s, while for women part of it is more recent. Changes are also reflected in our interviews in the virtual disappearance in the early 1950s of customs such as the adoption of future daughters-in-law and other forms of child betrothal, as noted earlier, and a reduction in the number of marriages of females of ages fourteen to seventeen and males of sixteen to nineteen. But at the same time there has been no clear trend upward in marriage ages in recent years in response to the late marriage drive, and as of 1973–74, 40 to 60 percent of males and 60 to 80 percent of females were marrying below the new minimum ages set by the government. Perhaps it is too early to render a final judgment here, since in many rural areas late marriage was only beginning to be vigorously pushed and enforced in 1972, that is, just prior to our interviews. But these data should warn us not to automatically assume that the late-marriage policy is being complied with in the countryside, or that any rise in marriage age is due solely to government pressure rather than to such things as long-term changes in educational enrollments and expectations or in the economic circumstances of peasant households. Clearly the average age of rural marriage has gone up, but it is not obvious what role official marriage policy played in this change.[17])

How do marriages of people below ages twenty-three and twenty-five occur today? Our informants describe a number of circumstances. In some localities the dissuasion against early marriage was still perfunctory in 1973–74, and after a few words of caution younger couples were allowed to register their marriages. In other cases, however, some deception is involved. Some couples falsify their ages. The commune marriage registration office seems to rely not on official household registration data on ages, but on the word of brigade officials, who supply couples with a letter of introduction (cheng-ming), giving their approval to the marriage. (With marriage to a partner from outside the commune boundaries, of course, the commune would have no records on the woman anyway.) The brigade cadres are not only very busy with production and other matters, but are also linked by kinship and neighborhood ties with one or both of the families involved. Our informants felt that it was not difficult for families intent on completing an ''early marriage'' to gain the signature of some friendly or harried brigade cadre.[18]

Another tactic is simply for the couple to go ahead and marry in a family ceremony, and then wait until they pass the required minimum ages before going to the commune to register their marriage.[19] Whatever commune officials say, Kwangtung peasants still regard the family celebration, rather than the registration, as validating the marriage. The bride changes her residence, and thus receives a private plot and grain rations from her new production team, and gives up those in her former team. Local cadres have to concur in these changes, but again this not generally a problem. In 89 percent of the villages for which we have information (N = 35) at least some cases of falsifying ages or marriage without registration are reported, and a number of our informants felt that commune cadres were not unaware of what was going on. Couples who marry before they register may, of course, start having children in the interim. The widespread existence of such deception should caution us against uncritical acceptance of figures on marriage ages (and perhaps also birth rates) given to visiting delegations by commune officials.

What sort of individual marries earlier or later? This question is of particular interest because in pre-1949 China the relationship between status and marriage age generally was the opposite of what it tends to be in contemporary Western societies. Persons from better off families had earlier ages at marriage, whereas in the West today marriage age tends to be later among high-status or upwardly mobile groups. It is a matter of some interest, then, to see whether today Chinese youths from better-off families marry earlier or later than others. Unfortunately we lack reliable family income data for our

Table 28

Marriage Age by Selected Characteristics of Bride and Groom (Gamma Statistics)

	Husband's class	Wife's class	Husband's education	Wife's education	Husband a cadre
Husband's marriage age	-.48*	-.09	-.22	-.78*	-.23
(N)	(74)	(48)	(43)	(32)	(96)
Wife's marriage age	.28*	-.10	.04	.01	-.39
(N)	(63)	(57)	(35)	(35)	(87)

Note: All substantial relationships in this table remain unweakened when statistically controlled for village and imformant characteristics.

Source: Marriage sample (1968-74 marriages only) with cases offered by informants as particular examples of early or late marriage excluded.

*p ≤ .10

marriage sample. We can, however, look at those who are advantaged or disadvantaged in other ways: in schooling, in cadre status, and in class labels. In table 28 we examine these relationships.[20]

Some of the associations in table 28 are weak, but on balance they provide some evidence for the continuation of the traditional Chinese pattern, but only for men. Men of the favored poor or lower middle-peasant class labels, with a fair amount of education, or who serve as cadres, are somewhat more likely to marry early than men with other characteristics. Men serving as cadres are also more likely to marry younger women, but former poor peasant males, in fact, marry somewhat older women than others do. The only other visible pattern is that women with more education than others tend to marry younger men. Looked at in terms of the age gap between spouses at marriage, these figures indicate that there is a particularly large gap between those former landlord or rich-peasant class males who marry and their wives, while there is a small gap between educated women and their husbands. To summarize, the clearest pattern in the table is that males who are somewhat advantaged tend to marry earlier than others. This finding is unexpected both in terms of the contemporary Western pattern of late marriage among the better-off, and in terms of the Chinese expectation that former poor peasants, well-educated youths, and rural cadres are likely to be more responsive than others to the government's appeals for late marriage. Instead we find a picture that fits the traditional Chinese pattern for men, and suggests we are still dealing with a "marriage market" situation, in which the advantaged are particularly desirable mates and can more easily (and thus earlier) find a spouse.

How do the characteristics of villages relate to average age at marriage? Do people in villages which are particularly prosperous or have many party members marry earlier or later than people in other villages? In table 29 we examine the association between our trichotomized marriage age variables and a variety of characteristics of our villages. (The Ns in the table refer to the number of marriages, not the number of villages. Again, only post-1968 marriages are considered, and the villages involved are those of the husband and his family.)

Table 29   Average Marriage Ages by Village
                                                      Characteristics (Gamma Statistics)

	Male Marriage Age	Female Marriage Age	Median N
Male marriage age	--		
Female marriage age	.64*	--	
Administrative			
Political density	.13	-.21	(91)
Political study	-.23	-.29	(76)
Urban-communications			
Urban proximity	.08	-.08	(91)
Urban youths	-.35	-.45	(62)
Communications	-.15	-.16	(88)
Nurseries	.06	-.14	(91)
Economic			
Collective affluence	-.10	.05	(91)
Household consumption	-.14	-.52*	(87)
Land/labor ratio	-.19	-.31	(85)
Remittances	-.31	-.13	(68)
Other			
Brigade size	.23	-.16	(76)
Team size	.15	-.30	(91)
Lineage composition	-.09	.01	(91)
Non-Hakka ethnicity	.01	-.33	(92)
Delta region	-.22*	-.25	(92)
Median N	(94)	(87)	

Note: All substantial relationships remain unweakened when controlled statistically for informant characteristics, other village traits, and for different personal characteristics of the bride and groom.

Source: Marriage sample.

*p ≤ .10

The relationships in the table are again on the weak side, making interpretations tentative. This is to be expected since marriage decisions primarily involve two individuals and their families, rather than entire villages. Nonetheless, the patterns in the table are of considerable interest. The first thing to note is that the majority of the coefficients in the table have negative signs; if we disregard the variables listed as "other," this is the case for sixteen out of twenty. What this means is that a variety of variables which we have assumed are indicators of "modern" or governmental or other antitraditional influences are, in fact, associated with somewhat earlier marriage ages. The strength of most associations is, as we have noted, quite modest. But looking down the table we can see that there is some tendency for villages with regular political study meetings, many sent-down youths, high communications exposure, high levels of average household consumption, high land-labor ratio, many families receiving overseas remittances, and a Pearl River Delta regional location to have both men and women marrying at earlier ages than other villages. Beyond this overall pattern we call attention to only two coefficients of special interest. The strongest coefficient, $-.52$, between high average household consumption and early marriage for women, fits a situation we will return to later: villages with high levels of family consumption serve as "magnets" for women in the surrounding area, and are able to entice their parents to part with their labor relatively early. The $-.09$ coefficient between male marriage age and lineage composition conceals an interesting pattern, in which teams composed of people of a single lineage have men marrying significantly later than either multilineage teams or single-lineage brigades. This again fits a situation we will note later, in which the difficulty of meeting a potential bride in single-lineage teams is somewhat greater than in the other two settings. These two relationships and the larger pattern of negative signs provide further evidence that marriage age is primarily responding to marriage market considerations, rather than political-communication-modernization influences. Villages where people are well-off, where there is not severe land pressure, where urban influences are close at hand, and so forth might be expected to be especially responsive to the government's pleas for people to delay their marriages. But people living in such villages will also be especially desirable mates for people living in other, less fortunate villages. When they or their parents wish to arrange a marriage they are less likely than others to have to go through a lengthy process of searching for and negotiating with potential spouses.

In sum, marriage in rural Kwangtung is taking place later than it did half a century or so ago, but there has not been much change in the last decade. We have examined some evidence that both individuals and villages which are advantaged in some sense tend to be characterized by earlier marriage ages. This does not fit expectations drawn from contemporary Western experience or theories of modernization or expectations expressed in the official media. But this pattern does coincide roughly with what we know about the pattern of marriage-age differences in rural China in the pre-1949 period.

The Process of Mate Choice

We are also interested in whether the traditional arranged marriage has given way to free choice of mates among rural youths. There is no reason to assume that this issue is closely related to the question of marriage age: either parents arranging marriages or youths who find their own mates may do so early or late.[21] In our interviews "blind" marriage, in which a couple does not meet until the day of the wedding, is a thing of the past. Very few of the specific examples of recent marriages provided by our informants fit this pattern. At the same time marriages resulting from the initiative of a young couple, followed by courtship, with little parental say (or even parental opposition) are also rare.

If young people are to take the initiative in finding mates, they must have some opportunities to meet eligible partners. Yet traditional customs restrict the range of eligibles or limit contact with them. Some of these customs are breaking down, but they still play an important role in limiting the development of youth initiative in marriage. One such custom is the lineage exogamy rule mentioned earlier. In 55 percent of the villages for which we have information (N = 51), marriage with someone of the same localized lineage is still tabooed. A similar attitude still prevails in many localities about marriage within the village. In such places one has to look for an "outsider," but today there are limited opportunities to get to know youths from other villages. Education through the lower middle-school level is now available in most places within each brigade, and most work activities are centered within the smaller production team. As we noted earlier, opportunities for jobs in towns and cities, which expand freedom of mate choice in many developing societies, are still quite limited in rural Kwangtung. Thus only a select minority of youths have opportunities for more than casual contacts with outside youths: primarily upper middle-school students, workers in commune-run factories, and Youth League and militia cadres. Briefer contacts occur in the projects for water control and land reclamation involving laborers from an entire commune or even from several adjacent communes. One informant saw work on these projects not as a revival of tedious corvée labor traditions but as a welcome opportunity to look for a potential spouse.

Even meetings with outsiders may yield little chance to get to know them well. This is because of another traditional custom; most villages still have taboos against pairing off or public displays of affection.[22] In many of our accounts youths report that they would be teased and ridiculed if they were seen alone often with a potential mate. One sent-down urban youth described his view of this custom:

> I discovered that in the commune men and women peasants, especially unmarried young men and women, very rarely conversed, and all were very shy. Although we intellectual youths all grew up in the city, when we were in this kind of rural setting we also did not dare to violate their traditional customs, and we also rarely conversed with girl members of the team. If we met them on the road, we acted like strangers, and passed them by without uttering a sound. In my several years there I never talked individually with a local young woman—this is the result of the feudal restrictions that young men and women receive.[23]

In some cases village opinion is expressed by more forceful ways than gossip or teasing, as another sent-down urban youth who was less cautious reports:

> In 1970, soon after we were sent down, we young men and women talked into the middle of the night, and the brigade accused us of illicit sex, and hauled us off to the militia headquarters. We laughed and denied it, and the next morning we told the brigade head, and he calmly persuaded the others, and only then did the big ruckus die down. The local peasants, when they see us males and females walking side by side, say we people from Canton are very bad, and have no shame.[24]

In such circumstances a youth who has his or her eye on a potential mate will find it difficult to initiate courtship, and any relations that do develop are likely to be very restrained.

These constraints on youth initiative are clearly on the wane. In some villages marriage with someone of the same localized lineage and more relaxed fraternization between the sexes have become accepted. Perhaps the same-lineage taboo was altered some time ago as the result of brave "pioneers," couples from the same lineage who fell in love and married against parental opposition and despite warnings of deformed children or other dire consequences. Only when these fears proved to be mistaken did other couples begin to follow the lead of such pioneers, although such marriages are almost always with members of other branches of the lineage.[25] Table 30 provides some evidence on the breakdown of the taboos against "in-marrying."

Marriage to people of the same village and lineage clearly increased through the mid-1960s, although there may have been a slight reversal of this trend recently.[26] Clearly, for a substantial minority of youths it is now possible to marry somebody from the immediate locality, and in such cases the opportunities for youth initiative are much greater than with "outsiders."

This declining taboo on same-lineage and same-village marriages is of particular interest because it has not been a response to official pressure. The Chinese government has not made any attempt to convince people they should marry their kinsmen, and we noted earlier that the 1950 marriage law specifically says on this point that local customs will be conformed to. But here customs are clearly changing, without any official pressure. Why, then, has this change occurred? We note first that this taboo operates against the natural tendency in any society for people to marry others who live nearby. In general it is easiest to find mates from among nearby acquaintants unless there is a strong force operating to prevent this. That strong force was provided before 1949 by corporate lineages. By guaranteeing that wives and potentially contentious in-law relationships came from outside lineage boundaries, the solidarity of the lineage and its ability to compete with other lineages for rural resources were upheld. Lineage elders played an important role in creating and supporting public opinion against in-marriage. The weakening of the taboo is one indication of the reduced importance of

Table 30		Changes Over Time in Closeness of Marriage Partners		
	Pre-1949	1950-58	1959-67	1968-74
Community of origin				
Same village	3%	21%	30%	23%
Same commune, different village	47	33	38	42
Outside of commune	50	46	32	35
(N)	(34)	(48)	(53)	(158)
Lineages of the couple				
Same lineage	0%	38%	44%	22%
Different lineages	100	62	56	78
(N)	(5)	(8)	(16)	(55)

lineages and their leaders in contemporary Kwangtung. Marriage to outsiders also served the purpose of building ties with people in other villages with somewhat different farming schedules, ties which could be used by families as a basis for labor exchanges during the busy farming seasons. With collectivized rather than private farming, these ties and exchanges are no longer so necessary. Perhaps most important, though, is the fact that young people from the same village have many new opportunities to fraternize with each other—in school, team labor, and mass organizations. These opportunities make it difficult to sustain mate choice based upon parentally sponsored matches with strangers. Together these important changes help explain the declining functions and untenability of the traditional taboos. Still, the taboos have not disappeared from all villages yet.

Where young people have little or no opportunity to find a mate themselves, they must rely on introducers. A variety of people play this role: friends, former classmates, relatives, or one of the surviving professional marriage arrangers (mei-jen). The latter, who are usually women, continue to operate in most of our villages (in 74 percent of them—N=46), and to receive fees for their services. But even where they operate, the percentage of marriages arranged by such matchmakers has clearly declined, as has the general reliance on introductions, as tables 31 and 32 show.[27]

We note that these tables, like our earlier figures on marriage ages, provide clear evidence for change over time but not for changes particularly concentrated in the period since the assault on "old customs" in the Cultural Revolution. The decade of the 1950s seems to have been more important for the changes dealt with here than has the Cultural Revolution and its aftermath. These tables also tell us that roughly one-quarter of all marriages in recent years have resulted from the free choice of youth, the rest involving some sort of introduction. (An introduction is not by itself proof of parental interference, since young people may seek out friends or relatives to help them find spouses.)

The professional matchmakers who continue to operate these days do so at

Table 31		Change over Time in Percentage of Marriages Involving Introductions		
	Pre-1949	1950-58	1959-67	1968-74
Introduction	100%	92%	71%	79%
No introduction	0%	8%	29%	21%
(N)	(5)	(12)	(28)	(106)

Table 32	Change over Time in Type of Introducers Used in Mate Choice		
	1950-58	1959-67	1968-74
Matchmaker	43%	27%	21%
Relative	29	35	33
Friend or acquaintance	14	8	24
None	14	31	23
(N)	(7)	(26)	(92)

some risk. In the official view their activities are denounced both as feudal (that is, traditional) and capitalist (that is, money-making). During intense political campaigns such as the Cultural Revolution, individual matchmakers are picked as negative examples and subjected to mass-struggle meetings, with their fees confiscated. However, during other periods they are left alone, and local cadres seem aware of public support matchmakers receive as people whose services are needed, given the obstacles to finding a mate which we have noted.[28] One informant recounted the local phrase used to underline their importance: "You can't sew without a needle." But nowadays more and more relatives and friends are taking the place of professional matchmakers. Often these are local women who have married out into other villages where they can keep an eye out for potential mates. Friends and relatives typically receive little or no payment, in contrast to the 30 to 50 yuan which the professional matchmaker charges. The government is not particularly opposed to these nonprofessional introductions.

(The initiative in arranging an introduction can come from many sources. In some cases, as we have noted, an individual uses his or her contacts; in other cases the parents decide it is time to find a spouse for their offspring, and they inform friends, relatives, or a matchmaker. In still other cases a relative or friend may spot a good match and propose it to both parties. In some cases youths in love "at a distance" ask their parents to arrange an introduction because they are too shy to approach the other party directly. Thus the relationship between introductions and the "free choice" of mates is complex. Even when the initiative comes from parents, the young couple has a substantial voice. In most cases mate choice involves double approval and a double veto power; both the young people and their respective parents must agree. Few young people are pressured into a match, and few couples marry in defiance of parental wishes. Defying his parents is particularly difficult for a young man; he depends upon his parents for housing, for funds to pay the costs of the wedding, and for help and assistance in later married life. For the woman the obstacles are more emotional than financial—she wishes to have a secure base back in her native village after her move to her husband's home. (Given the continuing restrictions on migration in the Kwangtung countryside, "running away to get married" is rarely possible.) However, there is clearly much variation in the relative influence of young and old in particular matches.)

We have divided our marriage cases into two categories, insofar as possible, on the basis of the available information. One category includes both marriages resulting from free choice without introductions and marriages resulting from an introduction in which the young people both agreed to the match and made substantial efforts to get acquainted with each other. This category we consider to be marriages in which the young couple played the dominant role in the process of mate choice. The other category involves marriages resulting from introductions, in which few efforts were made to get acquainted, whether the young couple freely gave their consent or not. This second category we consider to be cases in which parents dominated the decision.[29] From the data in table 33 we discern a clear trend over time toward greater say by the young couple, although again there has been little change in the most recent period. This trend is what one would expect given the decline in the role of introducers and the relaxation of the same-lineage marriage taboo. For example, while introductions usually involve people of different lineages and villages, marriages in which the young couple play the major role will occur as often as not between people of the same lineage or village, people who have known each other for some time.[30]

Who marries largely by their own choice, and who follows parental dictates? Such limited information as we have on the personal characteristics of couples is presented in table 34. To answer the question we have relied on two measures: both the generational dominance measure used in table 33 and the code for whether an introducer was used or not (from table 31).

The class origins of individuals do not have a strong influence on whether they will marry on their own initiative and without an introduction. "Bad

Table 33		Dominance in Mate Choice over Time		
	Pre-1949	1950–58	1959–67	1968–74
Parents	100%	83%	41%	38%
Young couple	0%	17%	59%	62%
(N)	(6)	(6)	(17)	(52)

Table 34

Degree of Free Mate Choice by Characteristics of Couple (Gamma
Statistics)

	Husband's class label	Wife's class label	Husband's education	Wife's education	Husband a cadre
Youth dominance in mate choice	-.02	.39	.41	-.02	.63[a]
(N)	(49)	(36)	(26)	(23)	(69)
Introduction not involved	-.35	.08	-.39	-.72*	.74*
(N)	(75)	(61)	(45)	(38)	(106)

Source: Post-1958 marriages from marriage sample, with cases offered by informants as particular examples of free or forced marriage excluded.

[a]Relationship weakened when controlled statistically for whether informant was a
native of the village, an educated youth returning to his or her home village, or an
urban youth sent to live in the village.

*p ≤ .10

class" males are slightly more likely to take the initiative in mate choice
than "good class" males, while "bad class" females are slightly less likely
than others to do so. Part of this pattern may be due to bad class males being
somewhat older at marriage than good class males, as we saw in table 28
(and their parents more likely deceased). Older youths are likely to have
more say in marriage decisions than younger ones. Bad class females tend to
be younger than others at marriage, and our informants picture them as more
likely to marry spouses from distant communities than other women, in
order to escape the stigma of their family backgrounds, and thus as more
likely to rely heavily on parental arrangements. The influence of education
and cadre service are generally stronger than class background, although the
pattern for education appears inconsistent. Well-educated males (but not
females) are more likely than others to have a dominant voice in picking a
mate, but well-educated males *and* females are more likely than others to
rely on introductions. This apparent inconsistency is resolved if we keep in
mind our earlier statement that introductions do not automatically imply
parental dominance. Educated youths have more contacts of their own outside the village who can assist them with introductions, and they are less
likely than others to marry the girl (or boy) next door. Many of the introductions on which they rely come through their own contacts, rather than their
parents', and even if their parents take the initiative the males, at least, are
somewhat more likely to make efforts to get to know their spouses-to-be.
Thus educated youths score low on mate choice without introductions, but

high (for males) on mate choice in which the young couple has the primary voice. Men who are cadres, on the other hand, are both more likely than other men to marry without an introduction and perhaps more likely to have the major voice in their marital decisions. It is uncertain how much this is due to cadres being ideologically less disposed toward following parental dictates, and how much to cadres having more opportunities to become directly acquainted with potential mates within and outside the community. We note that men who are cadres are also more likely than others to marry women of the same lineage (gamma=.80, N=84) and women from within the commune or brigade rather than outside (gamma=.48, N=295).

Do villages differ in the extent to which young people take the initiative in marriage matters? Why is there more free mate-choice or youth initiative in some communities than others? We examine these questions in table 35, where our measures of generational dominance in mate choice and the use of introductions are related to selected village characteristics.

Most of the associations in table 35 are weak or inconsistent, indicating that the majority of village characteristics have no clear relationship with the degree of free choice in marriage. The clearest pattern is the modest associations with brigade size, which indicate that in larger brigades young people have more say in marriages and are less likely to require introductions. This makes sense given our earlier remarks that the social field of young people is for the most part confined to their brigade (for schooling, some agricultural work, and many other activities). Those in large brigades will come in contact with more potential mates as a result of their daily activities than those in small brigades. The weaker associations with our three-category lineage composition variable conceal a pattern which can be interpreted similarly. Youth dominance in mate choice is more common in both multilineage teams and single-lineage brigades than in single-lineage teams, while introductions are relied on least of all in the multilineage teams. Again this relates to whether there are potential mates close at hand. Such potential mates are most available in multilineage teams, and least available in single-lineage teams, given the restrictions on same-lineage marriage discussed earlier.[31] The only other consistent pattern in the table is that villages with regular political study routines are somewhat more likely than villages without them to have free choice in marriage. Given the fact that other political and urban-communications measures do not have such an effect, it is not clear whether this reflects a set of "modern" ideas about mate choice communicated in such meetings, or simply the way these meetings provide structured opportunities for young people (and others) to get

Table 35   Freedom of Mate Choice by Village Characteristics (Gamma Statistics)

	Youth dominance	Introduction not involved	Median N
Introduction involved?	1.00*		
Administrative			
Political density	-.08	.18	(87)
Political study	.23	.49*	(71)
Urban-communications			
Urban proximity	-.10	.02	(86)
Urban youths	-.52*[a]	.02	(60)
Communications	.28[b]	-.66	(81)
Nurseries	.04	.26	(87)
Economic			
Collective affluence	.12	-.05	(87)
Household consumption	-.20	-.00	(86)
Land/labor ratio	.01	.32	(85)
Remittances	.32	-.01	(68)
Other			
Brigade size	.25	.48	(68)
Team size	-.06	.13	(87)
Lineage composition	.07	-.36*	(87)
Non-Hakka ethnicity	-.37[c]	.05	(87)
Delta region	.03	.33	(87)
Median N	(69)	(104)	

Note: Superior letters indicate relationships substantially weakened by statistical control for one of the following:

[a] Age of informant,

[b] Remittance dependency,

[c] Place of origin of informant.

Source: Same as table 34.

*p ≤ .10

together in the evening. The inconsistent associations of our communications scale mirror those we saw in table 34 for husband and wife education, and we recall that the proportion of youths in school is one of the indicators making up this scale. With greater schooling, youths are more likely to develop their own contacts in their village and adjacent villages in the same brigade which can be used for marital introductions. In sum, most of our characteristics of villages dealing with income, political structure (with the exception of political study) and access to most urban or communication influences have no clear effect on mate choice. What do seem to matter are factors which influence whether or not young people will have opportunities to meet or to secure introductions to eligible partners: factors such as the size of their brigade, the lineage composition of their locality, and their pattern of school attendance.

If an introduction is involved in finding a mate, agreement to the match is worked out in stages. The first step is for a preliminary meeting to be set up. Even earlier both sides make initial inquiries about the suitability of the intended person. Then the introducer (professional or amateur) arranges a meeting, often in a mutually convenient market-town teahouse, but sometimes in the home of one of the youths. The main purpose of this first meeting is to get the young couple's reaction to the proposed match. In some instances both sets of parents are present; in others just the girl and the go-between arrive to meet the boy and his family. The young couple meet for a brief and usually awkward conversation, though a few informants mention aggressive young women arriving prepared to "grill" the intended spouse. No agreement is expressed at this initial meeting.

Next comes the stage of consideration. Each youth tells his or her impressions to the parents, and if these are negative the matter will usually not be pursued further. If there is preliminary approval, the parents seek further information. The man's family is concerned primarily about the woman's character, health, and temperament, while the girl's parents are more concerned with economic matters. In some cases the woman's family sends an emissary to the boy's village to inquire about the economic status of the potential in-laws, the size of their house, whether there are many dependents in the family, and so forth. In a few places the custom is for the woman's parents to go directly to his home; there they are served a meal and allowed to poke around, even to the extent of checking the family's grain stores. Our informants imply that factors like attractiveness and education level are less important in mate choice than economic and personality factors. Individual personality and health factors are critical in the choice of the bride, since she will have to leave her home and fit into her husband's family. In selecting the groom, on the other hand, it is not simply his individual characteristics that are important, but those of his entire family, since at least initially the couple's livelihood will depend on the health of this larger unit.

As a result of this process of mate choice do individuals end up married to people similar to themselves? There is a traditional Chinese phrase about marriage choice: there should be matching doors and windows (men-tang hu-tui). In other words, people should, and they generally did, end up marrying someone of similar social status. There is, of course, nothing distinctively Chinese about this practice. This tendency toward what technically is called homogamy persists today, although the criteria of status have changed. Though lacking reliable income data, we can examine class origins, ethnicity, age at marriage, and levels of educational attainment. We have repeatedly stressed that class labels continue to play an important role in the Chinese countryside today, even though they are based on a family's economic status more than two decades ago. "Bad class"males may not be able to find a bride at all.[32] Our data on 125 marriage cases show that there is a clear tendency for former poor or lower-middle peasant males to marry women of the same status, and for sons of former landlords and rich peasants to marry women with similar labels. The association is quite strong (gamma=.58).

Though we have little systematic data on ethnic status in marriages, apparently most Hakka males marry Hakka females, and most Cantonese males marry Cantonese females, even when both groups live intermingled. Intermarriages between these two groups usually involve a Cantonese male and a Hakka female, as in the past, rather than the reverse pattern. This differential is understandable, since Hakkas are still considered by the Cantonese to have low status, and since villagers desire women to be subservient to their husbands (and since the expenses of acquiring a Hakka bride are generally less than for a Cantonese bride).

Homogamy is not restricted to class origins and ethnicity. Not surprisingly, men tend to marry women of similar, although somewhat younger, ages (gamma=.45—the age gap is about two years among younger men and somewhat larger among older men). Men also marry women of similar, but slightly lower, educational attainment (gamma=.73). Since informants did not mention age, ethnicity, or educational level prominently in discussing criteria peasants use in picking mates, we conclude that these factors enter mate choice at an earlier stage in the process, as they tend to in our own society. Generally only individuals within certain age, ethnic status, education, and class label ranges will be considered potential mates in the first place. Within this pool of eligibles, criteria such as economic status and personal character and health are then used in selecting a specific spouse.

We have not followed the process of mate choice quite to its conclusion, but we are in a position to draw together several observations. The most important of these is that a clear shift toward more voice by the young in marriage decisions has taken place. This shift is in line with official policy, but several of our findings suggest that it was not produced primarily by the diffusion of "modern" ideas about mate choice from the government to the people. First, part of the reason for more free mate-choice is the breakdown of the taboos against same-lineage marriage, a breakdown the government has not tried to bring about. Second, villages with more free mate-choice are not generally those we expect to be more in touch with official messages about such matters. Third, there has not been much further progress toward free mate-choice since the mid-1960s, although this ideal has received more stress than usual in the media since the Cultural Revolution. The patterns we have examined suggest that in considering freedom of mate choice the most important things are the opportunities young people have to meet or to be introduced to a potential mate. A young person who believes in freedom of marriage but lacks the contacts necessary to meet potential mates may have to choose between remaining idealistic but unmarried, or getting help from his or her family.[33] Official policies have helped young people to develop such contacts, particularly as a result of the expansion of rural education and the formation of other groups and organizations that bring young people together outside of their families: work groups, the rural militia, irrigation projects, and maybe even political study meetings. However, we stress again that these broader contacts are still restricted to a fairly narrow geographical range, primarily involving other members of one's team and brigade. The officially sponsored restructuring of rural life that has offered youth social contacts is, in our view, more responsible for the expanding voice of the young than are frequent and forceful communications of the official ideal of free mate-choice.

Marriage Finance

If the second round of inquiries about the potential mates is resolved favorably, another meeting is set up, and here the older generation plays the key role. Now the primary concern is with what bride price the man's family will have to pay. Since there is considerable debate and confusion in the literature on marriage finance in China before 1949, we need to consider some of the issues that bear on our findings. The Chinese Communists, we have noted, regard the payment of a bride price (at least a substantial one) as marriage by purchase; this is specifically prohibited in the 1950 marriage law. We have also noted that the party feels that, besides the general mercenary connotations of "buying" a bride, the bride-price custom perpetuated class inequalities, by allowing the well-off to acquire the most desirable brides, leaving poor males with the remainder, or unable to marry at all. According to recent work by anthropologist Jack Goody, however, true bride-price systems need not have all these implications.[34] In fact, these systems predominate more in economically unstratified than in stratified societies, particularly in West Africa, with bride prices forming a sort of rotating fund. Bride prices are constant from family to family, and a father uses the valuables taken in when a daughter weds to marry off his son or, if there is no son, to acquire an extra wife for himself. Some sons, particularly those with no sisters, must delay marriage and some even have to leave their home village in search of bridewealth. Polygyny and late marriage are promoted, but over a number of generations the sex balance among families is sufficient for no single class of families to gain significant economic advantage over others. Dowry systems, in contrast, almost always imply economic inequality, with parents using the dowry as a form of inheritance-in-advance to preserve their daughters' social status as well as their own prestige. Parents try to prevent their daughters from marrying males who do not bring a sufficient amount of inherited property to the marriage. Dowries stay within a limited economic stratum rather than being distributed among all segments of a community, and as a consequence dowries act to perpetuate differential status and wealth. Thus pure bride price, which appears to Western (and Chinese Communist) eyes as more mercenary, is actually compatible with egalitarian systems; while dowry, which to the same eyes appears more equal (allowing women a share of family property), implies inequality and efforts to preserve that inequality across generations.[35]

The bearing of this argument on the Chinese case is problematic, since traditionally Chinese peasants practiced a system that was part bride price and part dowry, with many class and regional variants. According to the rural surveys conducted by Buck and his associates around 1930, the average wedding expenditure, including bride price, for a male's family was 127 yuan, while the average female expenditure, including dowry, was 96 yuan. The ratio between these two quantities varied by region, being highest in the double-cropping rice region (which includes Kwangtung)—the figures were 305 yuan and 169 yuan—and lowest in the winter-wheat-Kaoliang regions (Shantung and nearby areas) and in the Szechwan rice area, where female wedding expenses exceeded those of the male. For China as a whole peasants generally had male wedding expenses about 50 percent higher than female expenses, but for those with very large farms female costs were about as high as male wedding expenses.[36] (This is as we should expect, given Goody's argument about the importance of dowries in preserving status differences.)

These generalizations do not exhaust the complications of the Chinese case. The major confusion arises because the valuables delivered by the groom's family in many cases did not serve as a true bride price in Goody's terms. Instead they were an indirect dowry—they were used to pay for a dowry, which returned with the bride on the day of the wedding. Thus in some instances, instead of having a surplus from the bride price with which to marry off their own sons, a bride's parents would have to spend it all, and some of their own resources, to provide their daughter with a dowry. The groom's family, which looks like it is paying a substantial bride price, might receive most of that expenditure back with interest, in the form of extra dowry expenditures from the bride's family (although part or all of this was controlled by the bride and groom rather than by his parents). Unfortunately, most accounts of Chinese marriage expenses before 1949 list gross estimates of total costs to both sides, without separating bride price, dowry, wedding feast expenditures, and numerous other gifts which flow among kin before, during, and after a wedding. One detailed account we do have deals with a particular "middle class" marriage in a village in Yunnan in 1940. The groom's family sent a series of betrothal and marriage gifts to the bride's family totalling 2,700 yuan. The bride's family ceremonially returned 10 percent of each preliminary gift, or 245 yuan, and then spent 4,250 yuan in all on the dowry. In this case there was a net movement equivalent to 1,795 yuan from the bride's family to the groom's family, so it clearly qualifies as a case of indirect dowry and dowry, rather than pure bride price.[37] The items included in dowries in various parts of China differed, but generally included clothing and personal effects for the bride, furniture, bedding, washbasins, and so forth, or in the words of the above account "nearly everything that the young couple will need in their daily life."

We do not have systematic information on marriage finance customs for all of China prior to 1949, but at the most general level we suggest that China should be classified primarily as having an indirect dowry system. Bride prices were strongly correlated with class, but ever larger bride prices among not-so-poor, and middle, and upper-middle peasants primarily went to pay for ever larger dowries which were returned at the time of marriage. It was only among the very poor that there was primarily a bride price with a minimal dowry, while among the rural elite dowries predominated, with these families trying to preserve both their own status and that of their daughters. Bride prices may have delayed marriages and supported concubinage, but from the standpoint of class structure the Chinese Communists should have directed their anger more at dowry than at bride price.

What has happened to marriage finance since 1949? From our interviews we can detect both persistence and change. First, in spite of the provisions of the marriage law, material considerations have not become incidental to marriage—far from it. We were told of only five cases of marriage which did not involve a bride price, and these were offered as unusual exceptions to local practice. In every village for which we have information, virtually all marriages involve a bride price (li-chin, or p'in-chin), although the amount varies. Bride prices are given even when a marriage is the result of free choice by the young couple.[38] We asked informants whether local cadres, who are responsible for enforcing the prohibition on bride prices, themselves give a payment in marrying off their sons, and the usual response was that they had to if their sons were to find brides.

Does current practice involve a true bride price, though, or an indirect dowry? Are the funds used by the bride's family to furnish a substantial dowry for their daughter or to procure a bride for their son? On these points there is clear evidence of change. Dowries are now of negligible value in rural Kwangtung; they seem invariably to be much smaller than the cash and gifts delivered to the bride's family by the groom's family. Let us look at the current set of customs by returning for a moment to our narrative of marriage negotiations.

The second meeting of the two families is where the adults negotiate over marriage finance. Here the bride's parents present a list of demands; typically for a certain number of sets of clothing for the bride, a variety of food items, wedding cakes (li-ping—sent out by the bride's family to announce the match), sometimes jewelry, and a cash portion. The monetary value of the total varies from village to village. Within any village there is usually a customary amount for the cash portion, but the list of goods is more flexible. In some of our marriage cases the total cost to the groom's family of goods and cash was only about 100 yuan, but in other cases it exceeded 1,000 yuan. The groom's family receives this list of demands, considers it, and then proposes a list of its own, usually somewhat reduced. When a bargain is struck, the match is agreed to. In some localities there is a formal betrothal (ting-hun), with part of the bride price or separate gifts sent to the bride's family, and the rest delivered just before the wedding.

Our informants are emphatic that today, unlike in previous times, there is no negotiation over the items to be included in a dowry. The dowry will, in fact, include some items from the bride price—clothing items and perhaps jewelry. These may be supplemented by combs, mirrors, vacuum bottles, and similar gifts from the bride's family and friends. But the total value of the present dowry is quite small, and stocking it requires little or no extra expenditures by the bride's family. Items that in many areas used to be part of a dowry (such as furniture and bedding for the bridal room) are now the sole responsibility of the groom's family. His family buys these items directly, rather than delivering money with which the bride's family purchases them for inclusion in a dowry. Thus a man's family may have substantial other expenditures prior to the wedding in addition to the bride price and wedding feast (expenditures on the latter will be discussed in Chapter 13). In a few localities the groom's family is supposed to supply not only furniture for the bridal room but new housing for the couple, which may cost another 1,000 yuan or more.

Today only a small portion of the bride price goes to form part of the dowry, and thus could be considered an indirect dowry. Another portion, primarily the food items, is used for a separate wedding feast held in the bride's home (see Chapter 13). Most of the cash is saved and in many cases forms part of the bride price used to marry off a brother of the bride. Several quotations from our interviews illustrate both the change in marriage finance customs over time and the current uses of these payments.

> In our locality the girl's family spent much more for a wedding than the groom's family. For this reason, before liberation, if you had many daughters, you would be greatly burdened later with wedding expenses, and people would therefore accept money and send some daughters to other families. There was the sadder fact that some people would kill such daughters as they were born. Also some parents in order to marry off their daughters had to sell land. This situation, continuing over time, led to males being more numerous than females, with the gap becoming quite large. Perhaps this is the main reason why at liberation, when they propagandized the marriage reform, there was a 180-degree change in the situation, and for males to find a marriage object became a hard problem. Those who had daughters to marry off saw their daughters become "money trees"—they could get as much as 200 yuan in bride price, and the average was even over 100 yuan . . . . As I reflect now on the past I think it is quite remarkable how much things have changed. I don't know whether to cry or to laugh.[39]
>
> If one has both a boy and a girl, the custom is that one first marries out the daughter, thereby getting a bride price, and then with this newly attained money one has the price to get one's son a wife. There is a local term for this. While I was in the village, there was even one case where this was carried to the point that two families in different brigades simply swapped daughters [into marriage with their sons]. There was no need to use money at all.[40]

It cost me 2,000 yuan to marry, but this is special, since I am an Overseas Chinese, and could spend money sent by my parents. And this 2,000 yuan does not include money spent on clothing, furniture, etc. . . . Poorer people use only 1,000 yuan or so. If I am a poor or lower-middle peasant and my son will be getting married, I start saving two years in advance. I raise a pig, save up grain, and make or buy furniture piece by piece. If bought all together this would cost over 1,000 yuan, but this is spread out over a long period of time. You can use the money from marrying off daughters to help in this. Also other relatives will help [with loans].[41]

In sum, our information points to the emergence of something like a pure bride-price custom, with dowry and indirect dowry becoming much less important. Most of the wedding expenditures of a bride's family are met out of the bride price, and there is generally money left over to put toward a bride price to get a wife for the family's son. The groom's family, in comparison, has to view the transaction as more unilateral than used to be true, since what they expend does not return to them by way of a dowry. This implies that the customs in rural Kwangtung today involve more "marriage by purchase" than in the past. How can we explain this shift?

If we follow Goody's argument, the decline of dowry may reflect a reduced salience of status differences based on landholding in the Kwangtung countryside. As land reform eliminated differential landholdings as a basis of inequality, the importance of dowries as a way of protecting the status of daughters through a sort of inheritance-in-advance presumably declined. Thus one reason for the decline of dowry may be that the rural social structure is now more equal in terms of property. What appears as more marriage by purchase may, in fact, have been fostered by the very egalitarian measures that the Chinese Communists counted on to help eliminate bride price.

There are probably other reasons for the decline in the dowry part of marriage finance. Dowries were traditionally displayed ostentatiously in a procession to the groom's home; given the current government's criticism of displays of wealth, such ostentation may be politically unadvisable. Additionally, dowries used to serve to strengthen bonds of cooperation and obligation with affines—with the wife's kinsmen. We have noted that these affinal bonds are less important in rural Kwangtung today, and we will discuss this further in Chapter 15.

There are other pieces to this puzzle, however. Rural Kwangtung now has a purer bride-price system, with valuables circulating around the community, received for daughters and expended for sons. Why do not Kwangtung peasants simply decide to avoid the burden of negotiations in which many families come out even, simply trading a daughter for a daughter-in-law? This question is of particular interest, since we are dealing here not simply with a traditional custom which has persisted despite official opposition but a custom which has changed markedly in a direction opposite to that desired by the government. (We will take up the matter of the burden of bride prices in relation to income subsequently.) It is clear that the need to accumulate substantial bride prices does cause inconvenience and problems for peasant families. Most of the problems the Chinese Communists ascribe to "marriage by purchase" are clearly visible today. Even if they have received a bride price for a daughter, they still need to meet other wedding expenses for their son. Much advance saving and borrowing is required, and poor families have a hard time marrying off their sons, and may go deeply into debt doing so. One Chinese document from 1963 describes a poor male lamenting, "with wives so expensive, I cannot get one even if I work myself to death at my farming."[42] The problems such men have in finding brides may keep the age gap between males and females at marriage larger than one would expect where youth have a voice in picking marriage mates.[43]

It is our contention that no custom which involves so much financial trouble, and even occasionally political danger,[44] can be simply a survival of "feudal" attitudes. The decline in inheritable land does not explain why the bride price itself remains substantial. We must look to other features of the rural situation to explain this—features which are not hard to locate if we follow Goody's arguments.

The payment of bride prices is part of a system of exchange in which what are gained are rights in women. In cultures with minimal bride prices, the rights gained by the husband's family are correspondingly less than in cultures with large bride prices. The rights transferred to the male's family vary from culture to culture, but in the Kwangtung case they seem fairly clear. What is transferred is partly rights to the fruit of a woman's labor. As in the past, in moving to her new home a bride ceases to be obligated to support her own parents, and her labors add to the income and property (housing, furniture, consumer durables, but no longer land) of her husband's family. Even if she and her husband divide from his parents' household, their property is not joint between her and her husband, in spite of the provisions of the marriage law, but belongs to the new corporate family of which her husband is the head. In the event of divorce or the death of her husband, if a woman remarries she forfeits all claims to his family property, a fact we will discuss more fully later. Thus, receiving a bride price implies acceptance of the transfer of the rights to the economic activity of a woman from her parents to her husband's family, with no establishment of independent rights to property in either household by the woman herself.

One might also argue that the importance of bride price has increased because one of the results of rural transformations in China has been an increasing mobilization of rural women to labor regularly in the fields. Evidence of this increasing mobilization can be pieced together from scattered rural surveys over the years. In Buck's survey, circa 1930, the average amount of farm labor performed by women in rural China as a whole was only 13 percent (with 80 percent performed by men and 7 percent performed by children). Peter Schran, in a detailed study of the effect of collectivization and communization on the rural labor force, concluded that from 1950 to 1959 the total number of work days expended in agriculture had been more than doubled, and that this had been accomplished by getting more days of work each year out of adults, but particularly out of women.[45] In the double-cropping rice region (which includes Kwangtung) the women's share was traditionally higher than in other regions—29 percent.[46] But a similar process of mobilization of women took place there as well. A traveler to parts of rural Kwangtung in 1973 reports that women now constitute over half of the agricultural labor force and participate in field labor only slightly less than men.[47] Though we have no precise estimates of the extent of women's participation in farm work in our data, our impression agrees with that just cited. In our villages virtually all women below the age of forty-five work regularly in the fields, and may contribute up to 40 percent or so of the total labor effort in agriculture.

We argue, then, that in Kwangtung as elsewhere women are now performing a larger share of agricultural work than they used to. Since family income now depends overwhelmingly not on landholdings but on the number of laborers and their level of earnings, women's labor should be more important to the family economy than formerly. Insofar as bride price payments represent, in part, the acquiring of rights to the fruit of a woman's labor, those rights should also be more valuable today. In short, we argue that bride prices remain substantial because the rights whose transfer they bring about continue to be important, and probably have even gained in value. A woman's parents now depend heavily on her earnings, and will not want to part with her without substantial compensation. A man's family, on the other hand, may be willing to pay such sums without seeking a commensurate dowry in return since they know that a new bride's earnings will, over time, more than compensate them for their initial expenditure.

There is substantial evidence from different cultures throughout the world that where women do much of the subsistence work there tend to be substantial bride prices, whereas in cultures where women do little such work, bride prices tend to be absent, and minimal exchanges or dowries predominate.[48] Furthermore, in Buck's data for seven localities in rural Kwangtung circa 1930, there is a rank order correlation of .57 between the share of farm work done by women and the ratio of the groom's wedding expenses to the dowry.[49] Thus across cultures and within pre-1949 Kwangtung there is evidence that more subsistence work by women is associated with more of a tendency toward "marriage by purchase." We might expect, then, that when women's labor becomes more valuable over time, as has been true in rural Kwangtung, a shift toward more of a true bride price will result. And this is what our data show.

Today the ratio of bride prices to dowries is clearly higher than in former times, but has the value of bride prices relative to peasant income also increased? Unfortunately, Buck's study does not say what average peasant income in Kwangtung was in 1930, and it gives only average male wedding expenses, without separating out the proportion of this sum that is bride price. We can take this figure for the seven Kwangtung localities in Buck's study, and we can also compute the current estimated average expenditures by the male's family on the bride price and wedding feast, using figures from thirty-six of our villages. We compare these two figures, not with average peasant family income in Kwangtung in the two periods, since we lack this statistic, but with estimates of the *national* average peasant family income. If we can assume that these national estimates are fairly accurate and that the ratio of Kwangtung peasant incomes to national peasant incomes has not changed markedly over this forty-year period, then these ratios will tell us how the burden of male wedding expenses relative to family incomes in Kwangtung has changed since 1930. Given the indirectness of this estimating procedure, the result should be regarded as tentative.

The average of the man's wedding expenditures for the seven Kwangtung locations in Buck's data was 230 yuan, and Buck estimated that net peasant family income for all of China was about 400 yuan at the time;[50] this ratio is .575. Our data from thirty-six villages yield an average family expenditure, for males, on weddings (not including new housing, which we assume was not included in Buck's data) of 728 yuan. A contemporary source gives an estimate of per capita net rural income for all of China in 1970 of 158 yuan.[51] An assumption of 4.4 individuals per family yields a figure of about 695 yuan for the net family income for all of China. Hence our ratio for the current period is 1.05, substantially higher than the earlier figure.[52] With the crudeness of this procedure we cannot be certain that the burden of male wedding expenses relative to family income has really increased dramatically (though this would fit the argument we have been developing), but we do feel safe in saying that this burden has not decreased over the last forty years—especially since today it is unmatched by a dowry of any substance.

Before closing our discussion of the functions of bride price in contemporary Kwangtung we should notice that other rights besides those in a woman's labors are transferred. As in the past, there are also the rights over a woman's children; they are regarded as belonging to her husband's family and kin, rather than equally to her and her husband. We will return to a discussion of these rights in the final section of this chapter.

Are there differences among individuals and communities in the size of the bride prices offered when marrying? Unfortunately we do not have information about the bride prices paid in as many cases as we had information about age of marriage and initiative in mate choice. Also, in many instances we only have estimates of the cash portion of bride price, rather than a total figure including clothing, food items, and so forth. It is our impression that when the cash portion is large much is spent on these other items also, but still estimates of the total value would be preferable. Because of our limited information we cannot examine bride prices in relationship to the personal characteristics of spouses, as we have done for marriage age and marriage initiative, but we do have enough information to examine village-to-village variation. We do this in table 36, using two kinds of estimates. One is derived from the reported value of the cash portion of bride prices paid in fifty-one specific marriages (dichotomized into 1 = 200 yuan or more, 2 = less than 200 yuan—so that a score of 2 is more "modern"), with cases coded in terms of the village in which they took place (the husband's village in each case). The second is an estimate by an informant of the average or customary size of the cash portion of bride prices usually paid in that village (again dichotomized at 200 yuan), information we have for forty-eight of our villages. Examined together, these two kinds of estimates should help us locate where high or low bride prices are paid.

The strongest associations in the table are with the level of household consumption and with the existence of nurseries (although the latter is weakened for our general village figures if we control for team size). Scanning the figures in both columns, we conclude that high bride prices are paid in villages which have low consumption levels, where collective nurseries are present, where there are few sent-down youths, and perhaps where there

Table 36   Bride Price Cash Portion by Village
                                                  Characteristics (Gamma Statistics)

	Low bride price cash portion[a]	Number of marriage cases[b]	Low bride price cash portion[c]	Number of villages
Administrative				
Political density	.17	(44)	.48	(43)
Political study	.29	(35)	.13	(36)
Urban-communications				
Urban proximity	.35	(44)	.05	(46)
Urban youths	.33	(32)	.58*	(33)
Communications	-.23	(42)	-.33	(41)
Nurseries	-.75*	(44)	-.54[d]	(42)
Economic				
Collective affluence	-.33	(44)	.08	(45)
Household consumption	.83*	(42)	.32	(43)
Land/labor	.14	(41)	.40	(38)
Remittances	-.38	(32)	-.22	(29)
Other				
Brigade size	.45[e]	(41)	-.25	(37)
Team size	-.17	(45)	-.41	(46)
Lineage composition	-.20	(45)	-.35	(47)
Non-Hakka ethnicity	-.10	(46)	-.57*	(46)
Delta region	-.02	(46)	-.16	(48)

[a]From marriage sample.

[b]Post-1958 marriages only.

[c]From village sample.

[d]Relationship weakened when controlled for team size.

[e]Relationship weakened when controlled by marital status of informant.

*p ≤ .10

is weak political life, high dependence on remittances, non-Hakkas, or people living in small teams or single-lineage brigades which are far from large cities but well exposed to official communications. We do not have a coherent interpretation to fit this entire pattern, and a number of the coefficients involved are fairly weak. We do see one fairly coherent pattern emerging, though. Bride prices are low in villages that have high consumption levels, have high land-labor ratios, and have more urban contacts than other places.[53] Peasants in such villages could presumably pay more than those in other localities, yet they pay less. One may assume that such villages act as magnets for young women, who are anxious to marry into them and able to persuade their parents to accept lower bride prices in order to enable them to do so. In contrast, villages with many families receiving overseas remittances tend to be economically "unhealthy" because of their dependency on outside funds, but they can, because of such funds, pay unusually large bride prices in their effort to attract brides, as one of our earlier interview quotations implies. We should also note, however, that Hakka villages, which are sometimes on the poor side, and which may have trouble attracting brides, turn out to give lower than usual bride prices. This may be attributable to non-Hakka women not usually marrying into such villages, so that these villages are not competing with wealthier non-Hakka villages to obtain brides. Thus at least in part high bride prices are characteristic of localities which have a hard time competing to attract brides, but which have access to extra cash, while low bride prices characterize villages into which families would like to marry their daughters.

We must now conclude our narrative of rural mate choice. We have noted that, once the bride price is agreed to, the match is settled, whether or not a formal betrothal is involved. We are uncertain how binding betrothals are these days, and the interval between betrothal and marriage varies widely. In some localities it is only a few weeks; informants claim that parents are anxious lest the other party change his or her intentions. In other localities the wait may be a year or more, with the bride's family making it clear that they are not willing to part with her labor sooner. Delaying marriage for this reason figures more prominently in our interviews than any desire to conform to the government's late marriage policy. Whatever the interval, the young couple is allowed to visit in order to become better acquainted. Commonly they visit each other's home (more often the male visiting the female), but they may meet and talk at the market town or go to the county town to buy items they will need later—and perhaps even go to the movies. By American standards these activities are quite reserved, with little privacy or physical intimacy (although many informants noted some cases of premarital sex and other exceptions to this pattern).[54] Though with most couples the partners do make some effort to get to know each other before the wedding day, this quasi-dating behavior takes place usually after the match has been agreed to, rather than before. As such, it functions more as a preparation for marital compatibility than as a way of screening potential mates. The final steps in arranging a marriage are the registration and the family wedding celebration. Both are discussed in Chapter 13.

We have now covered the major steps and customs involved in picking a mate today in rural Kwangtung. The dominating impression is that marriage follows modified versions of traditional practices, practices that are in some respects far removed from the official ideals of free romance, lack of financial considerations, and the absence of parental interference. Nonetheless, significant changes have taken place, particularly in the increasing role that youths play in marriage decisions.[55] Not all of the changes have been in the direction of increasing compliance with official marriage ideals, however, as we saw in our discussion of both the decline of lineage exogamy and of changing marriage finance. Through our discussion of these contrasting findings we have pointed to factors which help us understand the differential pattern of persistence and change in marriage customs—particularly factors affecting the competitive position of individuals and villages in the rural marriage market today and the structured opportunities young people have to meet potential mates. We conclude this chapter with a discussion of how some rural marriages are terminated.

Divorce and Remarriage

From our informants we receive the impression that most rural marriages are stable. Individuals expect, as in the past, to stay married for life, and both the local kinship structure and government policy favor such stability. Couples having marital difficulties do receive help and pressure from both kin and cadres, urging them to reconcile and avoid divorce. No doubt the process of mate choice contributes to stability. Young people have more say now, but their choice is based less on intense romantic involvement and more on assessments of compatibility than is the case in our own society. In most cases the partners can still expect to experience an increasing intimacy with each other after marriage, rather than following the Western pattern of intense premarital involvement which may gradually decline after marriage.[56] Also married persons do not live by themselves, but take on a set of obligations to other kin which no doubt helps to solidify their relationship.

Some of our informants claim that there have been no cases of divorce in their locality at all in recent years. But knowledge of local divorce cases is not evenly distributed, with about two-thirds of our married informants or those over age twenty-six able to describe divorce cases, while only about one-third of our younger, single informants can do so. Gossip about divorce cases seems to be part of the leisure-time conversation of the older, married informants but not of the young, which makes our information base somewhat uneven. We do, however, have some details on twenty-six cases of rural divorce, and on another nineteen cases of serious marital disputes which either did not result in a divorce or were still pending at the time our informants left. These cases allow us to make some preliminary generalizations.

In four out of five of our divorce and marital-dispute cases the wife initially demanded the divorce.[57] Even where the "fault" seems clearly to be on the woman's side (for example, if she is having an extramarital affair or is refusing to work regularly in the fields) the husband rarely initiates a divorce; he and his family either try for a reconciliation or make the wife so miserable she will ask for a divorce. Perhaps in rural eyes the party seen as responsible for breaking up the marriage is less the one who caused the problem than the one who demanded the divorce. This reluctance of males to initiate divorce may also reflect the sentiment in many villages that it is harder for a man to remarry today than for a woman (the reverse of the traditional pattern)—thus it is important to hold onto the wife you have. Males may also fear the loss of their bride price "investment."

The reasons cited in divorce cases vary greatly, but most commonly they are economic. One spouse charges the other with being lazy or eating too well—in other words with consuming more than they contribute to the family. The other spouse claims they cannot tolerate the poverty and bitter labor they are experiencing. In some cases prior deception is an issue. A bride claims the matchmaker led her to believe the man's family was well-off, while in reality they are quite poor. Sometimes illnesses or deaths in the family lead to a sudden drop in family livelihood, causing the wife to desire a divorce.

Another category of complaints involves sexual problems. One or both parties is detected in an extramarital affair. Or one of the partners is accused of being unable to have children—occasionally a wife says her husband is not even able to have sexual relations. Still a third category consists of political and legal problems. One spouse (most often the husband) gets in trouble with the authorities (either actual penal confinement or being made a frequent "struggle target" in mass campaigns). Or one spouse escapes to Hong Kong and refuses to return or to send back money. A final category of common problems revolves around family tensions: The husband and mother-in-law gang up on the wife, for instance, and she demands to be freed from their naggings and beatings.

When a marital dispute occurs, various attempts at mediation ensue. We have already noted that official policy requires prolonged mediation, even when both parties agree to a divorce. For a minor dispute mediation is informal, involving neighbors, relatives, and friends. If the dispute becomes serious more formal mediation begins. In most villages there is no "mediation committee," as there sometimes is in urban localities.[58] Instead the team leader or more often the brigade party secretary or some other cadre will investigate and urge reconciliation.

Few of the types of disputes mentioned (except for some political-legal ones) are regarded as sufficient grounds for divorce. We noted earlier that the marriage law of 1950 does not list specific grounds for divorce, but press articles and legal precedents over the years have conveyed information about what reasons are sufficient or insufficient.[59] The disputes mentioned above become sufficient grounds for divorce only when they lead to constant fighting and abuse between spouses that are not resolved by several rounds of mediation. To press her case, the wife may adopt the traditional response to marital misery—running home to her natal family (or, in a newer variant, running off to live with a new boyfriend). If the brigade cadres cannot resolve the dispute they throw up their hands and refer the matter to commune officials. The latter initiate a new round of mediation efforts, trying to get the couple back together. Only if commune mediation fails will a divorce be approved, and even then, generally, the agreement of both parties is required. If the husband is still opposed, commune officials may refuse to give their approval until the wife has succeeded in making him miserable enough to give his consent.

It is our impression that judgment at the commune level is the most important phase in the proceedings, although most of our informants had only vague information about the legal procedures beyond this. There usually is a county people's court hearing, but in most cases this is a formality to approve the judgment reached at the commune level. Only if the couple and lower-level cadres have not been able to agree on the disposition of children and property will the county people's court have a substantive judgment to make.[60]

There is thus a prolonged series of attempts at mediation on various levels which may delay for months and years the divorce of even those couples who are agreed on the matter. It is not clear that this policy is viewed by the peasants as an unfair obstruction of divorce. Rural public opinion seems to share the government's view that divorce is to be avoided if at all possible, and may have influenced that view in the 1950s. Our informants do give examples of successful reconciliations as well as of prolonged and bitter battles. In regard to mediation, at least, the official policy toward divorce seems to be followed fairly closely today.

Most divorces are followed fairly soon by remarriage, particularly by the woman. This also is true for young widows, for whom remarriage was traditionally frowned upon, as we noted earlier. Some portions of the rural population still feel that remarriage is wrong, but we were only told of a couple of cases of attempted interference in the remarriage of widows.

Young men may be reluctant to marry a widow, but there seem to be plenty of older bachelors, widowers, and divorced men who are eager to do so.

Most women who are divorced move back to their native village, or move rapidly into the home of a new spouse. Widows, in contrast, generally stay in the man's village and are entitled to support there until they remarry. As we noted earlier, most issues of child custody and property division are not specified in the marriage law but are supposed to be negotiated between the parties concerned. When the law and the courts step in, they are supposed to lean toward protecting the woman's rights. In rural Kwangtung, however, local customs regarding the negotiations still heavily favor the male side. In the majority of cases for which we have information, the male's family keeps custody of all children, and in other cases the children are divided, with the clear understanding that the woman can take away only those children agreed to by the male's family—generally a younger child or a daughter. Older male children remain in the male's family. The few cases in which the mother kept custody of all children were in some way special: the divorced husband was in Hong Kong, with an only daughter he did not want to be responsible for; a widow remarried locally, so that the children were not removed from the first husband's village; and so forth. In some cases we were told that commune officials did not give their approval to the divorce until the woman agreed that the children would stay with her husband. It is our impression that, while the courts may favor the woman's side, commune and brigade cadres tend to favor the man, as does rural public opinion generally. This is not too surprising, given the kinship ties that link a man's family to local cadres.

Disposition of family property is even more clearly biased than child custody, although today it does not include land. Women who have been married for some time will have contributed to the accumulation of family property: new housing, consumer durables, savings, and so on. In no cases in our interviews were women accorded individual rights in this property. Those who divorced, or widows who remarried out of a village, took only their clothing and other items they might own personally (for example, combs, jewelry). The family property remained with the husband or his family. This was the case even with the remarriage of one widow with no children—the house and the other family property went to her dead husband's brother rather than to her. (Widows still retain the right to the use of this property if they do not remarry.)

We feel, then, that widowed and divorced women may be remarrying somewhat more easily than in the past, but in doing so they usually forfeit claims to their children and to the family property they helped to accumulate (as was the case in the past). This forfeiture occurs in spite of official policy favoring equal rights for women and even special protection of these rights. We think this situation can be understood if we refer back to our earlier discussion of marriage finance. Bride price, we have argued, brings about the transfer of important rights in women from their parents' to their husbands' families. These are rights both in the children produced by the woman and in the fruits of her labor. Bride price is supplied, not by the husband, but by his family, and the rights transferred go not to him personally but to the larger family unit. The two families do not state these matters so explicitly in their negotiations, but it is implicit in the view of bride price as fair compensation to her parents. In the words of one informant, "I would sometimes joke with mothers about wanting so much money [for a bride price]. They would say that when they had spent so much time and money raising a daughter, it was not right to just give her away."[61] All parties involved—the bride and groom, both families, and even local cadres—grasp the nature of this transaction. A woman, upon entering a marriage and accepting a bride price, understands that she has certain rights and claims as long as she remains part of her husband's family. If she leaves via divorce or widowhood and then remarries, she forfeits those rights and takes with her only what her husband's family is willing to give—which in most cases is very little.

When a woman remarries and leaves her children behind and the family property intact, the husband's family is regarded as fairly compensated for the withdrawal of rights in her person. But the contract is not fulfilled if she leaves without providing fair compensation. The implicit marriage contract shows up most clearly in cases of divorces after short periods of marriage which have produced no children. In four such cases the woman and her natal family were told by the cadres that they had to repay part or all of the bride price they had received for her in order for her to receive a divorce. In these cases brigade and commune cadres reasoned that, although bride prices were illegal, one had been paid, and divorce would leave the husband's family without proper compensation for this payment. If a portion of the bride price was not returned, the man would find it difficult to afford a new spouse. In some of these cases repayment came from the woman's family, in others from her new husband-to-be. The parents of such women usually try to dissuade them from divorce, since they have already spent the bride price, perhaps to marry off a son.

Thus the emphasis in the marriage law on negotiation of rights over children and property leaves the door open for a continuing emphasis on patrilineal rights, even though the "spirit" of the law favors women. Local cadres support the claims of the man's family to these rights, even though ideally they are to be vigilant against bride prices upon which such claims are based. The result is that women, whose importance in agricultural work has increased over time, have not gained independent rights in family property and children, contrary to what one would expect from the Marxist argument about the liberating role of socially productive labor for women—an issue to which we shall return in Chapter 12.

We would also like to know whether divorces are more likely to occur in some villages than in others. The only piece of information we have on many of our villages is whether or not informants reported divorce cases in recent years, and the connection between this report and something like a divorce rate is obviously quite distant. In the absence of any other information, examination of our crude indicator may still be of some value. The relevant figures are presented in table 37. (Arbitrarily, a code of 1=no divorce reported, 2=some divorces.)

Table 37	Reported Divorce Cases by Village Characteristics (Gamma Statistics)	
	Recent divorce cases reported?	Number of villages
Administrative		
Political density	.35	(47)
Political study	.17	(41)
Urban-communications		
Urban proximity	-.28	(48
Urban youths	-.60*[a]	(36)
Communications	.09	(44)
Nurseries	.11	(46)
Economic		
Collective affluence	-.10	(48)
Household consumption	-.53*	(44)
Land/labor ratio	-.24	(39)
Remittances	.57*	(32)
Other		
Brigade size	.27	(39)
Team size	.23	(48)
Lineage composition	.26	(49)
Non-Hakka ethnicity	-.09	(49)
Delta region	-.04	(49)

[a]Relationship weakened when controlled for level of remittance dependency.

*p ≤ .10

The strongest associations in table 37 are those of reported divorce with household consumption level and level of remittance dependency (the other strong association with the percentage of sent-down urban youths living in a village is reduced when the value of remittance dependency is controlled for). These figures seem to represent the opposite side of the coin from the relationships we saw in table 36 in discussing variation in bride prices. Villages with high consumption levels tend to have few reported divorce cases, while villages which rely heavily on remittances to make ends meet have more reported divorce. Apparently the same types of villages that have difficulty attracting brides in (and who pay high bride prices to do so) also have trouble retaining their women. (The weaker associations with urban proximity, collective affluence, and the land-labor ratio also fit this pattern.) This finding conforms with our earlier comment on the predominance of economic causes of divorce.[62] The remaining associations in table 37 are fairly modest. The positive relationships between reported divorce and team and brigade size are likely to be due simply to the larger local units involved providing more couples in the "social field" of our informants, and thus more likelihood that divorce cases will come to their attention. We don't think that there is likely to be more marital instability in larger teams and brigades. Again we see no evidence that some sort of modernization or government influence factor explains these results—our political variables are if anything associated with more reported divorce, while urban contact and economic variables tend to be associated with less. We therefore find an interpretation based upon the "attractiveness" of a village to women in the marriage market more useful in understanding these results than an explanation based on modern or official contacts and influences.

Conclusions

In this chapter we have reviewed evidence on changing practice in regard to marriage and divorce in rural Kwangtung. The customs surveyed clearly show a mixture of change and stability. In interpreting this pattern we have found that official ideals are of limited value; in some areas there has been change in their direction, in others little change, or even change in the opposite direction. The officially directed social transformations of the 1950s, on the other hand—the confiscation of lineage property, the subsequent collectivization of family landholdings, the mobilization of women for regular agricultural work, and the expansion of education and other nonfamilial activities for youth, in particular—clearly have had an important impact, although in some cases an unintended one. In interpreting our results we have had to consider the effects not only of these social transformations but also of a variety of other features of the local scene: the size of each brigade, the ethnicity of its inhabitants, their reliance on overseas remittances, and so forth. We don't claim that the government's proclaimed marriage ideals, with which most Kwangtung peasants are quite familiar, have little impact. We do argue that their implementation depends to a very great extent on the concrete features of village life, features which support some changes and obstruct others.

11

Intrafamily
Relations

In studying rural China we want to scrutinize not only how family units form and dissolve, and how many children people have, but also the nature of relationships within the family, and how these have changed over time. Family relations are subtle and complex, difficult to study through on-the-spot observation, not to mention through recall "at a distance." Nevertheless, many of the most important questions one can ask about family change in China concern these internal relations, and we will try to piece together in this chapter such evidence as we have on three major themes: the division of labor among family members in performing daily tasks, the nature of key dyadic relationships within the family, and the ways in which children are reared.

The Family's Division of Labor
and the Daily Routine

The government's ideals as they pertain to the division of labor within families can be stated relatively simply. All ablebodied individuals, male and female, should be involved in collective production, helping to raise grain and other vital commodities. When there is a conflict between the demands of collective labor and the needs of the family, peasants should decide in favor of the collective or, in the words of the Cultural Revolution slogan, they should "destroy selfishness and establish collectivism [p'o-ssu li-kung].''[1] Within the family all members should pitch in to meet the burdens of collective and domestic work in a spirit of equality. In particular, men should be willing to share an equal load of domestic work with women (as women are sharing equally in field labor), and older family members should not place all of the household burdens on the shoulders of the young.

However, except for the goal of mobilizing women for regular agricultural labor (discussed in Chapter 10), these themes have not received strong or constant emphasis.[2] The press and local cadres have paid attention to removing obstacles to women working outside the home, including at some times and in some places promoting nurseries, sewing cooperatives, and other institutions to ease the burden of domestic work. But the goals of getting men to help more around the home and the old folks to stop tyrannizing the young have been the subject of more intermittent or passing concern. Ideals in these latter areas have been communicated to the rural population through examples in the press, contemporary short stories, and so forth, but compliance has not been actively enforced.[3] Given this uneven pattern of emphasis, it is interesting to see what the current pattern of division of family tasks is, and how it has changed.

Let us examine the activities of family members during a "typical" day. The length of the working day of Kwangtung peasant families varies with the seasons and the farming tasks, as it always has. There is no completely idle season, as Kwangtung's semitropical climate permits year-round farming. Local cadres try to fill any slack periods with land reclamation, canal repair, and other tasks. But Kwangtung peasants still recognize the alternation between busy seasons, when work in the fields may range from ten to twelve or more hours per day, and the slack periods of the year, when collective labor may consume six to eight hours or less. The timing of all activities during the day is naturally affected by these broad seasonal fluctuations.

During the slack periods the family may get up around seven or so, while in the busy seasons they will rise before daylight, often around five. The adult women of the family, particularly the mother, are the first to rise. They go to the kitchen to prepare food for the family's pigs and other animals, and then to fix the family's own breakfast. A variety of other tasks may be carried out in the early morning, depending upon the pressure of time. In most villages water has to be hauled from a stream or well for washing and cooking, and the private plot also needs watering. There also may be time to do some laundry. Most of these are tasks carried out by the adult women of the family, with some help from the older children. The father and grown sons generally get up half an hour or so after the womenfolk. During the slack season the men wash up and go out to work on the family's private plot; otherwise they share few of the early morning chores. In the peak agricultural seasons the ablebodied laborers in the family, male and female, may go out for an early morning stint of collective labor on an empty stomach, and then return home an hour or two later to eat breakfast. At such times a grandmother in the home is particularly valuable, both for cooking and for watching the children before school starts.

Throughout the day domestic chores are squeezed in around other activities. In Kwangtung villages today there are few institutions outside the family to help. We have already noted that when people's communes were first set up in 1958, private plots were eliminated, and communal institutions (public mess halls, nurseries, and so on) were established to help lighten the burden of domestic work and free family members for other activities. With the collapse of the Great Leap Forward most of these "sprouts of communism" were disbanded, private plots were restored, and individual families once again took over almost all domestic tasks. Since that time some teams and brigades have been able to reestablish some communal facilities. One example is the national-model Tachai brigade in Shansi Province, which now has collective nurseries, collective sewing and tailoring shops, and no private plots. But the expense of running such institutions has to be met out of local resources, with the approval of members, so they tend to be found only in well-to-do or model communes. We noted earlier that few of our Kwangtung villages have even collective nursery schools, and so the burdens of child care, laundry, meal preparation, and other domestic chores continue to fall on the individual family unit.[4]

Meals are almost always taken in the home, with family members sitting and eating together as a group, insofar as schedules permit (that is, more so for the evening meal than for the noon meal). In very few cases in our sample does the team set up a busy-season canteen out in the fields in order to avoid the loss of time involved in returning home for lunch. In most localities three meals a day are eaten, with either the mother or grandmother, or in some cases older children, doing the cooking. Although most meals are eaten jointly, in a number of places during the hot summer months family members fill their bowls with food and go wandering outside, looking for a cool place to sit and eat and chat with friends.

Team labor is divided into two or three labor periods, with cadres either announcing gathering times in advance, or calling people to work over the loudspeaker system. As noted in Chapter 10, most ablebodied women in rural Kwangtung work regularly in the fields, unless there is nobody else to care for their small children, or unless family income is sufficient to permit them to stay at home part of the time. Women work alongside other women, or mixed in with men, depending upon the task being performed. The pattern varies from village to village, but in most there are none of the enduring work groups of the type sometimes mentioned in the Chinese press: women's shock groups, youth experimental-plot work groups, and so on. Instead team members are assigned to different tasks on an ad hoc basis, with some work tasks done by individuals spread out in the fields, and others by short-term groups of shifting composition. A number of informants claim that there is much informal separation of the sexes in field labor during the slack periods, with men handling plowing and other heavy duties, and women doing weeding and other tedious tasks. In the harvest season rush, however, everyone pitches in side by side, although the tasks performed by men and women may not be identical. We find no evidence of the sort of "feudal" attitudes which have been reported to have limited female work participation in some places in the past: fear of seduction of women, fear of women "spoiling" the crops, and so forth. The team head assigns people to temporary work groups on the basis of both their skills and how well people can cooperate with others, and the latter principle may entail encouraging close kin to work together. But again these groups come together for specific farming tasks and then disperse, with members reallocated to other groups and tasks. There is also little reported in the way of production competition between work groups of the type sometimes stressed in the Chinese press and in the Soviet Union. Thus we see little evidence that the organization of work within the team acts to promote smaller solidarities or cleavages in any regular way, whether based on sex, kinship, or some other principle.

During their noon meal and rest period, family members again scurry around doing domestic chores. The males of the family go off to their private plot, and the women cook lunch, do the family wash, and clean up. If there is sufficient time after lunch, and depending upon the distances involved, women and children (who return home from school to eat) may go into the hills to cut mountain grass for use as fuel or for sale, or one or another family member may go off to market to make small sales and purchase necessities. In many if not most localities these activities require more time than is available during the rest period after lunch, and family members have to take part or all of the day off to engage in them. (As mentioned in Chapter 8, teams vary in number of days of collective labor required of their members each month, and in how they enforce such regulations.)

From what we have said thus far it should be obvious that there is still a fairly clear sexual division of labor within the family, even though this division is muted in collective work on the team's fields. If we designate as chores the following—child care, cooking, cleaning, clothes washing, and hauling water—then in most of the villages in our sample (72 percent, N=43) ablebodied men are reported to do few or none of these chores. In other villages husbands are reported to do some domestic chores, most often cooking, or occasionally tending a small child, but nowhere is there reported to be equal sharing of domestic chores between the sexes. Thus women in Kwangtung villages are subject to the "double bind" of working women in other countries, whether socialist or capitalist: even though they work full-time outside of the home, they still bear the major burden of domestic chores. The division is not so sharp, however, for either the very young or the very old. School-age boys and retired grandfathers both help with domestic chores more than fathers do. A grandfather may help to prepare meals or tend a grandchild, but it is also common for grandfathers to walk into town to visit a teahouse, or to go off to chat with other retired men during the day, leaving the grandmother tied down with babysitting and other chores.

When asked the reason for this pattern of minimal sharing of domestic chores by adult men, most informants attributed it simply to traditional attitudes of male chauvinism, although some said that the villagers felt that men, as the main income earners of the family, should be allowed to conserve their energies for team labor and private-plot work. (Or, in the case of aged males, that they deserved more rest after their long years of difficult field labor.) Our informants also give no indication that any special efforts were being made to get men to share more fully in domestic work, although the official ideal of equal sharing is known to all.

One of our female informants, a sent-down youth from Canton, gives the following picture,

> Women did all the housework such as cooking, washing, tending the children. In the morning before work, at noon, and in the evening from nine to eleven or twelve, the men would be gathered about in groups of three to five just chatting away. The women, meanwhile, were home working. . . . No, no one talked about men doing the work in the home. It was just about doing the heavy work in the fields that the women complained. We sent-down women pointed out that in Canton husbands helped with dishwashing and even cleaning up the diapers of the children. The village men just laughed and said they wouldn't be men any

more if they did that. The village women couldn't even think of such a change, so they didn't express any opinion.[5]

There is also some division of labor in the household's subsidiary economic activities. Tending and feeding the family's pigs and fowl are primarily the mother's responsibility, although here children and grandparents, and even occasionally the husband, help out.[6] Women and children are also, as mentioned, the main cutters of hillside grass, an important source of family fuel and supplemental income in many villages. Fathers are in turn the main laborers on the private plot, although they are assisted by their sons, and in some places by the womenfolk as well. Sixty percent (N=37) of our informants report that, except for early morning watering, private-plot work is monopolized by males. However, in some villages—particularly among the Hakka, whose women in traditional times kept their feet unbound and had a reputation for hard work and for being exploited by lazy husbands—women are reported to do as much private-plot work as men or even more.[7]

We have less information about marketing activities, but in this realm more equal sharing by sex seems to be common. For thirteen villages in our sample men are reported to do most of the marketing, in eleven villages men and women are reported to do the marketing with about equal frequency, and in four villages marketing is said to be predominantly the woman's task. Where there is some differentiation by sex in marketing activities, major purchases and sales are made at the initiative of the father, while daily purchases are made by the mother or by whoever has the available time. This pattern accords with the fact that it is still most common for the man of the house to manage the money. (In 65 percent of our villages, N=40, this is reported to be the usual pattern.)

We have been speaking of the modal pattern in the sexual division of labor—the pattern that is reported to be the most common throughout all of our villages. But of course there is much variation among families in the same village and across villages in who performs which tasks (as well as variation within one family over time). What sorts of villages are most likely to have men help with the housework, or women help on the private plot? We can examine such questions by looking at the associations of four measures with village characteristics. These concern whether men help with domestic work (almost none versus some), whether women help with private-plot work (almost none versus an equal or greater amount than men), who generally does the marketing (generally men versus equally or more often women), and who controls the family purse (generally the male, versus equal control or generally the female). The results are presented in table 38.

Table 38   Sexual Division of Labor by Village
                                                            Characteristics (Gamma Statistics)

	Domestic work division	Private plot work division	Marketing division	Family money management	Median N
Division of labor					
Domestic work division	--				
Private plot division	.61	--			
Marketing division	-.38	.11	--		
Family money management	.13	-.42	.69	--	
Administrative					
Political density	-.17	.04	.23	-.49[a]	(38)
Political study	-.76*	-.45	.03	.04	(35)
Urban-communications					
Urban proximity	.26	-.31	.15	.38	(38)
Urban youths	.94*	.49	-.14	-.04	(28)
Communications	-.24	-.05	.68*	.08	(37)
Nurseries	.13	-.66	.33	.57	(38)
Economic					
Collective affluence	.57	-.27	.14	.55*	(38)
Household consumption	.03	-.18	-.40[b]	.50	(37)
Land/labor ratio	.17	.10	-.32	-.03	(34)
Remittances	-.77*	-.42[c]	.41	.33	(26)
Other					
Brigade size	-.55	-.45	-.52	.34	(31)
Team size	-.33	-.04	-.06	.43	(38)
Lineage composition	-.07	-.26	.42	.37	(39)
Non-Hakka ethnicity	.13	-.71*	-.14	.72*	(38)
Delta region	.42	-.54	.03	.94*	(39)
Median N	(42)	(36)	(27)	(39)	

Note: Superior letters indicate relationships substantially weakened by statistical control for one of the following:

[a]Non-Hakka ethnicity,

[b]Informant's class label,

[c]Informant's education.

*p ≤ .10

The associations in the table are not very strong, but several deserve note. First, villages in which men do little domestic labor tend to be the ones in which women do little private-plot work, and villages in which men handle the marketing tend to be the ones in which men control the purse strings. (See the associations in the top panel of table 38.) However, all four items do not cohere; for example, villages in which men do little domestic work are not especially likely to be ones in which men handle the marketing—if anything women are likely to handle the marketing in such villages. Villages in which men do some domestic work tend disproportionately to be villages with many sent-down urban youths present, with no regular political study routine, with few families depending upon remittances, and perhaps with small brigades, a Pearl River Delta location, and collective affluence. These particular characteristics do not form an especially obvious pattern. For the next column we see a pattern in which private-plot work by women is particularly characteristic of Hakka women and in general of women in relatively poor villages outside of the Pearl River Delta. We see something of the reverse in the final column, in which women managing the household purse strings seems concentrated in the relatively affluent Cantonese villages of the Pearl River Delta region, and notably absent in the more isolated Hakka villages. For our marketing item the relationships are generally weaker and harder to interpret, and may be due to the operation of chance factors alone. Notable also in the table is the absence of certain patterns. There are no strong positive associations between political variables and measures of the division of labor by sex; the only strong relationships are negative, indicating more egalitarian patterns in villages lacking a strong political infrastructure. Our indicators of urban and communications exposure are generally inconsistent, rather than forming a clear pattern. Overall conclusions are difficult to state given the nature of the associations, but we note that the ethnic composition and regional location of a village are more often associated with variations in the sexual division of labor than are other village characteristics.

In the daily routine, again, children, especially daughters, come home after school and help around the house. Then in the late afternoon a daughter or a grandmother lights a fire for the evening meal. Women in the fields usually return home to help fix supper, and men either go home and rest or go to work on the private plot until supper is ready. The evening meal may be at six or so in the slack season, or as late as eight or so in busy periods, with a few localities scheduling short collective work periods after supper during the peak harvest period.

Evenings are generally free time. As mentioned in Chapter 4, most villages do not have any regularly scheduled team meetings, either for discussing production or politics. Instead, team or brigade cadres call meetings whenever they are required: to discuss work assignments and problems, to discuss work-point allocation, to announce and explain a new political campaign, and so forth. At some times, then, there may be several meetings in a week, but at other times there may be no more than one or two such meetings in a month. The image one often gets of China as a place with regular political study groups and constant meetings does not apply most of the time to large parts of the Kwangtung countryside.

When meetings are called the attendance varies. Generally all the able-bodied members of a team are expected to attend, although in some villages one representative from each family will suffice. In some localities it is mostly men who attend these evening meetings, with women staying at home with the children.[8] However, other informants report fairly equal participation, or even in a few cases a predominance of women attending, with children brought along and allowed to play at their feet. This tends to enliven the mood of such meetings, even if it does little for the orderliness with which issues are discussed.

If there is no meeting to attend, a variety of other activities take place in the evening. If a task-rate work-point system is in use, each family sends a member to the team headquarters to report on the tasks fulfilled by various family members during the day, in order to get work-point credit recorded accurately. Some individuals lounge around near the team headquarters, talking informally with friends and neighbors. Others wander off and chat with friends in the village. This is a time for relaxation and conviviality, mostly in small, informal groups of people of the same sex and near in age. Young men gather in the home of one of their number or in a "youth house" (a traditional institution which will be described in the final part of this chapter) to play cards and chat—about life in general, local young women, opportunities to earn extra income, and other topics. Older men meet separately in small groups to chat about the weather, production problems, village events, and so forth. Young women may stay at home to help their mothers, or they too may gather in groups in the evening—at the home of a girlfriend or in a "youth house"—to talk about the day's events, local romances, and so on. Married women and grandmothers are preoccupied with household tasks in the evening, and spend less time in group gatherings, although they may pause to chat with a neighbor. This pattern of differential evening socializing tends to reinforce the dominant position of adult men in the formation of village public opinion.[9]

There is little in the way of organized recreation or sports in most villages in the evenings, although once a month or so a movie or drama team visits the brigade and puts on a show. Those who live close to towns can, of course, avail themselves of additional opportunities there to see movies or engage in other recreation. Some villages also have youth clubs (not to be confused with the "youth houses" already mentioned). These have facilities for ping-pong and Chinese chess, and some books and pamphlets. In such villages young people, especially the males, congregate there in the evening rather than in individual homes. But most people have little energy or inclination for sports or other vigorous activities, and the evening hours are regarded as a time to relax and enjoy friendly conversations after a hard day in the fields.

All of these evening activities are, of course, limited by the season. During the peak periods of agricultural activity dinner finishes so late that all family members may simply rest at home afterward, chatting or listening to the radio while they finish last-minute chores. Then they turn in quickly, by ten or so if it is not too hot to get to sleep, for they know that they will have to be up the next morning before dawn for another very long day of work.

Dyadic Relationships within
the Family

Our discussion of the daily routine in Kwangtung villages tells us something about how family members relate to each other, but it still does not tell us much about the character and emotional tone of these relationships. Any changes in Kwangtung peasant families should be reflected in shifts in the character of the various dyadic relationships of which they are composed. We will focus on only four key dyads here: the relations between father and son, husband and wife, mother-in-law and daughter-in-law, and brother and brother.[10]

The existing literature presents a fairly consistent view of the general tenor of these dyads in the pre-1949 Chinese family, even though some particular points are in dispute.[11] The most important link within the family was generally that between father and son. The father had the obligation to raise his son and provide him with a wife and some inheritance, and the son in turn was obligated to show marked respect and subservience (filial piety) toward the father, support him in his old age, provide him with male descendants, and worship his spirit after death. From infancy onward the relationship was characterized by deference from the son, and some emotional distance, rather than by close companionship and open expression of affection. As the father got on in years he might gradually relinquish authority over day-to-day decisions to his son, but the grown son was still expected to consult his father and defer to the latter's demands and wishes.

The husband-wife relationship was colored by the predominant emphasis on the father-son dyad, as is often the case in peasant societies. The bride would, as we noted earlier, generally be a stranger from outside the village, marrying in by arrangement, rather than as a result of courtship and romantic involvement with her future husband. The bride's obligations within her new family were as much to her husband's family as to her husband himself: to willingly perform household chores under the direction of her mother-in-law, to defer to the authority of the father-in-law, and to provide the family with male heirs. The mother-in-law-daughter-in-law relationship is the one most often described in the literature as subject to exploitation and conflict, and in any case of dispute the husband was expected to side with his parents rather than his wife, and to demand the submission of the latter to familial authority, if necessary by the use of physical force. The husband and wife might over the years develop feelings of mutual affection and companionship, but in public, and even in front of other family members within the household, they were expected to refrain from any display of affection.

The tension and harsh treatment a woman sometimes received from her mother-in-law are reasons commonly cited for a woman running home to her parents or demanding division of the family. But by bearing children, especially sons, by showing proper obedience and diligence in performing household chores, and simply by children growing up and parents-in-law dying, a woman earned a secure place and much informal power within the family. Finally the marriage of her own son would bring into the family a younger woman she could dominate, as she herself had been dominated earlier in life.

Brothers were expected to support each other and to maintain family prestige in conflicts with the outside world, and the ideal was to have several married brothers all cooperating together under the father's direction (or even after his death) in maintaining the joint family economy. However, given the traditionally high rates of infant mortality, the majority of families could not hope to maintain this ideal. Older brothers were expected to be protective of their younger siblings, and younger brothers in turn were expected to show some deference toward older siblings. Underneath the cooperative veneer existed inevitable tensions, perhaps particularly in poorer families. If more than one son survived, family property would eventually be divided equally (or with a slight extra share for the oldest brother). Struggles over shares in family income and over future inheritance could produce simmering feelings of resentment. These were often regarded as being aggravated by conflicts between the various sisters-in-laws, whose jealousy over the position of their own nuclear units within the larger family led to squabbles with other women of the household, and sometimes to demands for family division even before the death of the family patriarch.

There are, of course, other dyads of potential interest, such as those betweeen mother and son, brother and sister, or grandparent and grandchild, but the ones we have already touched on are not only the most important but are the only ones about which we have much contemporary information from our interviews. We are interested in the following pages in seeing whether there has been much change in the content or tenor of these dyadic relationships. Official Chinese policy in regard to these relationships has already been noted briefly at the outset of this chapter. The ideal is a change away from the traditional patriarchal relationships toward a more egalitarian pattern of mutual help and respect. In particular, the subjugation of the young, especially of young brides, is supposed to change toward a pattern of close and cooperative relationships in which the voice of every family member is respected equally. This implies a change in both the importance and the character of the father-son tie and a closer and more important husband-wife tie. We are interested in seeing whether these expectations have been met in rural Kwangtung. We might note again that our peasant informants seem to be generally aware of these official ideals, but that no special campaigns or administrative efforts have been mounted to enforce compliance.

Fathers now do not train their sons for future work on the family farm (other than for the family's small private plot and for subsidiary economic activities), and sons in adulthood will spend most of their working hours in shifting labor groups under the supervision of people other than their fathers. As noted in Chapter 9, it is also common now for sons to divide from the family within a few years after marriage, rather than to try to remain together until the parents die (or at least the father does). But we have also noted that some contemporary influences reinforce the father-son tie. Sons for the most part stay at home working in the fields after they finish school, and they need the family's support and approval to marry and to build additional housing. In the limited-family private economy sons, while young, continue to receive orders and training from their fathers, and until the family division they expect their fathers to control their earnings and the uses to which those are put. (One informant referred to this control as a father's "iron abacus.") Most parents end up living with one son (often, but not necessarily, the youngest), and all sons bear responsibility for support of their parents in their declining years. The forces affecting this key relationship are complex.

Our male informants describe themselves as distant from, and even somewhat fearful of, their fathers. As we discuss more fully in the final section of this chapter, now as in the past fathers tend to become remote and severe in their dealings with their sons, and sons are rarely rebellious or disrespectful toward their fathers. Even as sons finish school and start agricultural work and then marry there is no sharp change in their relationship with their fathers. But a gradual change does occur as the father recognizes his son's growing maturity and responsibility by increasingly consulting him in financial and other decisions. The father is still the head of the family, and relations are not close or cordial, but the pattern of deference and discipline is gradually eased. A further easing occurs when the son divides his family from his father's. The grown son now manages his own family economy without direction from the father, although it is still considered proper for the father's advice to be sought on important matters. The two generations continue to live in close proximity, perhaps still in the same house (family division implies separate budgeting but not necessarily separate houses), and they continue to cooperate in matters like child care and constructing or renovating housing. Thus the relationship becomes a less hierarchical and more egalitarian one over time, although the independent son is still expected to show signs of respect for his parents, and especially for the father, even though he is no longer under their direct control.

In most localities this pattern of formalized respect combined with a more egalitarian power relationship is reported to continue up until the death of the father. But others report further changes once the father retires from field labor and becomes economically dependent upon his sons. It makes a difference whether the son is living in a stem family with the aged parents, or has formed an independent household earlier. For those sons who are still part of their father's household (and this includes almost all of those who are only sons) there are real authority issues involved. Some informants report cases of fathers who no longer work on the commune fields, but who still maintain close control over the family purse strings, perhaps until they die. Such fathers continue to demand respect and deference from the grown son and his family, even though the main income-earning power rests in the younger generation. But most fathers turn over control of the family funds to their grown sons, either gradually or when they themselves retire from full-time field labor (occasional or part-time field labor may continue until death for those who remain healthy). The aged father then becomes dependent upon both the labor and the decisions of his son, although he can continue to contribute to both through help on the private plot and through fatherly advice. Most such fathers continue to receive formalized respect from their sons, but our informants report a few cases of sons and their wives grumbling and complaining about having to support old folks and put up with their needs and moods. Such cases seem to be in the minority, however, since older relatives can assist in child care, domestic chores, private-plot work, and other activities. Sons who have divided their households from the parents at an earlier date do not face the problem of the aged as directly. They have to share in the economic support of their aged parents, but they do not have to respond to the daily needs and complaints of the old folks, cook them special food, and so forth. Thus the pattern of respect without subordination can be more easily maintained. At the same time their separation does not prevent them from benefiting from the child care and other help that old folks provide.

In sum, father-son relations become somewhat relaxed as the son matures, although they never become really close. Most sons continue to show respect for their parents even in their declining years although the actual power of their parents over them is not great. In most cases the relationship continues to be seen as a mutually beneficial and rewarding one. Support of even disabled parents is seen as a fairly automatic obligation, as it has always been in Chinese culture, and even those who resent the burden continue to bear it. There is no rebellion of the young or rejection of parents here, and probably the present nature of this dyad does not represent much of a change for most families. (In wealthy and powerful families the father was perhaps an autocratic patriarch in the past, but among the poor the same kind of softening of parental authority with age often took place.)[12]

A number of recent influences affect the character of the relationship between spouses. As we noted in Chapter 10, these days fewer couples than used to be the case start marriage without prior acquaintance. Although parents continue to play a major role in marriage decisions, increasing numbers of marriages in Kwangtung are of people from the same village and lineage, so that the new bride is less often a "stranger." The new wife's obligations are also altered somewhat, since she is expected to work regularly in the team's fields, rather than at home under her mother-in-law's direction. Still, she does in almost all cases start out married life in a household headed by her parents-in-law. Even those who take the initiative in choosing their own mates generally have not developed the close personal ties that would occur if more of a "dating culture" existed.

There are indications in our interviews of elements of both continuity and change in husband-wife relations. One thing that has changed little is the pattern of reserve between spouses. Husband and wife are expected not to display any affection for each other in public, and their activities outside of the family tend to be separate: the husband lounges and chats with his male peers, while the wife gathers with other village women. When they do go somewhere together (for example, to a brigade meeting or the local market) our informants report that they walk one before and one behind, rather than side by side (and certainly not hand in hand). In general there still seems to be a strong belief that spouses should preserve some emotional distance in public.

Perhaps the beginning of some move toward closer conjugal ties may be indicated by the kinship terms used between spouses. The traditional distance and reserve between spouses is reflected in some villages by the avoidance of using personal names in addressing each other. Either husband or wife will just start talking, assuming the partner will know he or she is being addressed. Or one will call out "wei!" (hey!) to attract the other's attention. However, the use of a mate's personal name is also common; in some villages this is done mostly among young couples, in others among couples of all ages. Addressing spouses by their personal names is not a totally new, or for that matter a revolutionary, development,[13] but it does seem to convey slightly more intimacy than the "no name" and "hey" forms of address.

Perhaps a clearer indication of change is visible in another set of terms, those spouses use in referring to each other when talking to third parties. There are three traditional sets of terms of reference which our informants report are still in common use: "my man" (wo ti nan-jen) and "my woman" (wo ti nü-jen), "my old man" (wo ti lao-kung) and "my old lady" (wo ti lao-p'o), and "X's father" and "X's mother" (where X is the name of their child). The personal name of one's spouse is not generally used in talking to a third party, and any one village may currently have several or even all of the above terms in common use. But there is one additional form of reference for a spouse that is becoming increasingly common: the officially espoused term "wo ai-jen" (my beloved), which is used by either mate in talking about the other. Some informants claim this term is not used in their village at all but is strictly an urban term. But in other villages (50 percent, N = 36) either young couples or even couples of all ages are reported to use this term (along with some traditional ones). The use of this term seems to symbolize greater mutuality and intimacy than the traditional terms, although admittedly at least in public behavior no dramatic shift toward more affectionate and close husband-wife contacts is visible. (Again, informants who had grown up in Canton or in other cities were surprised at the degree of distance shown between rural spouses when in public.)

Within the family we have already noted some continuing kinds of sexual inequality. Women continue to be burdened with most household chores in addition to their field labor. The husband is generally viewed as the family head and the main decision-maker. He tends to exercise ultimate authority on matters such as disciplining and educating children and on family finances, although in day-to-day affairs much of this authority is delegated to his wife. Even where the husband takes charge, however, there is generally considerable consultation and discussion with other adults in the family, including the wife. Husbands today have less control over property to support their authority, and need not be so concerned with keeping a large household together. The wife is expected to follow the will of her husband in important matters, but at the same time in most villages she is not required to make exaggerated displays of deference toward her spouse (for example, waiting to eat until after he has finished). The relationship today is clearly not one of real equality in terms of either power or domestic burdens, but neither is it one of husbands lording it over their wives in an autocratic fashion. Earlier accounts of village life in China differ in their picture of the husband's authority—in some cases he is shown as an absolute dictator, in others as a gatherer of family advice and opinion.[14] On balance the patriarchal features of the family seem to have softened slightly, although the husband is still clearly the head of the family.

Our informants vary in their descriptions of the amount of conflict between husbands and wives, and the frame of reference for their comments is often ambiguous. Some describe the relationship as quite amicable and cooperative, while others describe frequent arguments and even occasional beatings. We have already noted in Chapter 10 the variety of causes of marital conflict cited by our informants: finances, sexual infidelity, the discipline of children, in-law conflicts, and so forth. Most disputes between spouses are described as arising over "small issues" and then escalating into a verbal confrontation or fight, after which tempers cool and relations return to normal. Every village has a few cases, though, of spouses who are regularly at each other's throat. In severe conflicts the relatives and neighbors or even local cadres try to mediate, although there is a general feeling that marital conflicts are difficult to resolve, and it is best to let them work themselves out over time. The interest of all parties in maintaining the marriage seems to promote this gradual healing process, except in extreme disputes. Some husbands do beat their wives, but our informants do not convey the impression that this is widespread or frequent, or that it receives social approval. But while wives may not be seen as requiring periodic beatings, neither are the occasional wife-beaters hauled out by cadres for

criticism and punishment. Again, outsiders usually try to avoid getting involved and hope that the problem will blow over. In sum, we gain an
impression of spouses living in situations which are economically tight and
conflict-producing. Husband-wife ties do not seem as intense or openly
affectionate as in our own culture, and in the eyes of our urban informants
arguments and shouted rebukes among rural spouses are more common than
among urban spouses. But relations between husbands and wives still seem
on balance cooperative and generally amicable, with no clear or common
pattern of abuse and mistreatment of wives by their husbands. Again,
whether the current situation represents much change or little depends which
earlier account one reads.

As in accounts from pre-1949 villages, our informants report the mother-
in-law-daughter-in-law dyad as the most frequent source of family disputes.
The mother-in-law may get angry at her son's wife because she is not doing
enough of the housework, because she complains about how the old lady is
treating the children, because she takes food gifts and goes to visit her natal
family too often, or simply because she does not show enough respect
toward the husband's parents. One of our informants gives the following
picture:

> The most frequent arguments are between the mother-in-law and
> daughter-in-law. This is because this pair is together more than husband
> and wife, and it is easier for conflicts to arise. This happens because the
> older woman tries to control everything and tries to be very strict. The
> younger woman chafes under this control. This is the most common and
> obvious reason.[15]

The daughter-in-law usually has her own complaints: that the older woman is
not doing enough of the housework, is not supervising the children properly,
talks too much, or simply nags the daughter-in-law too often. As in the past,
many of our informants mention this type of conflict as the immediate cause
of many family divisions, with wives complaining and urging their husbands
to set up a separate household. (We note that our informants do not give as
prominent a place as do past accounts to conflicts between sisters-in-law,
since most couples now divide the family relatively soon after marriage,
generally before or as soon as another brother gets married.)

Our informants see this type of conflict as being handled when both
women go out of their way to help in domestic chores, and when the younger
woman shows some respect for and humors the quirks of the older woman.
And in fact some informants do mention that in the majority of families

harmonious and cooperative relations usually reign, with neither woman trying to establish absolute dominance and to subordinate the other. But even where there is frequent conflict we do not receive the impression that new wives are expected to serve their mothers-in-law like domestic slaves until they demonstrate their son-bearing abilities; the obligation and income-earning potential of the wife's labor on the team's field are accepted. Since those in the parental generation control less property today than in the past, they cannot as easily hold it over the younger couple; and if relations are strained the mother-in-law may be able to move in with another son. This remains a conflict-prone dyad, but in today's conflicts the young wife seems to be in a stronger position than in the past.

One especially critical question in comparing the strength of the husband-wife bond with the bond between the husband and his parents concerns what stand a man takes when his wife and his mother fight. We have already mentioned the traditional expectation, reinforced by community opinion, that the man should side with his mother, and should demand the submission of his wife. Is this the case now? This is an area in which substantial change appears to have taken place, although our evidence is fragmentary. Only 20 percent of our informants (N = 25) say the husband will support his mother in such a conflict, and even some of these claim this is due less to a feeling that it is the man's filial obligation to do so than to a recognition that the mother is old and set in her ways, while the wife can more easily adapt and accept defeat. At the same time only 24 percent say that the husband will generally side with his wife. The remainder (56 percent) say that the husband will not automatically take either side. There are two strategies mentioned. The husband may try to mediate the dispute from a neutral position. Several informants mentioned in this context the officially sponsored norm of "supporting the one in the right, rather than supporting the one most closely related to you" (pang-li pu pang-ch'in). The other strategy is to leave the scene of the fray; husbands often try to avoid getting drawn into the conflict. What this pattern suggests is not the replacement of the parent-son tie by the husband-wife tie, but rather a balancing of two equally important relationships. In contrast with accounts of traditional villages the husband-wife tie clearly has gained in strength and importance, but in most localities it is balanced against, rather than clearly superseding, the ties between a man and his parents.

We have noted in the preceding pages that there is a substantial variation from village to village in the reported nature of husband-wife ties. We have tried to classify villages in our sample in two respects: whether village husbands will reportedly support their mothers, remain neutral, or support their wives in the case of a mother-in-law-daughter-in-law dispute; and whether the term "ai-jen" is absent or used by at least some couples in the village. We can examine in table 39 whether these classifications are related in any systematic way to characteristics of our villages.

First, we note that these two crude measures of husband-wife ties are not closely related to one another; the relationship is in fact negative, with couples slightly less likely to use the term "ai-jen" in villages in which husbands are reported to side with their wives in disputes. Given this pattern and the small numbers involved in most associations in table 39, we cannot expect to make sweeping conclusions about where conjugal intimacy is developing most rapidly.

The item concerning whom the husband sides with in a dispute follows a fairly consistent pattern, although the number of villages for which we have data is small. The husband is reported more likely to side with his wife rather than with his mother in villages which are distant from Canton or Swatow,

Table 39		Husband-Wife Relations by Village Characteristics (Gamma Statistics)	
	Supports wife	"Ai-jen"	Median N
Husband-wife relations			
Husband supports wife (versus mother)	--		
Use of "ai-jen"	-.44	--	
Administrative			
Political density	.32	-.18	(30)
Political study	-.08	-.62*	(28)
Urban-communications			
Urban proximity	-.72*	-.31	(29)
Urban youths	-.78	-.54	(22)
Communications	-.31	-.12	(29)
Nurseries	-.94*	.23	(29)
Economic			
Collective affluence	-.51	.24	(29)
Household consumption	-.10	-.60*	(29)
Land/labor ratio	.11	-.45	(27)
Remittances	.18	-.30	(21)
Other			
Brigade size	.37	.41	(25)
Team size	-.48	-.28	(30)
Lineage composition	-.09	.02	(30)
Non-Hakka ethnicity	-.69*	-.15	(31)
Delta region	-.32	-.22	(31)
Median N	(24)	(34)	

*p ≤ .10

have poor collective economies, are composed of Hakkas, and lack nurseries and sent-down youths.[16] Clearly this pattern does not fit a notion that either economic development or communications and urban contacts promote stronger husband-wife ties. We also did not find, contrary to our original expectations, that men were more likely to side with their mothers in brigades composed of a single lineage (see the lineage-composition associations). We suppose that the pattern we found is attributable to the fact that in poor, isolated, relatively uncommercialized villages, parents before 1949 and still today have fewer resources with which to motivate obedience from sons than is the case in well-off suburban villages. The final item dealing with the use of the term "ai-jen" follows a somewhat similar pattern. Couples are most likely to use the officially approved term "ai-jen" in villages which lack regular political study routines, are removed from urban influences (especially sent-down youths), have poor household consumption patterns and land-labor ratios (but relatively large brigades). Here Hakka villages are not especially likely to use the term "ai-jen." Again prosperity, communications, and urban contacts do not seem to be associated with the adoption of this "modern" term, and this finding is especially surprising since "ai-jen" is clearly a term whose use is more widespread in urban areas and whose dissemination is fostered by official communications media. Perhaps this is an indication that officially espoused terms and concepts can only be expected to "take" when local conditions favor them, and local conditions which foster the use of the term "ai-jen" (for example, a lack of resources monopolized by parents) may be absent in those villages which are most fully exposed to communications and urban contacts. This pattern throws into doubt the notion that the diffusion of "modern" ideas about family life is a crucial factor in the changing husband-wife relationship.

Our informants differ on how close brothers tend to be nowadays, but the modal response is that this relationship is "ordinary," that is, neither especially close nor especially marked by conflict. In the words of one informant:

> The relations of brothers are captured by the common saying "When young they are two brothers, when grown they are two different households." They don't say brothers are like an arm and a leg together, or other expressions of closeness. As far as I could see, in the entire village there were only two or three cases of grown brothers who had close, mutual-aid relationships.[17]

Brothers are expected to protect each other and to stand up for the family honor in fights with other children, but for the most part they play in separate age-graded groups, rather than together. An older brother may, of course, be assigned to baby-sit for his younger siblings, and adolescent brothers will work together under the father's direction in the family private economy and contribute their earnings to the general family pot. But they do not remain a cooperating unit in a single household for long after they marry. After the division from the parental family, each married brother depends mainly on the efforts of his immediate family to do well, and brothers may differ in household income fairly markedly.

At the same time inheritance is less of a problem than it used to be. Inheritance involves housing, furniture, tools, and consumer durables, but not the commodity which used to be so vital—land. (At the time of family division the private-plot lands are divided up, but this is not land that can be bought and sold, and the team controls this division.) When family property is divided, the traditional principle of equal division among sons still applies, and our informants do report some examples of conflicts between brothers, particularly over housing (which, as we have noted, is still privately built and owned). But anxiety over future property shares does not seem to color the relationship betweeen brothers in most families. As each brother divides his family from the parental home, his share of housing and other property is discussed and agreed upon by the family, with other kin or in rare cases even with team cadres mediating any disputes. So brothers cooperate in certain limited ways (for example, in the support of aged parents), but they often have more frequent interaction with other males in the village, and at the same time there is less likelihood now of protracted and bitter fraternal disputes over property. This, then, seems to be the basis of the "ordinary" quality of the relationship today. It seems that the collectivization of agricultural land has removed some of the most important causes of both cooperation and conflict among brothers.

We have now reviewed four major dyadic relationships in the contemporary Kwangtung peasant family and are in a position to make some limited generalizations. One problem in an analysis of this type is that there are a number of different elements which can contribute to the "importance" of any particular dyadic bond: a sense of obligation or indebtedness, affection, close interaction and cooperation, shared values, and no doubt other factors. Weighing the importance of one tie against another or examining descriptions of a single relationship at different periods in time may be like comparing apples and oranges. Our generalizations must therefore have a tentative quality.

We have in the preceding pages observed important elements of continuity in family relations: the reserve between spouses in public, the distance maintained in father-son relations, the unequal power and burdens of husbands and wives, and respect for the aged, to mention only a few. But we feel we also detect a few important changes: a somewhat closer relationship between spouses, less subordination of the wife to her mother-in-law and perhaps of sons to fathers, and a more "ordinary" relationship among brothers. To return once again to our main point of focus, we want to stress that the husband-wife tie has not become the sort of intimate and mutual bond that it often is in American families, and it is even debatable whether there is as much sharing of domestic chores and consultation over decisions between husbands and wives as there is in this country. But at the same time the importance of the conjugal tie within the family has increased, while the hierarchical nature of the parent-son tie has moderated somewhat. Future research will have to investigate whether the current situation of husbands balancing their obligations to their parents and to their spouses is a stable one, or whether the conjugal tie and the interests of the immediate nuclear unit will continue to gain strength while the ties between parents and grown sons weaken.

The Socialization of Children

Traditionally, children were reared primarily within the family and learned adult roles gradually under the direction of parents and other adults. Only a minority of rural youths, primarily males, were exposed to any period of formal training in a nonfamilial setting, either in rural schools or as apprentices to merchants and craftsmen. Within the family, traditional descriptions convey a picture of an indulgent and affectionate early childhood followed, particularly for males, by a sharp change toward demanding and austere discipline in preparation for adult responsiblities. In rural schools and in the home the virtues of absolute obedience to parents and other family elders were stressed, and disobedient children received physical punishment as a corrective. Some authorities feel that this pattern of early indulgence followed by authoritarian severity produced a distinctive set of Chinese personality traits: a craving for order and discipline in interpersonal relationships and a desire to be subordinate to a strong authority figure. But those who stress the importance of early socialization for adult personality, and who describe a conflict between traditional Chinese character and the activist style of the Maoist revolutionary ethos, fail to consider whether or how methods of childrearing are changing in China today.[18] We can present the beginnings of such an examination in the pages that follow. We are interested, in particular, in whether the role of rural parents in childrearing is being significantly reduced in comparison with former times, and in whether the tactics parents use in raising and disciplining their children show any signs of change.

Official Chinese Communist ideals in the area of childrearing include a number of elements. First, collective child-care facilities (nurseries and kindergartens) are to be more widely available, and formal education through at least primary schooling is to be universalized, as noted in Chapter 6. The latter goal receives much more stress than the former, however, and authorities seem quite willing to live with a situation in which most preschoolers are cared for by their families.[19] While much early child-care remains within the home, official media do try to encourage changes in the way parents rear their children. Corporal punishment is strongly disapproved of, and for more than a generation parents have been advised (as have readers of American women's magazines and child-care manuals) that "persuasive education" is much more effective in training children.[20] Parents are expected to prepare their children for adult roles, but now this should entail less emphasis on obedience to parents and more emphasis on larger societal obligations. Parents should not keep their children at home to help with the chores when they should be in school or engaging in political or other activities, and parents are not expected to try to enforce old ways on children who have been exposed to new and different ideas outside of the family. But, as noted earlier, young people are still encouraged to respect their parents (providing they have not committed a serious political error), to help them with household chores, and to support them in their old age. Thus a somewhat milder form of parental authority is supposed to replace the filial piety and obedience, enforced by beatings, which were characteristic of an earlier era. Again, no special campaigns have been aimed at changing patterns of childrearing, although these official ideals have been widely disseminated. Although most of our interview material on childrearing in rural Kwangtung focuses on structures and behavioral patterns, rather than on the attitudes and values being transmitted (due to the methodological constraints discussed in Appendix 1), we can still get some idea from these materials of the extent of change and persistence in the rearing of children.

As we have noted, most mothers in Kwangtung villages work regularly in the production-team fields, and after childbirth they resume work after about a month, although often they are assigned at first to light jobs which do not take them far from home. In our sample, village nurseries and kindergartens are the exception, rather than the rule, being present in only 19 percent of the villages for which we have information. In Chapter 4 we noted that these institutions are almost completely confined to large and wealthy areas in the Pearl River Delta region. Even where they exist they are reported to be more like group baby-sitting arrangements than moral training institutions. In other words they do not present a radically different and, say, highly politicized environment for child care when compared with the family. One woman who was a kindergarten attendant in 1968 describes the scene:

> Children were crying all the time. When all collected in one place they got bored, but once you let them out they would run away and you would have to spend your time chasing them down. There was just one room for the nursery and not many toys or books. This village kindergarten was really very different from the city kindergartens. It was only occasionally that we could try to teach them songs. The children from age three to six were all together. There was no separation by level as in the city. Primarily the children were just rounded up [kuan-ch'i-lai le] while their parents went out to work. To the peasants the goal in life is just to grow up so one can start working and producing more food. Unlike in the city, there is no schedule of activities. Things just happened.[21]

Also, even where nurseries and kindergartens exist, only a portion of the local population uses them, with others caring for their children at home. In the bulk of the villages in our sample, where there are no nurseries at all, a variety of ways are found to care for the young children while allowing their mothers to work in the fields. The most common is for the paternal grandmother (or, less often, the grandfather) to serve as baby-sitter during the day. The mother nurses the infant when she comes home for meals, and at other times a hungry child is carried out to the fields by the grandmother, to be nursed there by the mother. (Bottle-feeding has made few inroads. Nurseries make similar arrangements to facilitate nursing.) If no grandparents are available, an older woman in the neighborhood may serve as a baby-sitter, usually for pay. One or two work points per day are taken out of the earnings of the mother and transferred to this woman's account in the team's books. Another common arrangement already mentioned is for an older sibling, most often a sister, to watch the infant during the day. In some cases this is a sibling as young as six or seven, but some parents have a child delay the start of schooling until eight or nine or later to help out (or pressure a daughter to drop out of school before graduation). The Chinese press has proclaimed that children should be allowed to bring their infant siblings to school with them, in spite of the distraction this may cause, in order to promote universal attendance while not interfering with family-assigned child-care duties.[22] In our sample of villages this idea has not been vigorously promoted, and some youths still stay out of school rather than take their infant charges to class with them.

When neither nurseries, grandparents, nor older siblings are available, and use of a neighbor is unacceptable for one reason or another, the mother has to cope as best she can by herself. In some localities she carries the infant in a baby carrier into the fields as she works, or places the baby under a nearby bush, although obviously neither arrangement allows her to work as well as women not so encumbered. Finally, in some places carrying a child out into the fields "is not the custom," and a few mothers stay at home and out of the work force until the infant is weaned and mobile.

The earliest years of life for the child seem, as in the past,[23] to be relatively pleasant. The infant receives a great amount of attention and has its needs attended to on demand, while few constraints are placed upon it. Most of the attention comes from the womenfolk of the family: the mother, grandmother, and older sisters. Fathers are described as occasionally holding and even playing with infants, things they rarely do with older children. Weaning is begun around the age of one year, or slightly before, and seems to be relatively gradual, with solid foods increasingly replacing the mother's milk. Some children are not weaned until about two years old, and there are unusual cases of children who, because of health problems, are allowed to continue to nurse to supplement their solid food up to the age of four or five. Toilet training is, by American standards, even more relaxed, as it has traditionally been in China. Up until the age of four or five, children wear traditional trousers with a split crotch, and in the summer they are allowed to run around naked. They are expected to squat whenever and wherever they feel the urge, even in the house, and the family dog is called over the dispose of the mess. A few drops of water on the packed earth or concrete block floors is an additional sanitary measure. At around the age of four or five, children begin to be urged by their parents to focus their squatting in the local latrines, but even then the change is enforced gradually and patiently. There is, of course, considerable doubt today among Western social scientists about whether the timing and severity of the training in these basic bodily functions is as crucial for later personality development as it was once thought to be.[24] But if such training has a formative influence, we can detect little change in our data from the patterns described for pre-1949 China. Kwangtung peasants do not seem to be weaning and toilet training their children earlier or more abruptly than they used to, nor are they being urged by the cadres or the mass media to do so. Such matters are left up to the family.

The life of the toddler in our villages seems to be one of lax supervision but fairly harsh discipline. Once children are weaned and able to get around on their own, they are not kept at home but are allowed to roam and play about the village. Their parents have little time to supervise them during the day, and grandparents and older siblings will not be able to keep detailed track of all their wanderings. It is thus a relatively carefree period but also a potentially dangerous one, since it is not difficult for a toddler to get hurt or to fall in a local pond and drown.[25] But when toddlers are disobedient or get into trouble, parents or other caretakers are strict in a traditional sense. Spanking (ta) and scolding (ma) are the mainstays of discipline, and some informants even claim these are the only techniques used to discipline children. A naughty child is yelled at, cuffed on the ear or rear, or beaten with a bamboo rod. There seems to be little reliance on the techniques of persuasion, praise, or withdrawal of love which are favored by child-care authorities in both China and America. The Chinese government's campaign since the early 1950s against corporal punishment of children may have reduced reliance on this tactic in urban areas and even in rural schools, but apparently not in homes in rural Kwangtung. The sent-down urban youths among our informants were surprised and even shocked by the heavy reliance on physical punishment in rural homes. They saw this reliance on scolding and spanking as a result of the low educational level and general lack of sophistication of rural parents. But they also mentioned the heavy work burdens of peasants, which leave them with little time or patience for lengthy persuasion and explanation sessions.

What kinds of naughtiness are most feared by Chinese parents? Our respondents claim that parents are most worried about fighting and stealing. Stealing might be either from the collective (fruit from the brigade orchard) or from other families (vegetables from a private plot). A child caught stealing from the collective might cause a public reprimand to be given to his parents for not rearing the child better, while stealing from another family could provoke an interfamily feud. The latter seems to be a source of greater anxiety, although this is only a rough impression. Fighting with other children poses similar dangers. When we asked for examples of conflicts between families, the most common response was to mention cases where one child beat up another, the latter's father intervened or retaliated, and the affair escalated into a shouting match or even a physical fight between the two sets of parents. The most feared kinds of misbehavior, then, are the ones that can lead to conflicts between families, rather than, say, acts which violate abstract moral standards or harm socialist property. Kwangtung peasants live and work in close contact and cooperation with their neighbors, and now as in the past parents are extremely anxious to protect the harmonious relationships they have with others. Indeed, one could argue that the collectivization of agriculture has made harmonious relations more important than before, since family income is now more dependent on cooperation with neighbors. So not only the techniques of discipline but the acts which are punished most severely show strong elements of continuity with the past.[26]

Any older member of the family can discipline a child; however, our informants felt that the main burden of discipline falls on the mother, in spite of her busy work schedule. When team labor is completed, the mother spends most of her time doing domestic work around the house, while the husband is off working on the private plot or resting the chatting with neighboring menfolk. At such times it is mainly the mother who watches the children; she scolds or spanks them for misbehavior, and it is to her that children come with their questions and problems. As the children grow older, especially as they approach school age, the father tends to become more remote and harsh in his relations with them, a shift which is commented upon in the literature on Chinese childrearing before 1949. Both consciously and unconsciously fathers strive to encourage respect from their children, and even fear. In the words of one of our informants,

> My children are scared of me, so I can get them to behave easily. Most children are scared of their father, but not of their mother. Fathers are strict—they don't say much, and they believe the strong, silent treatment is best. They don't often lose their tempers and curse, though, or the child would get used to it. If the mother spanks the child and he cries, the father will say, "Why are you crying? Stop that crying!" And the child will stop. Fathers are more venerable [tsun], while mothers are more sympathetic [ts'e]. Fathers rarely joke with children or play with them. No father would play ping-pong with his child—we just don't have that custom![27]

The father is the ultimate disciplinarian in the family, and he will intervene in cases of major misbehavior, although for lesser matters he leaves things in the hands of the mother. Since village children still spend a great deal of time at home doing tasks for the family, parental discipline remains highly salient in their lives.

Grandparents and older siblings also discipline the child, particularly when the parents are out at work. When the parents are at home, however, they usually take charge, and we have noted that some disputes between the mother and the grandmother center on how strictly or leniently the other woman is disciplining the children. Other kin and neighbors do not play an important role in child discipline, as this would again threaten village harmony.

The techniques and style of family discipline (as opposed to the attitudes passed on, about which we have less information) in comtemporary Kwangtung villages do not seem markedly different today from the picture we have of China in earlier days, or of Taiwan today. The main burden of rearing children is clearly still centered in the home, and team, brigade, and commune authorities do not seem to pay much attention to how children are being reared and do not generally give advice or intervene. Only in an extreme case—a father beating a child so badly as to seriously injure or kill it—do our informants report commune authorities taking action against parents. (This might be judged an instance of change, since published sources tell us that before 1949 parents had the de facto power to beat or even kill a child without suffering official penalties.)[28] Again, social scientists are no longer certain how crucial for later personality development the earliest six years or so of life are, but insofar as these years have a crucial formative role it seems that the "new men" (and women) in Kwangtung villages will have to be created on the basis of a fairly traditional early childhood.

Children begin helping around the house at an early age. Some children as young as five or six help to feed the family fowl and clean house, and in a few villages they are even reported as helping to prepare meals at this age. As they get older, particularly after they start school, they take on heavier tasks: hauling water from a stream or well, feeding the animals, cooking, doing laundry, tending younger siblings, and helping with the private plot. The sexual division of labor we have already described emerges at this time, although it is not yet rigid and sharp. In a few villages boys and girls are reported to do equal amounts of domestic labor, but in the large majority girls are reported to bear the heavier burden. Girls are felt to be naturally more obedient and responsible, while boys are seen as somewhat mischievous and unruly.

The labor provided by the children is quite important to the family economy, as noted in Chapter 9. By aiding with child care and other duties and by earning a few work points from the team, youngsters can begin to contribute to the family economy long before the normal age for beginning full-time labor (normally sixteen). For this reason there are economic pressures on poor parents to keep their children out of school. In recent years a liberalization of rural school regulations has eliminated the upper age limit for starting primary school, thus making it possible for parents to delay sending a child to school without forfeiting his or her chance to an education later, although over time there is clearly an upward trend in enrollments, as noted in Chapter 6. Even after children start school they may attend irregularly, responding to the changing pressures of work at home, or may drop out early. The shortening of academic careers is more common for girls than boys, which reflects the greater value placed on the labor of daughters while they are young, even though eventually it will be the sons who will be the main income earners. School and brigade cadres respond to these problems by sending teachers to peasant homes to encourage them to get their children to attend school, and for poor families, by waiving the tuition charged by rural schools. But the major economic consequence of children attending school is not the cost of tuition but the lost labor the children could provide, and teachers and cadres cannot easily answer the claim of poor peasants that they need to keep their children at home to help out. Rural schools also try to accommodate themselves to these problems by not scheduling extensive extracurricular activities; it is assumed that children after school have to go home to help out their families. School authorities, in fact, support familial obligations by presenting stories and model examples of students who are diligent in performing household chores.

The normal age for entering school is seven, and we noted in Chapter 6 that most brigades in Kwangtung have a primary school, often with attached lower middle-school classes as well. Especially in recent years, then, children have been able to attend through lower middle school while living at home. Only in order to attend upper middle school do they have to leave home, generally to board at a school in the commune town. Since in most villages 90 percent or so of the young people go to primary school (although they may start at a later age than seven, and not all continue through graduation), while only a small minority of students go on to upper middle school, for most rural youths getting an education does not mean leaving the local community and the influence of, and responsibility toward, the family.

Still, the change from the pre-1949 situation in which less than a majority of rural males and few rural females received an education to the current pattern in which virtually all youths of both sexes receive some schooling is clearly a major one. In the pages that follow we will consider whether the nature of this widely available rural schooling conflicts with the training youths receive in the home and if the schooling is experienced by parents as a threat. We do not have very extensive information about the content of rural education or about how rural teachers see their role; we can say something about the role rural parents feel schools have in rearing their children. Some discussions of schooling in China and other "totalitarian" societies give a picture of schools as the primary locus of the state's battle with parents for the minds of their children. Schools present young people with a new set of ideas and values that conflict with those held by their parents: loyalty to the state and the party, sexual equality, political activism, atheism, and so forth. Over time the younger generation is won over and may even begin to proselytize the new values within the family, or report on the traditional behavior and values of family members, thus causing a loss of influence and great fear and anguish for the parents.

The testimony we get from our rural informants does not square with this sort of picture. Rural schools are not viewed as Trojan horses, introducing strange new values into the community and the home. Instead they are viewed primarily as institutions where useful knowledge is transmitted, particularly basic skills in reading, writing, and arithmetic. In recent years rural schools have been required to orient their curricula more toward agricultural training than was formerly the case, but our informants felt that young people learned how to farm by doing it and observing others, not by formal instruction inside or outside of the classroom. Schools are also supposed to be a major source of moral and ideological training, but the emphasis on such training does not seem to be very threatening to parents. Some of the moral training that is carried out in the school, in fact, reinforces themes stressed in the home—discipline, hard work, cooperativeness, avoidance of fighting, and so forth. Schools also teach children the basic terms and ideas of Maoist political culture, but these seem to be regarded by parents as "useful knowledge" much like the three Rs, since success in later life will require familiarity with the political catechism of contemporary China. In this respect parents in Chinese villages seem like the adaptive and future-oriented parents in the Soviet Union of an earlier era, as described by Inkeles.[29] We heard no tales of young people coming home and criticizing their parents on the basis of new values learned in school, or reporting on their parents or criticizing them publicly to the authorities, although such cases are sometimes mentioned in the Chinese press.[30] Our informants gave varying judgments about whether young people today are more disrespectful toward their parents than they used to be "in the old days," but even those who detected such a change attributed it more to the busy work schedules of rural parents than to the corrosive influence of new values learned in the school. Most of our informants judged that there had not been any particular decline in the amount of respect youths show to older people (67 percent, N = 33, gave this general response). So on balance we see little evidence that the parents sense rural schools as rivals or threats.

Parents are relatively uninvolved in the schoolwork of their children, and in many cases they would be ill equipped to offer advice and guidance, since they may have had little or no schooling themselves. Schools do make efforts to develop close ties with families through two separate practices: the parents' meeting at the school (not too different from such meetings in our own culture), and the teacher's home visits (an institution modelled on Soviet practice).[31] Actually, in our accounts the parents' meetings are few and far between, and parents rarely go the the school to inquire about their children's progress. The teacher's home visits, however, are considerably more regular—usually once per term at least, and more often to the homes of children with particular problems in school. In such visits the teacher reports on the schoolwork and behavior of the student over the recent period, praising the progress and asking the parents' help in correcting deficiencies. The primary goal seems to be to encourage parents to provide the proper conditions in the home to support school learning. These visits are not seen by parents as an intrusion but either in a neutral light or as a welcome opportunity to find out how the children are doing. Since at least some of the teachers come from the local area, or have been recruited from among sent-down urban youths who have lived in the village for a few years, they need not be seen as hostile outsiders. In spite of these practices, however, it is our impression that the ties between home and school are not particularly close. The instruction in the school and the character training in the home go on without much apparent conflict or intimate connection. One of the most important sources of nonfamilial influence in our own culture, the student peer group, seems to be relatively unimportant for those who do not go beyond lower middle school. As mentioned before, rural schools do not organize extensive extracurricular activities, and youths have little free time to play with their peers after school. Much of their free time is spent, not in the company of friends from school, but at home helping with the chores, or doing miscellaneous jobs for the production team.

In sum, the picture we get of the role of schooling in rural Kwangtung is as follows. Schooling provides useful knowledge (political as well as academic) but not things which are absolutely indispensable for later life as a farmer. Therefore some parents feel they can delay or shorten the school careers of their children in order to cope with family economic problems, without fear that the young people's futures will be ruined. Insofar as moral and character training are carried out in school, they are seen as largely congruent with such training in the home, rather than in conflict with it, although it is not entirely clear to what extent this is due to the adaptive behavior of parents in accepting new values and to what extent to the accommodating measures taken by teachers to support family authority. Parents see some value in the kinds of knowledge children learn in school, and they do not see schools as sources of hostile ideas or places where their children are weaned away from family loyalty and obligations. Thus there seems to be some division of labor between the school and the family in childrearing, but relatively little of the conflict over the control of young minds which the "totalitarianism" concept presupposes.

Most of the things we have been saying about rural education do not apply with equal force to those who go on to upper middle school. These students do generally live away from home, visiting only on weekends and holidays and developing more of an active peer-group life. Yet even the upper middle school does not ordinarily serve as a route toward independence from the family. Graduates, it would appear, generally return to their villages (and homes) to farm, rather than going on to higher schooling or urban jobs. (They are termed "hui-hsiang" or "returned-to-the-village" youths.) The restrictions we have previously noted on migration to the cities and direct admission to universities, and the as yet small employment role played by rural small industries, insure that more rural youths remain in the village after their education than is generally the case in other developing or industrialized societies. Many of the specialized positions that make use of skills learned in school are ones that do not require departure from the village— jobs as team or brigade accountants, barefoot doctors, primary-school teachers, and so forth. In general, then, rural schools do not appear as serious competitors with the families for the minds of young people, and they also do not represent a major threat to family loyalty and obligations by providing an independent route to future jobs.

In the preceding pages we have been presenting evidence for our view that the new institutional arrangements in the Kwangtung countryside have not dramatically altered either the predominant role of the family in childrearing, or the ties and obligations young people have toward their parents. Further light on the strength of these ties comes from examining a traditional institution which still exists in a number of our villages: the youth house. In at least eight villages in our sample,[32] mainly in the Pearl River Delta region, this interesting institution still exists, although under a number of different names—most often youth house (ch'ing-nien-chien), or male room (nan-wu-tzu) and female room (nü-wu-tzu). Vacant houses or sheds in the village are turned over for use as youth houses. Adolescent youths of each sex move out of the parental home and into a male house or a female house (the institution is not coeducational), and where the custom exists most youths follow it. A village may therefore have several youth houses for each sex, and young people live there with their peers until they marry. The historical origins and reasons for this institution are not clear to us, and our informants simply report that "it is the custom." (We are not aware of a similar custom in other parts of China.)[33] To the cynical Western mind these youth houses seem to offer opportunities for youthful rebellion and experimentation in gambling, sex, and other kinds of behavior disapproved of by both traditional and revolutionary morality. But our informants deny that this is the case. When youths move out into these houses they remain within the village, under the watchful eyes of both parents and other villagers. They continue to help with the chores at home, they generally eat at home, and their earnings from the team are turned over to their parents. In most cases, then, the youth house is little more than a place to chat and spend the night, and obligations and ties to families are not significantly reduced. After marriage males return to live with their parents (and females move to the homes of their in-laws), without any apparent adjustment problems due to this interval of youthful "freedom." Thus institutional arrangements which to the Western eye seem to provide potential conflict with parental control over the young are not completely new in rural Kwangtung, but now as in the past not much actual conflict results, and strong family ties and obligations continue.[34]

We have argued here that children below the age of seven or so seem to be reared in ways that have not changed very much since 1949. Clearly, beyond the age of seven more changes are apparent. But we have also argued that the expansion of formal education has made less of a difference in the lives and orientations of rural young people than one might think. School authorities take pains not only to avoid conflict with familial authority but to stress values that parents strongly approve of: hard work, discipline, harmonious relationships with others, and helpfulness around the home. Rural schools do not seem to have been affected much by the disrespect for authority and lack of discipline reported in urban schools in recent years. Policies affecting education and the graduates of schools, particularly in recent years, have the effect of orienting people toward returning to their villages and their families after graduation, rather than escaping to the city.

When all of this is said, it still must be acknowledged that there remains potential for conflict between the school and the family over some of the ideas and values stressed by the school. Students do hear sexual equality espoused in the schools while observing the continuing inequalities affecting rural women, and they do learn the tenets of scientific atheism while observing fellow villagers worshipping the ancestors and other spirits. But still the result does not seem to be frequent or sharp conflict or parental hostility to schools. Perhaps this can be attributed to this type of conflict not being a new phenomenon in Chinese history. For centuries rural schools taught Confucian rationalism while the village environment sustained folk magic and mysticism.[35] Individuals and communities seem able to compartmentalize things in such a way that new ideas can be accepted and accommodated without, for the most part, weakening traditional notions about family loyalty and obligation or, for that matter, the critical role in childrearing that the family still plays.

The discussion in the preceding pages makes it clear that one of our potential directed-change mechanisms from Chapter 2 is based on a misleading premise. The reliance on child socialization as a mechanism for social change assumes that dramatic changes have taken place in this realm since 1949, changes which are producing young people with very different personalities and values who will participate in the remaking of the larger society. We argue here that for rural Kwangtung this assumption is unfounded. Changes have occurred, but much about the nature of childrearing, and particularly the role of the family in childrearing, appears relatively unchanged. Socialization does not, of course, end with childhood, particularly in China. Throughout their adult lives Kwangtung peasants will be exposed to a variety of influences designed to change their attitudes and values: from the mass media, movie and drama teams, political campaigns, and so forth. But these change efforts will be aimed at people who in their preschool and school years have not had to make sharp reorientations away from the kinds of expectations and obligations placed on young people by their families in previous generations.

In family relations in general the picture we get is one of a great deal of carry-over from the pre-1949 period. The position of the wife in disputes is somewhat stronger now, a new term (meaning "beloved") for one's spouse has gained some acceptance, the authority of older family members has softened somewhat, access to formal education has been greatly expanded, and so forth. But much of what we have described here involves persistence: for example, in the domestic burdens of women, in the reserve between spouses in public, and in the pattern of early indulgence followed by stern demands and frequent spankings in rearing children. Long-standing regional and ethnic differences in family roles are also still clearly visible. Certainly part of this persistence is attributable to official policy never having given great priority to the attempt to enforce changes in relationships within families; press stories frequently deal with this topic, but there is little official pressure, and local cadres do not act against child-spankers or husbands who do no household chores. Where changes are visible they are not concentrated in those villages which have the strongest political infrastructures or which are most accessible to communications and urban contacts. This pattern suggests that other factors besides the government's ability to disseminate and enforce new family norms are involved in this mixed pattern of persistence and change in family relationships. Changes in the internal order of the family have depended on such province-wide phenomena as the collectivization of agriculture, the mobilization of women as full-time laborers, the shortage of nursery schools, official restrictions on mobility, and the decline of joint households; and on such village-specific factors as whether or not aged parents have traditionally had strong financial resources with which to maintain their authority.

12

The Changing Role of Women

Our aim in this chapter is to draw together in one place the impressions we have gained of the changing role of women in rural Kwangtung, and to speculate upon the meaning and explanation of those impressions.

We have noted a variety of ways in which the position of women relative to men prior to 1949 was an inferior one.[1] Women had very little in the way of property rights, they were supposed to subordinate themselves to men all of their lives (to fathers, husbands, and sons), they had limited economic and social roles outside the home (especially in wealthier classes), they received little education, and they were sometimes subjected to child marriages, concubinage, infanticide, and miserable marriages—conditions from which women had few escapes. The picture is not all black, since women sometimes received an education and achieved public prominence,[2] poor women played vital economic roles, and most women had a powerful influence within the household and, indirectly, within the larger village community. Particularly as women aged, their authority increased while, according to some authorities, that of their husbands waned, so that for all intents and purposes some older women ruled the family roost.[3]

Nonetheless, reformers of every stripe in early twentieth-century China demanded an end to the subjugation of women, and considered that subjugation an intimate part of the evils of Confucian family relations that had to be changed for China to enter the modern world. One who held this view was

Mao Tse-tung, one of whose earliest writings dealt with the misery of women forced into marriages against their will.[4] At various times after that Mao returned to the theme that Chinese women, who "hold up half of heaven," must be accorded equality with men. In fact Mao showed more concern for improving the role of women than he did for the general reform of family relations. This emphasis was incorporated into a number of policies and programs, from the 1950 Marriage Law to a more recent stress on equal pay for equal work and on promoting women into leadership positions. Yet at the same time it is true that the emphasis on sexual equality has fluctuated over time during the past quarter century, with more stress on women's rights and duties in the larger society at some times, and more stress on their traditional domestic and familial obligations at others. Critics note that the party has been more concerned with mobilizing women for labor outside the home than it has been with assuring women full equality in other realms.[5] Nevertheless, even though many changes were well under-way before 1949, most observers agree that dramatic changes have taken place in the role of women in China since then.[6]

Against the background of the traditional subordination of women and the current emphasis on sexual equality, we want to examine changes in the role of women in rural Kwangtung. We are concerned with interpreting the general pattern of change and continuity in women's roles in domestic, political, economic, and other spheres. This concern leads us to consider one general and one more specific question. At a general level, we are interested in the extent to which different aspects of women's rights, powers, obligations, and burdens change together or separately. Does an improvement in treatment at home or in income-earning potential lead to improvements in the division of domestic chores or in women's influence in the wider community? Or can and do these things vary separately, so that a change in one realm produces no change in another?

The more specific question stems from a theme in the Marxist literature on the family. According to Engels, the key to the subordination of women is their exclusion from socially productive labor (while they remain chained to private domestic labor).[7] Once women participate equally with men in productive labor they should progress toward general equality with men. An adaptation of this argument is often applied to the situation of American women today. If women work outside of the home, says this argument, they will gain skills and self-respect, have control over their own incomes, not be so dependent upon their husbands for financial and psychological support, and begin to demand and acquire an equal say in family decisions and an equal division of domestic burdens. Their increasing economic influence will eventually gain them equality in political and other realms outside of the family. In either version of this argument women's work outside the home is seen as having a key role in breaking down barriers to sexual equality throughout society. We have already noted that there is evidence that the role of women in agricultural labor in Kwangtung and in China generally has increased since 1949. We want to examine in this chapter particularly whether this change in women's farming activities can be related to other changes in the role of women. Does the rural Kwangtung case lend support to the notion of the key liberating role of women's productive labor?

First, we have noted that women's participation in agricultural labor is fairly regular. Although we do not have any precise measures of the proportion of labor contributed by women in each of our sixty-three villages, our informants claim that most women below the age of forty-five or so work in the fields almost every day. They may work a few days less a month than men, and some women return from work earlier than men to cook the family meals. Women do begin to retire from active field labor earlier than men—after the birth of grandchildren, or by the age of fifty-five or so in any case, while men usually work full-time until around age sixty. But with these qualifications, women in Kwangtung are involved in agricultural labor on a day-to-day basis and not just during periods of peak agricultural activity, as appears still to be the case in some northern Chinese villages. Women in Kwangtung play almost as important a role as men in agricultural labor outside the home. Thus in terms of Engels's arguments, we should expect the most important obstacle to sexual equality in our villages to have been removed.[8]

Women do not receive equal pay for their field labors, but it is hard to say whether this is because they contribute less than men or because they are discriminated against (or both). Where task rates operate, as they did in many places in 1973–74, one's work points depend only on the completion of certain tasks, rather than on group judgments of individual strength, skills, and other factors. Thus if a woman can complete as many tasks as a man in a given period, she should receive the same pay. However, discrimination can still enter a task-rate system through the work assignment and task evaluation process. If certain tasks are assigned work-point values that are abnormally low (in terms of the actual work required), and if women are usually assigned to those while men get picked for more "rewarding" tasks, then a woman working equally hard will end up with fewer points than a man. When time rates are used, women in most villages receive about two points less than men for a day's work (for example, six to eight points instead of eight to ten), although it is hard to say whether this reflects accurately a real skill and strength differential. Our general assumption, however, is that the level of discrimination against women in remuneration is small—women may earn almost as much as men, and a few women earn more than most local men. So women's increasing role in agricultural labor has resulted in some sort of roughly comparable increase in women's earning power.

One part of the argument for the key liberating role of women's productive labor is that by engaging in such labor women gain control over their wages and are less dependent upon their menfolk economically. But we noted in Chapter 11 that this does not happen in Kwangtung. Team payments are handed over to the family head or his representative; payment is regarded as earned by members of the corporate family unit rather than as disposable income for each individual member. The family head is usually a male—unless no senior male is present. Family members (male or female) who want funds for some purchase or for other use must ask the family head or the manager of the family funds. This manager is not always the family head and may be a woman, but we have no indication that this is more likely to be the case when women contribute a larger share to family finances than otherwise, or that women manage the family funds more commonly now than in the past. (We saw in Chapter 11 that in Hakka villages, where women have a tradition of agricultural labor and still do more work on the income-earning private plot than women elsewhere, they are *less* likely than women in non-Hakka villages to manage the family funds.) In any case the money manager, whether male or female, is regarded as the caretaker of funds for the family as a corporate unit, rather than as a private owner of those funds. Misuse of money can bring criticism from other family members, regardless of sex. Women work in the team's fields as individual members of the labor force, rather than under family supervision, but when we consider the consumption and use of the income they earn, the corporate family unit still reigns supreme. Farm labor does not lead to independent incomes for women (or for men). The failure of earning power to translate into control over earnings is not a complete surprise, since similar phenomena have been reported in other Chinese cultures and in many peasant societies.[9] When women regard themselves as working in order to contribute to the family economy, rather than to satisfy their individual needs, they are unlikely to demand that they retain full control over their earnings.

What about women's political role and influence in the wider community? In this realm also we see no clear tendency for women's increased role in labor to translate into heightened political power and community influence. As noted in Chapter 7, in 1973–74 most teams and brigades had at least one woman cadre, and a few had two or three at either level. The most common situation was to have a brigade women's federation chief serving among six to eleven brigade cadres who were otherwise all male, and a lone woman serving as women's team head at the production-team level. Our findings are in contrast with press accounts for some model areas in Kwangtung and elsewhere in China where 25 percent or more of the rural cadres are said to be women.[10]

However, there has clearly been some increase in the proportion of women cadres in rural China in recent years. During the 1960s, Kwangtung villages usually had brigade women's federation chiefs, but the women's team head post is a newer, generally post–Cultural Revolution phenomenon. Our informants imply that the increase in women's representation resulted from pressure from above, symbolized by exhortative quotations from Mao Tse-tung and by recent attacks on the male chauvinism of Confucius, rather than emerging gradually as a consequence of women's enlarged role in field labor. Some informants claim that higher authorities recently sent down a directive that each team and brigade must include at least one female cadre, with an eventual goal of 30 to 40 percent female representation.[11] It seems clear that China's leadership had come to the conclusion that women would not attain a greater role in local leadership without fairly specific administrative pressure being applied from above.

As we noted in Chapter 7, most team and brigade women's cadres are serving in "women's work" posts, rather than exercising general leadership. They focus their attention on encouraging women to work in the fields and on organizing birth control propaganda, rather than on political and economic affairs. Informants note that when localities were pressured to add women cadres, they usually did so by adding a women's team head, rather than by selecting women to replace some of the existing male cadres. Although the title seems to imply that these women lead other women into the fields, in actuality field labor is not regularly carried out in groups formed along sexual lines. The team head, almost always male, has the primary responsibility over both men and women for labor assignments and other matters. The women's team head does sit in on team cadres meetings, where she may introduce a female perspective on some issues, but most of our informants saw this post as a form of tokenism.

Some of the reasons for the limited progress toward sexual equality in local leadership, in spite of vigorous pressure from above, have already been noted. Women are more burdened with household chores than men, and are less available for time-consuming cadre duties. Because women also move out at marriage, new brides will not have built up the relationships of mutual trust upon which selection for local leadership depends.[12] The women's federation also does little to foster women's political voice. The national hierarchy of the women's federation ceased to function during the Cultural Revolution, as did other mass associations, and had only begun to be reorganized in 1973. Brigade women's chiefs did not disappear during this period, although some of our informants claimed that their villages had women's chiefs but no functioning women's federation. Even where this organization exists, however, it has little general influence and lacks a dynamic leadership role in relation to local women. The federation organizes some birth control propaganda, it encourages women to work in the fields, and it holds meetings every year on March 8, International Women's Day. Before the curtailing of the marriage reform campaign in 1953, the women's federation in some places did play a forceful role in helping women to confront husbands who mistreated them.[13] But today this organization is not much involved in the mediation of marital disputes or in the protection of women from abuse by their husbands. In general it is discouraged from acting as an advocate for the views of women, or from pressuring the local leadership to grant changes that would benefit women. Instead, the role of the women's federation is to organize and subordinate women to the general political, economic, and social goals of the party leadership. As matters stand now, then, women do not have a formal political voice that corresponds to their increased economic role.

We can examine variation from village to village in how well women are represented in local leadership posts. We noted for thirty-seven of our villages (all those for which we had sufficient information) how many women were serving as team or brigade cadres in 1973–74. If there was one or none at both levels, we assigned a code of 1 to the village; if either the team or the brigade or both had two or more women serving as cadres (as occurred in 46 percent of these villages), we assigned a code of 2 to the village. This code serves as our crude indicator of minimal or more than minimal inclusion of women in local leadership, and in table 40 we examine how this measure relates to characteristics of our villages.

Most of the associations in table 40 are weak, but they tell us that we are likely to find more women serving in local cadre posts where household consumption levels are high, where the team is a relatively large one, and perhaps where there are many sent-down urban youths and where the vil-

Table 40	Representation of Women in Local Cadre Posts by Village Characteristics (Gamma Statistics)	
	Women cadres	Number of villages
Administrative		
Political density	.10	(36)
Political study	.20	(31)
Urban-communications		
Urban proximity	.00	(36)
Urban youths	.39	(26)
Communications	.24	(34)
Nurseries	-.11	(36)
Economic		
Collective affluence	.02	(37)
Household consumption	.63*	(34)
Land/labor ratio	-.16	(33)
Remittances	.00	(26)
Other		
Brigade size	-.02	(30)
Team size	.50	(36)
Lineage composition	-.25	(37)
Non-Hakka ethnicity	-.08	(36)
Delta region	.35	(37)

*p $\leq$ .10

lages are in the Pearl River Delta region. At least the first two patterns can be interpreted by saying that it is easier to find women to serve in cadre posts where consumption levels are high enough to free women from some of their household chores and where there are a large number of families that might supply such women. The independent, but weaker, association with the percentage of sent-down urban youths might reflect the higher educational level of those youths, male and female alike, and their lack of familial obligations, which make them good candidates for small cadre jobs in the team, particularly as work-point recorders and accountants. On the other hand we also have the impression that urban women who settle down in the villages chafe at the subordinate role rural women assume, and on this point (even if not generally) they may try to subtly agitate among local women to demand more voice in public affairs. So this association in table 40 may be due to either the availability of urban women for service as cadres or their influence on local women (or both). This is not simply a matter of villages more in touch with urban contacts or communications leading the way in women's representation, as the weakness of the other urban-communications associations shows. Nor do our measures of the political infrastructure of villages have much to do with how well women are represented. What seems particularly important, then, is whether there is a sizable pool of women available locally who can be freed from their heavy domestic burdens to take up service as cadres.

What has happened to the informal influence of women? As we noted in Chapter 11, women traditionally, and in Taiwan today, have had substantial influence over village life, influence which is exercised for the most part informally, through gossip among other village women and pressure on their husbands. In that chapter we argued that the current organization of rural life does not foster this informal influence of women, and may even reduce it. Work groups are not permanent and are not generally based upon sexual lines, and heavily burdened rural women have little time to gossip with other women while they do their laundry. The most important informal groupings in the village are male: the older men who sit around in the evenings and chat about village affairs. Insofar as village opinion is formed and altered in these discussions, women are not included; most of the adult women are at home tending their children and doing domestic chores. (Some younger women of the village gather separately in the evenings to chat, but their solidarity will be ended as they marry out to different destinations.) Except for some of the birth control meetings and the women's meetings on March 8, we see little evidence that solidarity among women is being promoted today. Women are supposed to attend general team meetings along with men, although the burden of household chores often makes their attendance irregular. Unfortunately we have no detailed information about how much women speak out during such meetings in relation to men, and whether these meetings provide a meaningful new device for voicing women's points of view. Women undoubtedly continue to influence the community indirectly through their husbands, but still the evidence we have reviewed leads us to conclude that women's farming role has not given them increased informal influence in community affairs. We also see no evidence that rural women desire to band together to protect the interests of women as a group but are frustrated in doing so by the workings of the rural social structure. The continued predominance of family-oriented motivations in the midst of a changed political and economic structure seems to inhibit such desires.

In domestic labor the changes occasioned by the increased participation of women in agricultural labor appear to be minimal, although we do not have much information about what sorts of things peasant males used to do around the house before 1949. In most villages women continue to do the bulk of domestic work, and men do little. A division of labor of sorts does emerge between women of different generations, however, with the mother-in-law handling much of the child care and cooking during the day in order to enable the younger woman to participate in field labor. (Tasks outside of working hours are more often borne by the younger woman.) As long as men play only a minor role in tasks like clothes-making, child-tending, and cooking, women are unlikely to see their labor in the fields alongside of men as much of a "liberation." The "double bind" of field labor and domestic chores is one of the factors preventing women from becoming more involved in community leadership posts.

We noted in Chapter 11 that there is some dispute about the degree of authority and influence women had within the family before 1949. Some writers stress the autocratic nature of male authority, while others stress the way many women, especially older ones, effectively dominated families. Today men are still acknowledged as the family heads, and as the final arbiters of important family decisions, but women make many important day-to-day decisions and are regularly consulted by their husbands. Our informants mention both families in which wives are beaten and families in which the spouses have close and cooperative relationships. It is hard to say whether there has been much change in this picture. One clear sign of change we have noted concerns the treatment of new brides. We do not hear stories common in previous village studies—of new brides being abused and exploited by their mothers-in-law until they gradually win acceptance by proving their competence in domestic work and in their ability to bear sons. Instead, the transition into life in the husband's home is relatively smooth today. We have argued that this change does relate to the increasing role of women in agricultural labor. Since women work more in the fields now, and contribute in major ways to family income, it is important to insure that they are contented and productive workers, and this may explain why new brides receive better treatment than in the past. They also simply spend less time in the company of their mothers-in-law than in the past. Other factors in this change may be that the husband has more say in picking a wife now, and will be more likely to side with her in a dispute, and that more women are marrying men from the same village and even the same lineage than before, which means that they have family members living close by who can check up on how they are treated.

Thus while domestic chores are not being taken over by husbands to any significant extent, a wife—even a new one—can expect better treatment now, and can often count on at least the neutrality of her husband in the event of a squabble with her mother-in-law. The other side of this coin, however, is that older women are losing some of their former power, which depended in part on exploiting their sons' wives. Thus in this area we do not see women who work in the fields gaining, relative to men, but younger women gaining at the expense of older women. What is being affected is generational inequality more than sexual inequality. Women start out their marital lives in a more secure position today, but they cannot look forward to a leisurely old age in which they boss younger women around. In their declining years they will be kept fully occupied with domestic chores in order to enable younger family members to work full time in the fields. It is interesting to note that in Taiwan during the Japanese occupation increasing educational and occupational opportunities and increasing freedom of mate choice produced a very similar change, one reflected in a declining suicide rate for young women but in an increasing suicide rate for older women.[14]

In some other realms clear changes affecting women have taken place. One of these is education. Before 1949 there was a large gap between males and females in access to education, with very few rural women being literate. In 1973 girls still tended to drop out of school earlier than boys in most villages, but the gap had been dramatically reduced. Almost all girls are receiving some education, and in most villages the percentage of girls completing primary school seems only slightly lower than the percentage of boys doing so. It is less clear, however, what connection this trend has with the changing role of women in agricultural labor. Our informants do not perceive literacy or other school-taught skills as vital to a life in farming. In other words, the collapsing of the sex gap in education does not seem attributable to a process of peasant families and their daughters calculating that, since women do more work in the fields now, they will need more schooling, which local authorities should be pressured to provide. The expansion of schooling for women seems to have resulted primarily from governmental pressure and popularization of the ideal of universal education. The government, of course, may have calculated that women would be more productive agricultural workers if they spent some time in school; but, if so, this was only part of a larger calculation of the benefits of education for political, social, and other purposes. So the sexual differential in education has clearly declined, as in many developing societies, but if there is a connection between this decline and the increasing role of women in agricultural labor, it is a rather indirect one.

Young women clearly have more of a say in mate choice than they formerly did. An increasing proportion of them take some initiative in finding a mate; even when their parents lead the way, young women have a chance to meet and approve or veto the man chosen. But this is again more a shift in power between generations than it is one between the sexes—young men also have more say in picking their mates today.

We also argued that women are more able to initiate divorce today. Even though this power is resorted to rarely, it is clear that families can no longer use the assumption that marriage is unbreakable to keep young women in line. This change does seem to be related to the changed economic role of women. Women are now more able to support themselves, and they are an important asset to the families that control their earnings. The woman's parents may not pressure her as much today to endure an unhappy marriage, when they know she can help them economically after the divorce and can probably remarry readily.

However, we also noted that the growing ability of women to initiate divorce has not been accompanied by equal rights to the family property and children produced during the marriage. Women's increased economic role helps to explain the shift from an indirect dowry form of marriage finance to more of a pure bride-price form, involving substantial expenditures by the man's family. These bride prices seal the transfer of important rights from the woman's family to her husband's family. Thus women's increasing economic role has helped to make divorce (and remarriage) easier today, but by the same token it has helped to maintain the penalties (in loss of property and children) that women who divorce and remarry suffer.

We have drawn together here various aspects of the changing role of women in rural Kwangtung,[15] and they yield a rather complex picture. Women are working more regularly in the fields than they used to, and in connection with this trend marriage finance has changed, women have more ability to divorce and remarry, and new brides receive better treatment. During the same period, other changes affecting women have occurred, such as the decreasing educational differentials between the sexes and the increased representation of women in local leadership posts. We do not see these latter changes flowing directly from the increased economic role of women; instead, their accomplishment has required separate administrative pressure from the government. At the same time many aspects of the role of women, such as her primary responsibility for domestic chores and her need to exercise her influence on village affairs informally and indirectly, do not seem to have changed much at all. Finally, some of the changes which can be connected with women's changing work-role, such as those in marriage finance and in the solidarity among women, do not seem particularly favorable.

What can we conclude from this complex pattern? First, we consider the evidence sufficient to reject the notion that socially productive labor has some sort of crucial role in promoting general sexual equality. We find that women have made some gains in certain areas of social life, but in still other areas they have made no gains or have even lost ground. This does not mean that women's changing work role is unimportant, or even that it may not be a necessary precondition for progress in some areas. But clearly it is not sufficient: by itself, getting women out of their homes and into the fields does not produce general equality of the sexes. What other conditions might be necessary to produce broader equality—perhaps an ability of women to organize politically to pursue female goals, an equal sharing of household burdens, an end to patrilocal residence, a mobilization of women for long-term work outside the village as individuals or in groups with other women—we cannot specify with any certainty from our data. But work outside the home is not enough, and even has some negative consequences. Given these findings, we should be wary of those who point to the increasing work-obligations of women in China as evidence of their general progress toward equality. We also cannot assume that gains women have made in other areas—for example, in education—flow naturally from women's increasing role in production.

Our findings are also relevant to our more general question—whether there is a syndrome we can call "the status of women," in which women's economic, political, domestic, and other rights and powers improve or deterriorate together. We have seen that it is possible for one aspect of women's lot to improve while another fails to change, and still another worsens. There is simply no clear tendency for everything to change together. Instead, particular changes are accommodated to, and adjusted into, a pattern of life which may seem contradictory to us, but which is evidently not so for the women (and men) who experience it. We argue that a key to understanding this complex pattern is the continued dominance of familial orientations and obligations, rather than individual, class, or common-sex identifications. Potential changes are reacted to in terms of their implications for corporate family units rather than for individuals or for women as a group.[16]

One possible criticism of our argument would be that our analysis is premature—that changes in the economic role of women are too recent to have had their full impact felt. With the passage of time (and generations), this argument would have it, sexual equality in other spheres will begin to catch up with that in labor contributions. We reject this argument on several grounds. First, the mobilization of women to take part in agricultural labor dates back to at least the time of collectivization (1955–56), so that a new generation has already arisen without producing a dramatic change in the situation. Younger women are not producing a revolution in rural social relations and, so far as we can tell, are not even pressing for one. (However, large numbers of urban young women sent into villages since 1968, and accustomed to the greater equality of urban life, may provide a spark for some changes in the future.) In the Soviet Union we can observe an even longer time frame, and one careful comparison of family time-budget statistics in that country for the 1920s and the 1960s found no tendency for men to take over any greater share of domestic labor in the latter period, although in the interim almost all adult women entered the full-time labor force. In the Soviet Union, then, even a span of two generations does not reveal any tendency for women's work outside the home to affect the division of labor within the home.[17]

Finally, we reject the "not enough time" argument because it assumes the existence of something we see little evidence for: a tension between women's relatively equal role in field labor and her restricted role in other areas of social life. This tension is what is expected to lead women to demand overall equality, with them citing their important economic role as a justification. We stress again that we see women working in rural Kwangtung primarily in order to meet family needs and fulfill familial obligations, not to attain individual goals or to improve the lot of oppressed women. The fact that women do much field labor does not seem to lead them to resent their lack of control over their earnings, or their restricted role in village affairs. Thus we see no reason for saying that the present situation is unstable, and will be replaced in time with fuller sexual equality once new generations come along. To change this situation would require not just time but more fundamental shifts in the rural social structure, such as enabling women to organize to pursue female goals, ending the strong preference for patrilocal residence, or making other fundamental changes. In the absence of some such major changes in rural social life, the current pattern of men's and women's roles in Kwangtung villages seems an effective and stable adaptation of traditional social relationships to the reality of the present village and commune structure.

13

Life-Cycle
Ceremonies and
Ritual Life

*t*he richness of ceremonial life in Chinese culture has long served as a source of fascination for foreign travelers and scholars. Over the millennia of Chinese history, rituals were developed and elaborated, and in many ways they served to solemnify and reinforce existing social relationships. Indeed, according to the ancient Book of Rites (the Li Chi, a collection of earlier texts of Chinese ritual life, compiled during the Han dynasty), Confucius developed arguments for Chinese ritual life that are remarkably similar to those of Emile Durkheim more than two thousand years later. The sage is quoted as follows:

> According to what I have heard, of all things by which people live the rites are the greatest. Without them they would have no means of regulating the services paid to the spirits of heaven and earth; without them they would have no means of distinguishing the positions proper to father and son, to high and low, to old and young; without them they would have no means of maintaining the separate character of the intimate relations between male and female, father and son, elder brother and younger, and conducting intercourse between the contracting families in a marriage, and the frequency or infrequency (of the reciprocities between friends). These are the grounds on which superior men have honoured and reverenced (the rites) as they did.[1]

This quotation expresses a view that rituals and ceremonies are not important simply because they are a link with the past, but because they celebrate and reinforce core social relationships and values in the present lives of the Chinese people. Scholars have argued that the features of the spirit world which enter into such rituals are not simply an arbitrary collection of mythical figures dreamed up by generations long dead, but mirror the social world and the concerns of the living: the importance of family solidarity; the power and capriciousness of bureaucratic officials; the obligations and interdependence of generations; the uncertainties of death; and so forth.[2] In the worship of the gods and ancestors the entire system of Confucian and "feudal" social relationships which the current government has set out to destroy is brought to mind and celebrated. As the core features of peasant social structure and values change, the nature of ritual life should also be expected to change. But the other side of the coin is that rituals celebrate the status quo and may make it more difficult to bring about change. They orient peasants toward their obligations to families, kin groups, and the ancestors, rather than to the party and to the changed social order the party is trying to create. This role of rituals in promoting the status quo is one of the reasons for a revolutionary regime's opposition to traditional ceremonies. Insofar as such rituals orient the population to look backward rather than forward, to believe that man is at the mercy of the spirits and the existing order of things, and toward fatalism rather than activism, they represent a source of conservatism and inertia that can impede the effort to get people to reject the "bitter past" and struggle to remake the future. The government brands these rituals "superstitious," and lumps them together with various religious activities as, in Marx's term, "opiates of the masses."

> Religious and superstitious thoughts constitute a serious threat to socialist revolution and its construction. Socialist revolution aims to change the old social system of exploitation and oppression and to destroy classes. Of course this aim requires courage and revolutionary struggle. On the other hand, religion teaches people to seek happiness, solve the problems of life and reach the happiness of the afterlife through prayer. Therefore belief in religion must make revolutionary ardor fade.[3]

Mao Tse-tung in his famous 1927 "Report on an Investigation of the Peasant Movement in Hunan" indicted the system of religious authority in China as one of the four "thick ropes" (along with state authority, lineage authority, and masculine authority) binding the peasants in the feudal-patriarchal system. Mao felt that once these ropes had been cut by class struggle and revolutionary action, peasants would lose interest in traditional rites and ceremonies.[4]

Traditional rituals are opposed not only because of their purported role in encouraging fatalism and conservatism but also because they are seen as supporting the authority of traditional clan and class elites, who manipulate the rituals to keep poor peasants in subjugation. A critique in the 1960s during debates on the role of religion expresses this idea:

> Most temples and similar structures were built by wealthy people and bureaucrats. There were also some built on imperial orders. The promoters were in fact mostly "upper class" people. It is obvious that religion was also their tool for misleading the people. Otherwise, why should they spend so much money and exert so much energy to do these things? . . . Religion has a comparatively strong foundation. This foundation exists because of the presence of bourgeois elements and the continued influence which exploiting ideas have on people. This is the foundation on which religion exists.[5]

The argument implies that, once poor peasants are totally liberated from the influence of the old clan and class elites, and reoriented in the working-class political ideology of the new government, they should have no further desire to engage in traditional ceremonial life.

There is one other major reason the government opposes traditional ceremonials: they involve major expenditures of time and money in nonproductive activities, and these expenditures constitute a severe hardship for poor families. Surveys in rural China around 1930 showed that the major source of peasant indebtedness was not loans from landlords and usurers to pay for seeds and other production expenses, but loans for nonproductive uses, of which a prominent item was ceremonial expenditures. (In the region to which Kwangtung belongs 78 percent of the total credit was for such nonproductive uses.) John L. Buck estimated that in this period the average Chinese peasant spent about four months' net family income on a son's wedding, three month's family income on a funeral or on a daughter's wedding, two months' on a birthday celebration for a senior member of the family, and one month's on a birth celebration.[6] One particularly revealing critique on this issue appeared in 1958, concerning the burden of funeral expenditures in Shantung Province. The author, a provincial party official, claimed that about 3 percent of the arable land of the province was occupied by graves and tombs, that the lumber used in Shantung each year to build coffins would suffice to build 200,000 houses, that burial clothing required over 24 million feet of cotton cloth annually, and that the total expenditures on funerals in the province each year exceeded 51 million yuan.[7] Coping with these burdens was a serious problem for both families and agricultural collectives.

For all of these reasons, then, the Chinese Communists are determined to change ritual life in China. What is advocated is not the elimination of all rituals and celebrations, but the replacement of elaborate, expensive ceremonies, with their religious symbolism, by new, simplified and secularized forms. The number of festive occasions should be reduced and consolidated, with lesser events ignored. More important events, such as weddings, funerals, and major annual festivals, can be celebrated in new ways: with simple meals and modest expenditures, and with new political elites, rather than traditional ritual specialists, officiating. The media in China contain numerous examples of the new types of ceremonies. One of Mao Tse-tung's best-known articles, "Serve the People," was an address given in 1944 at a simple memorial meeting for a fallen comrade, and in this address Mao advocated such memorial meetings as a replacement for traditional funerals.[8] Weddings in which no large expenditures or feasts are involved, but instead center on a team or brigade meeting or simple tea party to welcome the new bride, are also cited as models to emulate.[9] A recent press article mentions an old woman in rural Kwangtung who, when confronted by a crowd of relatives who had come to celebrate her birthday, asked them to join her in a "meal of remembering past bitterness." Instead of a feast, the guests ate wild vegetables and other coarse dishes to remind themselves of how they had suffered in the old society.[10]

On these and other occasions, traditional celebrations are to be radically simplified or replaced by new, secular forms, in which a political message replaces religious elements. But official pressure to bring about such changes has not been intense or uniform. During periodic major political campaigns local cadres and activists are pressured to crack down vigorously on those engaging in traditional ceremonial life, and even during the lulls between campaigns some activities (for example, rituals led by traditional priests or involving entire lineages) may receive criticism or sanctions. But no special campaigns have been waged to change traditional ceremonies, and for the most part official goals in this area are communicated to peasants through "model examples" in the mass media, such as those cited above. Thus coercive tactics and administrative pressure have not been stressed much of the time, and communication and persuasion are expected to play the major role in bringing about change in this area. At the same time there have also been changes in the economic life of peasants, in the roles of women and the aged, and in other factors that may make traditional ceremonies more or less meaningful today. In this chapter and the next we will examine persistence and change in ritual life in rural Kwangtung. We start by examining ceremonies connected with life-cycle events.

Birth

Informants differ on whether there are any important prenatal taboos placed on women. In some villages pregnant women are not supposed to eat certain foods, to attend funerals, or to engage in certain activities (for example stepping over another person or over a carrying pole), and there are beliefs that violating these taboos will bring harm to the unborn child or others in the community. For example, one informant claimed that pregnant women were not allowed to eat dog or snake in his village, for fear the infant would be born with skin ailments or deformities. But generally these taboos seem minimal, or absent entirely, and they do not sharply restrict the activities of pregnant women. Most women work until shortly before giving birth, with their team assigning them to light work during the final weeks. Such information as have on prenatal taboos in Kwangtung before 1949 indicates a modest number of taboos and restrictions then also[11] (in comparison with some other societies), so it is not clear how much change has taken place here.

A substantial proportion (45 percent) or our informants report that deliveries now take place in commune clinics or town hospitals, or in delivery rooms attached to the brigade medical station. Those who do give birth at home are generally attended by a brigade midwife with some short-term formal training; a few poorer localities report deliveries with the aid only of experienced old women.

Some villages with deliveries in the home have minimal forms of postpartum taboos. The mother and child are expected to stay in the house for a period (often twelve days, sometimes thirty), and outsiders are not supposed to enter during this period.[12] Generally there is no team regulation about when women are required to resume field labor, and since in almost all villages they receive no paid maternity leave, it is simply a matter of a family receiving less income the longer the mother stays at home. The usual pattern is to resume field labor soon after the birth celebrations are concluded (generally after thirty to forty days), with the team again assigning light tasks at first.

Almost all informants (forty-one out of forty-three who supplied information on this point) report ceremonies held to celebrate the birth of children. In some localities there are two separate occasions, one a meal for very close kin twelve days or so after the birth, and a larger feast at the end of the month, called a full-month feast (man-yüeh-chiu or ni-yen). Relatives and friends are notified after the birth and in advance of the various festivities, in some places, still, by the sending of the traditional hard-boiled eggs colored red. The most important festivity is the full-month feast, involving perhaps four or five tables (about thirty or forty people). Those invited gather for a meal on the designated day, bringing gifts for the child—generally either cloth, clothing, or simply money in "lucky money" envelopes (li-shih or hung-pao). The maternal grandmother is particularly obligated in many localities, and may provide food gifts, a full set of clothing for the infant, or a back-pack baby carrier for the mother. Apparently there are no particular rituals observed now during this celebration; the infant is simply brought around for all to admire, and people eat. In some villages the traditional custom of shaving the head of the infant prior to this ceremony is still followed,[13] but no ritual specialists or worship activities seem to be required. These celebrations clearly indicate how important childbirth still is to peasant families.

In many localities the full-month feast is more elaborate for the first child, especially if it is a boy, and is reduced or eliminated altogether for later children, particularly if they are girls. The persistence of this traditional sexual disparity reflects how sons continue to be the primary guarantee of a family's future economic security, since daughters will marry out into other families. The expense of holding such a feast is generally modest compared with that of wedding feasts (generally under 100 yuan, perhaps only 40 or 50 yuan on the average), and we have noted that few "superstitious" elements are involved. Informants report that not only do rural cadres not criticize the holding of such feasts, but they hold them for their own children as well.

Naming customs vary widely from village to village, and summary statements are difficult. Children in some places are given names at birth, or at the full-month feast, or perhaps not until they start school. If no formal name is picked initially, children are given a baby name or nickname, sometimes of a joking or derogatory character (dog's son, little pig), and even when a formal name is bestowed, a nickname may be used more commonly until the child enters school, or even until he or she is ready to marry. How a child's given name is picked also varies. We have information on only thirty-six of our villages, and in eleven of these the parents or paternal grandparents pick the name at random, simply because of its sound or meaning. It is still customary in many villages, though, for siblings to have a repeated character in their names (a custom reported in sixteen villages). For example, several brothers share a common first (or second) character in their given names, while their sisters may all share a different common character. In some villages this sharing extends beyond the immediate family, and all males of the lineage have shared characters which vary for different generations.[14] Informants from such villages could recite the list of common characters for generations past and for several generations still to come. Even though this custom emphasizes lineage solidarity, it does not seem to have been criticized in the villages where it exists, and cadres and Communist party members follow this naming custom as well.

There is another traditional naming practice which occurs in a few villages in our sample (nine cases). In these villages fortune-tellers are consulted to pick a name which is not only propitious (which is important if the parents are illiterate), but which makes up for any deficiencies in the "five elements" (water, fire, wood, metal, and earth) which the child enters the world with. Where these fortune-tellers exist, only part of the community may consult them, while other parents pick names for their children on their own. These specialists (often blind people who covertly supplement their meager income by this activity) are not criticized most of the time, but some have been dragged out for struggle meetings during intensive campaigns, and put out of business temporarily or permanently. It is likely that free parental choice of names has gained over these traditional customs in time, although several informants said this trend was underway even before 1949, and the pressure even against the name-picking specialists has been applied only intermittently.

The customs surrounding birth do entail some expense, some "superstitious" elements, and even some support for lineage solidarity (and sexual inequality). However, on balance the threats posed do not seem very severe. Although these ceremonies are modified versions of traditional forms, rather than politicized observances, the primary stress is on the family and close relatives joining to celebrate the new arrival. The focus seems to be on eating and conviviality, rather than on worship or relating to past generations, and peasants do not go deeply into debt trying to have more lavish celebrations than their neighbors. So in this set of customs we see some slow changes, and apparently minimal concern on the part of higher authorities with accelerating the pace.

Weddings

The next important life-cycle ritual is the most important one: the wedding. As the process of finding a marital partner was discussed in Chapter 10, we will be concerned here primarily with the wedding itself. It is important to note, though, that in most cases whether a marriage is initiated by the youths or by the parents does not affect how elaborate the ceremony is. However a couple has been brought together, the wedding almost always involves considerable ceremony and expense. Simplified, secular weddings of the sort advocated in the Chinese press were reported to be completely absent or practiced by a very tiny minority of couples in all but two of the villages on which we have information.

After the match and a bride price are agreed upon by both families and the couple involved, the preliminaries to the wedding itself begin. If there is no formal engagement custom locally, the groom's family simply proposes a wedding date, and the bride's family responds. Nowadays the checking of the "eight characters" of the bride and groom to see whether the match would be suitable or in conflict seems not to be followed, although in a few villages fortune-tellers are consulted to pick an auspicious day for the wedding.[15] In most places, though, the boy's parents simply suggest a wedding date according to convenience in rural work schedules and income distributions, but the specific day will be one they feel is lucky. (It is common to marry on a date with a nine in it, since nine is a homophone for long-lasting.)

We noted in Chapter 10 that the customary time that elapses between the agreement to a match and the wedding varies a great deal from place to place—from only a month or so to more than a year—and that during this interval a couple may engage in proto-dating behavior. There is no set rule about when a couple should register their marriage at the commune office. Some couples do this several weeks in advance of the wedding, and some only a day or two ahead of time. (We also noted before that couples below the ideal marriage ages may have the family wedding first, and only get the marriage registered months or even years later, once the minima have been passed.) In a few cases registration may precede the wedding by several months. In this manner the security of the match is protected by the registration, while the girl's family continues to receive the benefit of her labors. During the interim period there may be mutual visiting, but sexual relations are not supposed to begin until after the family wedding, although in the eyes of the government the couple is already married.

The bride-price items generally are delivered a few days in advance, and the minimal dowry is brought back to the groom's house the day before or on the day of the wedding. On the wedding day the groom's family holds a feast, and in many localities it is customary for the bride's family to hold a separate feast as well. (Informants report that the feasts are separate even when the bride and groom come from the same village. The feast in the bride's home generally takes place on the day before or the morning of the wedding.) The size of these feasts varies from place to place and according to the wealth of the family and the number of relatives they have, but the groom's feast is generally considerably larger than the bride's. Our informants report grooms' feasts ranging from a minimum of five or six tables up to a maximum of thirty tables or more in some villages (with eight people at a table generally). With the larger feasts, the guests have to eat in shifts, with tables set up both inside and outside the house. Clearly one cannot engage in feasts of such size covertly. Informants again report that cadres give wedding feasts for their offspring as well, although these may be on a more modest scale than those of their neighbors. For the bride's family the modest feast does not constitute a major financial burden, since much of the food comes from the bride price supplied to them. For the groom's family, however, the burden of the feast is much more substantial (figures of 100 to 600 yuan were cited), and the small cash and other gifts brought by the guests only partially offset this expense.

The other major event of the wedding day is the arrival of the bride (ying-ch'in), and the coordination of this with the male's wedding feast varies. Commonly the bride arrives just before or during the feast, but in some villages not until it has concluded, and sometimes not until the guests have eaten and gone home. To fetch the bride, the groom sets out for the bride's home with a group of other young males on bicycles (or in boats, in areas where this is the more common mode of travel). In some localities the groom waits at his home while the young males go alone to fetch the bride. When the troupe gets to the outskirts of the bride's village, firecrackers are set off, and the young men dismount and proceed to the bride's home. There firecrackers may again sound, and the young males enter or try to enter. In some villages there ensue various teasing games in which the sisters and friends of the bride try to block the way and prevent her from being taken away. After suitable bribes (perhaps of 10 to 30 yuan) and performances, the males are allowed to enter. They request that the bride be delivered to them, and she finally comes out of her room.

Generally neither the bride nor the groom wears special wedding garments now, but simply new clothes of ordinary style. But as of old, in preparation for her departure, the bride has her hair combed and decorated with flowers or ribbons, often by an old woman from the village who has many sons and grandsons (she is called the "good luck lady," and symbolizes the hoped-for fertility of the bride).

The bride is seen off at the door by her parents and goes with her "sisters" to mount bikes for the return journey. In some localities she is carried between house and bicycle on the back of the marriage arranger or a "good luck lady," and in others one of the "sisters" holds an umbrella over her head. The exact meaning of these acts is unclear, but they are designed to protect the bride and preserve good luck, since the bride is viewed as very open to danger until she is incorporated in her new family. Informants report that the sedan chairs which traditionally were used to fetch brides were replaced at a fairly early date by bicycles, and these more modern conveyances do not seem to be decorated with protective charms or other traditional symbols.[16]

As the troupe sets out again, firecrackers are set off, and they sound again as the party arrives back at the groom's village. There all dismount and proceed on foot to the groom's house. In a few villages there are rituals to be followed in entering the house, such as having the bride step over a grain sifter or a pile of burning straw, acts which signify the transfer of her ties to the groom's family as well as the cleansing of any evil spirits picked up on the road.

After the bride enters the house the particular sequence of events varies. In some cases she and her female companions go directly to the bridal room (hsin-fang) and do not come out, except briefly for the bride to pour and offer tea to the guests, who give her envelopes of "lucky money" in return. In about half the villages about which we have information, however, there is some sort of more pronounced expression of subordination to the older generation. This is called the worship of the family hall (pai-t'ang), and may involve kneeling down to worship at the domestic ancestral shrine, and-or kneeling down or bowing to the husband's parents (and even in a few cases washing their feet to show subservience). However, these acts, particularly extreme forms of them, are less common than the toasting rituals (in which the groom takes part by serving wine). In some localities the bride joins the feast, while in others she is expected to remain in the bridal room with little or no food (or special food brought from her parents' home by her "sisters"). Throughout the ceremony the marriage arranger or good-luck lady instructs the bride on what she is expected to do next.

After the feast the guests disperse to their homes, or to the homes of relatives in the village, in the case of those who have come from far away. In the evening many of them return again for activities referred to as teasing the new couple (nao hsin-fang or wan hsin-fang), activities commonly held in thirty-seven of the forty-five villages for which we have information. While the older relatives dominate the daytime feast, now the younger relatives and friends play a more active role. Tea, fruits, and candy are served, along with cigarettes. The guests throw out challenges to the new couple, particularly to the bride: to sing various songs, to tell the story of their romance, to both smoke a single cigarette, to light cigarettes for all present, to answer riddles, and so forth. This activity continues into the middle of the night, and the new couple is by custom not allowed to complain or to ask people to leave. Only after the guests have tired of their fun and have left of their own accord can the couple be alone together.

A few days after the wedding (often, but not everywhere, on the third day) the bride returns to visit her own family. She takes along presents of food, and in many localities the groom accompanies her. Usually she is required to return to her husband's home on the same day, signifying that her primary obligations have now been shifted to his family. In some places a few days after the wedding the bride's parents come to her new home for a meal, and her visit back to her natal family takes place somewhat later. With the bride's return from this visit the wedding ceremonies are concluded, and the bride is expected to begin a full round of field labor and household chores.

What has just been described is the dominant process and ceremony of marriage in villages all over Kwangtung, but there are exceptions to this pattern. Some families do hold smaller and simpler ceremonies, and a few parents economize on bride prices by directly exchanging daughters (as brides for their respective sons).[17] In our interviews, however, it is very rare to hear of weddings which follow the ideals espoused in the official press: the couple, having fallen in love, decides to marry, goes to register the marriage, and then returns to set up house. In the press this is generally done with little ceremony or expense at all, although a small tea party for friends (more than relatives) may be held, or the team or brigade may call a meeting to welcome the bride and present her such "modern" wedding gifts as a hoe or a set of Chairman Mao's works. We also have no accounts of the sort of quasi-religious political rituals connected with marriage (bowing to portraits of Chairman Mao, and so on) which have sometimes been reported.[18] In most villages what movement there is in the direction of official ideals consists simply of less elaborate and expensive family celebrations, rather than politicized forms.

Curiously, one secondary wedding pattern which is reported in some villages (a few cases in twelve villages, many cases in two villages) is at variance with both traditional customs and with the ideals expressed in the press. This is called the traveling marriage (lü-hsing chieh-hun). In such a marriage the couple decides to wed and, generally with the approval of both sets of parents, opts to avoid most of the ceremonial expenses. The couple registers the marriage at the commune office and then goes off on a trip to

Canton or some other place for several days, during which their conjugal life begins—in our terms, they go on a honeymoon. Only after they return do they hold a meal for relatives and friends, and this is generally modest in size. This traveling marriage is clearly a break with traditional practices, since sexual relations begin after the registration and before any family ceremony. The conflict with official ideals is more debatable, since the modesty of the traveling marriage is in keeping with the government's goals. But the honeymoon trip is not, so far as we know, advocated in any of the many official pronouncements on ideal revolutionary marriage, and some expenditure and feasting is still involved. The trip may stem from the variety of "enlightened marriage" customs developed among the urban educated classes in China before 1949.[19]

What has changed about rural weddings, and what has persisted? Here as elsewhere in our study we find a mixed picture. Although the elements of traditional weddings which the government brands as superstitious have not been eliminated completely (for example, wedding dates with a nine in them, the use of "good luck ladies"), they seem clearly on the wane—for example, in the reduced role of fortune-tellers in judging whether the match is suitable. Weddings do not now involve any worship in the lineage hall, or other elements which would directly focus on lineage solidarity. (It is our impression that even before 1949 rural weddings were largely a domestic affair, and did not usually involve celebrations by the lineage as a corporate group.[20] However, some lineage sanctification was involved—for example, to make sure that marriages with people of the same lineage did not take place.) We are unable to say whether the guests at weddings include a higher proportion of friends rather than relatives than they used to, but it is clear that relatives are still the main participants, and that the team and brigade have not become the organizational basis for wedding ceremonies.[21]

In terms of expense, consumption, and resulting financial burden, we have already noted in Chapter 10 that little progress toward the official ideals has been made and that perhaps the burden has increased. For the male's family the combined burden of the bride-price and wedding-feast expenses relative to household income seems, if anything, greater now than it was in this area in the 1930s. Because of these expenditures, which may exceed the annual income of many families, people who are poor still have some trouble finding a bride for their sons, and families may go deeply into debt staging a wedding.

We can also examine some of the changing symbolism of the wedding celebration. First, we note that relatively elaborate and expensive cere-

monies emphasize the crucial importance of marriage and the family in village life. Informants say that this is an event that happens to you once and
affects the fortunes of the family from then on. They voice traditional
concerns that they will "lose face" with neighbors and relatives if they do
not have an elaborate wedding, even if this means risking disapproval from
higher authorities. Particular elements of the celebration, such as the holding
of separate wedding feasts for the two families, the hindering of the bride-
fetchers, and restrictions on the length of the bride's visit home after marriage all emphasize the transfer of a woman's primary obligations to her
husband's family at marriage, as in the past. However, the rituals by which
the new bride expresses subordination to her in-laws—by kneeling down
before them, by serving them tea the next morning, and so on—seem less in
evidence today. Here we see a reflection of the trends we sketched in
Chapters 11 and 12: new brides are in some ways a more important resource
today, but they do not start their married lives in such a subordinated position. Still visible, but clearly on the decline as well, are the fertility symbols
used in weddings. We have noted the occasional use of "good luck ladies"
with many sons and grandsons, but other customs mentioned in traditional
accounts, such as the ritual preparation of the marriage bed (for example, by
a priest's blessing, by young boys bouncing on it), are generally absent.
Perhaps there is less anxiety about having sons today, given improved health
standards and the increasing proportion of children who survive. So the
symbolic aspects of the wedding continue to emphasize the importance of
marriage and of obtaining a bride as events that should be rejoiced in, but
some particular elements are now less central.

Old Age and Death

In most localities there is no firm rule on the age at which people can retire
from work in the production team's fields. The main constraint is economic
rather than administrative, since the team does not provide any retirement
pay or pensions (except to those with no sons). In poor families old people
work in the fields well into their sixties and beyond, while in better-off
families they retire earlier. The most common pattern is for men to ease out
of the labor force by about sixty, and women by fifty or fifty-five. In some
localities women retire even earlier than this in order to tend their
grandchildren, and since collective nurseries are generally lacking, team
cadres cannot object very strongly.

In many villages it is still customary to celebrate the decennial birthdays of old men and women (at fifty, sixty, seventy, and so on) with special feasts to which relatives and friends are invited. The old person may wear a new set of clothes sewn by a daughter, but other than this there is little in the way of special ceremony. We do not have precise figures, but it is our impression that both the scale and the expense of such old-age feasts (shou-yen) are more modest than birth celebrations, not to mention weddings. In some villages this celebration is now largely gone.

Burial seems to be virtually universal today in the Kwangtung countryside, with the cremation espoused in the official press making few inroads. We were told that in forty-one of our villages there were no cremations, in five villages there were a few cremations, and only in one village had cremation been generally adopted. The five villages with a few cremations involved "special cases" of various sorts—the death of a commune cadre, the death of the local parent of a prominent provincial official, and so forth. Most villages are located too far from the existing crematoria (which are reportedly not present in all of Kwangtung's county towns) to conveniently use them even if the demand existed, and in such places there is of course no pressure to popularize cremation.

When an old person is ill and about to die, relatives are notified. Apparently traditional feelings that people should die at home motivate relatives to bring patients home from commune or town hospitals when death is imminent. At home the dying person is often taken out of the bedroom and placed in the parlor of the house, with feet pointing inward and head pointing toward the door.[22] In a few villages it is reported to be the custom to carry dying people out and lay them in the old lineage hall, even though these halls have otherwise been converted completely to new uses (as meeting halls or storage rooms). After the dying person has been moved, the preparations for the funeral begin. Some families have bought and stored a coffin in advance, but if not a relative will be dispatched to purchase one. Coffins vary in cost in the shops from 20 or 30 to over 100 yuan, and a privately made coffin may cost 300 yuan or so. Informants generally claim that the coffins available in the shops now are not as good as in "the old days," being made out of wood scraps (and, in a couple of villages, out of concrete).

When a person dies, the body is turned around, with feet facing the door, and the funeral activities proper begin. Generally now there are no Buddhist monks or nuns called in to officiate at funerals. In a fair number of villages Taoist priests (called nan-wu-lao) were active up until the Cultural Revolution, but many of these were attacked then and have since become inactive. In some instances older relatives substitute in reciting the funeral incantations (nien-ching). This is in keeping with the general trend for family members, rather than ritual specialists, to do most of the organizing and officiating in contemporary ritual life. The oldest son and other relatives go to a nearby lake or stream to "buy water" (mai-shui). This involves the heir collecting a basin full of water and then throwing coins into the stream in exchange. This water is then used to wash the body of the deceased or simply the face. After this the body is dressed (sometimes in several layers of clothing), and the formal mourning begins.

Generally the body is only kept at home overnight, and burial takes place the next day. Fortune-tellers are seldom used now to pick an auspicious time for encoffining or burial. During the time the body remains at home the family and relatives stand and kneel alongside it, with the older women wailing their grief in a loud, sing-song voice. In some localities the relatives wear ordinary clothes, perhaps with only an armband or hemp belt to indicate mourning, but in many villages (twenty-five in our sample) full mourning-dress, with hats, shirts, skirts, and belts of hemp or other coarse white material, is donned.[23]

The body is put in a coffin in the evening or the next morning, and just before the burial procession sets off the coffin is nailed up and taken outside. As in the past, graves are scattered in the hills (if hills are nearby), but in a few localities they are now concentrated in hillside graveyards. In twenty-two villages in our sample geomancers are still hired covertly to pick grave sites and directions in accord with traditional feng-shui principles, but even in such villages not all families consult them.[24] It seems more common for the family itself to pick a site, based upon general notions about what spots are good or bad, notions which are in turn grounded in popular knowledge of feng-shui. In some localities there are part-time specialists hired to dig the grave, or the team assigns members for this task. Otherwise family members or relatives dig the grave themselves.

The funeral procession sets off toward the grave in a definite order. In most cases there are no priests or monks to lead the way, but in some localities there are still gong-beaters and horn-blowers who take this role. Sometimes there are individuals who walk in front holding banners, poles, or incense burners, often led by someone strewing "streams of money" (hsi-ch'ien) and-or firecrackers in the path of the procession, to appease and frighten the evil spirits. Then comes the coffin, and then the oldest son, close kin, and more distant kin and friends. In some villages things are not so elaborate, and the procession consists simply of the coffin, perhaps preceded by a single firecracker-setter, with the various relatives and friends following in order behind. In some localities the procession stops half-way to the grave, and the more distant kin and all the women, who customarily are not allowed at the graveside ceremony, turn around and go back to the village by a different route.[25]

At the grave the coffin is put in the earth, and often incense (which has to be purchased on the black market, unless mosquito incense is used in its place) and paper ingots (yüan-pao—generally homemade) are burned, sometimes with firecrackers set off as well. The oldest son and then other kin throw handfuls of earth on top of the coffin, and then the procession returns home (again, according to custom, by a different route). The gravediggers complete the burial. The participants in the funeral often bring small funeral gifts to the family of the deceased, and this family in turn is obligated to serve them a meal after returning from the grave. After this meal the participants disperse homeward.

We have no systematic financial estimates, but the costs of the funeral seem intermediate between those of the birth celebration and a wedding (usually under 300 yuan, and probably only 50 to 150 yuan on the average). We believe that some decrease in funeral expenditures over time has occurred, particularly as a result of the reduced cost of coffins and the general absence of paid priests and readers of incantations. In view of what we have said earlier about marriage expenditures, the cost of funerals *relative to marriages* has certainly declined. (By our estimates Kwangtung families may spend on the average about 15 percent as much on a family funeral as on a son's wedding; in Buck's data from villages in seven Kwangtung localities around 1930 the figure was about 55 percent.)[26]

After the funeral the mourning clothes are generally taken off, although they may be donned again for later memorial rites within the first year. In some localities further memorial activity takes place only on traditional holidays, particularly during the Ch'ing-ming and Ch'ung-yang festivals (see Chapter 14). But in other villages at intervals of seven, fourteen, twenty-one and on up to forty-nine days after the funeral, the family lights incense in their home and puts out food offerings to the deceased.[27] In some places the anniversary of the death date or the birthday of the deceased may also be observed with worship and offerings in the home.

Ancestral tablets in the lineage hall are generally gone now, but many families establish ancestral tablets or surrogates for them at home for their deceased relatives. In four villages in our sample the ancestral tablets that were destroyed by Red Guards during the "smash the four olds" stage of the Cultural Revolution have been replaced by newly carved tablets, which are generally hidden away when not in use. In other places people use paper tablets, with the names of the deceased written on slips of red paper and hung on the wall in the traditional place.[28] In other villages photos of the deceased suffice, and are presented with offerings much as the traditional tablets were. In twenty-four of our villages one of these forms of replacement of traditional ancestral tablets was reported, but in a further twenty-nine villages no tablets or tablet surrogates were reported, although families may still put out offerings and burn incense in front of an empty wall where the domestic shrine used to be. (Domestic ancestor worship is reported present in some form in thirty-seven villages, and absent in sixteen.)

The funeral, then, is largely traditional in form, although simplified. One reads in the Chinese press of funerals that are a collective and not a family affair, secular memorial meetings (chui-tao hui) in which brigade cadres give speeches about the contributions of the deceased. But in our accounts funerals are almost always a family affair in modified traditional form. Where "modern" memorial services are reported they are again special cases: commune cadres, a peasant killed while protecting commune property, and so forth. However, we did run across occasional cases of "hybrid" funerals, involving both traditional and new elements. Here is part of the account by one informant of a funeral in the spring of 1973:

> The younger sister of the deceased came back to mourn—she had to hold a sugar-cane stalk in her hand, and at the gate of the village she changed into mourning clothes, and then she could enter the village. After the kin had all returned, on the second day after the death, they took him for burial. CYC [the son] invited the brigade cultural-recreational group members to come and act as drummers, and he invited another team member to take charge as the burial official [wu-kung]. When they entered the door, CYC gave each a li-shih [lucky money envelope]. The wu-kung put the corpse in the coffin, added some paper ingots [yüan-pao], and then nailed on the coffin lid. When the funeral procession went out, they carried the coffin first past the door of the old lineage hall for a ceremony in which the kin of the deceased set out three small cups of wine and three kinds of meat as a memorial. The mourners all had to scatter wine on the ground [tien-chiu]. This was the traditional custom to follow, but this time a small bit of new ceremony was added. After the wine scattering, the brigade security defense chief led everyone in singing "Do Not Forget Class Suffering," and then the security defense chief went on to say that the deceased had been a laborer, and that in the past when poor people died they couldn't have memorial rites, and they couldn't even afford a coffin, so we shouldn't

forget class suffering. After the song was sung, firecrackers were set off, and then the drums and flutes and gongs sounded, and the funeral party set off for the grave.[29]

Traditional funeral activities are not criticized very often. Village cadres may not engage much in worship activities, such as incense burning, but members of their families, such as their wives and mothers, often do.[30] When a team or brigade cadre or local party member dies, the funeral will not differ much from those of ordinary peasants.

Several years after the burial (generally from three to seven years), the custom of reburial of the bones is still generally followed in the villages from which our informants came (it was reported absent in only three villages). Family members, or part-time specialists who know the required techniques, dig open the grave and carefully take out the bones of the deceased, clean them, and place them in an established order in a pottery urn (referred to as a "golden pagoda"—chin-t'a). The urn is then partially reburied in the hillside. This reburial custom seems to be followed whether or not the family has had good fortune since the person in question passed away. However, recent fortunes may determine whether the urn is placed in the same location as the earlier grave or moved elsewhere. If it is moved, the new site is usually picked by family members on the basis of their general knowledge of feng-shui principles, although in a few places geomancers are covertly consulted. The final stage of traditional reburial, in which a tomb is built to hold the urns of a family's ancestors, is now absent, although most families did not observe this stage even before 1949.

Most informants could not explain very clearly the reasons for reburial, now or in the past, but simply regarded it as the customary thing to do. According to students of the subject, reburial was practiced in this part of China because feng-shui is believed to act through the bones of deceased ancestors to help or harm descendants. Thus special care has to be taken in the preservation and siting of these bones. Although the custom seems clearly to stem from traditional "superstitious" beliefs and to have no modern rationalization, it is reportedly not criticized by rural authorities. Again, local cadres generally rebury the bones of deceased kin, as do their neighbors. The reburied bones are visited and presented with offerings at Ch'ing-ming and perhaps other festivals, but for our purposes the reburial completes the final stage in the life cycle.

From our examination of the pattern of funeral activities, it is clear that elements that the government considers superstitious are more prominent than in other life-cycle rituals—understandably, given the great uncertainties and anxieties surrounding death. Although funerals have not been secularized and politicized, the role of ritual specialists has clearly decreased sharply from former times. Geomancers, fortune-tellers, and incantation readers are not completely gone, but they operate under severe restrictions. Thus much of the "superstitious" activity is now organized and carried out by the relatives themselves rather than by ritual specialists. Relatives are again the main participants in old-age feasts and funerals, but, as with the weddings, in most villages activities explicitly emphasizing the lineage are generally absent, and the immediate family and close kin are clearly the focus. The financial burden of these last rituals is more modest than for a wedding, although given the low incomes of Kwangtung peasants expenditures of 100 yuan or so are still substantial. The elements of traditional funerals that are preserved emphasize that family obligations and inter-dependence transcend generations. In the peasants' eyes, present family fortunes depend on past efforts of the deceased, are affected by his or her passing, and will continue to be influenced by proper care for the ancestral spirits in the future.

Overall Patterns

The dominant impression we receive is one of change toward modified and somewhat simplified versions of traditional activities, but with a considerable gap between current practice and official ideals. But this pattern is not uniform, and some elements of these rituals have changed more than others. What explains these differences?

Parts of the puzzle have been touched on in preceding chapters; in particular the role of collectivization of agricultural land and the increased participation of women in field labor in perpetuating or even increasing wedding expenditures. But we need to consider other forces as well. Part of the pattern we have found is attributable to the variable pressure that comes from higher authorities. In general, a harsher official line is taken against ritual specialists and the manufacturers of ritual objects (incense, and so on) than against ritual activities engaged in by ordinary peasants. At the time of land reform these specialists were given the label of "religious practitioners" and were considered part of the exploiting classes. At various times since then they have been pressured to abandon their specialties and to rely on agricultural labor to live. When caught plying their trades during intense political campaigns, they are drawn out for mass struggle meetings. One of our informants, in fact, had been a covert manufacturer of incense sticks who had been "struggled" so often his life became unbearable, and he decided to escape to Hong Kong. In rural ritual life, then, for the most part the policy followed conforms to the view expressed in 1963 by Ya Han-cheng: "We must strictly distinguish between the people's theist ideas and spontaneous superstitious activities and the activities of those engaging in superstitious trades who swindle money and goods from the people through superstition."[31] The specialists can be dealt with by coercion, but persuasion should be used in the longer-term effort to change the behavior of peasants, and this means considerable tolerance toward "superstitious" practices.

Part of the reason for the persistence of traditional rituals also turns on the role of local cadres. We have noted throughout this chapter and elsewhere that cadres at the brigade level and below engage in many of the same traditional activities as their neighbors. Even when a cadre avoids participating, members of his family and close kin are involved, and cadres seem reluctant to crack down too vigorously. One informant bluntly states, "In general cadres don't pay attention to birth and death ceremonies and so forth—these are very ordinary matters, and they don't bother to interfere."[32] The judgment by cadres that these are "ordinary matters" is based on an assessment that these activities are of minor concern to commune and higher-level authorities. Apparently such things as birth celebrations and bone reburials are not seen as presenting a serious threat to the political, economic, and social goals rural authorities are trying to pursue.

We also noted that the lineage as a corporate group is unimportant in life-cycle celebrations. The role of lineages in ritual life before 1949 is none too clear to us, and seems to have varied from place to place, depending partly on the resources (land, halls, and so on) that lineages commanded. With the confiscation of lineage lands and the transformation of most ancestral halls into new uses during the land reform campaign, the role of lineages as a corporate focus of ritual life declined. One's close kin, in contrast, remain very important in these ceremonies. Except in one respect, there has been no official pressure on people to associate less with their relatives and more with unrelated friends and neighbors. This one respect concerns former landlords and other "class enemies." They live under a political cloud today and are ostracized. In some places they are not invited to the life-cycle events of kin from the "good classes," and they may in turn invite few people to their own celebrations. They must be careful not to engage in very visible or expensive traditional rituals, for they, like the religious specialists, are still considered "enemies" and are likely to be drawn out for "struggle." So even though life-cycle celebrations reinforce kin ties, the focus is not on the lineage itself, and those who played a leading role in lineage rituals before 1949 play no such role today.

There has been little success in popularizing secular rituals in which brigade or team cadres officiate. Partly this may be due to local cadres having made little effort toward such popularization. But we also note that these officially espoused rituals are designed to be simple and frugal. As such, they may not meet the desire of peasants to stress family events. The immediate family is still the basic unit in rural life today, and provides much of the status, emotional support, and economic security that peasants enjoy. In Kwangtung, village change is still closely tied to biological and meteorological rhythms and recurrences, as in other peasant societies, and technological and other "modern" sources of change have not completely taken over.[33] Life-cycle rituals serve to mark the importance of transitions in the family unit and the interdependence of generations; modern rituals do not do this very well, in peasant eyes. For this reason, even when official pressure to eliminate traditional rituals is exerted, peasants often ignore it and drag their heels, or wait until calmer times to resume the traditional celebrations. Thus these rituals continue to be practiced not simply because of the force of tradition or the laxity of official enforcement, but because they celebrate events which are still very important to Kwangtung peasants.

We have noted throughout this chapter that particular customs survive in some villages while they have died out in others. What is the overall pattern? What sorts of villages are likely to have traditional celebrations of life-cycle events, and what other villages show modified forms? We can answer these questions with the data in table 41. There we examine the association of village characteristics with eight separate life-cycle customs, each coded dichotomously into "traditional" and "modern" forms.

Naming customs	1 = generational character and-or fortune-teller choice
	2 = parents' or grandparents' free choice
Wedding cost	1 = over 1,000 yuan generally
	2 = under 1,000 yuan generally[34]
Wedding feast size	1 = 10 tables or more generally
	2 = 9 tables or less generally
Worship at groom's home as part of wedding	1 = yes
	2 = no
Traveling marriage	1 = no cases locally
	2 = some cases or common

Old-age birthday feasts	1 = generally held
	2 = none or a few
Ancestral tablets presently used	1 = yes
	2 = no
Geomancer used presently	1 = yes
	2 = no

We see first in table 41 that our eight life-cycle items are generally, although not perfectly, interrelated. The closest relationships are among our traveling marriage, old-age birthday, and geomancer items (average gamma = .89) and among our wedding feast size, wedding worship, and ancestral tablets items (average gamma = .69). Given the number of items in this table and their interconnections (as well as the crudeness of our data and the small numbers involved), we can make the most sense out of the table by examining it by row, rather than by column. In this way we focus on whether particular village characteristics make a difference in general life-cycle customs.

The relationship between the administrative-political characteristics of villages and these measures is generally negligible or negative. This means that having more party members, a poor and lower middle-peasant association, regular political study, and so forth are not related to "modern" life-cycle activities, and in a few cases seem related to more traditional rituals. Our item for urban proximity generally has positive signs, although the relationships are all fairly weak. Being close to Canton or Swatow produces at best a very weak tendency to have more "modern" life-cycle celebrations. The presence of many sent-down urban youths shows a contradictory pattern, as does our measure of local exposure to mass communications. In the latter case villages with much media exposure are more likely to have parents picking names for children and to have worship activities absent from weddings, but are more likely today to employ geomancers in burials. The presence of collective nurseries is more consistently related to modern celebrations, although only the association with the presence of traveling marriages is very strong. On balance there does seem to be some relationship between our urban-communications measures and modern life-cycle celebrations, but it is modest in size and inconsistent.

Similarly mixed results come from examining our economic measures. Collective affluence is generally, but weakly, associated with more traditional life-cycle activities, except that in rich villages naming customs are likely to be more "modern." Our measure of average household consump-

Table 41   Life Cycle Rituals by Village
                                                  Characteristics (Gamma Statistics)

	CN	WC	WFS	WW	TM	OAB	AT	G	Median N
Life cycle rituals									
Child naming	--								
Wedding cost	.27	--							
Wedding feast size	-.14	-.09	--						
Wedding worship	.61	-.11	.80*	--					
Traveling marriage	.27	.71	-.26	.11	--				
Old age birthdays	-.14	.45	-.40	.51	.91*	--			
Ancestral tablets	.20	-.20	.83*	.34	.00	.50	--		
Geomancers	.41	-.17	-.14	.56	.89*	.87*	.41	--	
Administrative									
Political density	-.02	.03	.00	.00	-.33	.20	-.42	-.07	(33)
Political study	-.08	-.82*	.35	.06	.11	-.23	-.43	.20	(30)
Urban-communications									
Urban proximity	.10	.39*	.23	.27	.28	-.07	.04	.18$_a$	(34)
Urban youths	.08	.62	-.60$_b$	-.50	.08	-.27	.18	.45[a]	(25)
Communications	.63*	.06	.45[b]	.63*	-.12	-.06	-.35	-.61*	(32)
Nurseries	.59[c]	-.05	.04	.36	.78*	.30	.31	.36	(33)
Economic									
Collective affluence	.58*	-.21	-.26	.05	-.19	-.26	-.07	.14	(34)
Household consumption	-.05	.32	-.39	-.36	.37	.00	-.17	.12	(33)
Land/labor ratio	-.40	.47	.44	.48	.12	-.14	.18	.59*	(31)
Remittances	.33	-.47	-.20	-.32	-.52	-.68*	-.57*	-.62*	(24)
Other									
Brigade size	-.38	-.20	-.59	-.27	.26	-.33	-.30	.00	(27)
Team size	-.16	-.50	-.35	-.32	.27	-.13	-.22	-.24	(34)
Lineage composition	.30	.00	.22	.13	-.17	-.01	.03	-.10	(35)
Non-Hakka ethnicity	.56	-.60	-.62*	-.32	.07	-.62*	-.59*	-.23	(34)
Delta Region	.38	.11	-.57*	.00	.29	.13	-.27	.41[a]	(35)
Median N	(35)	(27)	(30)	(32)	(35)	(30)	(46)	(33)	

Note: Superior letters indicate relationships substantially weakened by statistical control for one of the following:

[a]Informant's class label, [b]number of hours of interview, [c]household consumption.

*p ≤ .10

tion in our villages shows a weak and inconsistent pattern—if anything, villages with high consumption are more likely to have traveling marriages and weddings with moderate costs, but are more likely to have large feasts and worship at the wedding.[35] Localities with a high land-labor ratio are generally somewhat more likely to have modern life-cycle festivals, while villages with many families receiving remittances are consistently likely to hold more traditional celebrations (in both of these cases with the exception of the naming-custom item). Thus our economic items point in different directions. This indicates that economic well-being does not in any simple fashion lead people either to forget the old rituals or to observe them more elaborately. We feel that life-cycle ceremonies tend to be somewhat more elaborate in the traditionally wealthy but densely settled areas in the plains and river valleys, and simpler in hillier regions where the land-labor ratio is higher.[36] The stronger and more consistent pattern for remittances indicates an additional factor, with remittance dependency associated with more elaborate celebrations. However, we are not certain to what extent this represents remittances as a ready source of funds for rituals (an economic factor) or the social pressure exerted by relatives outside of China (some of whom periodically visit the village) to maintain traditional forms (more of a social factor). In any case we can see in these figures the influence of long-standing economic differences within rural Kwangtung.

Among our other variables, large brigade size and team size are both associated more often than not with more traditional celebrations, although the strengths of these associations are generally modest. These relationships may indicate some sort of social-pressure effect, with those having large circles of important social ties feeling more obligation to maintain traditional celebrations, particularly at weddings. But the associations with the lineage composition of a locality are generally weak or nonexistent; individuals who live in brigades or teams composed solely of kinsmen are not more likely to engage in traditional celebrations than those who live in multilineage units. Thus if village social pressure helps to maintain traditional activities, it does not require that the villagers all be one's kinsmen. Our measure of whether or not villagers are Hakkas shows a fairly strong and consistent pattern. Except in the cases of naming customs and traveling marriages, Hakka villages are more likely to engage in simple or "modern" life-cycle rituals—to have modest wedding celebrations and to lack old-age birthday feasts and ancestral tablets, in particular.[37] The final code for region shows an inconsistent pattern, with delta villages more "modern" in some ways (particularly naming customs and traveling marriages) but more traditional in others (wedding feast size). This is probably due to the offsetting influence on delta villages of the urban-communications and economic-terrain variables already discussed.

How can these relationships be summarized? Stated very crudely, a village is most likely to have modern life-cycle activities if it is composed of Hakkas, has few people receiving overseas remittances, has more land per laborer than is common elsewhere, has small teams and brigades, and is exposed to influences from urban centers and official communications. Traditional forms predominate for the opposing terms of these dichotomies: in non-Hakka villages with many families receiving remittances, with land shortages but traditionally high rice-yields, large brigades and teams, and low exposure to urban-communications influences. This pattern gives no support to the notion that traditional activities are rooted in poverty and in weak political organization, or that with economic improvement and the consolidation of local political organs these customs can be readily changed. Some villages that are quite isolated and poor (particularly Hakka ones) seem by our measures quite "modern," while others which are well-off (especially if part of their wealth comes from remittances) and have strong local political organs engage in more expensive or elaborate traditional celebrations than their neighbors. The lack of a pattern for our political-life variables does not mean that politics plays no role in the changes in ritual life. Administrative sanctions—the confiscation of lineage property, the penalties employed against ritual specialists, and so forth—have had a powerful impact on life-cycle ceremonies. Higher-level priorities and pressures are important in producing change, but the political characteristics of particular villages are not so important. In other words, the degree to which higher-level goals and priorities get transmitted and implemented in the lives of peasants depends less on features of village political organization than on other local characteristics.

We have examined life-cycle rituals and have found that they have changed somewhat since 1949—particularly toward more of a domestic focus, with ritual specialists rarely involved—but that they still take recognizable forms. The pattern of change and persistence in these ceremonies cannot be fully explained by official goals and priorities, and reflects how the changed rural social structure makes some traditional ceremonies less important now but others as important as ever. We have also found that the villages which show greater or lesser change in ritual life are distinguished more by their ethnic and other social characteristics than by their political traits. Now we must examine the other major set of rituals: those connected with the annual cycle of festivals.

14

The Annual Cycle
of Festivals

*t*he ritual life of rural China revolves not only around the cycle of birth, marriage, and death but also around the annual changes of season and farming tempos. As for peasants elsewhere, the heavy burden of agricultural labor in China is periodically broken by feasts and religious observances, in which thanks are given for past blessings and prayers for future harmony and prosperity are offered. The long stretch of Chinese history produced an elaborate set of annual festivals oriented toward the harvest and toward the triumvirate of gods, ghosts, and ancestors.

The Chinese Communists oppose the traditional festivals for many of the same reasons that they oppose life-cycle celebrations. They claim that the festivals orient the populace to traditional lineage, kin, and community groups and the elites within them. For example, in many communities some of the annual holidays involved collective worship and feasting in lineage halls or local temples organized by lineage elders and ritual specialists.[1] Festivals also involve the expenditure of large amounts of time, money, and food—expenditures the government regards as nonproductive. Excerpts from a 1958 article about a county in Kweichow Province with many different minority groups illustrate these concerns:

> In the past, antiquated rules and oppressive customs were countless. A rough estimate showed that there were some sixty superstitious regulations contained in their folklore. For example, every year before plowing a "living guide" had to lead the way before the masses would com-

273

mence farming. As a result, production was frequently delayed. . . . In addition, there have been too many religious festivals, including many national days, during which production has been at a standstill. Because of superstition and festivals, production has been discontinued more than 100 days annually, and in some areas 138 days. As each nationality maintains different festivals, numerous conflicts arise from these divergences. . . . The reactionary class had in the past used these evil customs and rituals to enslave the people.[2]

Official opposition to festival celebrations has involved many of the same tactics used against life-cycle celebrations, since more or less the same set of spirits, practitioners, and ritual objects is involved. The confiscation of lineage lands in the land reform campaign and the transformation in the uses of most lineage halls and village or local temples eliminated the facilities and resources used in many celebrations. Propaganda has repeatedly been carried out against festival activities that have been seen as wasteful and superstitious. Periodically attacks on individual ritual specialists are mounted, and the manufacture and sale of ritual items have been restricted or banned. At times individual peasant participants in festival activities have been singled out for criticism and official sanctions. The official pressure exerted on festival life, as in so many other areas, has varied over time, reaching peaks during major political campaigns. When our informants mention particular traditional activities disappearing, the timing almost always corresponds with one of the major campaigns. However, the pattern in each village is different, with a particular activity disappearing in some places as early as land reform (1950–52) and continuing in others until collectivization (1955–56), the Great Leap Forward (1958–60), the rural socialist education campaign (1963–65), or the Cultural Revolution (1966–69).

In regard to individual annual holidays, a dual strategy was adopted. The Chinese Communists introduced new, secular, political holidays which, unlike the traditional festivals, follow the Western calendar.[3] At the same time they tried to discourage participation in traditional holidays by scheduling work as usual, and also by praising those who gave up old ways and by criticizing those who engaged in particularly open or blatant festival activities. The policy toward the most important traditional festival, Chinese New Year, has vacillated. At some times the government has encouraged people to ignore the holiday and to work during it to promote the revolution.[4] But more often the effort has been to co-opt and secularize it. The term "Spring Festival" (ch'un-chieh) has been popularized instead of the term "New Year" (kuo-nien or hsin-nien). Time off from work is granted, but work units organize sports and other recreational activities to draw people away from the traditional holiday pursuits. There are also cases of politicized versions of some traditional activities, as the following quotation shows:

> It has been customary to eat meat dumplings on the first day of the Spring Festival, but I purposely made steamed corn rolls. I said to the children, "We take this meal so as not to forget the past sufferings, so as to let you know that our great leader Chairman Mao has brought us today's happiness, and so as to make you become good children nurtured by Mao Tse-tung thought."[5]

For other holidays secular versions and activities have not been introduced; instead, peasants are urged to ignore them. Celebration of these other festivals is officially frowned upon, although people who engage in modest observances on their own time may not be harassed. However, activities during such celebrations that are viewed as particularly harmful may be criticized. One example comes from the 1958 article already cited about a county in Kweichow Province with several minority groups:

> Other customs such as eating the viscera of a bull, dragon-calling, slope-climbing, "retirement" of old fields, "retirement" for old cows and horses, "Mah-yüan-ti," maiden's lot, and others have all been abolished because they arc unfavorable to production and also are not meritorious.[6]

What has been the result of this change effort in the Kwangtung countryside? Our expectation, reinforced by the previous chapter, is that rituals which celebrate collectivities and values that are still central to peasant life will persist, while those that focus on groups and values that are no longer so salient will die away. In the pages that follow we sketch the general pattern of current festivals in our villages, dealing first with the traditional set of holidays and then with the modern.

Traditional Holidays

Chinese New Year falls between late January and mid-February by our calendar.[7] Traditionally, we are told, new year celebrations might last a month or more, from the middle of the twelfth lunar month to the middle of the first month of the new year. However, many ordinary peasants could not have taken this much time off from work, particularly in rural Kwangtung where the semitropical climate allows year-round farming. Currently production teams give their members a vacation (unpaid) for the Spring Festival, commonly of four to five days, but in some localities for as long as ten days to two weeks. Family preparations for the holiday begin before the formal start of the team vacation, and peasants increasingly take off from work on their own as the holiday approaches. The free markets are packed for the final sessions of the old year as individuals sell their produce and use the cash to buy food items for the holiday. Peasants kill domestic fowl and buy pork to provide meat for the unusually rich holiday fare.

At home family members engage in a general housecleaning and often sew new clothes for the children (less often for the adults). People in most villages paste red-paper couplets (tui-lien) outside, on either side of the main door of the house, and these contain felicitous sayings for the new year. In most villages the couplets with traditional phrases ("May the fields yield prosperity," "May sons and grandsons fill the hall") have now been replaced by new-style couplets with revolutionary slogans ("Listen to Chairman Mao," "Follow the Communist party"). A number of informants report that only such new-style couplets have been sold in the book shops since the Cultural Revolution. However, in about a quarter of our villages, people buy red paper and then write their own traditional sayings to post outside the door. In such villages neighbors may have couplets expressing very different sentiments, new and old, without any apparent concern or conflict.[8]

One other customary activity was the sending off of the kitchen god to report to the king of heaven on the conduct of family members during the past year. Throughout the year a picture of the kitchen god (and sometimes his wife) stared out at the household from a position on or near the family oven. About one week before the new year, food offerings and incense were placed before the kitchen god, and then his image was taken down and burned. He then went to make his report (bribed into benignity by the food offerings), and returned at the start of the new year, when a new kitchen god image was posted. Informants from nineteen villages report some such kitchen-god activity taking place today, although it is reported absent in twenty-one other villages. Even where this activity is carried out, it is often done covertly. The kitchen god may be represented in the house simply by a slip with his name written on it rather than by a picture, or a picture or name may be put up just before he goes to report, and the new kitchen god taken down and hidden away at the end of the holiday.

A few days before the holiday the cooking of special dishes begins, and peasants all know they will soon be eating the most bountiful meals of the year. The particular dishes vary a great deal from place to place but include pork, chicken and other fowl, and a variety of steamed and fried pastries, dumplings and cakes, many of them made with a special and expensive glutinous rice (nuo-mi) and filled with tasty delicacies. These serve not only as food for the family itself but as gifts for the period of visiting among kin which is soon to take place.

The commune also organizes certain activities in preparation for the Spring Festival. Often meetings are held in which peasants are warned not to engage in extravagance, "superstitious" activities, and gambling. The Chinese press also carries articles at about this time urging frugality in holiday celebrations. In a number of localities Youth League members are organized to take food packages and inquire about the welfare of families who have a member away in the army or a member who died in military service.

On the morning of the last day of the old year family members bathe and put on new or relatively good clothing. No work or other community activity is organized on this day, which is strictly a family occasion. Individuals who have been living and working elsewhere are expected to return for the year-end meal (t'uan-nien fan), when the whole family should be together. The meal itself commonly begins in mid-afternoon, and before this meal and before the morning meal on subsequent days family worship activity is still fairly common. In only two villages does worship in lineage halls still take place. But worship within the household is reportedly still common in thirty-seven of the fifty-three villages on which we have information. Where worship takes place it involves placing food offerings, candles, and incense in front of the domestic shrine and praying to the ancestors and various other spirits and deities. As mentioned in the previous chapter, the character of the family shrine now varies a great deal, from instances in which there is simply an empty wall on which spirit images and tablets used to be placed to a few villages which still have wooden ancestral tablets and pictures of some gods (for example, the Buddhist deity Kuan-yin; in 64 percent of the villages for which we have information [N=33] worship to some other spirits besides ancestral ones is mentioned). Many of the ritual items used (incense, paper ingots, and so on) are homemade or bought on the black market. In many of these thirty-seven villages not every family continues to worship, and among families that do, not every member is involved. In all but eleven villages this worship is carried out covertly, with some fear of criticism if discovered. However, many informants in the other twenty-six villages felt that local cadres were well aware that this activity was being carried out but usually chose to ignore it. In many cases, as we have already noted, even the mothers and wives of leading local cadres continue to engage in worship activities.

With domestic worship concluded (where it occurs), family members sit down for the year-end meal, which may take several hours. According to several informants, it is customary not to consume all the food put out for this meal, this signifying that there will be a surplus of food for the family to eat during the coming year.

On New Year's eve people stay up late, but they do not stay up all night, as was reportedly the custom in some parts of China. During the night firecrackers periodically crackle around the village, and their noise is heard off and on for the remaining days of the holiday. Some informants report that local authorities discouraged the use of firecrackers during the Cultural Revolution, but unlike incense they are still available, and their use is still very common throughout rural Kwangtung. Evidently firecrackers are regarded as having a secular interpretation—creating a noisy and joyful atmosphere—although in the past another purpose was stressed—frightening away ghosts.

On New Year's morning villagers get up early, often at dawn, to the sound of incessant firecrackers. After the morning worship activities young people inquire of the health of their elders, and the latter in turn pass out "lucky money" envelopes to the children, and sometimes to all unmarried youths. In most of our villages it is not customary now for the children to kneel or bow at the feet of their parents on New Year's morning, a custom reported quite recently in a village in another part of China.[9]

In at least fourteen of our villages (we did not inquire during our early interviews) meals on the first day of the new year (or at least the morning meal) are meatless. The term used (ch'ih-chai) indicates a Buddhist derivation, as an ordinary meatless meal would be referred to by the term ch'ih-su. There are also nineteen informants who report that on this day certain traditional taboos are observed: against sweeping, using knives, saying unlucky words, and so on. The pattern of activities later in the day varies from place to place. In some localities people visit village kinsmen and neighbors to pay their respects (pai-nien) and exchange food gifts, with "lucky money" again given to the children. In some localities visits to kin outside of the village also begin on the first day of the year, and wives take pastries, meats, and small fruit trees and set off to visit their parents and married brothers. In other villages there is reportedly little house-to-house visiting within the village, and visits to outside kin begin only on the second. If this is the case, then the rest of the first day will simply be free time. In half of the villages for which we have information, the commune authorities organize "modern" holiday activities to occupy this time: sports competitions, movies, and drama team performances. Peasants also have ways of their own of filling free time, and one of these is gambling. Informants from ten villages reported that men still gathered for gambling during the Spring Festival, even though it is strictly forbidden, with those being caught possibly subject to arrest and "struggle" meetings. According to our informants, gambling is confined pretty much to this one period during the year.

The rest of the holiday is occupied with family worship, feasts, visits to outside kin, and also the recreational activity organized by one's commune. There is often a customary rule about which days are auspicious for visits to relatives and which days inauspicious—the third day of the new year is considered the latter, with visits then likely to end up in arguments. The second is in many places considered the opening of the new year (k'ai-nien), but this is not the occasion for celebrations more elaborate than those on other days. In most localities the team starts work again on the fourth or fifth day, but a fair proportion of the work force is still off making outside visits during the first few work days. These people receive no special criticism for their tardiness but as usual receive no work points until they resume work. In many localities, before 1949, each day up until the fifteenth had some distinctive ritual activitiy connected with it, but nowadays much of the distinctiveness is gone, with rich meals and family worship simply continuing until the family resumes work and other normal activities. The only distinction regularly mentioned by our informants concerned the seventh, "man day," when traditionally the weather was looked to for some indication of whether the coming year would be an auspicious one for births or not. Now by the seventh most of the special holiday food is gone, and peasants drift back to work and the holiday is considered over.

The fifteenth day of the first lunar month is called Yüan-hsiao chieh, and it has been celebrated in much of China as a lantern festival. Among our informants a celebration on this day was reported in only a few villages (twelve), and in those, generally, on a modest scale: some household worship and a richer than average meal, often including small rice dumplings (t'ang-yüan). The team gives no vacation from work, and in most villages there is no celebration of any note on this day.

The next holiday in most villages is a major one: Ch'ing-ming, which falls in early April by our calendar. This is the occasion for traditional visits to family graves and for "grave-sweeping," and such activities are reported absent in only three of our villages. Nonetheless, most teams do not call off work, and family members have to take time off on their own. In its simple version Ch'ing-ming involves family members taking a shovel and perhaps some food items and setting off for the hills where their recent ancestors are buried. The shovel is used to clean weeds off the grave mounds, and the food is put beside the graves as an offering and then consumed. In more elaborate versions people take along paper ritual items (paper clothing, money, and ingots), incense, and firecrackers. After the grave is cleaned some sheets of paper money are spread out on the mound, food offerings are placed in front, incense is lit, and paper ingots and other items are burned for the use of the ancestors. Family members kneel and pray before these offerings, and then proceed home for a family meal.[10]

Even this more elaborate version, it should be noted, is more modest in scale than Ch'ing-ming observances reported in some past accounts for this area.[11] The absence of common lineage property and corporate funds is obviously one factor here. One of our older informants gave us a detailed account of the changes necessitated in Ch'ing-ming observances over the last quarter-century.

> This custom [of five days of collective processions and worship at the tombs of the founders of the lineage and its various branches] still existed in the 1950 Ch'ing-ming, but not in 1951, since there was no income from the common property—at that time the campaign to reduce rent and interest was just beginning [followed by land reform]. From 1951 to 1956 each son and grandson had to foot the bill himself to buy silver paper ingots, wax candles, incense, and firecrackers for use in Ch'ing-ming. In 1957 an overseas Chinese who lives in Malaya sent relatives in the village over 500 yuan to use in grave-sweeping, and this money was not used up until 1961. From 1962 to the present, again, each son and grandson had to use his own funds to worship the hillside graves. From Ch'ing-ming in 1951 to the present, although there is grave-sweeping, there is no gathering for banquets, and the sons and grandsons going into the hills to worship just take several dry cakes. From the start of the Cultural Revolution in 1966, there was no sale of spirit incense, and no spirit candles or silver paper ingots—only fire-crackers were sold.[12]

This quotation brings out another fact about observances at Ch'ing-ming and other holidays. Funds provided by overseas relatives continue to be important in financing celebrations in some villages. Relatives in Hong Kong and Macao, in fact, often travel back to their native villages in Kwangtung to sweep the graves of ancestors, and extra train-runs to the

Chinese border in Hong Kong are added for the major holidays. The government's desire, for both economic and foreign-relations reasons, to permit and even encourage visits home of overseas Chinese inevitably undermines the official drive to eliminate traditional rites.

Ch'ing-ming observances generally involve trips only to graves of the family's recent ancestors, not to those of the lineage founder, but in most villages in this area that was also the case in the past. In a few localities only males go to the graves for these Ch'ing-ming rites, but in other places both sexes participate. Even though in most places local cadres do not give time off from work for this holiday, they do not criticize peasants for taking time off for hillside worship. In fact, they and their families generally make grave visits as well, although often of the "simple" type.

The next important festival is the fifth day of the fifth lunar month (tuan-wu chieh), which is called Dragon Boat Festival in the West. Only two of our informants claim that this holiday is no longer celebrated. In many Kwangtung villages prior to 1949, particularly in the Pearl River Delta (and still today in Hong Kong) races between long dragon boats that pitted village against village were common on this date. These have been discontinued in most places, due apparently both to neglect (the failure to spend funds to make and repair the boats) and to official dislike for the intervillage enmities these races fostered. In four accounts, however, we were told that races were still being held on this holiday, or had been restored since the Cultural Revolution, although now they sometimes involve boats smaller than the traditional dragon boats, which often held twenty or more men.

In most villages in Kwangtung there is no team vacation on this holiday. The holiday activities center on a rich meal, whose special dish is the wrapped rice dumpling (tsung-tzu) for which this festival is well known. This holiday is also supposed to be good for bathing in fresh water, with health benefits being derived from an invigorating dip. On this day, as on other traditional holidays, many families place offerings and ritual objects out before the family shrine and worship there before their holiday meal. None of these activities except the boat races interfere with agricultural production in a significant way, and cadres as well as ordinary peasants take part in holiday celebrations.

In the seventh lunar month there are two less important holidays, and each of these is celebrated in at least two different ways in rural Kwangtung. On the seventh day of the seventh lunar month there is a holiday celebrated in seventeen out of thirty-nine villages on which we have information. In some Hakka villages it is not celebrated, but in others women go before dawn to a nearby river or pond to fetch water. This water, which is supposed to have special curative powers, is stored in the home and used for some time for drinking and for bathing the ill. Some informants claim that if the water-fetchers fail to return before sunrise the water becomes harmful rather than beneficial. In Cantonese villages this holiday is called the "entreating skill festival" (ch'i-ch'iao chieh), and is an occasion for young women to gather and practice their domestic arts and honor the fabled seven daughters of the emperor of heaven. However, in some of these villages curative water is also collected; it is called "fairy water" and its curative powers are said to come from the seven daughters.

A holiday on the fourteenth or fifteenth day of the seventh lunar month is celebrated in thirty out of forty-one villages. In Cantonese villages it is called either the Ghost Festival (kuei-chieh) or Yü-lan chieh, and involves feasting and making food and paper clothing offerings to appease hungry ghosts, who are believed to congregate at this time. In Hakka villages the holiday is usually called simply seven–fourteen (ch'i-yüeh shih-ssu), and is an occasion to offer thanks for the harvest and ask protection for the new crops.[13] Neither seventh-month festival today involves much interruption of the farming routine.

The next important holiday is the Mid-autumn Festival (chung-ch'iu chieh), which falls on the fifteenth day of the eighth lunar month. Only one of our informants claimed that this holiday was no longer celebrated. Again the team generally gives no vacation. Moon cakes are the pastry char-acteristically eaten on this holiday, and these are generally purchased rather than made at home. Several informants claimed that during the Cultural Revolution moon cakes were not available in shops but that the supply of them has since been resumed (although in rationed form in some places). The evening meal is an especially rich one on this day, and, as with other holidays, it may be preceded by offerings and worship at the family ancestral shrine. Then in the evening families set tables up outside the house on which they place moon cakes, fruit, taro, and candles. Family members sit around this table and "appreciate the moon" (shan-yüeh). This seems to involve in some cases a sort of worship of the moon, but in others simply chatting and enjoying the moonlight and food. This activity is clearly public and may involve some minor elements regarded as "superstitious," but it does not receive any criticism.

After the mid-autumn festival comes the ninth day of the ninth lunar month, called Ch'ung-yang chieh. In seventeen of the villages for which we have information this holiday is not celebrated, but in most cases this does not seem to be because it has been recently discarded. In most of these villages there is no mention of this festival ever being observed, while in those nineteen villages where it is observed it remains an important holiday. The most common form of this festival now is essentially a repetition of Ch'ing-ming. Families go to the graves, taking food offerings and ritual items for commemoration of the ancestors, again generally without an official day off from the team, and in some places this is the time for the reburial of ancestral bones that was described in Chapter 13. The collective trooping off to the grave of the lineage founder by entire lineages, which used to be the prominent feature of this holiday, is now gone. In four villages this holiday is celebrated in a different way, with the festival being simply a time to take food items and climb to the top of the highest hill in the area and have a picnic, perhaps with kite-flying as well, a variant noted in some traditional sources.[14]

The final major holiday of the year is the Winter Solstice (tung-chih) which, as the name suggests, falls on December 22. Again, generally, the team does not give a day off, but families kill chickens, buy pork, and prepare a big meal. Though there is a curious Cantonese saying that the winter festival is bigger than the New Year's, the celebration and the atmosphere are much more modest and seem always to have been so. Even if the celebration is modest, only three villages are reported not to observe this festival.

We have now discussed the nine most important traditional festivals which are currently observed by peasants in Kwangtung. Of these the Spring Festival, or New Year's (the two terms are used interchangeably by our informants), is by far the longest and most elaborate. Four other festivals—Ch'ing-ming, the Dragon Boat Festival, the Mid-Autumn and Winter Solstice—are celebrated in virtually every village, generally with some family feasting, domestic worship, and sometimes visits to kin. The Ch'ung-yang festival is similarly important but celebrated in fewer villages. The other three common festivals (the fifteenth day of the first month, the seventh of the seventh, and the fourteenth of the seventh) are both less universally celebrated and more modest in scope where they are celebrated. In addition to these nine festivals there are some other holidays observed in a few of our villages (fifteen accounts mention one or more additional holidays). Most commonly mentioned are the third day of the third month, the eighth of the fourth, the sixth of the sixth, and the first of the tenth (all according to the lunar calendar). These dates can be connected with lesser holidays mentioned in the literature on traditional Chinese festivals.[15] But often our informants could not recall the exact name or nature of these lesser festivals, which are now celebrated with little more than a richer-than-usual family meal, perhaps with domestic worship added.

Another set of holidays generally absent in our accounts is birthday celebrations for the village earth-god (t'u-ti kung or pa-kung) or other community patron deities. Traditionally most places had shrines to such deities, who were regarded as protectors of the welfare of the villagers. As the days of birthday celebrations for patron deities of various villages differed, in any locality there would be a round of mutual visiting and feasting during the year by those joining friends and relatives in the surrounding communities in their celebrations. These local shrines were also nested in a hierarchy, so that peasants might be involved in celebrations at local shrines and also at superior temples in market towns and in the county seat. Now the earth-god shrines are mostly gone—either in disrepair, or dismantled to yield bricks for new buildings—and celebrations to honor patron deities are generally gone. Thus the multifamily celebrations—in both lineage halls and community temples—which provided the religious framework for traditional community life are almost gone now, although domestic celebrations remain.

Though the major traditional holidays are still widely celebrated (with important modifications), lesser holidays seem either to have disappeared or to have lost much of their original meaning. The average number of festivals being observed in the villages for which we have information is seven, but the range around this is very wide—from two villages where we were told only the Spring Festival is now celebrated to one village where thirteen traditional holidays are still observed. (A collection of articles on Kwangtung folk customs in the 1920s gives comparable lists of holidays celebrated in different localities, and they range in number from seven to fourteen—a range similar to that for our own figures, except that we have more cases now where only a few major holidays are celebrated.)[16]

Although production teams do not generally give days off for any particular holiday except the Spring Festival, in fact many teams call a day off for one or more of the other traditional days, especially if they happen to fall during a slack agricultural work period. Also, when a sufficient number of team members decide to take time off for holiday activities, many teams decide it is not worth trying to continue production with the remainder. On none of the traditional holidays besides the Spring Festival are "modern" activities organized—sports competitions, meetings, cultural performances, and so on. We will return to examine in further detail the pattern of change in traditional festivals after we have discussed the set of post–1949 holidays.

New Holidays

Peasants in rural Kwangtung also observe a set of new holidays introduced by the Chinese Communists, some of which are shared with other communist and socialist countries. There are eight of these, although only three involve the entire community. The first is New Year's Day by the Western calendar. Teams give a one-day or two-day vacation for this holiday, and in many localities there is a half-day commune or brigade mass meeting at which the party secretary reads the New Year's editorial published in the national press, and various cadres speak on the excellent situation for the coming year. Adults attending the meeting receive work points, and the policy of giving work points to encourage meeting participation is followed for other new holidays as well.

The rest of the holiday period is simply free time, although the commune often organizes sports competitions between brigades and stages cultural performances. In some urban organizations it has been the custom to have special meat distributions before the major new holidays in order to give them a more festive atmosphere, but this is rarely done in the Kwangtung countryside. There is little in the way of family feasting or other celebrations during these holidays, and this clearly constitutes a major difference from the set of traditional holidays, where domestic feasting is the core activity. Nor do we find in our interviews evidence for the sort of "secular-religious" activities during new holidays which have been reported by others and in the press (for example, meals of "bitter remembrance for past class suffering" such as that mentioned at the beginning of this chapter, worship of Chairman Mao's portrait, and so on). The routine on this and other new holidays consists basically of meetings, organized recreation, and rest. The recreational activities are reportedly attended more by young people than by others, and many older peasants use this time to work on their private plots and catch up on domestic work.

The next holiday is International Women's Day, which falls on March 8. Typically on this day the brigade convenes women for a half-day meeting, led by the chief of the brigade women's association. Primary topics are late marriage and birth control, although women's general participation in work and public life are also discussed. In most localities the afternoon is free for women to return home for family chores, but in a few villages a collective meal for women is organized to celebrate this holiday. (This is the only exception to our generalization about the lack of feasting on new holidays, and it applies in very few villages.) For all other villagers there is no special activity on this day, and work proceeds as usual. (We asked our informants if husbands helped out more around the house on this day, as on Mother's Day in America, and the usual response was an incredulous laugh.)

The next holiday is International Labor Day on May 1. This is essentially a repetition of New Year's Day, with many communes organizing mass meetings and/or athletic and cultural activities. A one-day vacation from work is called. Three days later falls the Youth Festival (ch'ing-nien chieh), which commemorates the beginning of the student patriotic movement of May Fourth, 1919. Working youths are called to a brigade or commune meeting for half a day, to hear the party or Youth League secretary discuss the history of the May Fourth movement and the events it touched off, including the founding of the Chinese Communist party in 1921. Youths who are team laborers receive half a day's work points for attending, but there is no collective meal, and in most localities they are expected to return to work in the afternoon.

The next three holidays do not affect the ordinary peasant. June 1 is Children's Day, and schools organize skits and other activities in connection with it. However, there is no activity for parents or the commune at large. July 1 is the anniversary of the founding of the Chinese Communist party. Party members are convened for all-day meetings and celebrations, but other people are not invited. August 1 is the anniversary of the founding of the Red Army. In most places this occasion is not celebrated at all, but peasants living near an army base may be invited in to attend performances and celebrations. In a few localities on August 1 commune authorities do organize the same sort of visiting and inquiring after the welfare of military-related families that we described in connection with the Spring Festival. The rural militia, however, does not have any special activities on this date, which passes in most localities with little notice.

The final new holiday is the most important one of the year: National Day on October 1, celebrating the Communist victory in 1949. Production teams give one or two days off from work, and in most respects activities are similar to those on January 1 and May 1, although there are more slogans and banners in the streets and on major buildings. Until 1971 parades and fireworks were held on this day in many rural towns as they were in China's major cities. In that year the fall of Lin Piao and the ensuing political turmoil coincided with a new official policy in favor of simplified National Day celebrations, and the parades disappeared. Thus there is little now to distinguish this occasion from the other two major new holidays.

These new holidays, then, have quite a different tone from the traditional ones. They do involve vacations, with work points given for those who attend meetings. In nine of our villages, however, the three major holidays involve little else besides time off from work—the meetings, sports competitions, and performances reported elsewhere are generally absent. Where these other activities are organized, the extent of attendance and participation varies a great deal from place to place, and by age within each village. The new holidays do not involve feasting or other family-centered activity, and the events which are organized are public and involve either a subset of the local community or draw out individuals from many communities to participate in their activities. Nothing could better illustrate the differences in the structural principles underlying the old society and the new: village-centered, religiously oriented festival activity involving families as units combining with neighbors and kin versus multivillage political and recreational activity involving individuals as participants in nonkinship groupings. But of course both of these structural principles continue to exist together and to find support in the two sets of holidays in rural Kwangtung.

General Patterns

Almost all of our informants report that the traditional holidays are much more important to the peasants, and continue to have more of a holiday atmosphere, than the new festivals. They often cite the four or more days of vacation given at Spring Festival as evidence of official recognition of this difference, since none of the new holidays receive more than a two-day vacation. But peasants do appreciate the time off afforded by the new holidays, and young people particularly appreciate the organized recreational activities. While traditional holidays continue to be more important to villagers, our informants do generally report that the spirit and lavishness with which they are celebrated are much toned down from earlier days.

If we focus just on the traditional holidays, what about them has changed and what has not? One pattern we have already commented upon: though minor traditional holidays are less regularly or elaborately celebrated, the major ones are still observed almost everywhere. So the government's goal of having people forget the traditional holidays (except in the case of the Spring Festival) has been realized only partially. But there have also been changes in the kinds of activities engaged in during the traditional festivals and in their atmosphere, which has become less boisterous.

We can assess changes most effectively if we consider again the aspects of festival life which the government considers particularly harmful. One aspect we have noted is the traditional role of festival activities in promoting the solidarity of lineages, with lineage elders leading their kinsmen in large feasts and ancestral hall observances. These elements of traditional holidays have largely disappeared, along with other public or community-wide celebrations.[17] In a few villages the converted lineage halls and tumble-down temples have worshipers visiting them on holidays, and in some places people still make offerings at hidden images of deities and before sacred rocks or trees. In some places religious specialists enjoy an active but covert trade on holidays. But these are the exceptions, and in most villages holiday activities have a strictly domestic focus; public feasting and worship are gone. The elimination of the public ritual centers also affects the form of those celebrations that had a domestic focus in the past. Celebrations are now largely confined to the home and do not involve individual families going to make offerings in lineage halls and community temples.

The government also frowns on the "superstitious" and fatalistic attitudes fostered by festival rituals, because these are seen as obstacles to enthusiastic compliance with official policies. Here our evidence is less clear, but substantial change seems to have occurred. Many acts regarded as "superstitious" continue to be practiced in Kwangtung villages, such as the gathering of "fairy water" on the seventh day of the seventh month festival and the reburying of bones during the Ch'ung-yang festival. In other contexts in our interviews evidence of continuing peasant "superstitious" beliefs occurred: belief in supernatural causes of some illnesses, attribution of death to the violation of ritual taboos, and in some cases consultation by individuals with local shamans to seek remedies to personal problems (illness, infertility, and so on). The major continuing focus of supernatural concern is the ancestral cult, which involves worship in the home and at the graves, with food offerings and the burning of incense, paper money, and other ritual objects. Against these elements of continuity we note that most religious specialists are gone or operating under severe restrictions. Although ancestor worship is still present, traditional holidays now focus mostly on family feasting and relaxation, rather than on the performance of certain ritual acts to please the spirit world. Accounts from villages in contemporary Hong Kong and Taiwan often show villagers coping with a complex series of ritual acts and taboos designed to please or avoid offending a variety of supernatural forces. People in such villages rely on the casting of lots in temples, and on the advice of fortune-tellers, shamans, and spirit mediums to cope with their daily problems and decisions.[18] We did not ask our informants questions about a wide range of "superstitious" beliefs and observances, only about those involved in life-cycle and annual holiday celebrations. But our general impression is that the importance of such beliefs and activities in the daily lives of Kwangtung peasants is noticeably less. The ancestral cult does remain fairly strong, with peasants feeling obligated to make regular offerings to deceased kin and hoping for some beneficial influences exerted by ancestral spirits. However, even this central element of traditional Chinese ritual life is largely gone in a few villages and is not maintained by every family in other localities.

Our dominant impression, then, is that there has been a noticeable decrease in the importance of worship and "superstitious" acts in rural Kwangtung. Such beliefs and activities still exist, but their impact on the lives of peasants, and the obstacles they pose to social change, seem diminished. We admittedly lack full information on these points, but in our interviews there is little indication of cadres having difficulty mobilizing peasants for some new activity or project due to fears of offending local gods, disrupting the flow of feng-shui, or violating ritual taboos. The "superstitious" beliefs which remain may provide peasants with extra hope, solace, a sense of belonging, or explanations of their situation, but they do not seem to govern their lives. At least a substantial portion of the Kwangtung peasantry seems to feel that future prosperity and happiness depend as much or more upon obeying higher authorities and upon their own efforts as on sticking to time-honored ways and following ritual prescriptions. How large a change from traditional times this indicates depends upon whether one thinks that peasants before 1949 mainly relied on their own hard work to get along, and looked to ritual acts for a little "extra help," or whether one thinks that reliance on the supernatural was very powerful and limiting. Jack Potter argues, in fact, that Cantonese peasants believe in both the efficacy of hard work and in the determining role of fate and luck, much as the Western Calvinist ethic stressed seemingly contradictory themes of predestination and striving for success.[19] Whatever the earlier case, the attitudes and activities revealed in festival activity today seem not to pose a serious obstacle to official programs. In fact, one might argue that fatalism could support, rather than obstruct, peasant acquiescence to official programs. For example, a Kwangtung fisherman, discussing popular reactions to the Cultural Revolution ban on the sale of ritual objects and the Red Guard destruction of domestic ancestral shrines, indicates a kind of fatalistic acquiescence:

Having gone through many years of post-liberation propaganda against superstition, worshipers were not so boisterous, and they just worshiped at New Year's. [Then came the Cultural Revolution restrictions.] The older families didn't express too many complaints about the restrictions on worship—it was as if a flood had passed by which affected everyone.[20]

In sum, our overall impression is of a fairly adaptive peasantry, not so bound by a traditional set of beliefs and practices that they are unable to change when it is in their interests to do so, but at the same time striving to maintain practices which have substantial value to them.

A third aspect of traditional festivals under attack by the current government is the extravagant expenditures involved. Spending on the building of temples and on god images is unimportant now, although ritual items like incense, which must be obtained on the black market, are no doubt more costly today. We are less clear on whether the expenditures for feasts have declined, a decline whose calculation is made difficult by the shift from partially collective to strictly domestic celebrations. The decline of lesser festivals and patron deity birthdays and in the competitive element present in public feasts must result in some savings, and on balance we feel that some moderation in holiday expenditures has occurred.[21]

The burden of festival life, in the eyes of the government, also involves time taken away from agricultural labor. Here we also detect some changes. Of the traditional holidays only New Year's, Ch'ing-ming, and Ch'ung-yang now require time off from work, since the domestic feasting and other activities of the remaining festivals can be fitted around rural work schedules. Some individuals and families do choose to take the day off for marketing and family celebrations on other holidays, but this does not bring agricultural work to a standstill unless many people make the same choice. The shift from collective to domestic celebrations makes it possible, then, to reduce the time conflict between work and festival life. Rural authorities do not appear to see the remaining days taken off from work as a significant problem for agricultural production.

The pattern we have sketched in this chapter can be summed up by saying that in regard to each official goal—the attack on lineage solidarity, on "superstition," and on the burden of festival expenditures—there has been some progress. The most marked shift concerns the decline of lineage-based and other community-wide festivities. We noted a similar shift in our discussion of life-cycle rituals in the previous chapter, but for the annual holidays the reductions in expenditures and "superstitious" elements are even more apparent. The traditional festivals have not disappeared, as the government wishes they would, but they have been altered toward more modest and domestic forms. Now festivals involve primarily the gathering of family members for an especially rich and tasty meal, for enjoyment of the delicacies and conviviality afforded by the occasion. This association of festive events with family gatherings and especially sumptuous meals remains absolutely central in the lives of Kwangtung peasants, and provides a welcome break from the regular routine of back-breaking labor and very simple fare.[22]

Our explanation for this pattern of change covers many of the grounds cited in the previous chapter. First, at some times official displeasure with traditional festival life has been backed up with efforts to punish participants. Usually these efforts have not been very vigorous, or have been aimed mainly at ritual specialists and conspicuous public celebrations. One reason why these attacks on religious specialists have been fairly effective is that China before 1949 had very little in the way of an organized clergy. Most temples lacked full-time priests, and there were few ties linking temples, monasteries, and other religious institutions in different parts of the country. The imperial authorities had always taken great care to prevent the emergence of religious hierarchies which might rival their own authority,[20] and thus religious specialists had little in the way of organization and resources to use to fend off the post-1949 attacks on them. But the application of official pressure has not always been limited to the specialists. Periodically, especially during major campaigns, even ordinary peasants have some fear that they will get into trouble for worshiping or engaging in other holiday activities. So part of our explanation rests on the variable pattern of official sanctions.

But other forces besides official punishment have undermined traditional festival life. We have referred at various points to the difficulty of financing collective feasts and other activities after the confiscation of lineage and temple lands in the land reform campaign. In Taiwan and other Chinese localities where corporate lineage property is relatively unimportant, other means (various kinds of associations and systems of rotating payment) can be found to finance such celebrations, but these means may be difficult to organize in rural Kwangtung, due to official displeasure. We need also to consider the possibility that the motivation to maintain old festival activities has also decreased. Local religion represented community autonomy under the control of traditional local elites. When the new government instituted a much more penetrating administrative system, with new boundaries and solidarities and different types of local leaders, the focus of traditional community ceremonials disappeared. It is thus unclear to what extent the corporate focus of holiday rituals was forced out of existence or simply withered away gradually as it became less important in peasant lives.

While these changes have occurred, the salience of family activities and obligations remains great. One's family, as we have repeatedly noted, remains an important source of economic and emotional security, a unit whose vital role in peasant life is reinforced by traditional festivals. Domestic feasting allows people to pause and take pleasure in the fruits of their recent efforts as a family, and domestic ancestor worship stresses the way in which individual well-being depends upon the bonds of familial obligations which transcend generations. We see here also a key to the lesser salience the set of new holidays has in the lives of Kwangtung peasants. These new holidays lack precisely the core elements of the traditional set: domestic worship and feasting. Commune members still depend less for their well-being on the collectivities emphasized by the new festivals—all women, all youths, all members of the brigade or commune—than they do on their immediate kin. Thus the new holidays may be a welcome added set of rest days, but they cannot effectively replace the traditional festivals.

Which segments of the village participate most actively in festival activities? The view in the Chinese press, of course, is that it is primarily former landlord and rich peasant families that engage in elaborate holiday activities and encourage others to do so. A contrary view would be that village cadres, as the new rural elite, will reinforce their community standing by spending more on such occasions than others. Though we have little detailed information on this point, our impression is that both of these views are inaccurate. Both rural cadres and "bad class elements" operate under some constraints in their festival celebrations, cadres for fear of being criticized by their superiors, and bad class elements for fear of being criticized by the cadres and the peasants they lead. Both kinds of families reportedly adopt a tactic of trying to stay out of trouble by making sure they are not the most elaborate celebrants in the village. This tactic is noted by one of our informants from a former landlord family:

> We Chens didn't dare show any prosperity in our celebrations, since many of us were classed as landlords, so we had to hold smaller and semisecret celebrations, compared with other people. The Chens don't dare lead the way in traditional activity—they follow the poor and lower middle peasants. If the latter are open in traditional activities, then the Chens do them too, but not quite so openly. In campaigns former landlords can be criticized for superstitious activity, even by poor and lower middle peasants who do the same things all the time.[24]

As a result of these concerns, the most elaborate festival activities tend to occur in noncadre families of "good" class background who are well-off economically, especially if they have older family members living with them for whom these celebrations are particularly important.

Within particular families worship activities are more actively engaged in by the old, and particularly by older women than by others.[25] We suggest that worship activities are not simply survivals but that they have certain contemporary functions—for example, sanctifying family structure and authority, providing women with security in the "alien" homes of their husbands, and comforting the aged in the face of the uncertainties of death. While some of these concerns are not too important for today's young people, they may become increasingly so later in life. We predict, then, that while there may continue to be a gradual reduction in some religious activities in rural Kwangtung, the remaining celebrations will continue to be sustained as new generations enter later stages in life and find these activities of value. Finally, we need to consider whether there are certain characteristics of villages that make them more or less likely to sustain traditional holiday activities or to emphasize the new. We have used seven different variables to categorize our villages, two of which are scales which are in turn made up of several other measures. In all seven, a code of 1 is conceived of as more "traditional" and codes of 2 or 3 as more "modern."

1. Elaborateness of Ch'ing-ming activities (1 = elaborate, involving worship and ritual offerings; 2 = simplified, with no worship, or not observed).

2. Abundance and elaborateness of annual festivals. This is a dichotomous scale composed of the equally weighted average of five items: number of festivals in the seventh month currently celebrated, elaborateness of the Mid-autumn Festival, existence of Ch'ung-yang celebrations, elaborateness of Winter Solstice celebrations, and the total number of traditional holidays observed during the year. (1 = many and elaborate festivals; 2 = few or simplified festivals. Elaborateness refers to worship and ritual offerings, as with Ch'ing-ming. The average inter-item correlation of these five items is $r = .38$.)

3. Traditional activities during the Spring Festival. This is a dichotomous scale composed of the equally weighted average of four items: the presence or absence of household worship activity, of kitchen-god activity, of old-style door couplets (tui-lien), and of worship for other deities besides the ancestors. (1 = many traditional activities; 2 = few or no traditional activities. The average inter-item correlation among these four items is $r = .49$.)

4. The number of days of vacation usually granted for the Spring Festival

(1 = six or more; 2 = five or less).

5. The number of traditional holidays during the year for which vacations are given (1 = two or more; 2 = only one).

6. Organization of modern activities—sports competitions, dramatic performances, and so on—during the Spring Festival. (1 = none; 2 = some).

7. Elaboration of the three major modern holidays—New Year's, May 1, and October 1. (1 = no meetings, sports, or special food distributions; 2 = one of these three elements is reported; 3 = two or more of these elements are reported).

In table 42 we can examine how these different measures of festival life are related to village characteristics.

We note first that our seven festival variables consist of three types: those that tap the degree of elaborateness of traditional festival activities (1, 2, 3), those that tap official willingness to give time off from work on traditional holidays (4, 5), and efforts to organize modern holiday activities (6, 7). In the top panel of table 42 we see that only the items within this first group— Ch'ing-ming elaborateness, total festival elaborateness, and Spring Festival traditional activities—are very closely related. Villages that have simplified some parts of their traditional festival life tend to have simplified others. But such villages are not much more likely than others to have few days off on traditional festivals, or to have extensive modern holiday activities. In fact, some of the relationships are negative. This indicates that the new and old holidays are not mutually exclusive, such that if a village celebrates new holidays more elaborately than elsewhere it will celebrate the old festivals in a simpler fashion.

We now proceed to examine table 42 row by row, but with the three separate aspects of festival life kept in mind. Our political variables have weak and inconsistent relationships with festival life, but the balance is toward a positive relationship, particularly for political study (positive meaning more "modern" festival life where political life is better organized). Our urban contacts-communications measures all have weak and inconsistent relationships with festival measures except the presence of nurseries in a community, which is usually associated with more modern festival life. Collective affluence is weakly associated with festival variables, except that prosperous communities are likely to give few days off for traditional festivals (columns 4 and 5). This may indicate the importance of local labor discipline in raising economic standards. Localities with high household consumption levels and high land-labor ratios show an inconsistent but perhaps slightly negative relationship with modern festival life. Villages

Table 42

Annual Festival Celebrations by
Village Characteristics (Gamma
Statistics)

	CME	AFE	SFT	SFV	THV	MSV	MFE	Median N
Annual festival celebrations								
Ch'ing-ming elaborateness	--							
Annual festival elaborateness	.74*	--						
Spring festival traditions	.77*	.65*	--					
Spring festival vacations	.41	.29	-.38	--				
Total holiday vacations	-.47	.18	.51	.14	--			
Modern spring festival	.04	-.51	.31	.11	.03	--		
Modern festival elaborateness	.17	.28	-.20	.38	.05	.33	--	
Administrative								
Political density	.27	.26	-.07	.06	.09	.00	.27	(39)
Political study	-.50[a]	.30	.21	.34	.48	.19	.59	(37)
Urban-communications								
Urban proximity	-.18	-.12	-.02	.30[b]	.05	-.12	.15	(38)
Urban youths	.20	.24	-.09	.42[b]	-.40	-.39	-.32	(29)
Communications	-.02[c]	.35	-.11	.16	.37[d]	-.21	.23	(39)
Nurseries	.43[c]	.76*	.16	1.00*	.46[d]	-.26	.28	(38)
Economic								
Collective affluence	.04	.06	.20	66*	72*	.22	.26	(37)
Household consumption	-.48	-.07	.27	-.49*	.27	-.05	-.38	(38)
Land/labor ratio	-.15	-.14[e]	.18	.32	-.33	.05	-.08[f]	(36)
Remittances	-.66*	-.47[e]	-.40	.00	-.11	.35	.48[f]	(28)
Other								
Brigade size	-.86*	-.19	-.48*	-.18	.41	.08	-.57	(31)
Team size	-.09	-.11	-.06	.38	.32	-.11	-.12	(39)
Lineage composition	-.24	-.45	-.22	-.10	-.46	.63*	.32	(39)
Non-Hakka ethnicity	-.70*	-.44	-.40	.23	.57[g]	-.40	.19	(39)
Delta region	.17	.00	-.03	.35	-.23	.31	.42*	(39)
Median N	(40)	(43)	(48)	(38)	(35)	(37)	(37)	

Note: Superior letters indicate relationships substantially weakened by statistical control for one of the following: [a]remittances, [b]informant's education, [c]interviewer's origin, [d]collective affluence, [e]total hours of interview, [f]sex of informant, [g]informant's class label.

*p ≤ .10

depending heavily on remittances show a tendency to continue to engage in elaborate traditional festivals but perhaps to also have more extensive modern festival activities (and no clear tendency in regard to the number of days off for traditional holidays). Localities with large brigades tend to hold elaborate traditional festival activities, particularly at Ch'ing-ming, although their pattern on vacations and new holidays is less clear. Team size seems unimportant, except for a tendency for large teams to give fewer days off for traditional festivals. This fits our earlier observation that team cadres will call off work if they can't get a certain minimum number of people to show up—in small teams it will be harder to get such a minimum. Localities in which the entire brigade is composed of people of a single lineage are somewhat more likely than others to have elaborate traditional holiday activities and more days off but also to have elaborate modern festival activities. In Hakka villages the traditional festivals are celebrated more simply, but there is a weak tendency to take more time off for such festivals. Finally, though the relationships are generally weak, villages in the delta region are somewhat more likely to organize extensive modern festival activities.

Retracing our steps, we see that we most expect to find simplified versions of traditional holiday activities in Hakka villages, in villages with little dependence on remittances, where the brigade is small and composed of people of many surnames, and where nurseries are available. We expect to find fewer days of vacation given for these traditional festivals in villages with regular political study systems, with collective nursery schools, where the teams and brigades are prosperous, the teams are large, and the villagers are not Hakkas. We expect to find more extensive modern holiday activities organized in villages composed of people of a single lineage, where many people receive remittances, in the Pearl River Delta region, and perhaps where the teams and brigades are prosperous, where there are few sent-down urban youths, and where a regular political study system exists. We do not have a ready explanation for each portion of these findings, but we stress one pattern which we have seen before: the maintenance of traditional activities is most often found in non-Hakka villages in which many families receive overseas remittances. We assume that a pattern of elaborate celebrations in such villages has been maintained from before 1949,[26] and that both the cash and the continuing visits and contacts with overseas kin help to sustain traditional festival life (and perhaps make officials in such villages reluctant to crack down on such activities, for fear of alienating overseas relatives, with their influence and funds). The finding that large brigades and single-lineage brigades are more likely than other places to maintain elaborate traditional activities may indicate only that holiday festivities were more festive in such places in the past and remain so, even though activities today do not bring together entire brigades or lineages for celebrations. Finally, we note some patterns that do not appear in table 42: villages with elaborate traditional festival activities are not primarily the isolated backwaters with few party members and low levels of family income. As in other chapters, we do not find a pattern which corresponds to notions of political backwardness or lack of modernization, in any simple sense.

In conclusion, the patterns we have found in examining change and continuity in festival life in rural Kwangtung are similar in many ways to those arrived at in earlier chapters. Important changes have taken place, but traditional festival life has survived in modified form. The most important modification has been the shift away from collective celebrations toward a domestic focus, with some decline in "superstitious" elements and perhaps in resources expended as well. New festivals have taken hold, but they show no likelihood of replacing traditional festivals. The family feasting and ancestral worship which are still common in most villages testify to the continuing importance of family ties and obligations. The characteristics of villages which show simplified forms of festival life are things like Hakka ethnicity and low remittance dependency, rather than closeness to a city, high access to communications, or a high proportion of Communist party members.

4

communities
and change

15

Changing Patterns of Cooperation and Conflict

*t*he preceding part of this book was concerned with the question of how new political and economic structures shape family and ritual life. Before concluding we want to turn this question around. In this chapter we will examine the effects of new community and old kin and market solidarities on attempts to enlarge the size of rural production units.

As noted in earlier chapters, Chinese rural organization is in many ways a compromise between a bureaucratic system imposed from above and a natural system of villages, lineages, and neighborhoods. In a commune the basic unit of production and of income-sharing—the basic accounting unit—is generally the production team. The typical team consists of about thirty to forty households. It is a small village or a neighborhood within a large village, and it may also be a lineage or a lineage branch. Led by local officials, this somewhat traditional, somewhat modern unit has made collective farming acceptable to the Chinese peasant. The people with whom he or she goes to the fields every day and with whom profits and losses are shared at the end of the year are old neighbors and kinsmen. Old affinities help create new kinds of cooperation.

In spite of the many advantages of the small accounting unit, there are those within the Chinese government who see the eventual goal in rural organization to be one of moving the level of accounting up from the team to the larger brigade and commune levels of administration.[1] This change would have a number of alleged advantages. Larger units would have greater reserves for the acquisition of new machinery and other capital goods. Larger units might more rationally divide into specialized units such as repair teams and horticultural groups. Larger units would help equalize some of the gross differences in income that now exist among different production teams. These units would take on a more socialist character because they would include more people cooperating together, and this would pave the way for a change to full state property ownership in the countryside. Many of the difficulties of moving the unit of accounting up from the production team to the larger brigade and commune in the past were dealt with in Chapter 4. Here we want to point to a number of trends which we see working against any future efforts to raise the basic accounting unit to higher levels. First, there have been shifts in social patterns in the countryside which in some ways make villages more encysted and closed to outside contact than they were twenty years ago. Second, many communes have been so enlarged that they no longer encompass any meaningful social community which might be used for refocusing rural loyalties. These changes are discernable in contemporary patterns of conflict and marriages among production teams. Finally, there is some evidence that the growth of brigade and commune enterprises—a growth that is supposed to precede social and political change—is likely to be rather slow.

Policy Decisions and Social Interaction

Traditionally, Chinese villages were rather open to outside contact, at least at the height of the dynasties. Because land might be sold and transferred among people in different villages, the boundaries between the holdings of one village and those of the next were usually not distinct. A person from one village would often find himself in an irrigation or crop protection association with people from another village. Similarly, because he or she went to the market town every few days, the average peasant was familiar with peasants from a large number of villages who all attended the same standard market. With these people, the peasant often intermarried, cooperated for public works projects such as bridge and road building, and joined for money lending and other special-purpose associations. More broadly, the outward migration of village residents to distant towns and cities for merchant and scholarly endeavors guaranteed some identification with the outside world.[2] To borrow from Clifford Geertz's analysis of Bali village structure, the organizational planes in the traditional Chinese countryside tended to cross-cut one another rather than coincide.[3] The persons with whom a peasant was linked for purposes of residence, land management, marriage, and government administration were often different. The peasant was in an open network rather than in the sort of closed network that would promote factionalism. To the extent that these networks were aggregated, this occurred in the standard marketing community rather than at the narrow village level. However, in some parts of South China large lineages prohibited the sale of land to outsiders and kept all dispute management within the lineage.

Eric Wolf and G. William Skinner deal with this phenomenon in similar terms. Wolf notes that in some parts of the world, under a system of corporate ownership such as the *mir* in pre–Soviet Russia or of collectively imposed taxes as in Middle America after the Spanish Conquest, peasants developed defensive, closed communities. Such closed corporate communities restrict membership to people born and raised within their confines and may reinforce this restriction by forcing members to marry within their boundaries.[4] Noting the outward migration from, and the pattern of marketing in, traditional Chinese villages, Skinner argues that the Chinese village was usually open rather than closed. Outsiders were permitted, marriages bridged villages, and peasants were deeply involved both in their market community and the broader world outside. It was only at the ends of the dynasties when the social system began to offer fewer chances for upward mobility or outward migration and when trade declined that people began to turn inward and their villages became closed. During the most extreme stages, outside merchants and artisans were excluded, land boundaries between villages were more clearly demarcated, and villages walled themselves for defense against outsiders—a process well under way in the last half of the nineteenth and the first half of the twentieth century.[5]

During the 1950s and 1960s villages were in some ways opened up to the outside world. Government intruded on the village to an unprecedented extent. Radio broadcasts and rebroadcasts, film teams, and study groups exposed villagers to messages from the outside, as did improved roads and the growing prevalence of bicycles. These all increased vertical integration between the villages at the periphery of the society and the capital in Peking.

At the same time a number of government decisions had the unintended consequence of restricting horizontal integration among villages in the same locale. National horizons were expanded, while the local community was restricted. Four decisions should be singled out.

1. The process of collectivization. One decision which restricted horizontal integration among villages was simply the manner in which villages were formed into collectives. Prior to 1949, it was primarily villages with powerful lineages holding claim to large expanses of corporate land that remained closed to outsiders. The corporate interests of these powerful lineages were weakened in the early 1950s, as they were deprived of landlord leadership, arms, and their corporately held land. However, in the mid-1950s collectivization again gave natural villages and old lineages a corporate interest in land. Partly out of haste and partly out of a conscious effort to adapt to the natural patterns of cooperation and social organization in the countryside, the new collectives and the subsequent brigade and team units tended simply to enclose old villages and lineages. In Kwangtung, where lineages had been strong before, traditional loyalties found a new focus.

More important, multilineage units and small single-lineage units which previously had no collective property holdings were suddenly given new corporate interests in the protection of land, water, and other economic assets. Instead of individual families alone having opposing economic interests, whole villages or neighborhoods could stand in opposition, leading to new patterns of intervillage and interneighborhood conflict. When a farmer plowed too far across a boundary line, it was no longer just Old Wang whose livelihood was threatened but a whole village's.

While creating new kinds of conflict, collectivization also led to new patterns of cooperation. Traditionally, much of the cooperation among villages was organized along kinship lines, which crossed territorial boundaries. Indeed, it was advantageous to have ties through marriage in other villages so that families farming under different soil conditions and harvest and planting cycles might exchange labor.[6] Today by far the greatest amount of cooperation is simply within one's own production team. There is less need to mobilize kinsmen outside the village simply because the cooperation of fellow villagers is guaranteed by the collective interest everyone has in the success of the harvest. To an extent, then, the narrow administrative circle has replaced the wider network of kinship.

2. *The pattern of landholdings.* A second decision which helped to narrow the range of horizontal integration among villages was the tendency to rationalize the holdings of land among villages. We noted that, traditionally, landholdings of different villages were interspersed, and peasants were forced to cooperate with people in nearby villages in regard to irrigation, access, and the protection of crops against intruders. Though the evidence on this trend is spotty, it appears that both during land reform in the early 1950s and in the retreat from the Great Leap Forward in 1961, when the

ownership of land was returned to production teams, there was a tendency to consolidate land around villages. In large single-village brigades, the constituent teams might have some land that was intermixed. Otherwise, land became clustered about the village that was to manage it, and it became more and more possible to conceive of property lines between villages or, more precisely, of property lines between teams and brigades.[7] Teams and brigades might still be organized in large water-control projects but gone were many of the opportunities for day-to-day casual contacts with peasants from nearby villages which have helped to knit the larger rural society together.

3. Educational policy. A third, more recent policy which will tend to narrow the range of social contacts is the decision to place more and more schools within the village. In the early 1960s, as more youths began to attend lower middle school, most of them had to leave their home villages to go off to the commune seat or to one of the larger villages in the area. Similarly, other villages without a primary school, or with only four grades out of a possible six in primary school, had to send some of their children outside the village to attend school. While outside, these young people formed close ties with youths from other villages—ties which were potentially valuable as a basis for cooperation in adult life. Since the Cultural Revolution, however, there has been less opportunity to form these relationships. Villages—or at least brigades—have been urged by the government to become self-sufficient in education: we saw in Chapter 6 that most Kwangtung brigades now have a five-year primary school and a two-year lower middle school program, so that only the minority of youths who go on to upper middle school need leave the village. (In Chapter 11 we also argued that most graduates of even rural upper middle schools have to return to their native village, so that outmigration does not produce a network of local contacts throughout an area.) Youths continue to form some friendships with outsiders on water-control projects during the agricultural off-season, but the opportunities for forming intensive fellow-student bonds with outsiders have been sharply reduced.

4. Commune and market. A fourth factor which narrows the range of horizontal integration in the countryside is the difficulty of finding any meaningful social unit around which to structure the commune level of administration—a difficulty exacerbated by the decision in some places to make the commune include a very large population.

Traditionally, there was a significant intermediate unit of social interaction between the village and the local level of governmental administration in the county. The standard marketing community, centered on a market town which served some 7,500 people—or 1,500 households—with marketing sessions every three, four, or five days, was the locus of much social life in the countryside. Knit together in a network of marriage alliances and informal political ties, the marketing community was on occasion used to organize projects and to mediate public disputes.[8] The post-1949 government was cognizant of the role of the marketing community, and the commune seat today is almost invariably located in one of the larger market towns.[9] Nevertheless, it appears that the marketing community is increasingly losing ground as a possible base for social cohesion in the commune.

This diminishing potential of the market is explained only in part by the decline in free marketing activity. While traders are no longer free to roam from place to place, in most locales peasants do regularly market produce from their private plots, poultry raised at home, and mats, hats, and other handicrafts. The market teahouse still is the place where a prospective bride and groom are first introduced and where the village carpenter meets his potential customer. However, such traditional functions may be ignored in the drawing of commune boundary lines. This is particularly so in Kwangtung, where the quest for large administrative units seems to take precedence over any concern for cohesive social units.

Traditionally, the size of marketing areas in the major river basins and near cities was much smaller than in remote hill districts. The greater population density of the basins plus the greater commercialization near cities generated enough demand for markets to be rather densely distributed. A market in the plains near Canton traditionally served an area of only about thirty square kilometers, while a market in the more remote hills of Kwangtung served over a hundred square kilometers. In the hills, the cultivable land was so sparse and the population so dispersed that it took a wide expanse of territory to support a single market.

In Kwangtung, that traditional difference between suburban and hill areas has been obliterated by recent commune reorganizations. For a time between 1960 and 1963, Kwangtung communes were rather similar to marketing areas. But by the end of 1963, communes in the central part of the province had been reorganized into much more populous units, in general along the lines of districts (ch'ü) created in the 1930s and again used in the 1950s. As a result, the average area per commune is rather similar from one part of the province to another (see table 43).

The average commune population, in contrast, varies tremendously. The most populous communes are in counties adjoining Canton and Swatow. In

Table 43   Communes and Markets, Kwangtung
                                            Province, ca. 1973

	Average area per commune (km²)	Average population per commune	Average markets per commune
Four suburban counties	120	60,000	3.5
Nine central counties	110	35,000	3.0
Seven intermediate counties	135	25,000	1.4
Thirteen hill counties	120	15,000	1.1

Note: The four groups of counties are differentiated by proximity to Canton and Swatow and by terrain.

Sources: Press and radio reports and interviews. Details on these sources can be obtained by written request to William Parish.

these counties relatively level terrain, many roads, large numbers of bicycles, and other means of communication help compensate for the difficulties of managing the affairs of very large populations. Because of better transport, small markets within these counties had begun to disappear in favor of larger markets even before 1949. In other central counties to the south and southeast of Canton, few markets have disappeared, yet administration has still been reorganized into larger communes. In this zone, commercialization created a dense network of traditional markets. In consequence, the place where the peasant goes to sell household goods or buy daily necessities is often different from the place where he or she must go to register a marriage, apply to join the army, or perform other civil functions.

In the counties in the far southwest and southeast of the province, the disjunction between market and commune is not quite so extreme, but the population in any one commune is still rather large. Similarly, in the hill counties in the north and northeast of the province, though markets and communes tend to correspond, populations are still fairly large. Markets have not proliferated to keep up with population growth since 1950. Instead of the traditional 7,500 people and smaller number of adults who had the chance of at least a nodding acquaintance with one another through repeated contact every few days over the years in a market town, today's hill communes include an average of about 15,000 people.

Communes in Kwangtung may be a bit extreme. While the average commune population in Kwangtung is about 23,000, the average for the nation is only 13,000. In some provinces, there is a closer correspondence between communes and old market communities. But there is great variation from place to place in the degree to which the commune has the potential for becoming a solidary community. Throughout the nation, communes near cities are invariably much larger and more populous than those elsewhere.[10] Even when the population per commune is only moderate, old market boundaries may be pretty much ignored. In some places in North China where private plots have been abolished or so restricted that there is much less market activity than before, many markets have simply withered away from lack of activity.[11] In these places as well, then, there is little in the way of an intermediate natural social community to help promote loyalty to the commune as a whole.

It should be understood that much of the above discussion is conjectural. Projections are based on assumptions of what is likely to occur in social behavior, given certain structural changes in rural society, as well as on anecdotal evidence from interviews. There are, however, two sorts of more systematic evidence which point to the increasingly important role of the village community and the declining potential of larger units such as the commune as a focus of social interaction. The first sort of evidence concerns the pattern of rural conflict in Kwangtung.

Rural Conflict

Today, life in the Chinese countryside is much more secure than it was in the immediate prerevolutionary period. Gone are the armed bandits who harassed villagers, and gone are the lineage and ethnic feuds which, in the absence of government control, sometimes escalated into brutal physical fights. Nevertheless, some of the old disputes over water, land, and animals remain.

In most places, though it is a continuing source of petty squabbles, water is no longer a cause of major disputes. First, because of the extensive collective irrigation and reservoir projects, water is now ample in most parts of Kwangtung. Except for an unusually dry period around 1963, informants report a steady decline in serious disputes over water since 1950. One of the two water disputes reported in our results is in a region in which this problem has not yet been solved. The peasants there picked up tools to fight opposing villagers and had to be pulled apart by a local army unit. A second cause of the decline in serious disputes over water is that, increasingly, water sources are controlled by higher-level commune and county administrators. Before disputes become too serious, they are referred up to higher-level administrators for adjudication.

Disputes over land involve such cases as one unit plowing into another's fields and the opening up of new fields in previously uncultivated hill land whose ownership is disputed. Conflict over already cultivated land is probably less frequent today simply because lands are not dispersed and intermixed with the holdings of other villages. One land dispute reported in our results involved a brigade trying to reclaim land it felt the opposing brigade had unjustly acquired during land reform. Probably because "bad class" elements were blamed for fomenting the trouble, this dispute led to commune armed-militia intervention and arrests by the county public security bureau.

Disputes over animals occur when a cow, pig, or flock of ducks wanders into an adjoining unit's fields to munch on their crops. It usually takes repeated transgressions by an animal and eventual flailing and injury of the animal by the offended unit for this situation to become serious. However, even petty incidents can become inflamed when old enmities are involved. One case in particular caught our attention. Because of a cow's wanderings, a youth got into a fight with members of a rival brigade. There had been bickering between the two villages before 1949, and bad feelings remained so intense that there was still no intermarriage between the two villages. When other young men gathered, bearing tools and ready to fight, the women ran away and skirmishes began. Luckily, by nightfall the commune's armed militia arrived to pull the combatants apart. Similar incidents occurred in a few other villages.

Most disputes among brigades and teams, however, lead not to physical fights but simply to shouting and ill feelings. The issues involved are usually minor. Even when water is ample, one team may take it from an irrigation channel at such a fast rate that teams further down the channel are short of water and slowed in their work. Such problems are handled by the team heads arguing with one another or by calling a brigade or commune official to mediate. Some teams have members involved in large and serious conflicts with outsiders every few years. Elsewhere such conflicts are rare, with one or two leading members talking out any disagreements which arise. Another group of teams are said by the informants to have never been involved in even a minor dispute in the last five years.

Conflict, then, ranges in degree from physical fights through serious arguments and minor disagreements settled by team leaders down to a complete absence of conflict. Coded 1 through 4 for each production team between 1967 and 1973, this information provides material for an analysis of conditions favoring an *absence* of conflict (table 44). There is only one strong relationship in this table, but the essentially zero relationships are also revealing. Given official explanations which frequently blame conflict on

Table 44   Conflict by Village Characteristics
                                            (Gamma Statistics)

	Absence of Conflict	Median N
Administrative		
Political density	.14	(44)
Political study	-.10	(37)
Urban-communications		
Urban proximity	-.03	(46)
Urban youths	-.15	(33)
Communications	.04	(41)
Nurseries	.32	(45)
Economic		
Collective affluence	-.18	(48)
Household consumption	.04	(43)
Land/labor ratio	.15	(38)
Remittances	-.37	(33)
Other		
Brigade size	.04	(37)
Team size	.00	(46)
Lineage composition	-.46*	(48)
Non-Hakka ethnicity	-.06	(47)
Delta region	-.15	(49)

*p ≤ .10

class enemies and an absence of class vigilance, the lack of any relationship with our political density scale is striking. Informal comments by informants also suggest that villages with few landlords are no more likely than others to be free of conflict.

The one strong relationship is with the lineage composition of villages, suggesting that arguments can escalate into physical fights when old kinship enmities are involved. Table 45 gives a more detailed look at this relationship, showing that it is primarily those large, once proud single-lineage brigades that continue to be the most contentious. They are most contentious because they combine internal conflict among their constituent teams with even more conflict against outsiders, to whom they often lost large expanses of land during land reform in the early 1950s. Some of them have not forgotten their former power or the way their less powerful neighbors took the lead in attacking them during that campaign.[12]

Perhaps more important, however, the data suggest that production teams are all very similar in the extent to which they are in conflict with their neighbors (see the last three columns in table 45). Whether single-lineage or multilineage, they rarely have disputes that escalate into physical fights, and a number register no conflicts or only very minor disagreements with their neighbors. Where a nearby team is composed of members of a different

Table 45   Conflict by Lineage Composition of
                                            Production Unit, 1967-1973

| | Single-lineage brigades | | | | |
	Total conflict	Conflict with outsiders	Conflict with teams in brigade	Single-lineage teams in multi-lineage brigades	Multi-lineage teams
Physical fights	6	5	1	1	1
Arguments	6	0	7	7	8
Minor disagreements	3	5	3	4	2
No conflict	0	1	2	4	6
Total	15	11	13	16	17

Note: The first three columns, each for the same set of teams in single-surname
brigades, have varying totals because of incomplete information in the second and
third columns. Also, because the most serious incident of conflict (whether with
outsiders or with other teams in the same brigade) was used to code the first column,
the seriousness of conflict in that column is much greater than in the next two
columns.

lineage, this does not make serious conflict any more likely than when they
are kinsmen of the first team. On the other hand peasants are willing to come
to the defense of their team even when this brings them into conflict with
their kinsmen in other teams. Studies in both Taiwan and Hong Kong
suggest that lineage loyalties and rivalries are strongest when material interests are at stake.[13] The constancy across teams of different composition
implies that in contemporary China as well, it is the current economic
interests of the production teams that are paramount, rather than kin group
loyalties. As we argued in Chapter 7, the changes in rural social structure
have not simply resurrected old lineages. Our data indicate that collectivization gave all sorts of villages and neighborhoods a new degree of corporate
interest in protecting what is theirs. Kinship feelings may in certain circumstances contribute to team and brigade rivalries, but they are not an essential
ingredient. The degree of open and physical conflict which results from local
cleavages is much less than in traditional times, due in part to local units
being nested within an effective administrative system that can step in to
defuse or put down conflicts. Yet the loyalty and corporate interests thus
generated do to a degree hinder the reorganization of the countryside into
larger collective units.

Marriage Networks

The second kind of systematic evidence concerns the changing patterns of
marriage in rural Kwangtung. We noted that, traditionally, young people

were required to marry outside their own lineage and village, and as a result a dense network of ties across villages was sustained. Since 1949 the traditional taboos have been breaking down, and the marriage network has been shrinking—a quarter or more of contemporary marriages in our interviews involve fellow villagers or members of the same lineage. Today, when a wife goes to visit her kinsmen on holidays, she goes less often to other villages and increasingly to a house just down the lane.

Marriage within small, subbrigade villages is most common in multilineage teams, next most common in multilineage brigades which have single-lineage teams, and least common in single-lineage brigades (see table 46). Marriages bridging across different parts of a brigade have just the reverse frequency order, being most common in single-lineage brigades, not quite as common in multilineage brigades consisting of single-lineage teams, and least common in brigades consisting wholly of multilineage teams, in which the taboos against marrying within one's village have largely disappeared.[14] Insofar as marriage ties form one basis for other kinds of cooperation across villages, this means that it is precisely multilineage teams which will be the most inward-turning and the most difficult to organize into larger brigade-wide cooperative projects. Suggestive evidence on this point is presented in table 47. There the provision of brigade programs and resources entailing some cooperation is examined according to the lineage composition of each brigade. In every instance except one (lower middle schools), the brigades with multilineage teams show the lowest level of provision of these brigade facilities.[15] These data support our contention that where there has been a reduction in intervillage ties the focus on the interests of one's own team is strengthened, making efforts to broaden the scale of sharing and cooperation more difficult.

Table 46		Proximity of Marriage Partners by Lineage Composition of Production Unit	
Origin of spouse	Single-lineage brigade	Single-lineage team in multi-lineage brigade	Multi-lineage team
Same sub-brigade village	6%	17%	27%
Same brigade	18	16	9
Same commune	38	32	34
Outside of commune	38	35	30
Total	100%	100%	100%
Total N	(82)	(82)	(88)

Source: Marriage sample (post-1949 marriages only).

Table 47   Brigade Services and Institutions by
                                                        Lineage Composition, 1973

	Single-lineage brigades	Multi-lineage brigades with single-lineage teams	Multi-lineage brigades with multi-lineage teams	Association (gamma)
Had cooperative medical insurance by 1970	100% (of 5)	78% (of 9)	36% (of 11)	.84*
Had more than 10 doctors per 10,000 population	71% (of 7)	87% (of 5)	27% (of 11)	.64*
Had a lower-middle school	92% (of 12)	64% (of 14)	72% (of 18)	.28
Had tractor and/or water pump	54% (of 13)	50% (of 6)	24% (of 17)	.41
Had workshops or factories	64% (of 11)	73% (of 11)	50% (of 12)	.08

Note: Numbers in parentheses represent the number of informants who could supply
the specified information with respect to their former production brigades.

*p ≤ .10

Cooperation

However, new kinds of administratively induced cooperation have
developed in rural Kwangtung, and one must consider whether these may
offset the tendencies toward narrowing of social ties that we have described.
Building a multivillage reservoir to bring water to fields previously dependent on the vagaries of weather gives visible proof to peasants of the potential benefits of cooperation in larger units. True, quotas for laborers are
generally assigned production teams on the basis of the expected benefit
each team will receive for the project, but still the virtue of collective effort
with outsiders will be demonstrated. There are also many examples in our
interviews of small-scale cooperation among neighboring teams—
sometimes under the direction of higher authorities but more often flowing
from the friendship and informal contacts among team leaders. Teams lend
draft animals, water pumps, and tools to one another. Less often they lend
grain or money or even a few temporary laborers to help a lagging team
bring in the harvest. Some of this aid is repaid in cash, but more often meals
for laborers or the promise of reciprocation in the future suffice.

Teams are not, then, totally closed off or working in opposition to one
another. But much of peasant social life and cooperation remains narrowly
focused, and interchanges and mutual help spanning village boundaries are
intermittent at best. In Kwangtung only once in two or three years or so are

rural youths called to work for a week or two on a large irrigation project. With virtually all teams growing the same crops on very similar schedules, there are few times when a team has labor or tools it can easily lend to a neighbor. In turn these new forms of cooperation receive less support than in the past from social ties based upon marketing, schooling, and marriage.

One additional new ingredient in the rural situation may be more important for fostering broader cooperation—the development of brigade and commune industries and other enterprises. We noted in earlier chapters that brigades have taken on increasing responsibilities in recent years for running education and health care programs, and that there has been some increase in brigade-owned machinery and small industry (most of it very small—for example, repair shops, grain mills, and brick kilns). Other sources note increases in brigade-owned sidelines, such as orchards and piggeries.[16] Commune-run enterprises are also on the increase. For example, the model Tachai commune in Shansi Province has seven such enterprises: an agricultural implement workshop, a refractory plant, an aluminite plant, a small coalpit, an animal-breeding ground, a commune farm, and a motorized transport team.[17]

These developments have been seen by some as paving the way for peasant identification with these larger units. In 1975 Chang Ch'un-ch'iao, a now deposed member of the Politburo of the party, noted that among communes in the suburbs of Shanghai the proportion of income generated by commune and brigade enterprises was increasing (from 28.1 percent and 15.2 percent, respectively, in 1973 to 30.5 percent and 17.2 percent in 1974), while that generated by production teams was declining (from 56.7 to 52.3 percent).[18] Since communes and brigades are collective rather than state institutions, and as such retain most of their profits for discretionary use locally, he saw this trend making commune and brigade levels more important in peasant eyes. More and more peasants were being drawn out to work in these enterprises alongside people from other villages. Increasingly, production teams would become dependent upon funds flowing to them from the profits of brigade and commune enterprises.[19] These trends should lead peasants to look beyond the narrow boundaries of their own team and village. In the Tachai commune, where these enterprises are not as highly developed as in the Shanghai suburbs, the following view is reported: "In the past some people were of the opinion that the commune was an empty shell—that economically it was flaccid. Today, they see that only by relying on the commune can one get on the road to prosperity."[20] Some view these

changes, then, as paving the way for moving the basic accounting unit up to
the brigade and finally to the commune level.

It is necessary to emphasize, however, that the process by which commune and brigade levels become economically more dominant is at a very
early stage in most places. In Kwangtung, small workshops grew very
rapidly in the early 1970s, and by 1977 commune- and brigade-level
enterprises were said to account for 20 to 25 percent of all rural production in
the province.[21] This is an impressive figure, and except for Hunan just to the
north no other provinces have been mentioned as having such a high level of
commune and brigade output. However, this is a gross figure, and the net
figure, with production expenses subtracted, would probably not be so high.
Probably no more than a maximum of 5 percent of the rural population are
involved in brigade and commune enterprises. Kwangtung's gross figure is
still only about half of the unusually high figures for the Shanghai suburban
communes, and most resources continue to be dominated by teams. In the
future, growth rates in rural industry are likely to be more gradual than in the
early 1970s, in part because of restraints built into official policy. According
to this policy rural industry should not be allowed to expand unless it serves
agriculture. Rural industry and agriculture should grow together, with most
products of commune and brigade industry to be sold within the confines of
each commune and brigade. Only county and provincial industries should
produce for wider markets.[22] On balance we feel that it will be a long time
before these enterprises produce a changed economic situation that might
significantly counteract the narrowing focus of peasant social relationships.

Conclusions

In Chapter 4 we first described the goal of China's more radical leaders,
including Mao Tse-tung and more recently Chang Ch'un-ch'iao, to reor-
ganize rural life on the basis of higher levels of collectivization, and their
lack of success in pursuing this goal since 1958. Through the analysis
presented in this chapter we acquire new perspectives on the problems
involved. We have argued that the social transformations of the 1950s were
successful partly because they relied heavily on natural communities among
the peasants—groups of close kinsmen, neighboring poor-peasant families,
and so forth—and even though they sharply reduced the influence of corporate lineages per se. We note here that collectivization in 1955–56 in fact
created new property and other interests for these naturally based com-

munities to protect. Various trends over the years have narrowed the focus of peasant social ties around these low-level collective units. The sorts of natural networks and cooperative relationships that could serve as the basis for higher levels of collectivization have become weaker over the years, primarily due to the successes of the earlier transformations. In our view the main obstacle to the radical goal is not any ingrained selfishness or conservatism of peasants but the fact that their social ties and economic interests in some ways have been narrowed rather than broadened over time.[23] The effort to eventually transcend production-team interests has been reiterated by the new Hua Kuo-feng leadership group, but any future move in this direction will be affected by local lineage alignments, the size of commune and brigade units, their industrial wealth, and a host of other factors, rather than simply by the skill of local leaders in mobilizing the peasant masses.

16

Conclusions

t his study has reported a wide variety of findings on the Chinese effort to transform rural life and on the conditions which foster or impede that effort. Our aim throughout has been not simply to describe the current patterns of village and family life but to construct an explanation of how and why particular changes have occurred. Some of our interpretations will be clear to the reader already, but we are now in a position to draw our findings together. We follow the Chinese preference for presenting things in numerical sets. Our analysis has been guided from the start by four major questions. Which parts of past village and family life have changed, and which have endured? What has been the pattern of change in particular areas of village and family life over time? What sorts of individuals within our villages are most likely to comply with official policies? What sorts of villages show the most evidence of change (or the closest approximation to official change ideals)? In sifting information that bears on these questions, we have tried to determine what change process could account for our findings. In Chapter 2 we examined three major perspectives on purposive social change: the official Chinese Marxist or Maoist view, totalitarianism, and modernization theory. We dissected these and showed that each perspective emphasizes a distinctive combination of three specific change mechanisms: structural transformation, administrative sanctions (including coercion and material sanctions), and normative influence (including communications, childhood socialization, and mobilized social pressure). Chinese Marxism assumes that the structural transformation to a socialist economy prepares the way for most desired changes but that the latter still have to be fostered by special campaigns, which rely heavily on normative influence—communicating new ways and pressuring peasants to adopt them. The totalitarianism model sees no change occurring except in response to direct rewards and penalties, with physical coercion emphasized. Thus effective mechanisms to monitor compliance and administer sanctions are crucial. The modernization perspective again sees much change occurring indirectly, as peasants respond to transformations in the social structure around them, but with many "modern" social structures, rather than simply socialist economic structures, inducing change. Individuals change as they are exposed to "modern" structures and influences. We now want to summarize how well these general perspectives and specific change mechanisms fit our actual findings.

Which Parts of
Village Culture Change?

We start our summary by dealing with the question of which parts of past village culture and family life have changed most and least. Figure 4 presents a rough summary of our major findings on this question. At the top of the figure we give our general sense of the extent of administrative pressure behind various change goals. Those listed on the far left are goals behind which the government mobilized special change efforts through new administrative structures and procedures, with new coercive or economic sanctions, sometimes reinforced by special campaigns. Further to the right are change goals stressed in the mass media (that is, conveyed through normative influence) but not backed up by special administrative sanctions, and on the far right are changes largely ignored in official policy. The vertical dimension in the figure conveys our rough sense of the extent of change that has taken place in regard to each goal. Items listed near the top are things that have changed markedly and widely. Further down in the figure are partial changes, either ones that occur widely in our sample of villages but fall short of official expectations or changes that have affected some localities but not others. At the bottom of the figure are those parts of village and family life that have changed very little or have changed in undesirable directions, along with changes the government tried to introduce and then had to rescind. Within these three broad categories the order of listing does not reflect finer gradations in the extent of change.

Figure 4.

Parts of Village and Family Life Which Have Changed and Persisted by Extent of Administrative Pressure

	High Administrative Pressure	Mostly Normative Influence	Little or No Pressure
Much Change	1950s Structure: Land reform Collectivization New political organizations Decline of old classes Expanded schooling Improved agriculture Decline of professional introducers, religious specialists, temple life Decline of lineage solidarity and community ritual Post-Cultural Revolution reform of rural schooling, cooperative medicine, health care Birth control	Women working Decline in power of aged Female divorce & remarriage rights No concubines, child brides Decline of "superstition" and ritual objects More conjugal emphasis in family, better treatment of new bride New holiday activities	Earlier family division and less solidarity among brothers Less adoption Less cooperation with affinal kin Decline of cowry Less solidarity of village women Kinsmen and friends as introducers
Partial Change	Material equality Control of private sector, reduced marketing, shift in market schedules Less inter-village conflict Late marriage Political study meetings Women in cadre posts Women's education	More freedom of mate choice and youth initiative in marriage, decline of arrangers Rural nurseries Less domestic ancestor worship New festivals	Travelling marriages Intra-village and same lineage marriage Decline of old age birthdays Younger village officers
Negligible or Negative Change	Post-Cultural Revolution shifts in accounting, work points, grain distribution Great Leap Forward commune organization	Women's domestic work Unequal pay for women's work Corporal punishment of children Feasting for holidays and life cycle events Marriage finance--bride price Inheritance by sons only No child custody or property rights for women after divorce Burial and reburial customs Preference for male children	Patrilocal residence Low divorce rates Father-son reserve Pattern of family childrearing Husband-wife public reserve Male youth roots in village Stress on obligations to corporate family Familial support of and respect for the aged

What can we conclude from the information in figure 4? The most obvious and important point is that the extent of change does not correspond in any clear and simple way with governmental priorities and pressure. There are cases where the government applied special sanctions to induce change without much success (in the lower left-hand corner of the figure), and even more numerous cases of changes occurring without official pressure (in the upper right-hand corner). High governmental pressure is not inconsequential—most of those aspects of society against which strong administrative sanctions are applied do change, and even when programs have to be rescinded they may leave some trace of their influence. But normative influence without administrative sanctions is generally ineffective in inducing change—in the second column of the figure there are as many cases of failure as of success. We feel that the overall pattern in Figure 4 can only be understood in terms of the interplay between administrative sanctions and structural transformation. Peasants are clearly responding to something in addition to the government's direct change efforts, and we argue that it is solidarities, obligations, and interests built into the transformed rural social structure in which they live.

When the Chinese Communists came to power they confronted a complex natural village structure in Kwangtung. During the 1950s, using large infusions of outside manpower, financial resources, and widespread coercion, they succeeded in producing alterations in that structure. In part, this success was due to the great use of force in these early campaigns, but only in part. There were also local interest groups and natural communities welcoming these changes. In the early 1950s, poor peasants thirsting for land could be whipped into a frenzy for land redistribution and the extermination of landlords. In the mid-1950s, some of these same poor peasants with their aspirations aroused but still lacking land, tools, animals, and skills to make themselves prosperous could be relied on to lead attempts to form collectives. In addition, we have suggested, the introduction of these collectives was expedited by the use of parts of the existing social framework and solidarities—groups of kin residing together, cooperative work groups among neighbors, and so forth. Administrative sanctions worked then because they meshed with existing interest groups and natural solidarities in the countryside.

Once the rural social structures had been successfully transformed in the dramatic campaigns of the 1950s, however, the situation was altered considerably. The rural response to governmental pressure in later years was much more selective, and the previous tactic of mobilizing poor peasant activists was no longer so effective in bringing about change. The reason for this greater difficulty in the 1960s and 1970s, we suggest, is that earlier changes had produced a new social structure that altered calculations by peasants of their interests. It was no longer so easy to find simple interest groups in the countryside which favored this or that change, and the interest groups that did exist did not correspond to the old class labels. Important solidarities were formed that could to some extent resist as well as accept later proposals for change.

More specifically, the result of government-induced changes in the 1950s was a new agricultural cooperative (later commune) and party structure at the top, but at the base remained brigades and teams structured around kinsmen and neighbors living where they always lived and led by natives of each village. Not all of the existing solidarities were utilized, of course, and we have noted that the powerful corporate lineages of Kwangtung had their property confiscated, their ritual centers taken over for other uses, and their poorer members mobilized to struggle against and even kill lineage leaders. But the strategy of making use of some existing solidarities left important parts of the natural village structure in operation. The family as a corporate economic unit, generally headed by a male, remained the basic building-block of rural life, and kept many of its old functions (support of the aged, early child care, the organization of consumption and domestic work, animal raising, and the provision of housing) even as it lost parts of other functions (the organization of daily farm labor, later socialization of the young). Roots in native villages dominated by groups of patrilineally related males were reinforced by official migration, schooling, and other policies along with the surviving preference for patrilocal residence after marriage. Families and villages continue to vary widely in their economic levels in ways that make the term "commune" as it is used in the West seem inappropriate to the Chinese institution. The combination of new and old social units established in the 1950s remains in place in rural Kwangtung today, and the corporate family, the village, the production team, and the brigade are all important foci for peasant activities and obligations. We stress that this is not simply a case of old wine in new bottles. We have seen repeated evidence in our discussions of the decline of nepotism, lineage conflict, ceremonial life, and of other topics that the new structures have succeeded in shifting importance away from lineages and affinal kin ties and toward team and brigade boundaries, whether they correspond with lines of kinship or not. Still, the natural social units upon which the commune structure is based affect how it operates today.

When the government has tried to introduce changes more recently, their acceptance has depended on how they fit with new interest groups and social solidarities created by the structure built during the 1950s. Recent reforms in rural schooling, health care, and birth planning have been accepted because they were desired by large proportions of the populace. These reforms also worked because they did not threaten and even sometimes strengthened local collectivities. In both schooling and health-care reforms, the brigade gained in importance as an administrative level, with increased responsibilities and resources, and neither change threatened the interests of subordinate teams in major ways. (Some of the gains in responsibility were at the expense of higher-level commune and county administrations.[1]) The unsuccessful attempts at economic reorganization in 1958–60 and 1968–71, in contrast, violated people's sense of equitable reward for work and involved major redistributions of income and other benefits between richer and poorer families and teams, thus threatening the interests of those important collectives. Poor teams favoring redistribution were no more numerous than affluent teams threatened by reduction to a common average, and none of the resistance or acceptance fit the official analysis that former poor peasants would be for, and former landlords and rich peasants against, greater equality. Interests were defined not by old class labels but by new collectives with which peasants had come to identify. In these cases the new arrangements led to reduced work efforts and peasant grumbling, and higher authorities eventually relented. We have noted that in the long run gradual trends in commune industrialization, population pressure, and agricultural output may make it easier to introduce more egalitarian economic arrangements, but for the moment radical changes which bypass the collectivities with which peasants have come to identify are difficult to carry out.

Much of the pattern in figure 4 can be interpreted by reference to the indirect consequences of this combination of new and old elements in the transformed rural social structure established in the 1950s. For example, the decline in the power of the aged, reflected in such things as decreased control over the marriage choices of offspring and an earlier ceding of family headship to the son, has come about, in large measure, because parents no longer control all of the economic resources needed to establish a family (although they still control some, such as access to housing) and because much of the management of daily farm labor is done outside one's family. (No doubt the expanding education of the young also plays some role here.) Better treatment of new brides, the disappearance of child brides, and more female ability to divorce and remarry reflect the increased economic role of women as well as the greater freedom of marriage that exists today. That greater freedom of marriage reflects in part the increased opportunities that young people have to meet today—in school, in agricultural labor, and in political study and other meetings. Even changes not advocated by the government can be seen as flowing from the nature of the altered rural social structure. Early family division and more "ordinary" relations among brothers reflect the loss of family land and the reduction in the family farming enterprise. Reduced adoption flows in part from the improved health-care standards and the decline of infant mortality, and the decline in cooperation with affines reflects again the reduced role of the family farming enterprise as well as the effect of having new labor-sharing mechanisms built into the commune structure. The decline of the dowry reflects this weakening of affinal bonds, the elimination of classes based upon land ownership, and the growing economic importance of women, while the declining solidarity of village women stems from their increased farm-labor role and the "double burden" of also being responsible for most domestic work.

The indirect effects of contemporary rural social structure can also help explain what has not changed. In other words, the consequences of this structure are decidedly mixed relative to the government's preferred changes. We have already noted the ways in which the new loyalties built into this structure helped undermine the early communes and the post-Cultural Revolution economic reforms. The primary role of women in domestic work, corporal punishment of children, domestic ancestor worship, family feasting and traditional funerals all reflect the continuing importance of the corporate family in rural life and the relative autonomy given to the family to manage its own internal affairs. The continuing or increased importance of "marriage by purchase" and women's limited child-custody and property rights stem from the increased economic value of women, who continue to move at marriage into their husbands' families.

We see a number of the cases labeled as partial changes reflecting ways in which the contemporary structure affects particular customs in a contradictory fashion. For example, marriage takes place later now in part to allow more time for schooling and for daughters to contribute to their families economically, but if it takes place too late peasants are concerned about not having a daughter-in-law to help in arduous domestic chores, and about becoming old and possibly disabled before children are old enough to support them (as well as worried about the competition for eligible mates with other families and villages in the area). Freedom of mate-choice and increasing same-lineage marriages are fostered by coeducational schooling, collectivized work, and other activities, as well as by the declining power and resources of lineages and parents, but they are obstructed by the ways in which schooling and migration policies restrict the social field of most young people to the brigade and require that they depend on their families for housing and for the finances needed to celebrate a marriage. Peasants in deciding whether to practice birth control must balance improved chances for survival of children today and the short-term poverty that comes from trying to feed too many dependents against the realization that in the long run those who have several sons (not daughters, due to patrilocal residence) will be supported more comfortably in their old age.

We are essentially arguing, then, that if one wants to understand which parts of village and family life have changed and which have persisted, one needs first to refer to the ways in which governmental pressure was translated into transformation of rural social structure (broadly conceived) in earlier years and the indirect consequences that this modified structure has for peasant behavior today. We do not see all rural change as interpretable simply in terms of the earlier structural transformations, however. Administrative sanctions display a role in fostering some changes in the 1960s and 1970s. We see the hand of coercion in the decline of religious specialists and makers of incense and other ritual objects. Improved agriculture, health care, and expanded schooling reflect not only changes in rural social structure but also economic sanctions—for example, changes in rural-urban price differentials, the provision of new seeds and tools, and state subsidies for irrigation projects and medical and teacher training. Economic sanctions reinforce land scarcity and low infant mortality in getting official birth control policies adopted. Widespread distribution of free or low-cost contraceptives and financial incentives and penalties for those who comply with or violate officially specified maxima for fertility now enter family calculations.

Even normative influence may play a secondary or reinforcing role in inducing change. It is plausible to us, for example, that peasants uncertain about sterilization may find official reassurances that the operation will not interfere with their sex lives or weaken their labor power sufficient to tip the balance in favor of acceptance. However, direct change efforts through sanctions and influence are most successful when they reinforce changes already underway due to alterations in rural social structure, changes that do not threaten the current set of peasant solidarities and interests. Such successfully introduced changes in turn produce new elements in rural social structure to which peasants respond. Recent examples would be the local establishment of cooperative health systems and lower middle schools, which increase the economic importance of brigades and peasant access to these services while focusing peasant social ties more narrowly on their own villages. If a governmental change program threatens the interests of important rural solidarities, on the other hand, or calls for behavior that conflicts with the requirements of the social structure in which peasants live, that program is not likely to be successful, and strong administrative sanctions to implement it are likely to be self-defeating.

The Pattern of Change
Over Time

We will return to discuss other implications of this analysis after an examination of our other major change questions. Though our information on change over time is incomplete and often unsystematic, a picture of some complexity emerges. It is clear from our argument thus far that the major changes in the structure of rural life took place in the 1950s. There have been more recent changes in health care, education, and female leadership, but attempts to modify the commune economic organization have been minor or unsuccessful. For family and ceremonial life, generalizations are more difficult. We have argued that the rise in marriage ages and freedom of mate-choice took place primarily by the late 1950s, with little change recently. In regard to birth control the opposite seems true, with an increase in surviving children in the 1950s and a decrease more recently. The decline of child brides and concubines predates and was completed by the early 1950s. The decline of religious specialists, temple life, public worship, the use of ancestral tablets, and so forth seems to be centered during major campaign periods— land reform, collectivization, the Great Leap Forward, rural socialist education, and the Cultural Revolution, with change occurring earlier in some villages than others. Such ritual activities also show a characteristic pattern of temporary suppression followed by a partial revival—activities that are discontinued during a campaign are resumed later on, but at a more modest, discreet level. For wedding and holiday domestic feasts the picture is somewhat different. During major campaigns peasants may feel inhibited and hold less elaborate feasts, but after the campaign the feasts seem about as elaborate as before, if not more so.

How can we explain these contrasting patterns? Again we feel that a combination of change mechanisms has to be utilized in any explanation, with the indirect influence of structural transformations now more important than normative influence and administrative sanctions. The pre- and immediate post-1949 changes in rural social structure made later marriage, freer choice of mates, and same-lineage marriages more likely by the combination of declining parental and lineage resources and increasing education and social contacts of the young. More recent campaigns to delay marriage have not been matched by further changes in rural social structure which could counteract the remaining peasant motivations for marrying early—the desire for help with domestic work, for early-maturing offspring, and so forth. The situation in regard to birth control is different. Some earlier restraints on the number of children born and surviving were reduced by changes of the 1950s—in particular the reduction in infant mortality and the elimination of family land inequality, which delayed the marriages of some poor males in earlier times. With collectivized agriculture, peasants would not have to worry about having enough family-held land to support more children, and they may have wanted extra sons as insurance against the high infant death-rate long after this was necessary. In more recent times further reductions in infant mortality, increasing land pressure, new official rewards and penalties to enforce fertility reduction, and easy availability of contraceptive devices and information have begun to reduce rural birth rates. In other words, in this case many of the important changes in the rural situation have been recent ones. In looking at the changes in ritual life, we have noted that the confiscations of lineage and religious halls and property undermined public ritual life, while collectivization produced new sets of cooperative relations making those cemented by the old rituals less important. With repeated governmental efforts, including both mobilized social pressure and coercion, the remaining religious specialists and public ceremonies have disappeared from view. Similar tactics have been used in regard to wedding and holiday feasts, but their resiliency suggests that the family solidarity and status changes they celebrate remain more important than the solidarity of corporate lineages and temple associations. In sum, in different areas of rural life we see contrasting patterns of change over time, rather than a gradual disappearance of all old practices or the adoption of new patterns during major campaigns. These contrasts seem interpretable only if we continue to emphasize the interplay between administrative sanctions and community and family interests in a changing rural social structure.

Variations in Individual Change

We have even less systematic information about individual variations in response to change, but our findings again lend most credence to explanations emphasizing indirect structural sources of change. Chinese media lead us to expect to find rural party members, cadres, and former poor and lower-middle peasants leading the way and setting a positive example for others in the realms of birth control, late marriage, and freedom of mate-choice. A Western modernization perspective might lead us to expect that individuals with more education than others, more access to communications, and higher incomes would lead the way. In each case certain individuals are seen as more responsive to direct change-efforts than others. Neither expectation is borne out in our data—in some cases such individuals seem less in compliance with official policies than their neighbors. Nor do we find former landlord and rich peasant families playing an active role in preserving traditional ways. For example, landlord sons tend to marry somewhat later, not earlier, than other peasants, for reasons that are quite understandable given their poor position in the rural marriage market. Unfortunately we do not have much information on who is first in advocating things like the provision of a cooperative health-care system or more egalitarian work points, although we might expect that current family income and family size would be more important than class labels or cadre positions. In general we have found individual and family variations in adopting changes more interpretable in terms of concepts like position in the marriage market and field of social contacts structural considerations—than in terms of differential exposure to official ideals. With only rare exceptions, our informants do not paint a picture of villages divided into ''activists'' and ''backward elements.'' Instead individuals and families react to advocated changes as they affect them and their positions within village, team, and brigade life, and they may readily accept some changes while opposing others.

Rural cadres may take the lead in some matters but are concerned to avoid alienating their neighbors and relatives. Our informants say that team cadres are generally not very different from the peasants they are leading in their customs and behavior. Brigade cadres are seen as only slightly distinctive, perhaps a little more vocal in advocating new policies, but still not far removed in life-style from other peasants. It is only the commune cadres operating from the market town, many of them sent in from outside the local area, who are regarded as a different breed. Our discussion of individual variation provides an important clue to why mobilized social pressure has so little effect and why the government shrinks from the widespread use of coercion. In our discussion in Chapter 2 we said that the government uses administrative sanctions and normative influence to try to directly change peasant behavior. What we failed to focus on there was that finally this sanctioning and exhortation depends on team and brigade cadres. As noted in Chapter 7, these cadres are local people rather than outsiders, and their primary social ties and loyalties lie within the village rather than to the bureaucracy outside. They are tied to the people they are trying to lead by kinship and past histories of cooperation and competition, and if they cannot maintain the respect of local peasants they can easily be pressured to resign. They may want to please higher authorities, but if a given policy is one they know is unpopular with their neighbors, they may enforce it reluctantly or not at all. Even refusal to participate in wedding feasts and to pay bride prices may jeopardize their relations with, and authority over, local peasants. When the targets of local enforcement are a small and special part of the local community, such as former landlords or geomancers, local cadres may feel that they can safely use coercion; to do so would be much more risky if a large part of the community were the target.[2]

This reliance on local leaders and policy enforcers who are ''not very different'' is both a great strength and a weakness of the Chinese system of collectivized agriculture. Kwangtung peasants no doubt work more cooperatively and diligently under individuals they know and trust than they would under outsiders, and the problems of nepotism and local recalcitrance are still kept in check by the nesting of teams and brigades under commune and county levels, whose leaders, many of them outsiders, must review and approve lower-level decisions. But locally bred leaders are constrained by their ties with other villagers and cannot be depended upon to vigorously enforce every new policy. China's leaders are clearly aware of this problem, and at times when they want to induce particularly rapid rural change they send in outside work teams to temporarily take command from the local leaders. This strategy has its own costs, however, particularly the fact that when local cadres are displaced and perhaps disgraced it may be difficult to get peasants to assume these posts afterward. The Chinese Communists have built a rural system that works fairly effectively, but it is one that constrains their ability to introduce further changes.

Variations in Village Change

Our final major question is whether changes have occurred in some types of villages more readily than in others. At various points throughout our study we have examined how fifteen coded traits of our villages—administrative, urban-communications, economic, and other characteristics—relate to the pattern of compliance with official policies. These characteristics do not correspond in any exact sense with our specific change mechanisms, although some connections can be made.[3] We present a rough summary of all of our data on intervillage variations in table 48. We group the findings from earlier tables into three columns in table 48, for changes at the collective level (in work points, grain allocation, health care), in family life (birth control, marriage customs, family relations) and in ceremonial life (life-cycle and annual holiday ceremonies).

The first thing to note about table 48 is that several village traits make little difference in the aggregate for any of our three aspects of rural change—this is the case particularly for political density, the percentage of urban youths in a village, household consumption levels, and surname composition of a locality.[4] The first two of these are the most surprising. Despite

Table 48   Changes in Village Life by Village Characteristics (Average Gamma Values)

	Collective life	Family life	Ceremonial life
Administrative			
Political density	.02	-.01	.00
Political study	.28*	-.06	.00
Urban-communications			
Urban proximity	.23*	-.01	.11
Urban youths	.01	-.05	.03
Communications	.17*	-.11*	.11
Nurseries	.14	-.12	.42*
Economic			
Collective affluence	.16	.03	.11
Household consumption	.05	-.01	-.05
Land/labor ratio	.08	-.07	.12
Remittances	.02	-.10	-.36*
Other			
Brigade size	.02	.05	-.24*
Team size	.20	-.11*	-.09*
Lineage composition	.08	-.02	-.08
Non-Hakka ethnicity	.04	-.13	-.24
Delta region	.33*	-.02	.06
Number of relationships	(16)	(15)	(13)

Notes: Statistical controls indicated by superior letters in some earlier tables are ignored. One variable, local cases of recent divorces, is excluded from this summary.

Sources: Collective life: average of tables 6, 7, 9, 26 (cols. 1 and 2), 40, 42 (cols. 6 and 7), and 44. Family life: average of tables 22, 26 (cols. 3 and 4), 29, 35, 36, 38, and 39. Ceremonial life: average of tables 41 and 42 (cols. 1-5).

*In a sign test pitting number of positive against number of negative relationships, disregarding absolute size of the relationships, the probability of the observed number of positive or negative relationships occurring by chance alone is less than one in ten ($p \leq .10$).

isolated examples in our interviews suggesting their impact, the presence of
many urban youths locally does not produce much impetus for change. We
feel that this is because for the most part these urban youths are fairly isolated
and concerned about not making their rural sojourn any more unpleasant by
"rocking the boat." Political density is a scale composed of measures of the
proportion of local residents who belong to the Communist party, the proportion who are *not* labeled as landlords or rich peasants, and the presence of
a functioning poor- and lower-middle-peasant association, an organization
designed to solidify peasant class consciousness and expedite official programs. The consistently low associations this variable has with various
aspects of change supports our contention that the old 1950s' class
categories no longer delineate meaningful interest groups in the countryside.
A separate analysis (not reported here) showing the same low relationship
for party membership by itself supports our contention that local party members, like cadres, are so closely tied to the village that they cannot be
counted on to actively mobilize social pressure for changes resisted by
fellow villagers.

If we examine the columns in table 48 we can see different patterns for
each. For those kinds of rural changes which involve collective units—teams
and brigades taking on new programs and activities—the villages that stand
out are relatively affluent ones concentrated in the fertile Pearl River Delta
region, in close proximity to urban and communications influences, and with
regular political study systems. On balance this pattern fits most closely a
moderniza ion explanation of change, with villages which have traditionally
been most advantaged economically and in exposure to urban influences
taking the lead in adopting new collective programs and policies, while more
isolated or impoverished villages respond less readily.

When we look at the other columns in the table, however, the impression
is quite different. The striking thing about the family-life associations is that
they are generally close to zero, and more often negative than positive. So
village characteristics we supposed might provide some general impetus for
change do not do so in the area of family life. As earlier chapters show, this
summary table obscures how particular village characteristics strongly foster
one kind of family change while obstructing another, such that when we sum
up many relationships the positive and negative values cancel each other out.
Thus, for family life there does not seem to be any clear generalization we
can make about what sort of village will change most readily. Rather, it
depends on what aspect of family life one is discussing, with the factors that
are conducive to late marriage-age being different from those conducive to

men helping their wives with domestic work. In the chapters dealing with family life we found that in order to explain our results it was necessary to refer to such concerns as position in the marriage market, structured opportunities to meet potential spouses, and the resources traditionally controlled by parents, rather than to the general change perspectives introduced in Chapter 2.

In the final column of table 48 we see still another pattern. Villages with certain characteristics are generally distinctive in having a relatively simplified, secular ceremonial life, but these are not villages that stand out in either collective or family life. More often than not villages close to official ideals in ceremonial life are those composed of Hakkas rather than Cantonese, those organized in small brigades, those without important ties and income provided by overseas relatives, and those with collective nursery schools and kindergartens (these characteristics do not always go together—Hakka villages, for example, rarely have nursery schools). We have no ready explanation for why collective nurseries should be associated with simple ceremonial life, since our other urban-communications variables show much weaker patterns. The only idea that comes to mind is that both nurseries and frugal ceremonies imply some deemphasis on the crucial role of the corporate family organization. In regard to Hakka villages we assume that what is reflected here is the influence of past economic conditions, with pre-1949 Hakkas being unable to support as lavish a ceremonial life as their lowland, more prosperous Cantonese neighbors and continuing to observe a simpler ceremonial life today. But the difference may be more cultural than historical-economic in nature, and we must admit that our understanding of Cantonese-Hakka ethnographic differences is not sufficient for us to be sure of our explanation. The findings in this column for remittances and brigade size have been interpreted in Chapters 13 and 14 as the effect of having large sets of important social relationships that have to be included in ceremonial observances (and, in the case of remittances, relationships which provide resources to finance those observances). We see no evidence in this column that villages with a better developed political infrastructure, a more prosperous economy, or more exposure to modern influences are likely to adopt simplified forms of traditional ceremonies.

The findings from this summation of intervillage differences support the main thrust of our argument in response to the other three change questions. There are no villages here that are uniformly more "socialist" or "progressive" than others, any more than there are distinctly "socialist" individuals within villages. Localities show complex combinations of new and old practices and customs that are adopted in response to distinctive local conditions. The factors in the local situation that lead a village to readily adopt a cooperative health-care plan may not be conducive to reduced births or simpler wedding feasts. To understand these patterns we have to adopt a flexible and inductive approach, rather than assuming that all changes proceed in a uniform manner everywhere.[5]

Summary

What can we say then about how rural change has been occurring in Kwangtung? If we focus on our three general purposive change perspectives from Chapter 2, we can see that all fall short of conveying the complexities of the actual change process. The official Chinese conception is correct, in our estimation, in focusing on poor peasants' thirst for land and their interest in the initial equalizing effect of collectives. The official conception is also correct in focusing on the key indirect force for change represented by structural transformations of the 1950s. It is incorrect in interpreting willingness to change in the 1960s and 1970s primarily in terms of outdated class labels. It is also deficient in its failure to note features of the contemporary commune structure which provide support for many kinds of disapproved traditional behavior. Also, we feel that the official conception places too much faith in the power of communications and persuasion (that is, normative influence) to change peasant behavior. Only when and where the rural social structure is supportive of particular changes—as in the adoption of time-rate work points in large, wealthy teams with dense populations—is normative influence likely to be effective.

The totalitarianism perspective, or simply an emphasis on change through direct administrative sanctions, also provides an imperfect explanation of the pattern of change. Clearly coercion, in particular the mass killings of landlords, helped push through the major social transformations of the 1950s, and in less dramatic forms has been important recently in the suppression of religious specialists and geomancers and the destruction of ancestral tablets. A broad "carrot and stick" emphasis also helps us note that many change ideals, particularly in family and ritual life, lack special enforcing bodies, monitoring procedures and explicit sanctioning mechanisms, so that noncompliance is not rapidly or consistently penalized.[6] Such a perspective would also point to the problems of relying on leaders bound to the local community to enforce compliance. Yet, this perspective is still not helpful in explaining changes dependent mainly on normative influence or changes where there is no government effort at change, and many of the changes with which we are concerned are precisely of these sorts. Nor can it explain those failures where administrative sanctions have been vigorously applied, and it provides no explanation of why the government pushes vigorously in some realms and not others.

Finally, the modernization perspective is superior to the Chinese Marxist perspective in its broader conception of indirect structural sources of change. From the observation of the traditional male obligation to support aged parents and from the existence of private plots, private housing, and severe restrictions on migration, the modernization perspective leads us to predict that significant family and community loyalties will be maintained. Yet, there are many other aspects influencing the acceptance of officially espoused changes that do not fit sensibly along some modern-traditional continuum—the rise of team and brigade solidarities, the changing size of collective units, the increased economic value of women, and so forth. Except in regard to some aspects of collective life, villages which change are not generally those that are the most modern—those with the most brigade machinery, access to communications, proximity to urban areas, and so on. The modernization perpsective shares with the official Chinese view the assumption that there is an orderly continuum along which individuals and villages can be ranked, although in this case it is from traditional to modern rather than from backward to advanced or socialist. However, no such orderly continuum is visible.[7] What these arguments suggest is that the focus on "modern" structural changes is still too narrow. A broader and more general conception of rural social structure is needed.

Each of these three broad change perspectives misses the mark in important respects and cannot account for our findings. But guided by these observations, we are led to our own explanation of the nature of the rural change process, one suggested by our remarks earlier in this chapter. We see Kwangtung peasants responding primarily to their immediate social environment, with administrative sanctions and normative influence successful in inducing changes primarily when they reinforce emerging trends and the interests of important solidarities within the environment. In the early 1950s change occurred more directly, as the government used a variety of sanctions and pressures to mobilize poor peasants and other discontented groups for land reform, collectivization, and other dramatic transformations of rural life. Since that time, however, it has been more difficult to find discontented groups which the government could, or would be willing to, mobilize, and change has occurred more indirectly with peasants weighing exhortations and threatened sanctions against the evolving set of obligations and interests to which they are bound.[8] In planning their daily work, how they will raise their children, how they will celebrate weddings and so forth, peasants will consider their social environment and what kinds of behavior will be most rewarding within it. If they feel a traditional custom will provide satisfaction they will follow it even if they know that such behavior does not have official approval. On the other hand, if they feel a new form of behavior will be more rewarding in their local context they may adopt it, even if it is not a change advocated by the government. In the process they will not be particularly concerned about whether their behavior is consistent or inconsistent, advanced or backward, modern or traditional, but about whether it contributes to a life that is secure and satisfying. The calculations that peasants and local cadres make will be affected by structural considerations that are uniform throughout Kwangtung—collectivized agriculture, the heavy work-load of women, familial support of the aged, restrictions on mobility, and so on—as well as by factors idiosyncratic to particular villages and families—their financial resources, the size of brigade and team units, the ties and resources provided by overseas relatives, and so forth. The combination of structural considerations that encourages one change may work against another, and peasants will adopt distinctive combinations of old and new behavior in different types of villages.

Discussions of social change in China sometimes focus on whether man is "malleable" and can be made into a new, public-spirited socialist man, or whether human nature is inherently selfish and unchangeable. Our study leads us to argue that both alternatives are misleading because they are sociologically uninformed. They assume that individuals are guided in their actions by fixed, internal gyroscopes provided by values or human nature, and that they are unaffected by the changing social environment in which they life. This clearly is not reality. Attempts to institute brigade-level accounting failed not because of the inherent selfishness of peasants but because this proposed change threatened the interests of important collectivities built by the revolution, the production teams. On the other hand, peasants now cooperate in extensive ways with many local people who are unrelated to them not because they have absorbed new values which say selfish interests should be ignored but because the commune structure makes such broad cooperation rewarding to them and to their families. What matters is not so much the struggle between old and new values, selfishness and public-spiritedness, but whether structural transformations can be introduced which will make new forms of cooperative behavior rewarding to the peasants. The effect of collectivization and other changes has been to introduce an altered and somewhat broader set of rural collectivities with whose interests peasants identify, not to lead peasants to favor every change which will produce still broader cooperation and sharing.

All of our analysis to this point leads us to conclude that a fairly stable modus vivendi has been established between the Chinese government and the Kwangtung peasants. If we look at things from the government's point of view, not everything is as it should be. Peasants persist in many kinds of traditional behavior that the government feels should be eliminated, and a number of efforts to move rural organizations forward toward communism have had to be abandoned. Yet the commune system works fairly effectively. After decades of rural disorder, banditry, and lineage feuding, the Kwangtung countryside has become a generally orderly and peaceful place, and this order is maintained without the extensive use of police and military forces in most circumstances. Harvests have been increasing at moderate rates, and village material conditions are improving. Peasants work very hard, putting in many more total work days than they did before 1949, and they do not challenge the principle of party rule in the countryside. Much of the funding for investment in rural economic and social programs comes from the local collective units themselves, rather than from the state budget, allowing the government to maintain fairly low rural taxation rates while still pushing new development programs. The government has had considerable success getting certain changes introduced, of course—not only the structural transformations of the 1950s but also more recent educational reforms, cooperative health-care systems, rural small industry, and birth control. The areas in which peasants ignore official demands in massive ways are in most cases ones that do not threaten the political and economic integrity of the commune system and may even have hidden benefits—as in the case of lavish wedding feasts and traditional funeral ceremonies. Peasants presumably have to work harder to accumulate the required funds for these celebrations than they would if they were to follow the government's frugal alternatives. The use of vigorous direct-change mechanisms to penalize peasants for such behavior might alienate peasants and make them economically and politically less compliant. The kinds of structural changes which would undermine such traditional behavior are in most cases ones the government would not want to make for other reasons. For example, some sort of general old-age pension system might lessen peasant motivations to marry early, to bear several sons, and even perhaps to celebrate weddings in a lavish manner, but the state and commune would have to bear the huge costs of such a system, and the willingness of young people to maintain roots in their village might be undermined. Traditional ceremonial life could be reduced if remittances and visits from overseas relatives were forbidden, but this would in turn eliminate an important source of foreign exchange and alienate many influential Chinese living outside China. Similar comments can be made about the drawbacks, from the official point of view, of changing other elements of the contemporary structure—by easing restrictions on mobility out of the village, creating a more autonomous women's association, assigning outsiders to serve as team and brigade cadres, introducing a system of guaranteed wages (as in state farms) in the communes, and so forth. In each case some further changes in traditional customs might be fostered, but only at the cost of eliminating features of the commune organization which make it so successful in the official view. For all of these reasons the Chinese elite has generally been content to make only minor adjustments in the nature of the commune structure in recent years, and to allow peasants to continue to ignore many official ideals as long as they are willing to work diligently within that structure.

Looked at from the peasant viewpoint, the current system also seems to be acceptable, although not ideal. The communes do place many restrictions on peasant ability to seek out economic opportunities elsewhere; at home they are not free to plant the most profitable crops, they live a much more regimented life than in the past, and periodically they are confronted with campaigns which at least temporarily disrupt their established ways of doing things. Yet in most villages they are able to make a living that is more secure than in the past. They are able to feed their families, to feel secure that their infants will survive and will have access to at least rudimentary medical care and education, to find brides for their sons and accumulate sufficient funds to meet the social obligations of a village wedding, to hope that by hard work and efficient management of private economic activities they will eventually be able to build better housing and buy bicycles and radios, and to know that after they lose the ability to support themselves they will still have sons in the village who can support them and provide them with a proper funeral and memorial rites after they die. They also know that they are shielded to some extent from the shifting whims of higher authorities by local leaders they trust, individuals sensitive to the restraining force of village public opinion. Some of their important social relationships have been altered, but they can still have some assurance that they live among relatives and neighbors who will help to protect their interests and provide them with security amidst the tumult of a revolutionary society. They know that the strong sense of familial obligations which has played so central a role in their own lives will not be undermined by hostile counterindoctrination in rural schools or by migration policies orienting their offspring toward outside jobs and individualistic life in the cities. It is this sort of assurance that the natural roots that form the base of contemporary commune structure will not be destroyed that makes this structure acceptable to most peasants and provides them with the motivation for disciplined work and orderly cooperation that make the system as effective as it is. The peasants as well as the government have learned to live with the imperfect compromise of contemporary commune life.

Our analysis suggests that further marked changes in the character of village and family life can only come from further changes in the rural social structure, rather than from campaigns to combat old ideas and customs. Yet the current structure is a fairly effective one from the official point of view, and most structural changes would pose some threat to that effectiveness. Thus the current modus vivendi between the government and the peasants is likely to continue into the future, although gradual and incremental changes in the rural economy and health and educational situation can be expected to have some consequences. In the future gradual evolution of commune life the peasants are best seen not as ardent Confucianists or as modernizing men or as new socialist men, but as flexible, family-oriented individuals striving to deal with the unique set of problems and opportunities existing in their local village environment in order to maximize the security and satisfaction that this environment can provide.

Appendix 1
Methodological
Notes

*t*he primary data used in this study are the transcripts of interviews with sixty-five individuals from sixty-three different villages located in thirty counties in Kwangtung Province and in one southern county of neighboring Fukien Province. While we have checked information from our interviews with published sources at a number of points, there are many details which cannot easily be verified elsewhere. For this reason it is important for the reader to understand how our interviews were carried out and how we have used the information contained in them.

The Interviews

Our project did not start as a joint one. When Whyte applied for research funds he was unaware that Parish had already begun interviewing in Hong Kong on virtually the same topic. Both of us worked at the Universities Service Centre in Hong Kong; Parish in 1972–73 and Whyte in 1973–74, with an overlap of less than one week. The agreement to collaborate was worked out gradually and tentatively during 1973–74 by comparing interests, interview transcripts, and ideas. Eventually we were able to work out a satisfactory division of labor and agreement on issues of substance, but because we did not collaborate at the start our research procedures were not completely uniform. In particular, some of the topics covered in the interviewing outline of each researcher were not as fully covered by the other, although on most major topics our outlines were similar. The result of this initial independence is that on most points of interest we have information on fewer than the full sixty-three villages, though the pattern of omission should be fairly random and should not bias our results seriously.

A second difference between our procedures stems from the timing of our research stays. When Parish began his interviewing, the rising tide of legal as well as illegal emigrants produced by China's liberalization of its exit-visa regulations was just beginning to swamp the Hong Kong authorities, and welfare agencies helping the new emigrants to get settled were still wary about cooperating with foreign scholars. Parish had to use a laboriously built-up series of personal contacts and informal grapevines to locate people to interview. By the time Whyte began his work in late 1973 this situation had changed. A regular procedure had developed by which newly arriving refugees could turn themselves in and be taken to a central police station in Hong Kong. There they would be allowed to notify any relatives in Hong Kong to come and get them. Those not picked up in this fashion were sent by bus to dormitories run by relief agencies, where they were registered and allowed to live until they became established in Hong Kong. Whyte and his research assistants were able to develop close contacts with one such refugee dormitory, which served as the major source of interviews conducted during 1973–74. This centralized location made it possible to screen large numbers of recent arrivals by age, sex, county of origin, and other criteria in order to achieve some variety among those actually interviewed. In addition, officials in the dormitory could reassure refugees in advance about the nature of our interviews, so that they would have less reason for fear and conceal-ment than would refugees located by other means.

The actual interviewing procedures used by Parish and Whyte were simi-lar. Interviews were conducted in offices at the Universities Service Centre. Each researcher used a standard topic outline to conduct semistructured inten-sive interviews. Informants were asked to provide concrete information about a wide variety of aspects of village and family life. (Scholars may acquire copies of the interview outline by writing to either author.) This outline was not followed in any rigid order; rather, new topics introduced by informants were followed up immediately, and loose ends from other topics were attended to later. Generally informants were interviewed several times in sessions of three hours each until the outline had been completed. Occa-sionally an informant would show a lack of detailed knowledge or would not respond well to our questions, and we would terminate our interviews after only three or four hours. At other times a responsive informant would come back again and again to supply additional details and highlights, for a total of sixty or more interview hours. In all, our interviews totalled 988 hours, or an average of 15.2 hours per informant.

Interviews were generally recorded not on tape but in the form of detailed notes, which were typed into full transcripts immediately after the interviews. Most interviews were conducted by one person: either by Parish or Whyte or by one of the two Chinese research assistants. The assistants were used mainly to interview peasants who did not speak Mandarin—speakers only of Cantonese, Hakka, or Ch'ao-chou dialects of Kwangtung. (Younger peasants who have been to primary school or beyond will usually be able to speak Mandarin, while older and less educated peasants will not.) The detailed interview reports recorded by our Chinese assistants were translated into English along with the other transcripts. In a few cases a Chinese assistant helped one of the authors in an interview when communication problems developed.

Informants were generally paid standard fees for participation in these interviews. At the time the customary fee was HK $45 (US $9) for a three-hour interview. Although payment is less desirable in a Chinese context than developing a close personal relationship as the basis for an interview, it is unavoidable when large numbers of individuals are being interviewed, as in our project. It has become a fairly well-established practice in Hong Kong, and for recently arrived refugees with very little clothing or funds this money comes in very handy. Informants were told in advance that the interviewer had a set number of topics to cover, dealing with common experiences from daily life, and that as soon as this was done the interview would terminate. These instructions were designed to discourage falsification and unnecessary elaboration.

Methods of Analysis

The transcripts of our interviews form the raw materials for our analysis—a total of 1,318 pages of textual material. At many points we simply extracted the general pattern or its major variants from these interviews in a qualitative fashion to describe the current organization of Kwangtung communes, villages, and families. But we have also dissected these materials in order to subject some of our impressions to quantitative tests. To do this we had to construct a number of "samples" from our transcripts and code standard kinds of information for all units in these "samples." (We use quotation marks because these were not randomly drawn samples, and despite some checks reported below we cannot finally establish that they are fully representative.)

One such sample is our group of sixty-three villages. For each village we systematically noted on coding forms basic characteristics of the local team, village, and brigade as reported by our informants. By coding we mean that such things as the size of the brigade and its proximity to a large city were reduced to simple categorical variables (for example, 1 = under 2,000 people, 2 = 2,000 or more people; 1 = more than 150 km away, 2 = 75–150 km, 3 = within 75 km). These coded village characteristics were then used to construct fifteen primary *independent* variables, used to compare the sixty-three villages throughout our study, and a number of others. (The codes for these variables, and their interrelationships, are given in Appendix 2.)

We also coded information for each village on a wide variety of other topics: how births were celebrated, whether there had been any recent divorces, and so forth. These we consider our major *dependent* variables, our measures of variation in how much village and family life have or have not changed. Throughout the study we have statistically examined whether particular variations in rural organization, practices, and customs (our dependent variables) are related to, and could be explained by, differences in village characteristics (our independent variables).

Given the large number of relationships involved, shorthand ways of presenting our results had to be found. We choose for this purpose an ordinal measure of association called Goodman and Kruskal's gamma. To take an example from Chapter 4, we can consider whether production teams with relatively many Communist party (CCP) members are likely also to have a functioning poor- and lower-middle-peasant (PLMP) association. If every team with a PLMP association had a relatively high number of CCP members and every village team without a PLMP association had few CCP members, there would be a perfect positive association, and gamma would equal 1.0. If instead every team with a PLMP association had few CCP members and vice versa, there would be a perfect negative association, with gamma equal to −1.0. Should half the village teams with a PLMP association have many CCP members and half have few (and the same for teams with no PLMP association), then gamma would be zero. Thus, a gamma statistic in a table indicates the strength of an association. In this example the actual relationship between many local CCP members and a functioning PLMP association is gamma = .67, which means that these two traits tend to appear together—but not always.[1] In general we have paid little attention to gamma values weaker than ± .4 (.3 in Chapter 10, with a larger sample) unless there is a consistent pattern of signs for somewhat weaker gammas across several related dependent variables. We assume gamma values weaker than .4 indicate that the underlying association is essentially zero.

We also report by an asterisk in tables those associations which are of sufficient size to occur on the basis of chance alone less than one time in ten. Significance tests are not strictly appropriate to our data, which do not come from a random sample, as these tests require. We use these tests simply as one more aid in detecting relationships worthy of scrutiny as we scan a large number of tables and gamma statistics. In all cases we did examine the full contingency table for interesting patterns, even though the text often reports only summary gamma statistics and those associations which surpass the $p \leq .10$ significance level.

One additional procedure was introduced to deal with possible spurious associations in our data. Since the independent variables characterizing our sixty-three villages are interrelated (see Appendix 2), we had to know whether, for example, the association between the Tachai work-point system and the existence of nursery schools in a locality could be attributed not to the influence of nursery schools themselves but to location in a large populous team, since places that have nurseries happen on the average to be more populous (see table 7). This type of question was dealt with by a partial-association computer program which calculates new values of gamma be tween two variables after the effects of a third variable have been partialled out. In the above example, the gamma between Tachai work points and nurseries is .43 before control but only .25 after controlling for team size— thereby suggesting that the original association was spurious or attributable to team size alone. In other instances, control by a third variable leaves the original relationship unaffected or even strengthens it, implying that the original relationship was not spurious.[2] Many of our findings are based on this kind of internal statistical analysis of interview materials, using sixty-three individual villages as units of analysis.

For other parts of our analysis we had to construct other "samples." To answer such questions as whether couples who marry on their own initiative or without parental pressure have simpler weddings than other couples, one needs information not on villages but on separate marriages occurring within these villages. Such a sample was constructed using information on 344 different marriages in fifty-one villages. These marriages entered interviews in a variety of contexts but particularly when informants described a wedding they had seen or attended or the composition of their neighbors' households. Using this sample, we could check whether certain characteristics of a marriage—the year in which it occurred, the backgrounds of the bride and groom, even the village where it occurred—were related to another set of dependent variables of interest to us, particularly the age of bride and groom, the degree of youth initiative, and the kind of marriage finance involved (see Chapter 10).

For the analysis reported in Chapter 9 we constructed still another set of samples dealing with household structure and birth control. We noted the composition of 131 households of neighbors in twenty-one of our villages (comprising 623 individuals). This neighbor sample approximates a random sample of rural households, since it includes only households of miscellaneous neighbors, rather than households of any special type of villager. We also constructed a combined household sample which includes 249 households drawn from thirty-six villages, with a total of 1,233 members. This includes, in addition to the neighbor sample, all other household descriptions which occurred in the interviews—of local cadres, former landlords or rich peasants, rich or poor families, the informant's family, and so forth. (Both of these samples exclude households of urban youths sent to live in a village.) From this combined sample we extracted a special subsample of 129 currently married women aged eighteen to forty. These women (along with the reported number and ages of their children) are also used in Chapter 9 to analyze fertility trends. The procedure in each case parallels that with other samples—we analyze whether households or women differing in some basic characteristics also differ in things such as household structure and number of children. Finally, we have taken the rural cadres mentioned by informants as another sample for analysis of leadership characteristics in Chapters 7 and 12.

Problems of Selectivity and Bias

The general criticisms of refugee interviewing as a research method are well known.[3] Briefly, it is claimed that refugees are not representative of individuals who remain in China and often come from places and organizations which are below average in some sense (the selectivity issue) and that most are alienated individuals who have rejected Chinese society and cannot be expected to give an accurate account of that society (the bias issue). There is some truth in both of these charges, but in our view the advantages of refugee interviewing still outweigh the disadvantages. If used carefully to study certain kinds of topics these interviews provide more useful information than other methods.

All sources of information on China today are subject to serious problems of bias and selectivity. The places and institutions reported on in the Chinese media and visited by foreign delegations are predominantly model institutions, most of them located in well-endowed and modernized sections of the country. The messages in the media and in trip briefings are frankly exhortative and normative; they tell what China is trying to do and where she wants to go, more than how things stand now. Moreover, on many topics of interest to us the official media and tour reports are simply uninformative—they do not convey the detailed information about daily life and customs which refugee informants can provide. (Both authors made trips to China and can testify that, though this travel experience is worthwhile in many ways, it is of limited value in studying something like changes in wedding customs.) Furthermore, it would be a mistake to assume that most refugees are bitter anticommunists. It is our impression that for most refugees the reasons for coming to Hong Kong are not found in political ideology but in the search for some kind of opportunity—opportunity to get more education, to find a more rewarding job, to rejoin relatives living there, to find a spouse, and the like. The search for opportunity does not necessarily mean that refugees reject the entire society built in China since 1949. Most informants give a fairly balanced account of the good side as well as the bad side of rural life—of improving standards of health care, education, and so forth. Still, we cannot simply assume that the problems of bias and selectivity are unimportant. We have to find ways to detect and correct for distortions introduced by interviewing refugees so that we can take advantage of the rich potential of the method. Since refugees are not representative of the population in China and may have a variety of grievances and biases, how can we avoid being misled? Procedures to control for bias have been introduced both at the interviewing and at the data analysis stage. In interviewing, we picked topics for investigation which were sufficiently mundane and open to casual daily observation that fabrication and anxiety would not be major problems. Any former resident of a rural village can report on such things as how weddings are celebrated and can feel that this information is of little use, one way or another, to foreign governments and intelligence services. Guarantees of anonymity serve to protect the informant and his or her relatives still in China. Then, in the interview, we repeatedly pressed informants to give concrete examples and personally observed details rather than village hearsay and subjective impressions. For example, in analyzing the results of the rural birth control campaign in Chapter 9, we placed more reliance on specific examples of neighborhood women and the number and ages of their children than on general impressions of how local peasants were accepting the campaign.

We also introduced checks on bias in analyzing our coded data. Particular kinds of informants might give a distorted picture of rural life. There is sufficient variation in the backgrounds of our sixty-five informants so that we can perform "quality control" checks to investigate this possibility.[4] The following figures summarize informant background characteristics.

Sex: 54 males, 11 females.

Age: twenty or less—8, twenty-one to thirty—41, thirty-one to forty—10, forty-one and older—6.

Marital status: 48 single, 13 married, 4 of unknown status.

Class background: 30 "good" class (worker or poor or lower-middle peasant), 15 "intermediate" class (upper-middle peasant, urban petty bourgeois), 14 "bad" class (capitalist, landlord or rich peasant), 6 of unknown status.

Educational background: 29 primary school or less, 27 partial or complete lower-middle schooling, 9 some upper-middle schooling or more.

Place of origin: 34 village natives, 8 who returned to their native village after going outside to school, 23 urban youths sent to live in a village.

History of trouble with authorities: none—35, yes but minor—20 (generally individuals caught during prior attempts to escape to Hong Kong), yes and more serious—4, no information—6.

Length of time in Hong Kong: three months or less—46, three months to one year—12, one year or more—7.

Length of time since informant left the village: three months or less—39, three months to one year—13, one year or more—12, no information—1.

In comparison with the population living in Kwangtung villages, more of our informants are male, more are unmarried, and they are younger, better educated, somewhat "worse" in class background and relations with authorities, and more urban in origin. However, there are enough informants with other characteristics to provide substantial variety and to allow checks on background effects.[5]

The basic idea in controlling for the effect of background characteristics is to see if informants of one type supply information that is systematically different in some way from that for informants of another type, and to take this into account in interpreting results. Our informants tend to be young, male, single, relatively well educated, and so forth. Would a group of informants including more older people, more women, more married people, and fewer highly educated people have given a different picture of the nature of rural life? Similarly, do informants with distinctive kinds of negative experience have an "axe to grind" that leads them to give a distorted view of rural life? Interviews also vary in fullness and freshness—the number of years the informant lived in the village, the length of time in Hong Kong, the length of time that has passed since the informant left the village, the identity of the interviewer (Chinese or American—assuming that the latter were more affected by language and interviewer-bias problems), number of hours for the total interview, and number of pages in the total interview transcript. Can it be assumed that those who lived in the village longer, left only recently, had not spent much time in Hong Kong, were interviewed by a Chinese assistant, and who came back for long and detailed interviews provided information that was more accurate (of better quality) than others?

We deal with these questions in two ways. One way is to delete individuals who might have a distorted view of the world and then compare results before and after the deletion. For example, people from former landlord or rich peasant families and people with past serious political errors might be expected to denigrate and understate material conditions more than other informants. However, removing the information supplied by these informants leads to only marginal changes in our calculations. Average reported grain yields rise from 760 to 780 catties per mou, the average work-day value rises from .55 to .58 yuan, the average proportion of overdrawing households in a team declines from 20 to 15 percent, while values for the proportion of families with bicycles, radios, and good housing remains unchanged. In this realm, then, bias among those of "negative" background does not seriously distort our results.

Another more commonly followed procedure is to examine whether controlling for informant and interview quality-effects reduces the association between any independent and dependent variable. This is done by the partial association computer program, which calculates new values of gamma between independent and dependent variables after any informant bias has been partialled out. It may turn out that the original statistical relationship is sharply reduced by these controls, providing evidence that the relationship was spurious—attributable to the biases of our information. On the other hand, the original relationship may be unaffected or may even increase.

In general we have not found these "data quality" problems to be particularly serious in our study. The number of significant correlations between informant or interview codes and our dependent variables is not much larger than would be expected on the basis of chance alone. (For example, for the family-related variables in our village sample we would expect 39 significant associations out of a total of 390 correlations with quality control variables; 47 significant associations resulted.) Nevertheless, we have systematically checked the quantitative relationships reported in this study to see if they were artifacts of informant bias. Where statistical checks substantially reduced the associations reported, we have noted that fact in those tables and have modified our own interpretations accordingly.[6] These statistical checks allow us to say with some confidence that our final conclusions on various topics are not simply the result of our interviewing a group of informants who were unrepresentative of the population of rural Kwangtung or who because of negative backgrounds had a jaundiced view of rural life. The modest number of informant bias problems detected serves as validation of our original impression that individuals of widely differing backgrounds and points of view can describe social reality in similar terms if only the topics and questions are sufficiently concrete and mundane.

Even if informants from widely differing backgrounds give fairly consistent images of village life, there is still concern over whether the information we have gathered is representative of the general situation in Kwangtung villages or of only a small, selected subset of villages. We adopted three procedures to deal with this selectivity problem. First, we used refugees as informants rather than as respondents. Not the attitudes of the individual but his or her account of the organization and customs in his or her village is the focus. The technique is basically that used by ethnographers who do research on other cultures by talking to knowledgeable informants, although in our case this talking occurred "at a distance" from the actual villages concerned.[7] Since our unit of analysis is not the individual interviewee but rather his or her village, neighbors, leaders, and marriages, the essential question is no longer whether informants are representative (they surely are not) but rather whether the reported villages, neighbors, leaders, and marriages are representative (they may be so).

Second, throughout our analysis we are as much concerned with internal variation in rural life as we are in the average level of bride prices, political study systems, or school attendance. We want to know, for example, whether places with political study systems or abundant education give smaller bride prices or support other kinds of social change. So long as we are concerned with the relationship between two village characteristics,

having a precisely representative sample of Kwangtung villages is less important than having a sample with sufficient variability to cover the extremes
of conditions in the province. We believe we have such a sample. Though
some of the richest communes, especially the vegetable-growing communes
in the Canton suburbs, are not represented, our sample includes both quite
rich and very poor localities. Informants might be expected to have come
primarily from poor production teams. Yet, in our sample the most affluent
teams have work-day values of about 1.38 yuan and grain yields of 1,200
catties per mou, figures not much different from the 1.40 yuan and 1,400
catties per mou that seem typical in reports of visitors to model villages in
Kwangtung.[8] This comparison suggests that our sample does include "success stories." (In fact our sample includes a few model villages mentioned
in the press, and on one occasion we were able to have an informant view
and comment on a documentary film made of his home commune by a
foreign news team.) We are therefore confident that our sample includes
enough variation to make valid generalizations about how rural conditions
differ and why.

At times, however, we want to go beyond examining village variations
and say something about the "general picture" in rural Kwangtung. To do
this we frequently compare our results with published reports on particular
Kwangtung villages, noting similarities and contrasts. But we also have used
a third procedure that yields more precise estimates of how representative
our sample of villages is. This involves comparing aggregate or average
statistics computed from our data with statistics for all of Kwangtung compiled from Chinese sources. Six sets of statistics are available for 1973 (the
most common reporting year in our interviews), and they yield the following
comparison.

1. Each informant was asked what the grain yield in his or her production
team was in the previous year. Ranging from 330 catties per mou to 1,200
catties per mou, the average (median) annual yield in our production teams
was 760 catties per cultivated mou. According to Kwangtung Provincial
Radio, the average (mean) yield throughout Kwangtung Province in 1973 was
790 catties per mou, a figure only marginally higher than ours.[9]

2. Informants report private plots ranging from .20 to .29 mou per family
with an average (median) of .27 mou. Calculations from known population
and land figures suggest an average (mean) private plot of .26 mou in the
province (see Chapter 8).

3. Informants' reports on land per laborer in their home production teams

range from 1.0 to 11.8 mou, with an average of 3.0 mou. Calculations from known population and land totals give an average land-labor ratio of 2.94 mou.[10]

4. Asked whether their brigade had a functioning cooperative medical insurance program, 80 percent of our informants responded affirmatively. Kwangtung Provincial Radio agrees, reporting in 1973 that 80 percent of all production brigades had a cooperative medical program (see Chapter 6).

5. Informants report that their brigades had anywhere from one to ten barefoot doctors, yielding an average of 2.5 doctors per brigade. Again Kwangtung Provincial Radio agrees, reporting figures which imply 2.5 barefoot doctors per brigade in 1973 (see Chapter 6).

6. Though their estimates are not so precise, informants in the great majority of villages report that virtually all children of the age for primary school are in school, leading to an estimate on our part of over 90 percent enrollment. A radio report in 1973 indicates that 92 percent of such youths in Kwangtung are in school (see Chapter 6).

The close correspondence between figures aggregated from our informant reports and official Chinese statistics is quite remarkable, especially since the official figures were not available to us at the time we made our sample calculations. We still cannot say that our samples are in any exact sense representative. Some regions of Kwangtung are better represented than others (see Kwangtung map on pp. 24–25), and we have no figures on many other aspects of rural life with which to check for selectivity in our village, neighbor, and other samples. But given the checks we have performed, we are fairly confident that our villagers and peasant families are at least typical enough so that we can make some generalizations about rural life in Kwangtung. (We noted in Chapter 3 that we do not claim that our findings can be generalized to all of rural China, although our general impression is that Kwangtung is not so unusual that broadly similar patterns would not be found elsewhere.)

We feel we have made the fullest and best possible use of the data provided by our informants. Only such informants can provide the vivid detail and personal color about village and family life in China today that are essential to a study such as ours. Though as a source of systematic data these informant reports present a series of problems, we believe that by the procedures outlined above we have been able to control and eliminate many sources of bias, selectivity, and spuriousness. Many of our conclusions are still based on partial information from small numbers of villages and families, and we accept the fact that future scholarship may modify some of the details as better information becomes available. But without the possibility of conducting empirical social science research in China—which we do not see arising in the foreseeable future—we feel that careful refugee interviewing provides the richest source of information about contemporary Chinese social life. We hope the results reported here encourage other scholars to tackle the difficulties involved in using this source.

Appendix 2
Village
Characteristics
and Their
Interrelations

*t*hroughout this study our assessment of social change has relied primarily on fifteen coded village characteristics. Table A tells how the fifteen primary characteristics are interrelated; whether a village with many sent-down urban youths is likely to be near or far from major cities, to have high or low levels of remittance dependency, and so forth. All data refer roughly to the year 1973. The statistic used in this table is Pearson's product moment correlation r, and values which are likely to occur on the basis of chance alone less than one time in ten (p ≤ .10) are marked with an asterisk. The number of villages involved in the correlations varies in the range from twenty-eight to sixty; most are computed for forty to fifty-five villages. These correlations have been used to determine which independent variables need to be controlled statistically in order to detect spurious associations (see the discussion in Appendix 1).

The following variables were included.

1. Political density. A dichotomous variable, composed of the equally weighted mean of three separate measures: the proportion of families with a landlord or rich peasant label (1 = 20 percent or more, 2 = 19 percent or less); the percentage of local Communist party members (1 = under 3 percent, 2 = 3 percent or more); and a poor and lower middle-peasant association (1 = absent or inactive, 2 = present and active). For the final scale, 1 = low political density, 2 = high political density.[1]

Table A

Correlations among Primary Village Characteristics

	PD 1	PS 2	UP 3	UY 4	Comm 5	Nurs 6	CA 7	HC 8	LR 9	Rem 10	BS 11	TS 12	LC 13	NHE 14	DR 15
1. Political density	--														
2. Political study	.17	--													
3. Urban proximity	-.04	-.02	--												
4. Urban youths	.06	-.19	.30*	--											
5. Communications	.22	.16	.12	-.29*	--										
6. Nurseries	-.19	.12	.41*	-.15	.18	--									
7. Collective affluence	-.05	.20	.28*	.21	.11	.35*	--								
8. Household consumption	.12	-.08	.39*	.36*	.03	-.09	.15	--							
9. Land/labor ratio	.03	-.13	.22	.37*	.05	-.08	.05	.28*	--						
10. Remittances	.19	.47*	-.10	-.39*	.41*	.02	.12	-.03	.04	--					
11. Brigade size	-.06	-.02	.06	-.27	-.03	.11	-.15	.21	.09	.04	--				
12. Team size	.04	.25	.19	-.00	.05	.43*	.2	.15	.07	.13	.32*	--			
13. Lineage composition	-.08	-.07	.16	.04	.01	-.16	.08	.05	.06	.17	-.25	-.09	--		
14. Non-Hakka ethnicity	-.31*	.13	.24*	.01	.13	.28*	.31*	.19	-.18	.16	.32*	.02	-.09	--	
15. Delta region	-.01	.09	.58*	.20	.10	.41*	.59*	.29*	.02	.27	.17	.27*	.14	.43*	--

2. Political study. Whether there are regularly held political study meetings in the team. 1 = none, 2 = some or frequent.

3. Urban proximity. The closeness of the village to Canton or Swatow. 1 = over 150 km away, 2 = 75–150 km away, 3 = within 75 km.

4. Urban youths. The proportion of adults in a team who are urban youths sent down to live in the village. 1 = under 3 percent, 2 = 3 percent or more.

5. Communications. A dichotomous variable, composed of the equally weighted mean of three separate measures: reported primary-school attendance (1 = "low," 2 = most, 3 = virtually all local youths); type of radio network (1 = none, 2 = wired street-speakers, 3 = wired speakers in homes); and frequency of movie team visits (1 = once in two or three months or less, 2 = more frequent). For the final scale, 1 = low communications, 2 = high.

6. Nurseries. Whether a brigade or team had collective nurseries or kindergartens. 1 = none, 2 = either or both.

7. Collective affluence. A dichotomous variable, composed of the equally weighted mean of three separate measures: reported recent rice yields (1 = under 799 catties per mou per year, 2 = 800 or more); reported value of a day's work points (1 = .59 yuan or less, 2 = .60 yuan or more); and types of brigade machinery (1 = no tractors or pumps, 2 = either or both). For the final scale, 1 = low affluence, 2 = high.

8. Household consumption. A dichotomous variable, composed of the equally weighted mean of three separate measures: percentage of households in a team with their own radios (1 = under 10 percent, 2 = 10 percent or more); percentage of households in a team with bicycles (1 = under 20 percent, 2 = 20 percent or more); and types of team machinery (1 = no tractors or pumps, 2 = either or both). For the final scale, 1 = low consumption, 2 = high.

9. Land-labor ratio. 1 = less than 3 mou per adult laborer, 2 = 3 mou or more.

10. Remittances. The extent of remittance dependency in a team, as measured by the percentage of families receiving some remittances from outside of China. 1 = under 10 percent of all families, 2 = 10 percent or more.

11. Brigade size. 1 = under 2,000 people, 2 = 2,000 or more people.

12. Team size. 1 = under 200 people, 2 = 200 or more people.

13. Lineage composition. 1 = multilineage team, 2 = single-lineage team in a multilineage brigade, 3 = single-lineage brigade (in each case "single lineage" means less than 5 percent of families from another lineage).

14. Non-Hakka ethnicity. 1 = residents of villages are Hakkas, 2 = resi-

dents of village are Cantonese, Ch'ao-chou, or some other non-Hakka group.

15. Delta region. 1 = village outside of Pearl River Delta, 2 = village in Pearl River Delta (boundaries determined by county).

Besides these fifteen variables, our analysis of material equality (in Chapter 5) used several others. These are coded as follows:

16. Irrigation supply. 1 = major or minor seasonal water-supply problems, 2 = supply of water adequate the year round.

17. Terrain. 1 = hilly terrain, 2 = delta or plains land.

18. Brigade factories. 1 = no brigade workshops or factories, 2 = some or many workshops or factories.

19. Electricity. 1 = no electric supply, 2 = intermittent (with seasonal or daily interruptions) or regular electric supply.

20. Housing. 1 = straw, bamboo, and mud or mixed fired-brick and mud-brick wall construction predominant, 2 = fired brick or concrete block construction predominant.

21. Overdrawing. 1 = 20 percent or more of team households overdraw, 2 = less than 20 percent overdraw.

22. Team machinery. 1 = neither tractor nor pump, 2 = either tractor or pump, 3 = both.

23. Brigade machinery. Same coding as no. 22. Note that these last two were collapsed into dichotomies for inclusion in earlier scales.

Notes

CB	*Current Background* (U.S. Consulate, Hong Kong)
CN	*Chung-kuo hsin-wen* [China News] (Peking)
FBIS	*Foreign Broadcast Information Service* (Washington, D.C.)
JMJP	*Jen-min jih-pao* [People's Daily] (Peking)
JPRS	*Joint Publications Research Service* (Washington D.C.)
KMJP	*Kuang-ming jih-pao* [Brilliance Daily] (Peking)
NFJP	*Nan-fang jih-pao* [Southern Daily] (Canton)
SWB	*Selected World Broadcasts,* weekly economic summary (British Broadcasting Corporation, London)
SCMM	*Selections from China Mainland Magazines* (U.S. Consultate, Hong Kong)

357

SCMP   *Selections from the China Mainland Press* (U.S. Consulate, Hong Kong)

URS   *Union Research Service* (Union Research Institute, Hong Kong)

1   Introduction

1. We also utilized a number of procedures to minimize or filter out the problems of bias and selectivity that inevitably occur in a study using emigré informants. These are fully discussed in Appendix 1.

2   Perspectives on Purposive Change

1. No comprehensive official account of how rural change is induced is available, so what is presented here is our own brief summary and interpretation. We feel our summary is fairly objective, but brevity has led us to omit important side issues and terminology. For an account that mirrors our discussion on many points, see Chinese Communist Party Committee of Hui-ho Commune, Ch'i-tung County, "Destroy Old Customs, Establish New Styles," *Red Flag,* 1973, no. 2, translated in *SCMM,* nos. 747–48, 26 February–5 March 1973.

2. See *Tachai, Standard-bearer in China's Agriculture* (Peking: Foreign Language Press, 1972).

3. See Cyril Black, ed., *Comparative Modernization* (New York: The Free Press, 1976); Alex Inkeles and David H. Smith, *Becoming Modern* (Cambridge: Harvard University Press, 1974).

4. Inkeles and Smith, *Becoming Modern,* chap. 13. Note the modernizing role the authors say is played by agricultural cooperatives, with the Comilla experiment in Bangladesh and the Israeli moshavim as their examples.

5. This aspect is stressed in Daniel Lerner, *The Passing of Traditional Society* (New York: The Free Press, 1958); and in I. de Sola Pool, "Communications and Development," in *Modernization: The Dynamics of Growth,* ed. Myron Weiner (Washington, D.C.: USIA, n.d.).

6. This distinction between direct and indirect (environmental) approaches to purposive social change is common in the literature on this topic. See, for example, James S. Coleman, "Conflicting Theories of Social Change," in *Processes and*

Phenomena of Social Change, ed. Gerald Zaltman (New York: John Wiley, 1973).

7. Compare the typology of compliance mechanisms in Amitai Etzioni, *A Comparative Analysis of Complex Organizations* (New York: The Free Press, 1961). Our typology differs by placing direct economic rewards and penalties among administrative sanctions. Other more general economic changes (for example, increasing prosperity) we categorize with indirect structural transformations.

8. We note that Etzioni divides his normative power category into two types: pure normative power—based on the manipulation of esteem and ritualistic symbols, and social power—based on acceptance from peers. It is the latter to which our mobilized social pressure subtype corresponds.

9. We should mention in passing that one perspective that has been applied to the study of rural change in China utilizes an alternation between Etzioni's three compliance mechanisms. Change is seen as induced by campaigns in which an initial normative stage is followed by a coercive stage designed to check excesses, to be followed in turn by a remunerative stage emphasizing economic rewards where things return to some sort of normal state until a new campaign cycle is initiated. This argument is presented in G. W. Skinner and E. Winckler, "Cyclical Compliance and Rural Social Change in Communist China," in *A Sociological Reader in Complex Organizations,* 2d ed., ed. Amitai Etzioni (New York: Rinehart and Winston, 1969). Since we lack detailed information on the pattern of most changes over time, we will be unable to examine this argument directly.

10. It would obviously be preferable to have longitudinal data for each village to trace patterns of change over time. Being without such data, we must rely on the technique of comparing contemporary customs in our sixty-three villages with what we know to have been the "traditional" situation in this region, in order to estimate the extent of change. We recognize that this traditional benchmark is a crude one, that villages were changing in many ways before 1949 in response to commercialization, foreign penetration, and other forces, and that within Kwangtung the character of village social life varied from one place to another. We still feel, however, that certain rough generalizations can be made about such things as how marriage mates were selected and the role of lineages in ceremonial life in this region generally before 1949. Fortunately, the information of Kwangtung before 1949 is fairly detailed, and we will make ample use of monographs on lineages in this region authored by Maurice Freedman, portions of the massive rural surveys of 1929–33 directed by John L. Buck, and a number of Kwangtung ethnographies and customary compilations. In some cases we have later information as our benchmark for judging change, using works by Andrew Nathan, Michel Oksenberg, Robert Worth, and Janet Salaff which describe work-remuneration systems, village leadership, birth control, and marriages in rural Kwangtung in the early 1960s.

3   Kwangtung Province

1. John S. Aird, *Population Estimates for the Provinces of the People's Republic of China: 1953 to 1974*, International Population Reports, Series P-95, no. 73 (Washington, D.C.: U.S. Department of Commerce, 1974).

2. Our study will not attempt to deal with one of the most distinctive geographic regions of Kwangtung—Hainan Island. It is so distinctive—with tropical vegetation, sizable minority groups, and special administration—and represented so poorly in our interviews that we cannot adequately describe rural life there.

3. To the west of Canton in rural Nan-hai County, thirty-nine major and seven minor markets of 1691 expanded into seventy-three major and sixty-five minor markets by 1835. See *Nan-hai County Gazetteer* for these two dates. On types of markets, see G. William Skinner, "Marketing and Social Structure in Rural China," *Journal of Asian Studies* 24 (1964–65): 3–43, 195–28, and 363–99.

4. Specific village locations are not given in order to preserve the anonymity of our informants. One informant, not included in the map figures, actually came from southern Fukien Province just across the border.

5. There are other ethnic groups in Kwangtung which are too small and too poorly represented in our interviews for us to analyze them separately. One is a group of people in the Han River Delta near the city of Ch'ao-chou who speak the Min dialect, which they brought with them from neighboring Fukien Province. Another is the ethnic subgroup called the Tanka, or Egg-people, who live on boats. For the coding of the ethnicity of our villages, see Appendix 2.

6. Sun Ching-chih, *Hua-nan ti-ch'ü ching-chi ti-li* [Economic geography of South China] (Peking, 1959), in *JPRS*, no. 14,954, p. 52. Another major recipient was Mei-hsien, a predominantly Hakka county. Emigration from Kwangtung affected localities of many ethnic types. On the fluctuations in official policy towards overseas Chinese, see Stephen Fitzgerald, *China and the Overseas Chinese* (Cambridge: Cambridge University Press, 1972).

7. For example, *Hsin-ning tsa-chih* [Sun-ning magazine], bimonthly.

8. For the classification of villages with many and few remittances used in later chapters, see Appendix 2.

9. The major Western studies of the organization of lineages in this region are Maurice Freedman, *Lineage Organization in Southeastern China* (London: Athlone, 1958), and, by the same author, *Chinese Lineage and Society: Fukien and Kwangtung* (London: Athlone, 1966).

10. Ezra Vogel, *Canton Under Communism* (Cambridge: Harvard University Press, 1969), pp. 211–16.

11. Replies to the issue of representativeness can be stated more bluntly. 1. For the purposes of studying covariation between social change and background condi-

tions, the object of much of our analysis, it does not make all that much difference whether Kwangtung is completely "typical" or not. It is essential that we have variation in background conditions—a variation which is amply present in Kwangtung. 2. Even for the purposes of making general descriptive statements about social change, the conditions in Kwangtung are far from all being weighted against government-desired change. While a history of strong lineages, insider-outsider conflict, low levels of party membership, and continuing overseas contact could work against change, the greater than average level of education, health care, and urbanization should favor change. For example, in the government's recent birth control campaign, Kwangtung was among the first four provinces claiming to have reached the nationally targeted growth rate of 15 per 1,000 population. Uncritical assertions about Kwangtung's exceptional backwardness should be greeted with some skepticism. 3. Finally, the search for an absolutely typical province is ultimately futile. Each province has its own special set of circumstances, and Kwangtung is as good a province as any (and certainly a large enough one) with which to start. (For amplification of point 1 above and for a discussion of how representative our sample is of Kwangtung itself, see Appendix 1.)

4   Collective Agricultural Organization

1. On the structural transformation of agriculture, see Franz Schurmann, *Ideology and Organization in Communist China*, 2d ed. (Berkeley: University of California Press, 1968), chap. 7; Kenneth Walker, *Planning in Chinese Agriculture* (Chicago: Aldine, 1967); and, for Kwangtung, Vogel, *Canton Under Communism*. On the structure of contemporary communes see A. Doak Barnett with Ezra Vogel, *Cadres, Bureaucracy and Political Power in Communist China* (New York: Columbia University Press, 1967), pt. 3; Benedict Stavis, *People's Communes and Rural Development in China* (Ithaca: Cornell University Center for International Studies, 1974); Byung-joon Ahn, "The Political Economy of the People's Commune in China: Changes and Continuities," *Journal of Asian Studies* 34 (1975): 631–58; and Frederick W. Crook, "The Commune System in the People's Republic of China," in U.S. Congress Joint Economic Committee, *China: A Reassessment of the Economy* (Washington, D.C: U.S. Government Printing Office, 1975).

2. See Vogel, *Canton Under Communism*, p. 94. The term "cadre" refers to leadership personnel at any level in China and to salaried members of the state bureaucracy.

3. See Peter Schran, *The Development of Chinese Agriculture, 1950–1959* (Urbana: University of Illinois Press, 1969), p. 23. This brought the average farm for a family labeled as "poor peasants" up to about two acres in size. It is important to note that land reform did not equalize all holdings. Those families labeled as "middle

peasants'' and ''rich peasants'' were not brought down to the poor-peasant level, and they averaged about three acres and four and a half acres after land reform, respectively.

4. The number of pigs in China declined from more than 101 million in 1954 to 84 million in 1956, after collectivization. The average size of collectives was reduced from 344 households in 1956 to only 164 households in 1957. See Schran, *Development of Chinese Agriculture,* p. 30.

5. Other reasons for the relative smoothness of Chinese collectivization are detailed in Thomas Bernstein, ''Leadership and Mass Mobilization in the Soviet and Chinese Collectivization Campaigns of 1929–1930 and 1955–1956,'' *China Quarterly,* no. 31 (1967): 1–42.

6. The Sixty Articles are translated in Union Research Institute, *Documents of the Chinese Communist Party Central Committee,* vol. 1 (Hong Kong: N. p., 1971). We will refer to this document later simply as the Sixty Articles.

7. See ''Document of the CCP Central Committee, chung-fa (1971), no. 82,'' in *Chung-kung yen-chiu* [Studies on Chinese Communism] 6 (September 1972) and ''Document no. 22 of the CCP Ssuma District Committee,'' translated in *Issues and Studies* 9, no. 6 (March 1973). The way these changes affected the labor incentive system is discussed more fully in Chapter 5.

8. The visions for the future are laid out in Chang Ch'un-ch'iao, ''On Exercising All-round Dictatorship over the Bourgeoisie,'' *Peking Review* 18, no. 14 (1975): 4. Chang was purged as one of the ''gang of four'' in October 1976. The goal of eventually moving the accounting unit up to the brigade and then the commune was still being stressed after their purge, however.

9. Philip R. Lee, ''Notes on a Visit to China,'' mimeographed (San Francisco: University of California School of Medicine, 1973), p. 21.

10. The average Soviet collective farm (kolkhoz) has in recent years embraced four hundred or so households, a much smaller size than that of the average Chinese commune. However, there is less decentralization in the kolkhoz, with the farm chairman, often an outsider, directing the activities and managing the income for the entire unit. Thus, while the coordinating levels of the brigade and commune make the Chinese unit larger, the basic unit of daily farming operations in China, the production team, is only one-tenth as large as its Russian counterpart, leaving the Chinese peasant closer to the natural neighborhood and kinship groups with which he or she is familiar.

11. During the Cultural Revolution mass associations and the party itself ceased to function throughout the land, and all were in the process of slow rebuilding after 1969. The Poor and Lower-Middle Peasant Association was simply slower than most. The original rules of this association are translated in R. Baum and F. Teiwes, *Ssu-ch'ing: The Socialist Education Movement of 1962–1966* (Berkeley: University of California Center for Chinese Studies, 1968), pp. 95–101.

12. These wired broadcasting networks continue to develop rapidly. A recent source claims that in 1975 92.7 percent of the production teams in the entire country were reached by wired broadcasting, and 70 percent of rural households had loudspeakers within the home. *Peking Review* 18, no. 39 (1975): 30.

13. A Chinese source states that in 1974 the average peasant in Kwangtung attended more than ten film shows. See *Peking Review* 18, no. 45 (1975): 30.

14. For a visitor's description of a rural study meeting which supports the points made here, see Arthur W. Galston, *Daily Life in People's China* (New York: Crowell, 1973), pp. 100–101. For a more analytical treatment of village study meetings, see Martin K. Whyte, *Small Groups and Political Rituals in China* (Berkeley: University of California Press, 1974), chap. 7.

15. One of our informants, a sent-down youth, provides the following example: "The women there do not wear short-sleeved clothes—they feel that wearing short sleeves is for ghosts and not for people. Women also do not wear colored clothing. The only thing they have is black clothing. In the last two years, these women have been influenced by us sent-down girls, and they have started to wear westernized clothes, and two or three young women are wearing short-sleeved clothing. Some young males are wearing watches" (Interview TC-1, p. 4).

16. Except where otherwise noted, sent-down urban youth are excluded from subsequent tables on household structure, age structure, marriages, and incomes, and therefore do not affect these tabulations.

5   Material Equality and Inequality

1. See the discussion in Arthur Okun, *Equality and Efficiency: The Big Trade-Off* (Washington, D.C.: Brookings Institution, 1975).

2. The classic statement here is Milovan Djilas, *The New Class* (New York: Praeger, 1957).

3. See J. S. Adams, "Inequity as Social Exchange," in L. Berkowitz, ed., *Advances in Experimental and Social Psychology* (New York: Academic Press, 1965) 2:267–99.

4. See the Sixty Articles translated in Union Research Institute, *Documents of Chinese Communist Party Central Committee* (Hong Kong, 1971), 1:695–725.

5. The most extensive foreign accounts are S. J. Burki, *A Study of Chinese Communes, 1965* (Cambridge: Harvard University, East Asian Research Center, 1969); Keith Buchanan, *The Transformation of the Chinese Earth* (London: Bell and Sons, 1970).

6. See Hunan Province Revolutionary Committee, Agriculture and Forestry

Bureau, ed., *Nung-ts'un jen-min kung-she sheng-ch'an k'uai-chi* [Rural People's Commune production accountant] (Ch'ang-sha: Hunan People's Press, 1973); China People's Bank, Kwangtung Province Branch, ed., *Nung-ts'un jen-min kung-she sheng-ch'an tui k'uai-chi* [Rural People's Commune production team accountant] (Canton: Kwangtung People's Press, 1974); Liaoning Province, Financial College, Agricultural Economics Department, ed., *Tsen-yang tso hao sheng-ch'an tui ts'ai-k'uai kung-tso* [How to do production team financial and accounting work well] (Shenyang: Liaoning People's Press, 1973); Peking Municipality, Financial Bureau, *Nung-ts'un jen-min kung-she sheng-ch'an tui k'uai-chi ho-suan* [Rural People's Commune production team accountant tabulation] (Peking: Peking People's Press, 1973); China People's Bank, Kansu Province Branch, *Nung-ts'un jen-min kung-she k'uai-chi shou-ts'e* [Rural People's Commune accountant manual] (Lanchou: Kansu People's Press, 1972).

7. After the Stalinist policy of forced extraction from agriculutre had been modified, Soviet collective farms paid a 1961 tax of 7 percent of gross output. David W. Bronson and Constance B. Krueger, "The Revolution in Soviet Farm Household Income, 1953–1967," in *The Soviet Rural Community,* ed. James R. Millar (Urbana: University of Illinois Press, 1971), p. 250.

8. Burki, *A Study of Chinese Communes,* p. 20. Buchanan, *Transformation of the Chinese Earth,* p. 136. Graham Johnson, "Rural Economic Development and Social Change in South China," mimeographed (Vancouver: Department of Anthropology and Sociology, University of British Columbia, 1973), p. 13. In recent years village consumption levels have been further supported by long-term grain loans to poor teams (see Chapter 6).

9. C. K. Yang, *A Chinese Village in Early Communist Transition* (Cambridge: MIT Press, 1957), p. 230. The comparison with earlier practice is inexact due to varying accounting practices.

10. For similar Soviet trends in the 1950s and 1960s, see Bronson and Krueger, "The Revolution in Soviet Farm Household Income".

11. China People's Bank, Kwangtung Province Branch, *Rural People's Commune Production Team Accountant,* p. 89.

12. William Parish, China travel notes, Rural Small-Industry Delegation, July 1975.

13. See Audrey Donnithorne, *China's Economic System* (London: George Allen and Unwin, 1967), p. 448. Dwight H. Perkins, "Growth and Changing Structure of China's Twentieth-century Economy," in *China's Modern Economy in Historical Perspective* ed. Dwight H. Perkins (Stanford: Stanford University Press, 1975), p. 153. Again, for similar trends in the Soviet Union, see Bronson and Krueger, "The revolution."

14. Wei Min, "China's Tax Policy," *Peking Review* 18, no. 37 (1975): 25. The

Chinese motivations for not soaking agriculture to pay for industry involve not only a natural sympathy for peasants based on a rural revolution but also an acquaintance with the failures of old Soviet models, a knowledge of new Soviet models being adopted after 1953, and such a close margin of existence among Chinese peasants that an exploitative policy was untenable. See Anthony Tang, "Policy and Performance in Agriculture," in *Economic Trends in Communist China,* ed. Alexander Eckstein et al. (Chicago: Aldine, 1968).

15. T'ien Lin, "Pu ch'i nien pi yi-pai nien" [Supplement on 7 years compared with the previous 100 years], *Hsin-hua pan-yüeh k'an* [New China monthly], 1957, no. 15, p. 159. Christopher Howe, *Wage Patterns and Wage Policy in Modern China, 1919–1972* (Cambridge: Cambridge University Press, 1973), pp. 50–51. According to Howe, the consumption differential is somewhat smaller than the income differential, with rural consumption being about 75 to 80 pecent of urban consumption in the 1950s. However measured, the issue of whether the differential has narrowed in recent years hinges on increasing labor-force participation in cities. Urban women may have gone to work in new industries in sufficient numbers to significantly increase their family's income, thereby maintaining an almost constant per capita urban-rural differential.

16. This estimate of average income assumes a work-day value of .72 yuan, twenty-eight days of labor per month, and a private-sector income of 20 percent. Thus, $.72 \times 28 = 20.2$ and $20.2/.80 = 25.2$ yuan per month. The assumed .72 yuan average work day remuneration for rural Kwangtung is above the average of .55 yuan calculated from our interviews and designed to give a generous allowance for the possible unrepresentative nature of our sample. See Appendix 1 for a discussion of the issue of representativeness.

17. The Chinese gap was never as large as that in the Soviet Union before 1953. In that year an ablebodied collective farm worker earned only 18 percent as much as an average industrial worker, although changes in the post-Stalin period raised this figure to 75 percent by 1970. See Bronson and Krueger, "The Revolution," p. 228; David E. Powell, "The Rural Exodus," *Problems of Communism* 23 (November–December 1974), p. 8. In Taiwan per capita agricultural as a proportion of nonagricultural income was about 80 percent in the 1950s, but with industrial growth declined to about 60 percent in the 1960s. See Taiwan Provincial Government Information Office, *Nung-ye sheng-ch'an* [Agricultural production] (Taiwan, 1971), p. 113.

18. "Regulations Governing Household Registration," (Peking: Standing Committee, National People's Congress, 9 January 1958), translated in H. Yuan Tien, *China's Population Struggle* (Columbus: Ohio State University Press, 1973), appendix L.

19. Chang Ching-wa, "Why We Must Reduce Urban Population," *Kung-jen jih-pao* [Worker's Daily], 4 January 1958.

20. This conclusion is based on household censuses of four production teams and estimates from other teams in our interviews. Many rural areas also have educated youths from the cities living in them, as noted in Chapter 4.

21. William L. Parish, "Kinship and Modernization in Taiwan" (Ph.D. dissertation, Cornell University, 1970). A similar outmigration exists on Soviet collective farms, depriving them of their youngest and most vigorous members. See Powell, "The Rural Exodus."

22. Buchanan, *Transformation of the Chinese Earth,* pp. 136–37; Johnson, "Rural Economic Development," p. 12.

23. The way in which the variables used here were defined is explained in Appendix 2. The statistic used in this and later tables is the gamma statistic, whose meaning and interpretation are discussed in Appendix 1. In general it tells whether two variables are associated with one another in a consistent fashion, and gammas of ±.40 or thereabouts are particularly worthy of note, although with such a small number of cases they may not be judged as statistically significant. Recall also from Chapter 3 that the grain yields and work-day value measures will be combined in much of our later analysis, as parts of a "collective affluence" scale.

24. For an argument that in the 1960s the Chinese concentrated new inputs in "high and stable yield" areas, thereby exacerbating intervillage inequalities, see Benedict Stavis, *Making Green Revolution* (Ithaca: Cornell University Rural Development Committee, 1974). Whether intentional or not, Chinese strategy in this period became one of "building on the best" that John Gurley claims is typical of capitalist and Soviet development strategies but not of the Maoist one. See his article, "Capitalist and Maoist Economic Development," in *America's Asia,* ed. E. Friedman and M. Selden (New York: Random House, 1971).

25. One traveler in Kwangtung was told that only 20 percent of the agricultural work in the province was as yet mechanized. Amir Khan, trip notes, U.S. Rural Small Industries Delegation, July, 1975. Also see Leo Goodstadt, "Poverty Frequent Theme," *Far Eastern Economic Review,* 21 May 1973, pp. 50–51. Informants claim that even when a source of electrical power is available in the vicinity, local teams and brigades have to pay the costs of transmission lines and other facilities needed to connect with it. For comparison, we note that only half of Soviet collective farms were electrified in 1958, although the figure had risen to 95 percent by 1965. See Erich Strauss, *Soviet Agriculture in Perspective* (New York: Praeger, 1969), pp. 251–52. Chinese rural electrification has been comparatively rapid.

26. The association in our figures between the proportion of households receiving remittances and the reported local grain yields was gamma = −.33. The village with the highest proportion of families depending on remittances, 80 percent, was also the one with the lowest value of a normal day's work points, only .12 yuan. Keep in mind that our radio and bicycle variables are parts of a combined "household consumption" scale, which will be used in later analyses.

27. Interview TCT.

28. On the reluctance to allow peasants to abandon poor lands, see John Kenneth Galbraith, *A China Passage* (New York: Signet, 1973), p. 76.

29. Informants mentioned examples of males who tried to move into villages where they had no kinsmen, and who were eventually driven out by village ostracism and harassment. On the absence of significant numbers of men marrying into villages, see Chapter 9.

30. The term "collective" here refers to the collective agricultural units—team, brigade, and commune—as opposed to the state on the one hand and the private sector on the other. Elsewhere we will use the "collective" in this sense, unless we specify that we are referring to the collectives of the 1956–58 era.

31. At the end of the year the work points earned by all team members for their daily labors throughout the year are summed into a grand total. This grand total is divided into the yuan amount available for distribution, giving the yuan value of a single work point. For example, if the grand total of work points in table 1 were 157,450, the value of a work point would be .10 yuan (a "work day" = 10 work points − 1.00 yuan). This figure could then be used to calculate the income to be credited to each household by multiplying the total number of work points earned by all members of the household by .10 yuan.

32. The one mou of cultivated land per person given for the handbook example is near the average for our interview villages, as is its stated single water pump and no tractor. The grain yield given of 1,000 catties per mou is about 25 percent above the average for Kwangtung, while the work-day value of .72 yuan is 31 percent above the average for our interviews but is nevertheless the "typical" figure we used for Kwangtung in earlier estimates (see note 16 above).

33. Computed from visitor and press reports in Crook, "The Commune System," p. 410.

34. Burki, *A Study of Chinese Communes,* pp. 40–41.

35. Crook, "The Commune System," p. 410.

36. This conclusion is based on our combined Kwangtung household census, in which informants judged the relative economic position within their villages of 106 neighboring households.

37. There are certain limits imposed, however. For instance, cadres are not supposed to split up team lands into portions to be assigned to each household, with families receiving a share of any grain they produce from that land over a specified quota. This practice, called "contracting down to households," occurred immediately after the Great Leap Forward and apparently even in recent years, although since 1962 it has been consistently regarded as a serious violation of official policy. See "Comrade Chen Yung-kuei's Report," *Peking Review* 20, no. 2 (1977): 10; and, on Kwangtung, *FBIS,* F-26, June 1974. There is only one example in our

interviews of a team using this system temporarily in about 1972.

38. We do not distinguish here several subtypes of task rates and time rates. For the subtler differences among a large number of work-point systems, see Frederic W. Crook, "An Analysis of Work-Payment Systems Used in Chinese Mainland Agriculture, 1956–1970" (Ph.D. dissertation, Fletcher School of Law and Diplomacy, 1970, University Microfilms No. 72-2226).

39. Tasks are also assigned to groups of workers with appropriate divisions being made after completion of the task. For details, see Andrew Nathan, "China's Work-point System: A Study in Agricultural 'Splittism,'" Current Scene 2 (15 April 1964).

40. Family and lineage loyalties in Kwangtung may have exacerbated the tension, but it was common to villages throughout China. Even at Tachai, according to an educated urban youth at the county exhibition hall, daily meetings caused people to be excessively concerned with work points and caused a loss of time. Tachai now assesses points only once a year. William L. Parish, China travel notes, Rural Small Industry Delegation, 17 June 1975. See also Martin Whyte, "The Tachai Brigade and Incentives for the Peasant," Current Scene 7 (15 August 1969).

41. Chia Ch'eng-jang, "Using Mao Tse-tung's Thought to Command Labor Management," Nung-yeh chi-shu [Agricultural technology], 1967, no. 11, pp. 26–27.

42. William L. Parish, China travel notes, Rural Small-Industry Delegation, 19 June 1975.

43. "Reading Notes on the Soviet Union's 'Political Economics,'" Miscellany of Mao Tse-tung Thought [Mao Tse-tung ssu-hsiang wan-sui], in JPRS, no. 61269.2 (20 February 1974), pp. 281–86. Mao was commenting on a translated Soviet text and referring to industry, but his comments also reflect official preferences for agriculture.

44. It is not obvious that task rates always have to lead to more inequality than time rates, since a time-rate system could utilize very sharp differentials between the ratings of some team members and others. But in the way these systems are usually applied, Chinese authorities assume that task rates promote inequality.

45. "Document of the CCP Central Committee, chung-fa (1971), no. 82," Chung-kung yen-chiu [Studies on Chinese Communism], 6 (September 1972).

46. Interview PAP-1.

47. Interview TCP-1.

48. For details on the problems of interpreting a gamma of 1.0, see Appendix 1.

49. For partial statistics on increasing equality, see Marc Blecher, "Income Distribution in Small Rural Chinese Communities," China Quarterly, no. 68 (1976): 797–816. For further discussion, see Chapter 8.

6   Health, Education, and Welfare
      Policies

1. See Morris Janowitz, *Social Control of the Welfare State* (New York: Elsevier, 1976).

2. The exact list of guarantees has varied over time. This recent list is as misleading as earlier versions since, instead of getting housing, most old people (as a condition of getting support) must bequeath their own house to their production team. Because of this stipulation, some refuse to take five-guarantee support, preferring to support themselves in the last instance by selling their house on the private market. In those few instances in our interviews in which old people had no house of their own, they often borrowed a room not from the team but from a friend or distant kinsman.

3. *Chung-kuo ch'ing-nien* [Chinese Youth], 1954, no. 17, pp. 31–32; ibid., 1956, no. 22, pp. 23–24.

4. *JMJP,* 9 February 1957.

5. *Chung-kuo ch'ing-nien,* 1957, no. 2, p. 26.

6. For an example of such a marriage, see Jack Chen, *A Year in Upper Felicity* (New York: Macmillan, 1973), p. 76. On teams supporting old people who have daughters but no sons, see Jan Myrdal and Gun Kessle, *China: The Revolution Continued* (New York: Pantheon, 1970), p. 52; and M. J. Meijer, *Marriage Law and Policy in the Chinese People's Republic* (Hong Kong: Hong Kong University Press, 1971), p. 261.

7. Calculated from our census of neighbors, which showed that 10.5 percent of all people in the census were over sixty. Since the average team size in our sample is two hundred people, .105 × 200 = 21, and 1.24/21 = .06. We note additionally that in Kwangtung in 1964 there were fifty-nine old-age homes (yang-lao yüan) for military veterans (less than one per county) and 1,100 "respect the aged homes" (ching-lao yüan) for members of communes and other collective units who have no offspring to support them (that is, less than one per commune). *NFJP,* 24 September 1964, p. 3. Then and now, institutionalization of the rural elderly is very rare.

8. This information comes from interviews conducted by Yeung Sai-cheung after we had left Hong Kong.

9. For discussions of the political debates over education in general, see Donald Munro, "Egalitarian Ideal and Educational Fact in Communist China," in *China: Management of a Revolutionary Society,* ed. John Lindbeck (Seattle: University of Washington Press, 1971); Marianne Bastid, "Economic Necessity and Political Ideals in Educational Reform during the Cultural Revolution," *China Quarterly,* no. 42 (1970): 16–45; John Gardner, "Educated Youth and Urban-Rural Inequalities, 1958–1966," in *The City in Communist China,* ed. John Lewis (Stanford: Stanford

University Press, 1971); and Joel N. Glassman, "The Implementation of Education Policy in Communist China" (Ph.D. dissertation, University of Michigan, 1974).

10. Calculated from Leo Orleans, *Professional Manpower and Education in Communist China* (Washington, D.C.: U.S. Government Printing Office, 1961), p. 16; Nai-Ruenn Chen, *Chinese Economic Statistics* (Chicago: Aldine, 1967), p. 141; UNESCO, *World Survey of Education,* vol. 5 (Paris: Unesco Press, 1973), p. 78, and earlier volumes.

11. See the speech by Chang Hsi-jo in *Hsin-hua yüeh-pao* [New China Monthly], 70, no. 8 (1955), p. 62.

12. While the motivations for this shift were partly ideological, one can also argue that the expansion of the educational system of earlier years made the concentration on higher schools less crucial, and created a situation in which investment in lower levels would produce more returns. See the arguments in Joel Glassman, "Educational Reform and Manpower Policy in China 1955–1958," *Modern China* 3 (July 1977), and George Psacharopoulos, *Returns to Education* (San Francisco: Jossey-Bass, 1973).

13. This statement is based on personal communications with several recent visitors to China, who report that when a commune received a quota for the number of youths it could nominate for higher education in the years 1970–76, it most commonly selected urban sent-down youth living there, rather than educated youth who were native to the commune. In the fall of 1977 a new shift in educational policy was announced which significantly modifies the egalitarian thrust of these reforms. Henceforth 30 percent or more of the college students will be selected directly from secondary school, and college students will be chosen primarily on the basis of standardized entrance examinations, as they were before 1966. These modifications should enhance the advantage of better-educated urban youths. At the time of writing, however, the program of sending large numbers of urban youths to the countryside had not been abandoned.

14. One visitor reports the following fees for Ta-li Commune in Kwangtung as of May 1975:

	Tuition	Books and Stationary
	(per year)	*(per year)*
Primary School	6 yuan	2 yuan
Lower middle school	10 yuan	2 yuan
Upper middle school	14 yuan	3.40 yuan

Cited in Ronald Cheng, "Recent Conditions of Rural People's Communes," paper for Western Conference of the Association for Asian Studies, 1975.

15. This was stated by the Kiangsu minister of education in talking to a visiting delegation. See John Lewis, China travel notes (1973), p. 256.

16. A survey of villagers in South China around 1930 found that about one-half of the males but only 3 percent of the females over age seven had had some schooling. See John L. Buck, *Land Utilization in China* (Nanking: University of Nanking Press, 1937), p. 373. Considering that older people in our sample would have been in the younger age cohorts of a 1930 sample, the two sets of figures can probably be reconciled, although the education of older women in our sample is slightly understated.

17. According to radio reports, 92 percent of Kwangtung primary school age children were enrolled in 1973 and 95 percent in 1974. (These figures include urban areas. Rural figures alone would be 2 to 4 percentage points lower). *SWB*, FE/4369/311/6, 10 August 1973; and *FBIS*, 10 May 1974, p. H9.

18. UNESCO, *Statistical Yearbook, 1973* (Paris: Unesco Press, 1974), table 1.4; Republic of China, Ministry of the Interior, *1973 Taiwan Demographic Fact Book* (Taipei, 1974), table 25; A. Chandra Sekhar, *Census of India, 1971: All India Census Tables,* series I, part II Special (New Delhi: Office of the Registrar General, [1972]), table C-III. Except for Turkey (total urban and rural population) and Taiwan (one rural county—Yünlin), statistics are for the total rural population in each country. The Kwangtung figures come from our table 8, rather than official statistics.

19. Leo Orleans, "Health Policies and Services in China, 1973," Testimony for the Subcommittee on Health of the Committee on Labor and Public Welfare, United States Senate (Washington, D.C.: U.S. Government Printing Office, 1974), pp. 24–26. For a lucid discussion of the policy issues of health care, see David M Lampton, *Health, Conflict and the Chinese Political System* (Ann Arbor: Center for Chinese Studies, 1974).

20. From interviews, and from Keith Buchanan, "The People's Communes after Six Years: Notes on Four Communes in Kwangtung Province," *Pacific Viewpoint* 6 (1965): 61.

21. "Canton Forum of Medical Personnel on Tour in Rural Areas," *URS* 49, no. 22 (15 Dec. 1967): 289–303.

22. *Ch'ih-chiao yi-sheng tsa-chih* [Barefoot doctor's magazine], bimonthly (Peking, 1973–). See a summary of the contents of a barefoot doctor's handbook in Victor Sidel and Ruth Sidel, *Serve the People: Observations on Medicine in the People's Republic of China* (New York: Josiah Macy Foundation, 1973), Appendix H.

23. This is exactly the same percentage reported for the 108 barefoot doctors in Kwang-li commune in Kwangtung, from notes for the Westinghouse Television Company documentary, "Commune," made by Paul Steinle and Peggy Printz in May 1973.

24. *SWB*, FE/W577/A/15, 1 July 1970 gives a figure of 47,000 barefoot doctors in Kwangtung, or 1 per 851 rural residents, and 2.3 per brigade. According to a June

1973 statement to a visiting delegation, there were 51,000 barefoot doctors in Kwangtung by that time, or an average of 1 per every 784 people and 2.5 per brigade. See Leo Orleans, "Health policies and services," p. 27.

25. Myrdal and Kessle, *The Revolution Continued,* pp. 110–11.

26. According to one report, about one-fifth (300+/1721) of the communes in Kwangtung have set up joint cooperative medical systems with their brigades, so that the entire population of the commune joins the same insured pool, and greater equality of medical services is offered. See *SWB,* FE/W735/A/2, 1 August 1973.

27. Statement by Chang Hsiu-chen, vice-chairman, Liu-chuang brigade, Chi-li-ying commune, Honan, in William Parish, China travel notes, Rural Small-Industry Delegation, 26 June 1975.

28. The most common fee is .30 yuan per month, or 3.60 yuan per year per person. See also Rewi Alley, *Travels in China: 1966–1971* (Peking: New World Press, 1973), p. 374.

29. According to Chinese reports, 80 percent of brigades in Kwangtung had cooperative medical plans by March 1973, with the figure rising to 93 percent by February 1976. See *SWB,* FE/W716/A/1, 21 March 1973; *CN,* 23 February 1976, p. 6.

30. Interview TKP-3, p. 7.

31. Interviews CSP-1, p. 22; PAP-2, p. 24, TSP-2, TSP-3, p. 23. An article in the *People's Daily* notes that, in one brigade, "medical expenses in excess of 100 yuan are to be covered by the individual patients through consultations with production teams and on the basis of the financial conditions of the patients concerned. In such cases, the excess portions may either be reduced or exempted after they are discussed by the poor and lower middle peasants" (translated in *CB,* no. 872 [8 Dec. 1968], p. 8).

32. See, for example, Barbara Tuchman, *Notes from China* (New York: Collier Books, 1973), p. 11.

33. Of the various estimates, we conclude that Robert Worth's are most consistent with everything else that we know about health care and population growth rates. See Robert M. Worth, "Recent Demographic Patterns in Kwangtung Province Villages," unpublished paper, n.d.; Leo Orleans, "China's Population: Can the Contradictions be Resolved?" in U.S. Congress Joint Economic Committee, *China: A Reassessment of the Economy* (Washington, D.C.: U.S. Government Printing Office, 1975), p. 77; Janet Salaff, "Mortality Decline in the People's Republic of China and the United States," *Population Studies* 27 (1973): 551–76.

34. On the basis of a reanalysis of the rural surveys directed by John Buck circa 1930, a recent study concludes that the infant mortality rate then was about 300 per 1,000. See George Barclay et al., "A Reassessment of the Demography of Traditional Rural China," *Population Index* 42 (1976), p. 618.

35. Salaff, "Mortality decline."; Committee on Scholarly Communication with the People's Republic of China, *Report of the Medical Delegation to the People's Republic of China* (Washington, D.C.: National Academy of Sciences, 1973), p. 55.

36. Donald Bogue, *Principles of Demography* (New York: Wiley, 1969), pp. 556–58.

37. Robert Worth, "Health Trends in China since the Great Leap Forward," *China Quarterly,* no. 22 (1965): 181–89. For a similar pattern on Taiwan, see Republic of China, Taiwan Provincial Government, Health Department, *Taiwan's Health* (for 1963 and subsequent years).

38. *Report of the Medical Delegation,* pp. 57–62; Sidel and Sidel, *Serve the People,* p. 92.

39. See Kun-yen Huang, "Infectious and Parasitic Diseases," in *Medicine and Public Health in the People's Republic of China,* ed. Joseph R. Quinn (Washington, D.C.: U.S. Department of Health, Education, and Welfare, 1973).

40. See Dwight Perkins, "Growth and Changing Structure of China's Twentieth-century Economy," in *China's Modern Economy in Historical Perspective,* ed. Dwight Perkins (Stanford: Stanford University Press, 1975).

7   Status and Power

1. Sources on traditional village leadership include Sidney Gamble, *North China Villages* (Berkeley: University of California Press, 1963), chap. 4; C. K. Yang, *A Chinese Village in Early Communist Transition* (Cambridge: MIT Press, 1959), chap. 7; Kung-chuan Hsiao, *Rural China* (Seattle: University of Washington Press, 1960); and Arthur H. Smith, *Village Life in China* (Boston: Little Brown, 1970, originally 1899).

2. See G. William Skinner, "Chinese Peasants and the Closed Community: An Open and Shut Case," *Comparative Studies in Society and History* 13 (1971): 270–81.

3. The classic study of these tendencies, based on the Yugoslav and Soviet experiences, is Milovan Djilas, *The New Class* (New York: Praeger, 1957).

4. The term for "class" and "class label" as used here is chieh-chi ch'eng-fen. In theory there is a distinction between personal class (ch'eng-fen) and class origins (ch'u-shen), but in practice this distinction is often lost, with ch'eng-fen used for both. For Mao's 1926 article, see *Selected Readings from the Works of Mao Tse-tung* (Peking: Foreign Languages Press, 1967), p. 11ff. The 1950 document, "Decisions Concerning the Differentiation of Class Status in the Countryside," is translated in *CB,* no. 52 (10 January 1951): 2–20.

5. Overseas Chinese were originally labeled as "overseas Chinese landlord" or "overseas Chinese rich peasant," but these labels were later simplified by the omis-

sion of the landlord and rich peasant references. See Stephen Fitzgerald, *China and the Overseas Chinese* (Cambridge: Cambridge University Press, 1972). The 1950 documents stated that those classified as ordinary landlords or rich peasants could be reclassified under a favorable label if they behaved themselves for three to five years, but this provision was never carried out.

6. For the policies and documents governing those under ''control'' as class enemies, see Jerome A. Cohen, *The Criminal Process in the People's Republic of China, 1949–1963* (Cambridge: Harvard University Press, 1968), pp. 276–95. On the general class-label policy, see Richard Kraus, ''The Evolving Concept of Class in Post-Liberation China'' (Ph.D. dissertation, Columbia University, 1974).

7. This pattern is recounted from our interviews, but it conforms to the official policy set forth in article thirteen of the 1950 ''Decisions Concerning the Differentiation of Class Status in the Countryside.''

8. In one sample of twelve North China villages in the 1930s, 15 percent of village headmen were in their sixties, while the average age was forty-eight. See Gamble, *North China Villages,* p. 323. In one earlier North China sample of 435 settlements, 37 percent of all headmen were over age sixty while the average age was fifty-five— data supplied by Gilbert Rozman from the 1875 *Ch'ing County Gazetteer,* Chihli Province. The figures in our table conceal variations in typical ages of different functionaries. Poor- and lower-middle-peasant association representatives and team custodians tend to be older, respected peasants, often in their fifties and sixties. Team security officers and militia leaders, in contrast, average twenty-seven years in age. The pattern of cadres retiring from office when they ease out of regular field labor is supported by a comparison of our figures with those collected by Michel Oksenberg on the backgrounds of leaders of sixteen Kwangtung villages in the period 1962–65. Our figures for the average ages of various cadres are virtually identical with Oksenberg's figures, which they could not be if officers in power in that period had stayed on in their posts. Except for more female representation and slightly more party members, the distribution of other characteristics—education, length of service, and class background—remained virtually the same between the 1965 figures and our 1973 data, suggesting a stable response to the structural needs of field management, collective accounting, and the like. We are grateful to Michel Oksenberg for the opportunity to examine his raw data, which formed part of the study he reported in ''Local Leaders in Rural China, 1962–1965: Individual Attributes, Bureaucratic Positions, and Political Recruitment,'' in *Chinese Communist Politics in Action,* A. Doak Barnett, ed. (Seattle: University of Washington Press, 1969).

9. This is stipulated in Article 50 of the Sixty Articles governing people's communes.

10. One line of argument holds that universally peasants perceive the world as providing a relatively fixed set of goods or a single fixed pie. If one's neighbor gets

more from the pie, then one's own family necessarily gets less. This assumption of a fixed pie causes peasants to be extremely jealous of any new advantage acquired by their neighbors and causes much of the gossip in villages to be about perceived changes in relative material advantage. See George Foster, "Peasant Society and the Image of the Limited Good," *American Anthropologist* 67 (1965): 293–315. The link between one's own piece and a neighbor's piece of the pie is even more direct under collective agriculture than in other peasant societies, since leaders and team members are all being paid out of one unified budget. Accordingly, we are reluctant to accept vague complaints about corruption as anything more than gossip unless these complaints are supported with concrete examples of corrupt behavior. Hence, our benign assessment of corruption in spite of some complaints.

11. E. Yuchtman, "Reward Distribution and Work-role Attractiveness in the Kibbutz—Reflections on Equity Theory," *American Sociological Review* 37 (1972): 582. For Chinese examples, see Rewi Alley, *Travels in China, 1966–1971* (Peking: New World Press, 1973), pp. 341, 345, 346, 354, 362, 363; and Jan Myrdal, *Report from a Chinese Village* (New York: Praeger, 1965), chap. 13.

12. A similar set of rewards and motivations is described for those holding the unpaid leadership posts in Israeli kibbutzim. See Yuchtman, "Reward Distribution."

13. One of the few studies of length of service of traditional village leaders, reporting on northern Chinese villages, points to the conclusion that today's brigade leaders serve longer than village elders did there in the 1930s, while other contemporary officers serve shorter terms. See Gamble, *North China Villages*, p. 323.

14. See the discussion in John W. Lewis, *Leadership in Communist China* (Ithaca: Cornell University Press, 1963), p. 238.

15. On the appeal of rural factory jobs even when they do not pay much more than agricultural labor, see Editing Group, *Shanghai chiao-ch'ü nung-ye hsüeh Tachai* [Shanghai suburban agriculture studies Tachai] (Shanghai: Agricultural Press, 1974), pp. 52–67. On the general question of the varying prestige of jobs, see Gordon White, "The Politics of Hsia-hsiang Youth," *China Quarterly,* no. 59 (1974): 491–517.

16. The exact percentages in table 16, being based on our relatively small mobility sample, are not that reliable. A larger sample of all adult males showed former middle-peasant sons in a middle position—still underrepresented in leadership posts but not so severely so in other nonagricultural positions.

17. Interview TCT, pp. 37–38.

18. For references to this literature, see James Coleman, "Inequality, Sociology, and Moral Philosophy," *American Journal of Sociology* 80 (1974): 739–64; and Charles Bidwell and John Kasarda, "School District Organization and Student Achievement," *American Sociological Review* 40 (1975): 55–70.

8   The Pursuit of Equality and
Peasant Satisfaction

1. Not having precise household and village income distribution figures for contemporary Kwangtung, the best we can manage is a hypothetical estimate. This
estimate multiplies the per capita work-point totals found by Marc Blecher in two
Kwangtung production teams (figures for 92 individuals) by the annual work-point
values in our village sample (forty-eight villages with known values), giving the
collective earnings of 4,416 hypothetical peasants. In other words we are calculating
what the overall distribution of peasant incomes for this sample of forty-eight villages
would be if each village had the same internal variations in work-point earnings as
Blecher's two villages did. When ranked by earnings, the richest fifth of these
peasants receive about 36 percent, and the poorest fifth receive 9 percent, of per
capita income distributions. These figures, if roughly accurate, indicate less income
inequality than in rural India, Indonesia, Malaysia, Thailand, Chile, Honduras, or
the Phillipines in the 1960s and 1970s, but more inequality than in rural Taiwan,
South Korea, Sri Lanka, Egypt, or Bangladesh. For relevant figures, see Marc
Blecher, "Income Distribution in Small Rural Chinese Communities," *China Quarterly,* no. 68 (1976): 797–816; Norman T. Uphoff and Milton J. Esman, *Local
Organization for Rural Development* (Ithaca, N.Y.: Cornell University, Rural
Development Committee, 1974), p. 50; Shail Jain, *Size Distribution of Income*
(Washington, D.C.: World Bank, 1975). We feel that within Kwangtung over time
the contribution of within-village inequality has declined while intervillage inequality
has increased. Our figures are for collective income distributions alone, leaving open
the question of compensating effects of income from other sources. However, as
noted below, we feel that there is little tradeoff between private and collective
income earnings in Kwangtung—most families earn roughly similar proportions in
the private sector. As noted in Chapter 5, remittances are competitive with collective
earnings. Two factors tend to eliminate bias from this source: first, we have deleted
from our calculations one team with 80 percent of its families dependent on remittances and an exceptionally low work-day value of .12 yuan. And truncation at the
top end of our collective income figures due to sample bias will tend to offset any
remittance-induced biases at the lower end (on the representativeness of our sample
and the full range of work-day values therein, see Appendix 1).

2. If one assumes that team arable land averages about one mou per capita, and if 6
percent is distributed as private plots, the average family has 4.4 members, and one
mou = 666.7m^2, .06 × 4.4 = .26 mou per family or .26 × 666.7 = 173m^2, and
the square root of 173 is roughly 13 meters. These figures correspond closely with
informants' reports of local plot distributional formulas, which were said to provide
family plots of between .20 and .29 mou, with a median size of .27 mou.

3. In some localities, such as the model Tachai brigade and Hsiyang County in
Shansi Province, private plots have been dispensed with altogether. In other places,

such as much of northern Honan, simple private plots have been replaced by curious hybrid "collectively cultivated private vegetable plots" which supply vegetables for families free of charge. See Chen, *Upper Felicity,* and the Delegation on Rural Small Industry, travel notes, 1975. We found no incidence of comparable changes in rural Kwangtung.

4. On the time and care involved in feeding the family pig as well as a discussion of subsidiary work for women and children, see Chen, *Upper Felicity,* pp. 57–60, 154–56, 254–55, 309–10; Myrdal and Kessle, *The Revolution Continued,* p. 38. Pigs, unlike foul and vegetables, cannot be sold legally in the free peasant markets.

5. Walker, *Planning in Chinese Agriculture,* p. 34.

6. Buchanan, *Transformation of the Chinese Earth,* pp. 142, 157. S.J. Burki, *A Study of Chinese Communes* (Cambridge: Harvard University, East Asian Research Center, 1969), p. 40. Graham Johnson, "Rural Economic Development and Social Change in South China," mimeographed (Vancouver: University of British Columbia, Sociology and Anthropology Department, 1973). The 20 percent figure cited by Burki as an average has been used in all our peasant income estimates.

7. David W. Bronson and C. B. Krueger, "The Revolution in Soviet Farm Household Income, 1953–1967," *The Soviet Rural Community,* ed. James R. Millar (Urbana: University of Illinois Press, 1971), p. 234.

8. Some villages in our sample never changed from their traditional three-day cycle of markets. Others switched from the three day to five day schedule but then changed back to the three-day schedule around 1970 or 1971, citing the inconvenience and overcrowding produced by less frequent markets.

9. Since black market rice is three times as expensive as that allotted through one's home team, individuals who go outside to work without having the team's permission (and rations) will find a large part of their wages eaten away by the need to buy food on the black market. Examples of team-supervised outside income earning also appear in Chen, *Upper Felicity,* pp. 169–70, 270–72.

10. On the 1960s situation, see C. S. Chen, ed., *Rural People's Communes in Lien-chiang* (Stanford: Hoover Institution Press, 1969) and *URS* 27, nos. 7, 8 (1962).

11. *Nung-ye sheng-ch'an* [Agricultural production] (Chunghsing New Village: Taiwan Province Information Office, 1971), pp. 6–7. *Taiwan Statistical Data Book, 1965* (Taipei: Executive Yuan, Council for International Economic Cooperation and Development, 1965), pp. 18, 24.

12. Among sixteen developing nations in Asia, China ranks fourteenth—Uphoff and Esman, *Local Organization for Rural Development,* pp. 33–35.

13. Ibid.

14. These results rest on a questionable assumption of a 2 percent population

growth rate since 1953. We will argue in the chapter on birth planning that the Kwangtung population growth rate was considerably greater than 2 percent in the mid-1960s. But it was below 2 percent in other periods, giving a population total in the 1970s similar to that used in table 18. See John S. Aird, "Recent Provincial Population Figures," *China Quarterly,* no. 73 (1978), p. 24.

15. Food and Agriculture Organization, *Production Yearbook, 1974* (Rome, 1975), tables 3, 12. These statistics on unmilled grain, because they ignore the greater loss rates in milling rice, overstate Kwangtung's advantage somewhat. See also Dwight H. Perkins, *Agricultural Development in China, 1368–1968* (Chicago: Aldine, 1969), p. 303.

16. This figure is for the double-cropping rice region which includes Kwangtung. See Buck, *Land Utilization,* p. 246.

17. The number *per person* was actually somewhat higher than in 1930, but we have assumed a smaller 4.4-member household in 1957. Kuangtung Province Statistical Office, *Kwangtung sheng kuo-min ching-chi chien-she ti wei-ta ch'eng-chiu* [Great accomplishments in building Kwangtung Province's civilian economy] (Canton, 1958), fig. 13. The 1955–56 slaughter of pigs at the start of collectivization, noted in Chapter 4, was a temporary phenomenon, and by 1957 the number of pigs exceeded pre-1955 levels.

18. *Peking Review* 14, no. 1 (1971), p. 17.

19. On inheritance rights, see Articles 12 and 14 of the 1950 marriage law.

20. On housing loans to tidewater areas, see Ezra F. Vogel, China travel notes, 14 June 1973, and interview PYP1, p. 2.

21. Interviews TCP1, p. 11; TKM, p. 5; TCT, p. 23; PAP1; HYH; TML, p. 4. Costs reported to visitors range from 600 to 2,000 yuan: Myrdal and Kessle, *The Revolution Continued,* pp. 47–48; E. L. Wheelwright and Bruce McFarlane, *The Chinese Road to Socialism* (New York: Monthly Review Press, 1970), p. 194; Vogel, travel notes; Peggy Printz, "The Chen Family Still Has Class," *New York Times Magazine,* 14 November 1973; Ruth Lor Malloy, "The 'New' China Has an Old Face," *The National Observer,* 19 May 1973, p. 1; Chen, *Upper Felicity,* pp. 195, 373.

22. Figures for 1930 come from the double-cropping rice region in Buck's survey. For 1973 the figures are simply informant judgments about the predominant type of local housing. The villages sampled are not all in the same parts of Kwangtung in the two periods, making the comparison inexact. Both in 1930 and today, many of the tamped mud or mud-brick walls have a foundation and corner pillars of fired brick or stone. See Buck, *Land Utilization,* 443–44.

23. Chinese studies show labor inputs (number of labor days per year) more than doubling with collectivization in the mid-1950s. See Schran, *The Development of Chinese Agriculture,* p. 69. Thus peasants are working much harder now, and the yields per hour of labor must be quite a bit lower than before 1949.

24. But in the 1974–76 period, when radicals were trying to regain control of central government policy, inappropriate crops may have been imposed on some teams from above. At least, this is what interviews by John Unger in 1975–76 and press criticisms in 1978 of such "harmful deviations" would suggest.

25. A partial list of the defects of the Soviet kolkhoz system in its early years would include a brutal collectivization campaign, initially highly extractive grain delivery quotas and nearly confiscatory grain purchasing prices, farm leadership predominantly by outsiders paid according to state wage standards rather than work days, planting directives arbitrarily imposed by the outside party and agricultural bureaucracy, controls of farm machinery by outside agencies, and an unwillingness to decentralize farm management and economic accounting.

9   Household Structure and Birth Control

1. One recent article describes the effort of authorities in Ting-hsien in Hopei Province to promote matrilocal marriages because these marriages favor birth control (families with daughters only will not have to worry about being left alone in their old age), lower the number of "five-guarantee households," enable more women to serve as cadres (since ties of trust are not broken by a marriage move), and undermine male favoritism in general. See *JMJP*, 14 March 1975, p. 3. The newspaper *NFJP*, published in Canton, printed two articles on a village promoting matrilocal marriage in the same period (on 18 January and 8 February 1975) (translated in *URS* 29, no. 13 [13 May 1975]), but very few other press references to matrilocal marriage have come to our attention.

2. "Joint family" refers to a structure in which several married brothers live together in one unit with their parents. This contrasts with a stem structure, in which parents live with only one married son, and a nuclear structure, in which each couple lives separately. Other combinations are, of course, possible, but these are the ones with which we will be primarily concerned.

3. The custom of adopting a daughter-in-law as a child, while traditionally not viewed as favorably as the ordinary marriage of young adults, did allow families to make sure at an early age that a son would have a spouse, to save on the expenses of a wedding, and to train the daughter-in-law in obedience from an early age. The custom was quite common in some parts of pre-1949 Kwangtung and nearby provinces. See Arthur Wolf, "The Women of Hai-shan: A Demographic Portrait," in *Women in Chinese Society,* ed. Margery Wolf and Roxane Witke (Stanford: Stanford University Press, 1975). The elimination of such "child brides" was a theme stressed by the Chinese Communists after 1949.

4. Sidney Gamble, *Ting Hsien: A North China Rural Community* (New York:

Institute of Pacific Relations, 1954), p. 39; George Barclay, *Colonial Development and Population in Taiwan* (Princeton: Princeton University Press, 1954), p. 211. Few females, even among the poor, never married. The Chinese Communists outlawed concubinage after 1949.

5. These conclusions are based upon demographic estimation procedures pioneered by Ansley Coale and others. See Ansley Coale, "Estimates of Average Size of Household," in A. J. Coale et al., *Aspects of the Analysis of Family Structure* (Princeton: Princeton University Press, 1965); and William L. Parish and Moshe Schwartz, "Household Complexity in Nineteenth Century France," *American Sociological Reveiw* 37 (1972): 154–73.

6. Two technical points: (1) For reasons that we can only begin to guess at, the composite household size for rural Kwangtung from recent visitors' reports is nearer to 4.5 than our 4.8. (2) Because it apparently includes an over-sampling of wealthy households in Chieh-yang County, Kwangtung, the Smythe estimate comes up with more joint and stem households than other studies for the 1920s and 1930s. The tables which follow suggest that there has been a true decline in household complexity, but table 19 may exaggerate that decline somewhat. Smythe's study is based on a subsample of John Lossing Buck's 1929–31 rural survey.

7. The smaller number of spouses per household in 1973 is largely the result of there being more female-headed households with absent husbands than in 1930. See table 21.

8. In order to have sufficient cases to show the full range of household relationships, tables 20 and 21 use our combined household sample rather than just the neighbor sample. Because the combined household sample includes a number of local cadres who have larger families, the average household size of the combined sample is 5.0, and the complexity of households in 1973 is slightly overstated. This does not change our basic generalizations in this section, however.

9. Ch'en Ta and Sun Pen-wen, "Population," in *Chinese Economic Yearbook,* 2d ed. (Shanghai: Commercial Press, 1935), pp. 8–12.

10. Among husbands of these women, a few have left for jobs outside their home village while their wives were forced by strict migration laws to stay behind. A few other husbands have fled to Hong Kong, a few have been divorced, but most have simply died.

11. Only a few older ones are left and no new ones are being acquired. In Taiwan, infant daughters-in-law disappeared very rapidly due to economic change alone, without government pressure. See Arthur Wolf, "Adopt a Daughter-in-law, Marry a Sister: A Chinese Solution to the Problem of the Incest Taboo," *American Anthropologist* 70 (1968): 864–74.

12. In our combined household sample only 24 percent of "bad class" families had a stem or joint structure (N = 29), compared with 42 percent of former middle-

class peasants (N = 33) and 36 percent of former poor and lower-middle-class peasants (N = 144).

13. See William Parish, "Socialism and the Chinese Peasant Family," *Journal of Asian Studies* 34 (1975): 622–25. The effect of preference for sons is also clearly visible in studies from Taiwan. See Ronald Freedman, "Trends in Fertility, Family Size Preferences, and Practice of Family Planning: Taiwan, 1965–1973," *Studies in Family Planning* 5 (1974): 280.

14. In this realm, in contrast to some others, the government has to try to persuade peasants to focus on the short-run difficulties of supporting many children and to ignore the security offered by collectivized lands and the long-term benefits that aged parents with many sons to support them receive.

15. John Aird, "Population Policy and Demographic Prospects in the People's Republic of China," in U.S. Congress, Joint Economic Committee, *People's Republic of China: An Economic Assessment* (Washington, D.C.: U.S. Government Printing Office, 1972), p. 294; interview with Dr. Ou, Family Planning Commission of Canton, August 8, 1973 (in the travel notes of a visiting public health group led by Victor Li). For more detailed accounts of shifting population policies in China over the years, see Pi-chao Chen and Ann Miller, "Lessons from the Chinese Experience: China's Planned Birth Program and Its Transferability," *Studies in Family Planning* 6 (1975): 354–77; and H. Yuan Tien, *China's Population Struggle* (Columbus: Ohio State University Press, 1973).

16. Robert M. Worth, "Recent Demographic Patterns in Kwangtung Province Villages," unpublished paper, n.d.

17. Such a system is implicit in the following sources: Graham E. Johnson, "Rural Economic Development and Social Change in South China," mimeographed (Department of Anthropology and Sociology, University of British Columbia, 1973), pp. 47–50; interview with Dr. Ou; interview CSP-1, p. 17.

18. Indicative of the change is the statement by a male brigade leader to a visitor: "Before, I thought planned births was just an ordinary slogan [yi-pan hao-chao]. Now I realize that it is something for which the party committee must take direct personal responsibility [chih-chieh ch'in-tzu chua]" (from 1975 travel notes by someone who wishes to remain anonymous). Recent press accounts denounce earlier male cadres' attitudes that "revolution and production were very hard tasks whereas family planning was a soft task, and it would be all right, as long as the women cadres and the health departments grasped such work." (*JMJP,* 30 July 1973.)

19. The form in Figure 1 is a translation of one acquired in 1973 in a suburban commune outside Wuhan by a public health group led by Victor Li. These forms and the group pressure rituals accompanying them are more typical of urban areas. See Pi-chao Chen, *Population and Health Policy in the People's Republic of China* (Washington, D.C.: Smithsonian Institution, 1976), pp. 95–105, and Han Suyin,

"Population Growth and Birth Control in China," *Eastern Horizon,* no. 12 (1973), p. 5. The national program for planned births is three-pronged, calling for delayed marriage, greater spacing of births, and stopping of births after the second or third child. In Kwangtung by 1974, the first and third prongs of this program were being implemented in at least some villages; the middle one was not.

20. Johnson, "Rural economic development,"; Carl Djerassi, "Some Observations on Current Fertility Control in China," *China Quarterly* 57 (1974): 40–62.

21. The provincial birth-planning commission has a budget to be used to subsidize commune hospitals for sterilizations at the rate of 3 yuan for men and 5 yuan for females. Some hospitals are simply passsing on these subsidies to patients. Interview with Dr. Ou, Chen and Miller, "Lessons," p. 358, and interview STP-1, p. 15.

22. In published sources, Kwangtung ratios range between 4:1 and 6:1. See Johnson, "Rural economic development,"; Chen and Miller, "Lessons," p. 361. In our own interviews there were about six female sterilizations reported for every vasectomy.

23. Interviews STP-1, p. 15; KNP-1, p. 16.

24. Fifteen criteria for successful family-planning programs are suggested in Robert Lapham and W. Parker Mauldin, "National Family Planning Programs: Review and Evaluation," *Studies in Family Planning* 3, no. 2 (1972). Of these, Leo Orleans find that the Chinese implement thirteen. See his article, "China's Experience in Population Control: The Elusive Model," prepared for the Committee on Foreign Affairs, U.S. House of Representatives, September, 1974, pp. 43–44.

25. Kwangtung Province and Chieh-yang County Revolutionary Committee Planned Birth Small Leadership Groups, eds., "The Red Sunshine of Ch'en-liao's Planned Births Is Good" (Kwangtung Province Scientific and Technical Display Press poster, 1975). Note that the 1965 birth rate reported for this locality falls within the range estimated from Robert Worth's study of 33 to 47 per 1,000 for rural Kwangtung.

26. Johnson, "Rural Economic Development."

27. Interview with Dr. Ou.

28. Interview HYH, p. 20. National leaders repeat similar, if less violent, stories of son preference. Edgar Snow, "A Conversation with Mao Tse-tung," *Life,* 30 April 1971, p. 47; Soong Ching-ling, "Women's Liberation in China," *Peking Review* 15, no. 6 (1972): 7.

29. Interview STP-1, p. 15.

30. We are grateful to Professor Worth, Department of Public Health, University of Hawaii, for the use of original data from his study.

31. Several technical points are in order. The regression equation which fits the 1965 Kwangtung data is: CHILDREN $= 1.41 + .22$ CURRENT AGE $- .25$

MARRIAGE AGE − .08 EDUCATION. Part of the decline in births is the result of rising marriage ages, which will be discussed in Chapter 10. In all Chinese statistics, age reckoning can be a problem, since the traditional scheme considered a child to be one year old at birth. We tried to question older informants who might use the traditional scheme closely, and we feel that few cases not based on Western reckoning slipped through. The sex ratio of children in our sample is 111 boys to 100 girls—a bit high, but within the bounds of likelihood for a sample of this size. All of the differences between 1965 and 1972 figures are statistically significant—that is, differences of these sizes would occur on the basis of chance alone less than one time in twenty. The 1973 figures are based on our combined household sample, rather than on the smaller and more representative neighbor sample. However, statistical examination showed that this did not bias the results reported here. (See Appendix 1 on the differences between samples.)

32. We do not feel that very young children are being underreported in these data, as was often the case in earlier Chinese censuses. Girls are most likely to be omitted, but the sex ratio for the 0–9 age group here is 102 to 100, which is about normal. The decline could also be exaggerated if informants were rounding ages upward or using traditional Chinese age reckoning. We tried various calculations involving shifting ten-year-olds back into the lower age category, and the population profile was still flatter than that in 1953, supporting the argument we present here. The 1953 figures are of course for all of China, but we have no reason to believe that rural Kwangtung at that time had a flatter age pyramid than the national average.

33. Interview FKP-1, p. 14.

34. Kwangtung Provincial Radio in *FBIS,* 17 June 1976, p. H-13. We remain somewhat skeptical of the precision of official figures on birth control. We will see in the next chapter that some rural marriges are not officially registered when they occur, and these may produce children that are not counted initially. We are also not certain whether local cadres who pressured to keep peasants from having more than three children will accurately report all fourth and subsequent children. Nevertheless, the evidence for a substantial reduction in fertility seems conclusive, even if the current statistics are slightly lower than reality.

10   Marriage and Divorce

1. For a review of the evolution of Communist and Nationalist family law, consult M. J. Meijer, *Marriage Law and Policy in the Chinese People's Republic* (Hong Kong: Hong Kong University Press, 1971), pt. 1, and M. van der Valk, *An Outline of Modern Chinese Family Law* (Peking: Henri Vetch, 1939). For evidence on the enthusiasm for family reform in the early Nationalist period, see P'u Liang-chu, et al., *Essays on the Reform of Folk Life in Kwangtung* (in Chinese) (Canton: Customs Reform Society, 1930).

2. For a review of evidence that industrialization and urbanization tend to produce a conjugal family emphasis (with the authority of extended kin reduced and the husband-wife tie becoming the most important bond), see William J. Goode, *World Revolution and Family Patterns* (New York: The Free Press, 1963). Evidence for China is reviewed in Part 6 of the Goode volume and in Martin King Whyte, "The Family," in *China's Developmental Experience,* ed. Michel Oksenberg (New York: Praeger, 1973).

3. For relevant comparisons, see John L. Buck, *Land Utilization in China* (Nanking: University of Nanking Press, 1937), pp. 378–81. Virtually all Chinese females married, most of them by age twenty-four, while a small percentage of males, probably less than 3 percent in South China, did not. Estimates about the percentage of males remaining unmarried depend on assumptions about the death rate among single men. For a very low unmarried estimate, see the reanalysis of Buck's data in George Barclay et al., "A Reassessment of the Demography of Traditional Rural China," *Population Index* 42 (1976): 610.

4. Ch'iao Ch'i-ming, "A study of the Chinese Population," *Milbank Memorial Fund Quarterly* 12 (1934): 173–74; Frank W. Notestein, "A Demographic Study of 38,256 Rural Families in China," *Milbank Memorial Fund Quarterly* 16 (1938): 65.

5. See Ch'iao Ch'i-ming and Wang Chung-wu, "Population" (in Chinese) in *Chinese Economic Annual,* 3d ed., sect. 2 (Shanghai: Commercial Press, 1936), p. B-25; and George W. Barclay, *Colonial Development and Population on Taiwan* (Princeton: Princeton University Press, 1954), p. 221.

6. See the discussions in F. R. Johnston, *Lion and Dragon in Northern China* (New York: E. P. Dutton, 1910), chap. 10; Sidney Gamble, *Ting Hsien: A North China Rural Community* (New York: Institute of Pacific Relations, 1954), p. 37; and Barclay, *Colonial Development,* pp. 222–30.

7. A translation of the marriage law appears in Meijer, *Marriage Law and Policy,* Appendix 8.

8. See the discussions in Meijer, *Marriage Law and Policy;* and C. K. Yang, *The Chinese Family in the Communist Revolution* (Cambridge: MIT Press, 1959).

9. A survey by Gail Henderson, a graduate student in sociology at the University of Michigan, yielded only two such *People's Daily* editorials on marriage reform in 1953, on February 1 and May 6.

10. Meijer, *Marriage Law and Policy,* p. 309.

11. See the discussion in Meijer, *Marriage Law and Policy,* chap. 9. On the tolerant attitude toward marriage presents and celebrations as well as parental involvement in mate choice see *How to Manage Marriage-Registration Work Well* (Peking: Village Reader Publishing House, 1963), translated in *Chinese Sociology and Anthropology* 1, no. 2 (1968–69).

12. See, for example, *URS* 79, no. 13 (1975).

13. C. S. Chen, ed., *Rural People's Communes in Lien-chiang* (Stanford: Hoover Institution, 1969), p. 203.

14. Consult *How to Manage Marriage-Registration Work Well*. For an example of this policy in operation, see the divorce case witnessed by Felix Greene in *Awakened China* (Garden City: Doubleday, 1961), pp. 195–207.

15. Ch'iao and Wang, "Population," p. B-27. For South China generally the ages were somewhat higher: 20.7 for males and 18.7 for females.

16. Of course it could be argued that there was a backlog of older bachelors in 1950 that the land reform enabled to marry, so that the initial average marriage age for males would rise, rather than fall. We have no way to check on this possibility with our few cases from this period.

17. We note similar processes in Taiwan with average marriage ages shifting upward from 18.1 for females and 24.0 for males around the turn of the century to 22.6 and 26.7, respectively, in recent years. See Chung-hua min-kuo, T'ai-wan sheng hsing-cheng tang-kuan kung-shu t'ung-chi shih, *T'ai-wan sheng 51 nien lai t'ung-chi t'i-yao* (Compendium of fifty-one years of Taiwan provincial statistics) (Taipei, 1946), p. 190; Republic of China, Taiwan Provincial Government, Department of Civil Affairs, *The Monthly Bulletin of Population Registration Statistics of Taiwan* 1, no. 10 (1966): 20.

18. The marriage registration handbook cited in note 11 above mentions the practice by brigades of supplying letters of introduction for couples but cautions commune registration officials that this does not mean they can omit all investigations. Apparently this caution is often ignored.

19. One recent account of a village in Honan Province mentions an example of a male marrying below the *legal* age (he was only nineteen). When the couple was refused registration by the commune they went ahead and married in a family celebration anyway, and soon produced a child. See Jack Chen, *A Year in Upper Felicity* (New York: Macmillan, 1973), pp. 77–78. As noted earlier, court precedents have accepted such "common law" marriage since the 1950s.

20. In this and subsequent tables marriage ages have been collapsed into three categories. For males, these are 20 or less, 21–27, and 28+; for females, the categories are 19 or less, 20–22, and 23 and over. For class labels there are also three categories: 1 = former landlord or rich peasant, 2 = intermediate label, and 3 = former poor peasant. For husband's education, 1 = incomplete primary or none, 2 = primary, and 3 = more than primary; for wife's education, 1 = none, 2 = primary or incomplete primary, and 3 = some middle schooling or more. Husband's service as a cadre is a simple dichotomy: 1 = no, 2 = yes. Not enough cases involving party members or women serving as cadres were available for analysis.

21. For example, the gamma association between male marriage age and whether or not an introducer was used (1 = yes, 2 = no) is only .27 (N = 71), and for

female marriage age it is −.01. These associations could easily occur by chance alone.

22. On the strength of this taboo in another area of China before 1949, see F. L. K. Hsu, *Under the Ancestor's Shadow* (New York: Columbia University Press, 1949), pp. 26–27. On the influence of the same-lineage marriage taboo and resistance to courting behavior in a village in North China today, see Chen, *Upper Felicity*, pp. 72–74.

23. Interview KYP-2, p. 3.

24. Interview TeC-1, pp. 3–4.

25. Some informants mention the same-lineage taboo breaking down before 1949. The lineage branches referred to here are corporate subdivisions of a lineage, most of which are based on descent from several sons or grandsons of the founding ancestor of the lineage. A lineage village may contain several such branches, each with several hundred to a thousand members.

26. In the lower half of table 30, pre-1958 marriages are judged in terms of current commune boundaries. For comparison, a study of 129 marriages in a Taiwan village in the 1960s found 20 percent of males and females marrying within the same village, 24 percent in the same township (a unit comparable in some ways to a mainland commune), and 55 percent outside their township. See Chuang Ying-chang, "The Adaptation of the Family to Modernization in Rural Taiwan," (in Chinese), *Bulletin of the Institute of Ethnology*, no. 34 (1975), p. 92. Intravillage marriage is similar but extratownship marriage is greater than on the mainland, supported one suspects by greater ease of transport and more education outside one's home village in Taiwan.

27. Not enough pre-1949 cases were available for inclusion in table 32.

28. On the acceptance of the professional matchmaker's role in a Honan village, see Chen, *Upper Felicity*, pp. 73–74.

29. These categories are modified and collapsed versions of ones used by Janet Salaff in "The Emerging Conjugal Relationship in the People's Republic of China," *Journal of Marriage and the Family* 35 (1973): 705–17. We note that Salaff estimated about half of the marriages in rural Kwangtung in the period 1958–67 involved primarily youth initiative, an estimate similar to our figure for the same period. In our figures, examples offered by informants to specifically illustrate free or forced marriage have been excluded.

30. In thirteen cases of post-1959 same-lineage marriages, twelve involved youth dominance, while this was true of only half of the fourteen different-lineage marriages for which we have information. Eighty-three percent of twenty-three post-1959 same-village marriages involved youth dominance, while this was true of only 41 percent of twenty-nine marriages with partners from another commune.

31. Consistent with this interpretation, one-third of the multilineage teams and one-half of the single-surname brigades are sited within large, single-village

brigades. Brigade and village social ties form a dense network in these places, whereas all single-lineage teams are isolated by themselves in independent villages not providing ready social ties to their larger brigade.

32. This is also the view expressed in Chen, *Upper Felicity,* p. 104.

33. Young people who believe in free mate-choice but continue to accept parental choices due to limited opportunities to find a mate are common in many societies moving away from arranged marriage. See, for example, Jack M. Potter, *Capitalism and the Chinese Peasant* (Berkeley: University of California Press, 1968), chap. 7 (about Hong Kong); and Ezra F. Vogel, "The Go-between in a Developing Society: The Case of the Japanese Marriage Arranger," *Human Organization* 20 (1961): 112–20.

34. Jack Goody, "Bridewealth and Dowry in Africa and Eurasia," in Jack Goody and S. J. Tambiah, *Bridewealth and Dowry* (Cambridge: Cambridge University Press, 1973). Using arguments from Goody's brief piece extensively, we will not cite individual page references. We us the term "bride price" to mean the same thing as Goody's "bridewealth," as the former term is more common in discussions of China.

35. According to Goody, the use of dowry has many other implications, including an emphasis on female virginity, monogamy, and arranged marriage. The first and third were characteristic of traditional China while the middle was violated to some extent by elite concubinage. We note that this mixture of bride-price and dowry systems in China had broad similarities to the mixture in economically stratified traditional India—see Tambiah's essay in Goody and Tambiah, *Bridewealth and Dowry.*

36. Buck, *Land Utilization,* pp. 468–69.

37. Fei Hsiao-tung and Chang Chih-i, *Earthbound China* (Chicago: University of Chicago Press, 1945), pp. 256–58. For an even more detailed example from contemporary Taiwan in which male and female exchanges just about match, even though *total* male expenditures are twice that of *total* female expenditures, see Myron Cohen, *House United, House Divided* (New York: Columbia University Press, 1976), p. 176.

38. In our data, the relationship between low bride-price cash (under 200 yuan) and the lack of an introduction is gamma = .25 (N = 37), and with youth dominance in mate choice the association is only gamma = .05 (N = 27). Neither figure is statistically significant.

39. Interview TPP-1, p. 9. (The informant is a sixty-five-year-old woman, widow of a former landlord.)

40. Interview TCT, p. 32.

41. Interview FKP-1, p. 12.

42. Chen, *Rural People's Communes,* p. 213. Bride prices there ranged from 400

to 2,000 yuan. We also note that urban males sent down to live in villages have a hard time marrying, as they lack local family and kin to help them pay a bride price (as well as lacking housing, a mother who can baby-sit, and so on). Sent-down females, in contrast, are in some demand, since they will accept smaller or negligible bride prices. They are jokingly referred to as "state-price brides."

43. One ordinarily expects that with increasing freedom of mate choice the gap in marriage ages between spouses will decline. See Goode, *Family Patterns,* pp. 40–48. Yet we saw in table 27 that pre-1949 studies placed the age gap between spouses in the range of 3.1 to 3.4 years, while our data for post-1968 marriages yield a figure of 3.7 years. This is in keeping with Goody's argument that true bride prices keep the gap large, since much time is needed by the male and his family to accumulate the required valuables. Of course, other factors can affect the age differential at marriage.

44. There are a few instances in our interviews of individuals being criticized for giving bride prices, and of brigade threats to confiscate bride prices. We were also told that in some places rural cadres tend to give cash, but few goods, in their bride prices, in order to be less conspicuous. However, usually there is little danger involved.

45. See Peter Schran, *The Development of Chinese Agriculture, 1950–1959* (Urbana: University of Illinois Press, 1969), chap. 3; *Nung-ts'un kung-tso t'ung-hsün* (Rural work bulletin), no. 3 (1958), p. 26.

46. Buck, *Land Utilization,* pp. 292–93. In the seven Kwangtung localities sampled in Buck's study, this percentage ranged from 5 to 38 percent (*Land Utilization,* statistics volume, p. 305). As would be expected, the highest percentages were in Hakka and lowest in Cantonese countries. See Myron L. Cohen, "The Hakka or Guest People," *Ethnohistory* 15 (1968): 237–92.

47. Graham Johnson, "Rural Chinese Social Organization: Tradition and Change," *Pacific Affairs* 46 (1973–1974): 562. The higher rates of female labor participation in Kwangtung compared to those in other provinces continued to be reported in studies done in the 1950s. See *Hsin-hua pan-yüeh k'an,* no. 94 (1956), pp. 63–65; *Hsin-hua pan-yüeh k'an,* no. 140 (1958), pp. 94–97. For a picture of lighter female participation in a northern province today, see Chen, *Upper Felicity.*

48. See Dwight Heath, "Sexual Division of Labor and Cross-cultural Research," *Social Forces* 37 (1958): 77–79; also Ester Boserup, *Women's Role in Economic Development* (New York: St. Martin's Press, 1970).

49. Computed from Buck, *Land Utilization,* statistics volume, pp. 305, 408–12. In an unpublished paper that uses these same data for all of China, Betty Lin finds a strong association between bride price (male's wedding expenses with indirect dowry [female expenses] partialled out) and the proportion of farm labor done by women, as we do for Kwangtung alone.

50. Buck, *Land Utilization,* p. 468.

51. Benedict Stavis, *Making Green Revolution* (Ithaca: Cornell University Rural Development Committee, 1974), p. 58. That the units of currency in the two periods are different does not affect the comparison.

52. If there is a bias here, it should be working against our conclusion. Stavis's peasant family-income estimate is probably too high, since it is based largely upon figures from communes visited by foreigners, which are likely to be unusually prosperous "model" communes. If this is so, it tends to reduce the value of the current ratio and minimize any increase over former times. In Chapter 5 we estimated Kwangtung peasant per capita income to be roughly 128 yuan and family income to be 564 yuan, figures smaller than Stavis gives, although we expect Kwangtung to have rural incomes higher than the national average. Using these figures, we conclude that the average Kwangtung peasant family today actually spends about 130 percent of its annual income on the expenses of a son's marriage—considerably more than is implied by our procedure in the text, which uses national income estimates as a base in calculation.

53. With informants claiming that rural women are eager to marry into communes in the suburbs of large cities, there must be a stronger "urban attractiveness" than the tabular figures show. Since the first dividing line in our urban proximity variable is at 75 km from Canton or Swatow, it will not detect an effect that holds strictly for suburban communes.

54. In spite of later marriage ages today and increased contact between young males and females, illegitimacy does not seem to be a common problem. We argue that the conservative atmosphere of peasant families and villages is still fairly successful in controlling sexual behavior among rural youth. However, exceptions do occur.

55. Other changes than those involved in the "major" traditional marriage pattern were mentioned in Chapter 9: the virtual disappearance of child betrothal, adopted daughters-in-law, and concubines.

56. On the fragility of romantic love as the basis for a lifelong marriage relationship, see, for example, Sidney M. Greenfield, "Love and Marriage in Modern America: A Functional Analysis," *Sociological Quarterly* 6 (1965): 361–77.

57. One Chinese press article from 1957 reported that 82 percent of all divorce cases were initiated by women. See Goode, *Family Patterns,* p. 317.

58. On the work of these committees, see Stanley Lubman, "Mao and Mediation: Politics and Dispute Resolution in Communist China," *California Law Review* 55 (1967): 1284–1359.

59. For instance, childlessness is not felt to be sufficient grounds. See the discussion in Meijer, *Marriage Law and Policy,* chap. 11.

60. A 1963 document specifies that the work of divorce registration should be handled at the commune level, with the county having the right to review and approve the commune's decision. See *How to Manage Marriage-Registration Work Well,* p. 17.

61. Interview TCT, p. 66.

62. However, this pattern does not conform to an expectation drawn from Goody's argument, that where higher bride prices are paid, the husband's family will gain more secure control over the woman (see Goody, "Bridewealth and dowry" p. 12). (Our comparison, of course, involves different villages, while Goody's involves different cultures.) This points to an important distinction from the African case, where marriages occur between communities that are economically similar, and where bride prices are fixed in value by custom. In rural Kwangtung today communities and families differ in wealth and "desirability," and so variable bride prices enter into the competition for mates while the rights transferred are fairly uniform.

11   Intrafamily Relations

1. See, for example, *JMJP,* 16 March 1968, 6 February 1969; *KMJP,* 11 April 1968; *Peking Review* 13, no. 47 (1970).

2. We have located only a few press articles over the years which focus on the need for men to help with housework. See, for example, *JMJP,* 29 January 1954; *Hung-Ch'i,* no. 12, (1973), pp. 20–21. Even the goal of mobilizing women to work outside the home has been deemphasized during periods of economic contraction. See Delia Davin, *Woman-Work* (Oxford: Clarendon Press, 1976).

3. For a brief time in 1969–70 there was an effort to establish "Mao Tse-tung's thought family-study classes." These were described as fostering egalitarian family relations by organizing younger members of the family to criticize the "backward" ideas of their elders. However, this effort was short-lived, and most of our informants had never heard of such family-study classes in their localities. See Martin King Whyte, *Small Groups and Political Rituals in China* (Berkeley: University of California Press, 1947), p. 140.

4. One partial exception to the pattern of family-based domestic work in Kwangtung is that most sewing of clothes is not done by each family but by taking store-bought fabric to a neighbor who has a treadle sewing machine.

5. Interview TCY, p. 3.

6. See Chen, *Upper Felicity,* pp. 57–60, for a similar pattern in another province.

7. Foot-binding was forbidden after 1911 and had disappeared among younger women long before 1949. Contrary to Davin's assertion in *Woman-Work,* p. 10, Cantonese foot-binding was common. In a similar ecological (rice-growing) setting

in 1905, 68 percent of the Hokkien women in Taiwan had bound feet, while only 1.5 percent of Hakka women there had them. See Committee of the Formosan Special Census Investigation, *The Special Population Census of Formosa, 1905* (Tokyo: Imperial Printing Bureau, 1909), p. 134. The latter source was brought to our attention by Richard Barrett.

8. On conflict in a village elsewhere in China over who should attend such meetings, see Jan Myrdal and Gun Kessle, *China: The Revolution Continued* (New York: Vintage, 1970), pp. 132–38.

9. A study from Taiwan places great importance on how the informal public socializing of women (for example, while doing laundry) gives them solidarity and a means of influencing village public opinion, thereby helping to offset their lack of formal power in family and village life. See Margery Wolf, *Women and the Family in Rural Taiwan* (Stanford: Stanford University Press, 1972). It is our impression that this sort of group socializing and opinion formation among women is weak in contemporary Kwangtung, where both a shifting pattern of work groups and a very hectic daily schedule interfere with the sort of stable ties among women and leisurely gossip that Wolf describes.

10. Maurice Freedman sees these dyads as the most crucial ones in determining the nature of Chinese family relations. See, *Chinese Lineage and Society: Fukien and Kwangtung* (London: Athlone, 1966), chap. 2.

11. See the discussions in Marion J. Levy, Jr., *The Family Revolution in Modern China* (Cambridge: Harvard University Press, 1949), chap. 4; Francis L. K. Hsu, *Under the Ancestor's Shadow* (New York: Columbia University Press, 1949), chap. 3; Martin C. Yang, *A Chinese Village: Taitou, Shantung Province* (New York: Columbia University Press, 1945), chap. 6; Francis L. K. Hsu, "Kinship and Ways of Life: An Exploration," in *Psychological Anthropology*, ed. Francis L. K. Hsu (New York: Dorsey Press, 1961); and Freedman, *Lineage and Society*.

12. See Yang, *A Chinese Village*, p. 57; Margery Wolf, "Child Training and the Chinese Family," in *Family and Kinship in Chinese Society*, ed. M. Freedman (Stanford: Stanford University Press, 1970).

13. See Y. R. Chao, "Chinese Terms of Address," *Language* 32 (1956); and John McCoy, "Chinese Kin Terms of Reference and Address," in Freedman, *Family and Kinship*. However, some writers say that the wife's personal name was dropped after marriage, and not used by her husband in addressing her. See C. K. Yang, *The Chinese Family in the Communist Revolution* (Cambridge: MIT Press, 1959), p. 111.

14. C. K. Yang, *Chinese Family*, paints a fairly dark picture of male dominance over their wives, while Martin Yang, *A Chinese Village*, depicts a situation of substantial consultation and mutual influence.

15. Interview TCY, p. 2.

16. Examination of partial gamma associations reveals that each of these variables was strongly associated with our "husband support" measure, even when the others are statistically controlled.

17. Interview TKP-4, p. 12.

18. We have in mind here particularly Richard Solomon's provocative study, *Mao's Revolution and the Chinese Political Culture* (Berkeley: University of California Press, 1971).

19. Collective nurseries and kindergartens are seen as freeing more women for outside work and providing collective political and moral training not available in the home. However, the superiority of this kind of care is not seen as sufficient to warrant a major campaign to universalize collective pre-school care. This was the position taken by Hsiao Ching-jo, an official of the State Council Group on Science and Education in a briefing on November 22, 1973. Martin K. Whyte, China trip notes, Early Childhood Education Delegation.

20. For example, New China Women's Publishing House, *Tui hai-tzu ti ku-li ho tse-fa* [On the reward and punishment of children] (Peking, 1956); Anhwei Education Dept., *Fei-chih t'i-fa yü pien-hsiang t'i-fa, p'ei-yang er-t'ung tzu-chüeh chi-lu* [The abolition of corporal punishment and disguised corporal punishment, the development of the child's self-conscious discipline] (Hofei, 1953).

21. Interview TKM, p. 1. A similar rural-urban contrast is described in William Kessen, ed., *Childhood in China* (New Haven: Yale University Press, 1975), pp. 66–69.

22. See, for example, *JMJP*, 17 July 1974, 5 September 1974, 6 March 1975.

23. See the discussion in Solomon, *Mao's Revolution,* chap. 3; Arthur H. Smith, *Village Life in China* (Boston: Little Brown, 1970; originally published in 1899), chaps. 22–23; Wolf, "Child Training."

24. For example, see William H. Sewell, "Infant Training and the Personality of the Child," *American Journal of Sociology* 58 (1952): 150–59.

25. For published reports of such dangers to rural children, see *JMJP* 29 May 1955, 16 May 1956; Rewi Alley, *Travels in China, 1966–1971* (Peking: New World Press, 1973), p. 340; Chen, *Upper Felicity,* p. 199.

26. A recent report from another part of rural China mentions "hearty smacks" being given for "hitting a neighbor's boy or raiding the larder," with cursing used for lesser kinds of misbehavior—all this in spite of official disapproval. See Chen, *Upper Felicity,* pp. 105–6.

27. Interview FKP-1, p. 10.

28. See Levy, *Family Revolution,* pp. 76, 242; C. K. Yang, *Chinese Family,* p. 93. A couple of cases of cadre intervention to deal with child abuse occurred in our interviews.

29. Alex Inkeles, "Social Change and Social Character: The Role of Parental Mediation," *Journal of Social Issues* 11 (1955): 12–23.

30. See, for example, *Peking Review* 13, no. 47 (1970); *JMJP*, 27 February 1975.

31. See F. Vigdorova, *Diary of a Russian Schoolteacher* (New York: Grove Press, 1960).

32. Not being aware of this institution when we began interviewing, we did not systematically inquire about it, and accordingly may have overlooked these houses in a number of other villages.

33. Spencer and Barrett stress a connection between this institution and both strong lineages and avoidance rules between adolescent brothers and sisters. However, not being as localized as youth houses, these factors are an insufficient explanation. Robert Spencer and S. A. Barrett, "Notes on a Bachelor House in the South China Area," *American Anthropologist* 50 (1948): 463–78.

34. In many early modern European peasant villages a variety of kinds of all-village youth activities and social gatherings existed, and there, too, we are told that these did not pose a threat to adult moral standards, such as premarital chastity. Edward Shorter, *The Making of the Modern Family* (New York: Basic Books, 1975), chap. 4. There as in China the virtual absence of life-chances outside the village and family context appears to be the crucial factor.

35. This conflict is discussed in C. K. Yang, *Religion in Chinese Society* (Berkeley: University of California Press, 1961).

12   The Changing Role of Women

1. For general discussions, see Marilyn B. Young, ed., *Women in China* (Ann Arbor: Center for Chinese Studies, 1973); Margery Wolf and Roxane Witke, eds., *Women in Chinese Society* (Stanford: Stanford University Press, 1975).

2. For examples of such unusual women, see Nym Wales, *Women in Modern China* (Paris: Mouton, 1967); and Mary Backus Rankin, "The Emergence of Women at the End of the Ch'ing: The Case of Ch'iu Chin," in Wolf and Witke, *Women in Chinese Society.*

3. This is the argument presented in Martin Yang, *A Chinese Village* (New York: Columbia University Press, 1945), pp. 56–57.

4. See Roxane Witke, "Mao Tse-tung, Women and Suicide in the May Fourth Era," *China Quarterly*, no. 31 (1967).

5. For critiques of the one-sided nature of party policy toward women, see Janet Salaff and Judith Merkle, "Women and Revolution: The Lessons of the Soviet Union and China," in Young, *Women in China;* and Sheilah Gilbert Leader, "The Emancipation of Chinese Women," *World Politics* 26 (October 1973).

6. For a brief summary of earlier trends, see William J. Goode, *World Revolution and Family Patterns* (New York: The Free Press, 1963), chap. 6.

7. See Frederick Engels, *The Origin of the Family, Private Property, and the State* (Chicago: Charles H. Kerr, 1902).

8. Marxism sees other changes as fundamental, of course—in particular the elimination of male domination of productive property ownership. This elimination has occurred in China with the socialization of agriculture, although it might be argued that the combination of preexisting patrilineal kin groups with patrilocal postmarital residence does not break the control of males over agricultural land as thoroughly as some other arrangement might.

9. See Janet Salaff, "Working Daughters in the Hong Kong Chinese Family: Female Filial Piety or a Transformation in the Family Power Structure?" *Journal of Social History* 9 (1976): 439–65. A study of Guatemalan peasants-turned-factory-workers notes, "The most common arrangement is for the wife to turn over to her husband almost all of her income, keeping back a small amount over which she has control. This kind of handling gives the husband the same control over domestic economy as if his wife were not a factory employee earning a rather large income." See Manning Nash, *Machine Age Maya* (Chicago: University of Chicago Press, 1958), p. 70.

10. See *JMJP*, 1 December 1973, 3 December 1973.

11. Since we have not seen the text of such a directive, which was said to date from the early 1970s, these reports must be treated as tentative.

12. Adopted future daughter-in-laws, who may on this account have supplied more than their share of female cadres in the past, are disappearing from the scene. (See the argument in Norma Diamond, "Collectivization, Kinship, and the Status of Women in Rural China," *Bulletin of Concerned Asian Scholars* 7, no. 1 [January–March 1975].) One strategy to deal with the first problem would be to foster matrilocal marriages, which would keep women in villages where they are well known. Yet we noted in Chapter 9 that very little effort has been made to encourage such marriages. However, we saw in Chapter 10 that more women are marrying within the village and lineage than in the past, and this trend should contribute to the breakdown of this particular obstacle to women serving as local cadres.

13. The most frequently cited source on the militant role of the early women's federations is Jack Belden, "Gold Flower's Story," in his book *China Shakes the World* (New York: Monthly Review Press, 1970), pp. 275–307 (originally published in 1949). See the discussion of the women's federation in Delia Davin, *Woman-Work* (Oxford: Clarendon Press, 1976), chap. 2.

14. See Margery Wolf, "Women and Suicide in China," in Wolfe and Witke, *Women in Chinese Society.*

15. We do not deal here with women's role vis-à-vis men in religious rituals, which will be touched on in the two chapters that follow.

16. These conclusions—that socially productive labor by women has no general liberating influence and that there is no unitary status-of-women syndrome that improves or deteriorates in a consistent fashion—fly in the face of much popular wisdom about sex roles. However, they are in line with an increasing amount of research on cultures other than China's. See Martin King Whyte, *The Status of Women in Preindustrial Societies* (Princeton: Princeton University Press, 1978); Joan Scott and Louise Tilly, "Women's work and Family in Nineteenth-century Europe," *Comparative Studies in Society and History* 17, no. 1 (1975); Elizabeth Zelman, "Women's Rights and Women's Rites: A Cross-cultural Study of Womanpower and Reproductive Ritual" (Ph.D. dissertation, University of Michigan, 1974).

17. Michael P. Sacks, *Women's Work in Soviet Russia* (New York: Praeger, 1976).

13   Life-Cycle Ceremonies and Ritual Life

1 The Li Ki (Li Chi), translated by James Legge, in *The Sacred Books of the East*, ed. F. M. Muller (Delhi: Motilal Banarsidass, 1966), 28:261–62. In Durkheim's view rituals celebrate the importance of society and social norms, and the nature of the rituals varies according to the structure of the society. This is a perspective we will rely upon heavily in this chapter and the next. See Emile Durkheim, *The Elementary Forms of Religious Life* (New York: Macmillan, 1915). The Confucian perspective does differ in emphasizing the values transmitted in rituals rather than simply their social aspect.

2. These arguments are cogently presented in Arthur P. Wolf, "Gods, Ghosts, and Ancestors," in *Religion and Ritual In Chinese Society,* ed. Arthur P. Wolf (Stanford: Stanford University Press, 1974).

3. Chou Chien-jen, "The Question of Breaking Down Religion and Superstitions," *KMJP,* 21 April 1964, translated in *Religious Policy and Practice in Communist China,* ed. Donald E. MacInnis (New York: Macmillan, 1972), p. 191.

4. See MacInnis, *Religious Policy,* pp. 9–10.

5. Chou, "Breaking Down Religion," p. 192.

6. See John L. Buck, *Land Utilization in China* (Nanking: University of Nanking, 1937), pp. 462, 468. For Kwangtung the expenditures were considerably higher.

7. Article by Chao Chien-min, *JMJP,* 17 June 1958, in MacInnis, *Religious Policy,* p. 315.

8. *Selected Readings from the Works of Mao Tse-tung* (Peking: Foreign Languages Press, 1971), pp. 310–12.

9. See, for example, MacInnis, *Religious Policy,* pp. 330–32; *URS* 79 no. 13 (1975); *KMJP,* 18 January 1969; *JMJP,* 24 January 1972, 20 November 1972.

10. "Old Aunt Wu Celebrates Her Birthday," *NFJP,* 21 January 1970, in Mac-Innis, *Religious Policy,* pp. 334–35. "Meals of bitter remembrance" are a part of many model celebrations, as we will note in the next chapter. The parallel with the symbolism of the Seder of the Jewish Passover is obvious.

11. See *Kuang-tung feng-su chui-lu* [Kwangtung customs miscellany] (Hong Kong: Ch'ung-wen Shu-tien, 1972). Being a collection of articles on Kwangtung customs in dealing with marriage and burial reprinted from journals of the later 20s and early 30s, largely *Min-su Chou-k'an,* this source will be used extensively below under the title *Miscellany.*

12. *Miscellany,* p. 391, mentions similar, not very restrictive taboos during this period. See also Marjorie Topley, "Cosmic Antagonisms: A Mother-Child Syndrome" in Wolf, *Religion and Ritual.*

13. Cf. J. Doolittle, *Social Life of the Chinese* (New York: Harper and Brothers, 1865), 1:120–26. The hair the baby is born with is believed to stem from the mother, and now it should start growing its own. This custom seems to illustrate the mother-child tensions discussed in Topley, "Cosmic antagonisms"

14. Also reported in Arthur H. Smith, *Village Life in China* (Boston: Little Brown, 1970; originally published in 1899), p. 181. We note that Mao Tse-tung had brothers named *Tse-*ming and *Tse-*t'an. His own sons were named *An-*ying and *An-*ching.

15. On the exchange of horoscopes (eight characters) traditionally, see Liu Wan-chang, "Canton's Old Wedding Customs," in *Su-yüeh ti hun-sang* [Marriages and funerals of Soochow and Canton] (Taipei: 1969; another collection of articles reprinted from ca. 1928–29), pp. 45–47; "Tung-kuan Marriage Customs Record," in *Miscellany,* p. 207. Obviously this change reflects the increased freedom of mate choice discussed in Chapter 10.

16. Criticism of these bride-fetching customs is offered in *NFJP,* 9 February 1975, translated in *URS* 79, no. 13, pp. 150–51. A Hong Kong observer reports recent Kwangtung bride-fetching observations in Hsiao Mu, *Chu-chiang san-chiao-chou chi-yu* [Pearl River Delta travel notes] (Hong Kong: Ch'ao-yang Press, 1973), pp. 101–2. For a general discussion of wedding rituals, and their grounding in ancient texts, see Maurice Freedman, "Ritual Aspects of Chinese Kinship and Marriage," in *Family and Kinship in Chinese Society,* ed. M. Freedman (Stanford: Stanford University Press, 1970). Also see V. R. Burkhardt, *Chinese Creeds and Customs* (Hong Kong: South China Morning Post, 1953), 1:95.

17. Several cases of bride exchanges between former landlord families occurred in our interviews, the exchange being a solution to this problem of finding brides.

18. See an early (1956) example of such quasi-religious ceremonies in W. R. Geddes, *Peasant Life in Communist China* (Ithaca: Society for Applied Anthropology, 1963), p. 25; see also George Urban, ed., *The Miracles of Chairman Mao* (London: Tom Stacey, 1971), p. 176.

19. See Olga Lang, *Chinese Family and Society* (New Haven: Yale University Press, 1946). Traveling marriages in contemporary rural Kwangtung are also reported in Hsiao, *Chu-chiang,* p. 103.

20. One source, however, does imply that weddings involved "clan banquets" held in the ancestral hall. See Robert Spencer and S. A. Barrett, "Notes on a Bachelor House in the South China Area," *American Anthropologist* 50 (1948): 467, 474.

21. A shift from lineal relatives and other kin toward more of a focus on friends as wedding participants is reported in a Kiangsu village in 1956. See Geddes, *Peasant Life,* pp. 25, 30.

22. On the importance of body placement before and after death, consult the *Li Chi,* 28:173ff; and *Miscellany,* pp. 53ff.

23. The mourning clothes worn do seem to be both less elaborate and colorful and less carefully demarcated for different types of relatives than is the case in contemporary Taiwan. See Arthur P. Wolf, "Chinese Kinship and Mourning Dress," in Freedman, *Family and Kinship.*

24. For discussions of the techniques and meaning of feng-shui (geomancy), see M. Freedman, *Chinese Lineage and Society: Fukien and Kwangtung* (London. Athlone, 1966), chap. 5; and Jack M. Potter, "Wind, Water, Bones and Souls: The Religious World of the Cantonese Peasant," *Journal of Oriental Studies* 8 (1970): 139–53. Families are free to pick grave-sites on unused hillside land, but if the commune or government decides to bring a grave area into use, families will be requested to move the remains of their ancestors to new locations.

25. *Miscellany,* p. 59, reports the traditional ban on women going to the grave. The exclusion of women from some traditional rites was also commented upon by Mao Tse-tung in his 1927 report on the peasant movement in Hunan (MacInnis, *Religious Policy,* pp. 8–9).

26. Buck, *Land Utilization,* statistical volume, pp. 408–12.

27. Though ancient texts mention a mourning period of up to three years, this was never the usual practice. A report of Canton funeral customs in the 1920s mentions the same forty-nine-day period that we were told about in 1973–74 (*Miscellany,* p. 59).

28. Traditionally wooden ancestral tablets were only found in the ancestral hall, and paper tablets were kept at home in the domestic shrine. Thus the real change here is not using paper domestic tablets, but the practice of some families of keeping wooden tablets in the home rather than in the ancestral hall. James Watson, personal communication; see also N. G. H. Nelson, "Ancestor Worship and Burial Practices," in Wolf, *Religion and Ritual,* p. 268.

29. Interview TSP-3, p. 16.

30. Not all cadres abstain from personal participation, and this fact is not confined

to rural areas. According to a 1967 Red Guard document from 1962–64, Tseng Sheng, the mayor of Canton, carried out traditional worship and memorial rites on repeated occasions after the death of his mother. See MacInnis, *Religious Policy,* p. 289.

31. Cited in MacInnis, *Religious Policy,* p. 39. This policy reflects Mao Tsetung's 1957 analysis of how to handle "contradictions" among the people and also harks back to his 1927 statement: "It is the peasants who made the idols, and when the time comes they will cast the idols aside with their own hands; there is no need for anyone else to do it for them prematurely." (Quoted in MacInnis, p. 9.) Of course this policy is not always followed—witness the "casting aside" of ancestral tablets in 1966 by Red Guards, rather than by the families that worshipped them.

32. Interview PYP-2, second set, p. 6.

33. Victor Turner emphasizes these latter factors in explaining why life-cycle rituals are more emphasized in some cultures than in others. See his book *The Forest of Symbols* (Ithaca: Cornell University Press, 1967), p. 93.

34. This coding of wedding costs, like the other variables in table 41, is based on informant estimates of the general practice in their village as a whole, and includes bride-price and wedding feast expenditures, payments to marriage arrangers, and so on, but *not* new housing and furniture.

35. We recall from Chapter 10 that the bride-price cash portion tends to be lower in villages with high household consumption than elsewhere. This may enable people in such villages to only spend moderate amounts on weddings even though their wedding feasts are relatively elaborate.

36. A simple terrain variable not included here (delta or plains versus hills) showed a fairly consistent positive association with these ceremonies, meaning simpler ceremonies in hilly regions.

37. These differences probably do not reflect greater Hakka receptiveness to post-1949 changes but prerevolutionary cultural differences. In the case of ancestral tablets, at least, Hakkas generally did not have such tablets in the home but only in the ancestral hall, unlike the Cantonese. James Watson, personal communication.

14   The Annual Cycle of Festivals

1. See Donald R. DeGlopper, "Religion and Ritual in Lukang," and Stephan Feuchtwang, "Domestic and Communal Worship in Taiwan" in *Religion and Ritual in Chinese Society,* ed. Arthur P. Wolf (Stanford: Stanford University Press, 1974). For a denunciation of the visiting of ancestral tombs by lineages, see *NFJP*, rural edition, 18 April 1964, translated in Maurice Freedman, *Chinese Lineage and Society; Fukien and Kwangtung* (London: Athlone, 1966), pp. 181–82.

2. *Min-tsu t'uan-chieh*, 14 June 1958, in Donald E. MacInnis, *Religious Policy and Practice in Communist China* (New York: Macmillan, 1972), pp. 183, 186.

3. Opposition to elaborate and "superstitious" holiday observances was also a feature of the early reform programs of the Chinese Nationalists—programs they continue today in Taiwan with seemingly little direct effect. See Wolfram Eberhard, *Chinese Festivals* (London: Abelard Schuman, 1958), p. 4, on the early programs.

4. See "Spring Festival in Shanghai," *Far Eastern Economic Review*, 3 (March 1966), pp. 413–15.

5. Peking Radio, 1 June 1969, cited in George Urban, ed., *The Miracles of Chairman Mao* (London: Tom Stacey, 1971), p. 155; cf. also Raymond L. Whitehead, "Liturgical Developments in China's Revolutionary Religion," in MacInnis, *Religious Policy*, pp. 339–41.

6. In MacInnis, *Religious Policy*, p. 185.

7. Though not explicitly noted for each holiday, the discussion that follows relies heavily on several basic sources for comparisons with pre-1949 holiday activities. V. R. Burkhardt, *Chinese Creeds and Customs* (Hong Kong: South China Morning Post, 1953), 1:75–77; Tun Li-ch'en, *Annual Customs and Festivals in Peking*, 2d ed., trans. Derk Bodde (Hong Kong: Hong Kong University Press, 1965), pp. 1–2, 25, 42–43, 69, 172, 340; *Kuang-tung feng-su chui-lu* [Kwangtung customs miscellany; hereafter *Miscellany*] (Hong Kong: Ch'ung-wen shu-tien, 1972), pp. 25–26; Eberhard, *Chinese Festivals*, pp. 73–75. Likewise, though not always explicitly noted, our account of contemporary Kwangtung customs is parallel at several points with Jack Chen's description of current practices in a village in Honan Province—*A Year in Upper Felicity* (New York: Macmillan, 1973), pp. 146–51. However, Chen finds more emphasis on the traditional solar (as opposed to lunar) holidays than we find in contemporary Kwangtung (see pp. 160–65). Comparisons with contemporary Hong Kong practices are provided by Morris I. Berkowitz, F. P. Brandauer, and J. H. Reed, *Folk Religion in an Urban Setting* (Hong Kong: n.p., 1969), pp. 48, 54–64.

8. For another example of a "struggle" between old and new tui-lien sayings—this time in Kiangsu Province—see *JMJP*, 27 January 1975.

9. Chen, *Upper Felicity*, p. 150.

10. This holiday continues to have some significance in cities as well. It was on this day in 1976 that police tried to disperse a large crowd that had gathered with memorials to honor Chou En-lai, thereby touching off the T'ien an men riot and a political crisis.

11. Cf. Hugh Baker, *A Chinese Lineage Village, Sheung Shui* (Stanford: Stanford University Press, 1968), chap. 2; Jack Potter, "Wind, Water, Bones and Souls: The Religious World of the Cantonese Peasant," *Journal of Oriental Studies* 8 (1970): 144.

12. KNP-1, p. 8. In most villages in this area Ch'ing-ming activities have long been conducted by individual families rather than entire lineages, although rites for lineage founders take place at other times. James Watson, personal communication. See Daniel H. Kulp, *Country Life in South China* (New York: Teacher's College, 1925), pp. 300–301.

13. The two patterns for each holiday correspond closely to those described in the Hong Kong study, *Folk Religion in an Urban Setting*, by Berkowitz et al.

14. *Miscellany*, p. 69.

15. For example, Burkhardt, *Chinese Creeds and Customs*, 3:154–60, mentions the "3-3" date as the anniversary of the Spirit of the North, the "4-8" festival as the occasion for washing of Buddha images and for the boat people to celebrate the birthday of Tan Kung, the "6-6" holiday as a Buddhist observance known as airing the classics, and "10-1" as All Souls Day, celebrated in North China by visits to graves.

16. *Miscellany*, pp. 9ff., 170ff., 339ff.

17. Though such activities were still being actively denounced in the Kwangtung press in the 1960s, changes in the direction indicated were already underway by 1951. See C. K. Yang, *The Chinese Village in Early Communist Transition* (Cambridge: MIT Press, 1959), pp. 187–96.

18. Potter, "Wind, Water, Bones and Souls"; and various papers in Wolf, *Religion and Ritual in Chinese Society*.

19. "Wind, Water, Bones, and Souls."

20. Interview TKF-1, p. 2.

21. As late as 1949 in one Kwangtung village, community celebrations consumed huge sums of money while lesser sums for an irrigation reservoir and a literacy class could not be raised. See C. K. Yang, *Religion in Chinese Society* (Berkeley: University of California Press, 1961), p. 16. Today, the order of priorities for community expenditures is completely reversed. Public rituals, to the extent that they are held, are cheaper in part simply because the traditional opera troupes which used to perform at these events have been suppressed in favor of "revolutionary opera."

22. Similar changes have occurred in capitalist settings. See Jack Potter, *Capitalism and the Chinese Peasant* (Berkeley: University of California Press, 1968), pp. 171ff., for an account of gradual change in Hong Kong, and Berkowitz et al., *Folk Religion in an Urban Setting*, p. 68, on more dramatic change following forced residential relocation in Hong Kong.

23. For a discussion of the long history of imperial attempts to restrict and control religion, see Yang, *Religion in Chinese Society*, especially chap. 8.

24. Interview HFP-1, p. 9.

25. See Maurice Freedman, "Ancestor Worship: Two Facets of the Chinese

Case," in M. Freedman, *Social Organization: Essays Presented to Raymond Firth* (London: Frank Cass, 1967), pp. 97–98; Bernard Gallin, *Hsin Hsing, Taiwan* (Berkeley: University of California Press, 1966), p. 148. In the Soviet Union, two generations after the revolution the same pattern of religious rites sustained by older peasants and particularly women is visible. See L. Anokhina and M. Shmeleva, *Kul'tura i byt kolkhoznikov Kalininskoi Oblasti* [The culture and daily life of collective farmers of Kalinin District] (Moscow, 1964), p. 221; P. I. Kushner, *Selo Viriatino v proshlom i nastoiashchem* [Viriatino village past and present] (Moscow, 1958), pp. 226, 232.

26. A recent study on Taiwan indicates that Hakkas have a somewhat simpler ritual life than non-Hakkas (the non-Hakkas being Hokkiens, rather than Cantonese) whose ancestors came from Fukien Province. See Wolfgang Grichting, *The Value System in Taiwan 1970* (Taipei: n.p., 1971), pp. 208–9.

15   Changing Patterns of Cooperation and Conflict

1. See the arguments in Chang Ch'un-ch'iao, "On Exercising All-round Dictatorship over the Bourgeoisie," *Peking Review* 18, no. 14 (1975): 5–11. Though Chang Ch'un-ch'iao has been deposed as one of the gang-of-four, the necessity of eventually increasing the size of accounting unit has been restated by the present leadership.

2. See Daniel H. Kulp, *Country Life in South China* (New York: Columbia University, 1925); G. William Skinner, "Marketing and Social Structure in Rural China," *Journal of Asian Studies* 24 (1964): 3–43 and ibid. 24 (1965): 195–228; and G. William Skinner, "Mobility Strategies in Late Imperial China: A Regional-Systems Analysis," in *Regional Analysis,* vol. 1, *Economic Systems,* ed. Carol A. Smith (New York: Academic Press, 1976).

3. Clifford Geertz, "Form and Variation in Balinese Village Structure," *American Anthropologist* 61 (1959): 991–1012.

4. Eric R. Wolf, "Types of Latin American Peasantry: A Preliminary Discussion," *American Anthropologist* 57, no. 3 (1957).

5. G. William Skinner, "Chinese Peasants and the Closed Community: An Open and Shut Case," *Comparative Studies in Society and History* 13 (1971): 270–81.

6. On earlier patterns of cooperation in South China, see Feng Rui and Ping-hang Yung, "A General Descriptive Survey of the Honan Island Village Community" *Lingnan Science Journal* 10 (1931): 153–86; Kulp, *Country Life in South China;* and Hugh Baker, *A Chinese Lineage Village* (Stanford: Stanford University Press, 1968), chap. 7.

7. Interviews CTF, HYH, TCT.

8. Skinner, "Marketing and Social Structure."

9. In 1951, Yeh Chien-ying, then a top official in Kwangtung, reportedly stated in a guest lecture on rural administration to students at Sun Yat-sen University in Canton, "If you want to control men you grab their pigtails. If you want to control villages, you grab their markets [Yao chua jen, chiu chua pien. Yao chua ts'un, chiu chua hsü]." Interview CTY.

10. Frederick Crook, "The Commune System in the People's Republic of China," in U.S. Congress, Joint Economic Committee, *China: A Reassessment of the Economy* (Washington, D.C.: U.S. Government Printing Office, 1975), p. 376. Data collected by William Parish show that in the eastern provinces of Anhwei, Kiangsu, and Shantung there are communes as large as in Kwangtung, especially in level terrain near cities. In other provinces such as Hunan, Hopei, Szechwan, Shansi, and Shensi, communes are smaller—averaging 10,000 to 13,000 people—and correspond more closely to old marketing areas. There is a certain mystery about the statistics on the number of communes in Kwangtung at various points in time. Canton newspapers give the number as increasing from 1,065 in late 1960 to 1,600 in April 1963, and on up to 1,724 in August 1965 (see Ezra Vogel, *Canton under Communism* [Cambridge: Harvard University Press, 1969], p. 379), a figure which corresponds almost exactly to the 1,721 citied to visitors in 1973 (see Chapter 4 above). But by examining individual cases we have found that a considerable amalgamation of communes took place about 1963, and in addition several Kwangtung counties were ceded to Kwangsi Province in 1965. Thus the 1973 (and even 1965) figures should show a marked reduction in the provincial commune total. We can only suggest that either the figures cited by Chinese authorities have not been updated to reflect the real situation or the 1963 figure was in error.

11. Personal communications and William L. Parish, China travel notes, Rural Small-Scale Industry Delegation, Summer, 1975.

12. Only the informants' own teams and brigades are included in table 45. The generalization that single-lineage brigades are more contentious for the reasons given is also supported by additional informant descriptions of some single-lineage brigades other than their own. Press reports on lineage loyalty and lineage conflict include *Chung-kuo ch'ing-nien pao* [Chinese youth daily], 13 July 1963, p. 4; *JMJP*, 30 January 1969; Hupei Provincial Broadcast Service, 22 September 1972, cited in *China News Analysis*, no. 912 (1972).

13. Baker, *A Chinese Lineage Village*, p. 99; Emily M. Ahern, *The Cult of the Dead in a Chinese Village* (Stanford: Stanford University Press, 1973), p. 257.

14. Any apparent contradiction between the findings in table 46 and our discussion of in-marriage in Chapter 10 can be resolved by noting that in table 46 all of the same-brigade marriages in single-lineage brigades, and most of the same-brigade marriages in multilineage-teams occur within a single large village. Thus, if village size is ignored, same-village (as opposed to same-brigade) marriages are most likely

in multilineage teams, next most likely in single-lineage brigades, and least likely in single-lineage teams, which is what we said in Chapter 10.

15. Single-lineage brigades have more services than others not just because of lineage loyalties and intermarriage but also because they tend to be in the more prosperous delta region. Nevertheless, control by prosperity and delta location leaves the gamma relationships in table 47 positive and no more than .10 weaker than the associations before control.

16. See the discussion in Marianne Bastid, "Levels of Economic Decision-making," in *Authority, Participation and Cultural Change in China,* ed. Stuart Schram (Cambridge: Cambridge University Press, 1973).

17. *Hsi-yang pien k'ai Ta-chai hua* [Hsi-yang county begins all-around Tachai transformation] (Taiyuan: Shansi People's Press, 1973).

18. Chang, "On All-round Dictatorship," p. 6.

19. For example, one report on Yang-shih commune in Wu-hsi County, Kiangsu Province, notes that 47 percent of the profits from commune industry are reserved for industrial expansion. Most of the rest are granted to production teams within the commune for use in water-irrigation and drainage projects, field leveling, and soil improvement. A small amount also goes toward health, education, and cultural work in the villages. See Dwight Perkins, ed., *Rural Small-Scale Industry in China* (Berkeley: University of California Press, 1977).

20. *Hsi-yang pien k'ai Ta-chai hua,* p. 151.

21. *JMJP,* 11 December 1976, p. 3; *Peking Review* 20, no. 7 (1977): 7; *SWB,* FE/W887/A/2, 1975.

22. Perkins, *Rural Industry;* and *Shanghai chiao-ch'ü nung-yeh hsüeh Ta-chai* [Shanghai suburbs study Tachai] (Shanghai: Agricultural Press, 1974), pp. 52–58.

23. We refer here to a narrowing down toward the village and team. The analysis in this chapter is not meant to belittle the broadening of cooperation from individual families to the production team which collectivization produced. Within the team and within some brigades, cooperation has broadened, while wider networks of cooperation have shrunk.

16   Conclusions

1. On the increase in brigade authority, see Marianne Bastid, "Levels of Economic Decision-making," in *Authority, Participation, and Cultural Change in China,* ed. Stuart Schram (Cambridge: Cambridge University Press, 1973).

2. That small target-groups are much easier to change than large ones, using administrative measures, is a common theme in the literature on change induced

through the legal system; see, for example, Lawrence M. Friedman, *The Legal System* (New York: Russell Sage, 1975), p. 85.

3. For example, nursery schools seem to represent our childhood socialization subtype of normative influence, and the percentage of urban youths represents a form of communication of urban ideas. But political study can be seen as either a mechanism of communication pure and simple, or an indicator of the strength of the political infrastructure that can administer sanctions. Similarly, our communications scale has as one of its items a rough estimate of the proportion of local youths completing primary school, but schooling can be seen either as the way new ideas are communicated (a normative influence), or as a setting in which young people (especially those of the opposite sex) can get to know each other without the direct supervision of family members (a structural factor).

4. As table 48 indicates, it includes not only average gamma measures of association but also a test of chance results (a test of significance). Both visual inspection of individual gamma values which go into the summary measures and examination of these tests of chance suggest that summary gamma values of .20 or greater are indicative of moderate association. Values much below .20 accompanied by an asterisk indicate a large number of very weak individual associations which are fairly consistently tilted in one direction—all negatively, as it turns out. Also, values close to zero may conceal individual strong relationships that get lost in summary measures, because they cancel each other out (the relationship with one measure is strongly positive and with another strongly negative).

5. This generalization is further supported by an attempt at factor analysis of our dependent variables which shows no consistent factor structure. Indeed, in the area of collective life there are as many variables related negatively to one another as positively.

6. This perspective is elaborated in the recent literature on legally induced change; see Franklin Zimring and Gordon Hawkins, "The Legal Threat as an Instrument of Social Change," *Journal of Social Issues* 27 (1971): 33–48, and Friedman, *The Legal System*.

7. The items within collective life, being related to several "modernization" indicators, might be an exception to this generalization were they not lacking in any clear relationships to one another. See note 5 above.

8. What we are proposing, in technical terms, is that to understand Chinese rural change, one must combine "moving equilibrium" and "interest group" theory. In the 1940s and 1950s the rural social system was in disequilibrium or under strain, with major local interest groups (poor peasants, women, and others) eager for change. The changes of the 1950s solved the major concerns of these groups, creating a new equilibrium among interrelated social elements. Once this new equilibrium was established, it was difficult to find new strains, or interest groups, which could be used for further dramatic change.

Appendix 1
Methodological Notes

1. The gamma statistic does have a special characteristic that needs to be noted. A two-by-two table containing a cell with no cases yields a gamma value of $+1.0$ or -1.0. For example, the gamma computed from the following table would be $+1.0$, even though from an examination of the cells it is clear that the association is not perfect (that is, the two variables are not related in a necessary and sufficient fashion).

	Variable 1	
	12	43
Variable 2		
	0	4

(A necessary and sufficient association would exist only if the upper-right cell had 0 cases rather than 43.) Even more problematic, a single zero cell is very likely to occur when there are only a few cases in one row or column. In the above example there are so few cases in the bottom row that a zero cell could occur often by chance alone. Fortunately, tests of significance provide an indicator of this problem. Where gammas of 1.00 or -1.00 appear in our tables without an asterisk, which indicates a low probability of chance occurrence, the gamma can generally be ignored as stemming from the quirk described here.

2. Given cost constraints, we generally checked only for spuriously inflated associations by controlling two or more independent variables which are correlated more than $\pm.40$ with a single dependent variable. Spuriously deflated associations reduced by association with another independent variable that operates in a counterdirection were not checked. Our major effort is thus to avoid spurious claims to strong association. Generally, among a set of independent variables the one picked as the control variable was the one with the largest gamma coefficient with the dependent variable in question or with the largest number of significant associations with other independent variables. When controls reduced the original gamma by more than .20, we considered the association in question substantially reduced.

3. See Martin King Whyte, *Small Groups and Political Rituals in China* (Berkeley: University of California Press, 1974), Appendix 1; and Jerome A. Cohen, "Interviewing Chinese Refugees: Indispensable Aid to Legal Research on China," *Journal of Legal Education* 20, no. 1 (1967).

4. The techniques described here are adapted from those originally designed for use in cross-cultural anthropological surveys. See Raoul Naroll, *Data Quality Control* (Glencoe, Ill.: The Free Press, 1962).

5. A word is in order about our informants of urban origin. For some years it has been official Chinese policy to settle urban middle-school graduates in rural villages.

Twenty-three of our informants were such individuals. Since they were not natives of the locality they described, we were concerned whether they would have a detailed knowledge of their adopted villages. Because of this concern we tried to screen out urban youths who had only spent a brief period in a village or had frequently gone back to stay in the city. Those we interviewed varied in the length of their rural tenure between one and ten years; the average stay was five years. Most of these urban-origin informants thus had considerable opportunity to familiarize themselves with rural customs. In some cases these youths were our best informants—some became almost amateur ethnographers, questioning local peasants about the logic of their customs, and reporting the distinctive features of rural life in particularly vivid terms. We felt their accounts of village life could be included, then, although we did perform systematic checks to see whether they were giving a different picture of village life than rural-origin informants.

6. The following criteria were used. For any dependent variable the informant or interview codes that were significantly correlated (at $p = .10$ or better) were noted. Then all independent variables that had relationships with the same dependent variable of gamma $= .40$ or stronger were controlled for those informant characteristics.

7. See Margaret Mead and Rhoda Metraux, eds., *The Study of Culture at a Distance* (Chicago: University of Chicago Press, 1953).

8. See, for example, Keith Buchanan, *The Transformation of the Chinese Earth* (London: Bell and Sons, 1970), p. 141; Graham Johnson, "Rural Economic Development and Social Change in South China," mimeographed (1973), pp. 10, 12; Ezra Vogel, China travel notes, May-June 1973; Philip Kuhn, China travel notes, September 1974.

9. Based on *SWB*, 6 January 1971, A6; and Central Intelligence Agency, *China: Agricultural Performance in 1975*, ER76-10149, March 1976, p. 18. The mean is a strict numerical average; the median is the value such that half of the sample has lower values and half higher ones. When there are few cases involved, some of which may be unusually low or high, the median is preferable to the mean as a measure of the average tendnecy.

10. Kwangtung has a total of about 50 million mou of land. Its population is roughly 50 million, about 80 percent of which is rural, and there are about .425 laborers per rural individual. The computed land-labor ratio is therefore 50,000,000/ $(50,000,000 \times .80 \times .425) = 2.94$. These computations are based on the following sources: Liang Jen-ts'ai, *Kuangtung ching-chi ti-li* [Kwangtung Economic Geography] (Peking: Science Press, 1956), p. 21—cultivated land is 16 percent of total land; Frederick W. Crook, "The Commune System in the People's Republic of China, 1963–1974," in U.S. Congress, Joint Economic Committee, *China: A Reassessment of the Economy* (Washington, D.C.: U.S. Government Printing Office, 1975), p. 410—the average household has 1.87 labor units and 4.4 members, or .425 laborers per member.

Appendix 2
Village Characteristics and
Their Interrelations

1. The four summary scales (nos. 1, 5, 7, and 8) were constructed by taking the equally weighted average of the three constituent measures in each and then dichotomizing near the median score. Where information was missing on one or two of the constituent measures, an equally weighted average of the other measures was still used to compute the final score—a procedure made possible by the intercorrelations among constituent measures. (The average value of r = .30, .38, .42, and .43, respectively, for the items in these scales.) The number of villages with these scale scores is thus greater than the number for constituent measures.

Index

icy toward, 158, 161; procedures,
192–97; and remarriage, 193, 194–
95; traditional ideals regarding, 157;
village variations in, 197–98
Domestic work, 133, 201–9, 227–28,
242–43, 323, 326, 390 n. 2
Dowry, 181, 323, 387 n. 35; contents
of, 182–85; decline of, 183–85; display of, 185; indirect, 182
Dragon Boat festival, 281, 283
Durkheim, Emile, 248, 395 n. 1
Dyadic relations. *See* Family relations

Earth god, 284
Education. *See* Schooling, rural
Eight characters (horoscope), 253, 396
n. 15
Elders: respect for, 212–13, 229. *See
also* Leaders, rural
Electrification, rural, 56–57, 124, 355,
366 n. 25
Emigration, 26–27. *See also* Overseas
Chinese; Remittances, overseas
Engels, F., 236
Entreating skill festival, 282
Equality and efficiency, 47, 65, 69,
73–74, 117
Equality and equity, 47, 73–74, 117,
125
Equality and inequality, 2, 31, 34;
compared with non-Communist
Asia, 115, 376 n. 1; material, 47–72;
in medical care, 85–94; and peasant
satisfaction, 115–27; in schooling,
78–84; in status and power, 96–114;
in welfare distributions, 73–78
Ethnic groups, 23, 360 n. 5. *See also*
Cantonese; Hakka
Examination system, traditional, 96

"Face," concern for, 109, 260
Family, loyalty toward, 2, 246, 249,
293, 321, 326, 331, 336

Family, reliance upon, 95, 321
Family division, 75, 135, 211, 323
Family head: change in, 135, 322; gender of, 135, 238; power of, 106, 133,
238, 243
Family planning. *See* Birth control
Family relations: changes in, 211–21,
233–34; official ideals for, 132, 211;
traditional, 209–10. *See also* Brothers, relations among; Father-son
relations; Husband-wife relations;
Mother-in-law–daughter-in-law relations
Family size, 60, 380 n. 6; change in,
134–37; compared with the West,
132–33
Family structure: changes in, 134–37;
compared with the U.S., 134–35;
joint, 132, 134, 137, 379 n. 2;
nuclear, 134, 137, 379 n. 2; official ideals on, 131–33; stem, 134,
137, 212, 379 n. 2; traditional ideals
on, 132–33; village variations in,
137–38
Family study classes, 390 n. 3
Father-son relations, 209, 211–13
Feng-shui. *See* Geomancy
Fertilizer usage: chemical, 56, 124; organic, 93, 123
Festivals: cost of, 273, 290, 400 n. 21;
new, 274, 285–87, 294–96; official
policy toward, 273–75, 284; traditional, 275–84, 287–90; vacations
for, 284, 287, 293–96, village variations in, 293–96
Filial piety, 209, 222. *See also* Elders,
respect for
Firecrackers, 256–57, 278
First Five-Year Plan, 74, 78
"Five guarantees," 74–76, 105, 369
n. 2, 379 n. 1. *See also* Aged, support of the
Footbinding, 26, 390–91 n. 7